THE FAITH OF FALLEN JEWS

The
Faith *of*
Fallen
Jews

**YOSEF HAYIM
YERUSHALMI
AND THE
WRITING OF
JEWISH HISTORY**

Edited by DAVID N. MYERS *and* ALEXANDER KAYE

BRANDEIS UNIVERSITY PRESS Waltham, Massachusetts

Brandeis University Press
An imprint of University Press of New England
www.upne.com
© 2014 Brandeis University
All rights reserved
Manufactured in the United States of America
Designed by Richard Hendel
Typeset in Arnhem and TheSans by
Tseng Information Systems, Inc.

University Press of New England is a
member of the Green Press Initiative.
The paper used in this book meets their
minimum requirement for recycled paper.

For permission to reproduce any of the material in this book,
contact Permissions, University Press of New England, One Court Street,
Suite 250, Lebanon NH 03766;
or visit www.upne.com

Chapter 3 was originally published as "Baer's History, Translated and Revised" by
Yosef Hayim Yerushalmi. Reprinted with permission from *Conservative Judaism* 21:1
(Fall 1966) © Rabbinical Assembly.

Chapter 6 was originally published as "In Praise of Ladino: A Review Essay" by
Yosef Hayim Yerushalmi. Reprinted with permission from *Conservative Judaism* 27:2
(Winter 1973) © Rabbinical Assembly.

Chapter 9, "Assimilation and Radical Anti-Semitism: The Iberian and the
German Models" is reprinted courtesy of the Leo Baeck Institute, New York.

Chapter 16, "Gilgul," originally published in the *New Yorker*, is reprinted by
kind permission of the *New Yorker* and Ophra Yerushalmi.

Library of Congress Cataloging-in-Publication data appear on the last printed
page of this book.

5 4 3 2 1

CONTENTS

ACKNOWLEDGMENTS

The editors would like to thank the Columbia Institute for Israel and Jewish Studies, and its director, Professor Jeremy Dauber, for its generous subvention of this volume. It is especially fitting that the institute, which Yosef Yerushalmi headed for more than a quarter-century, has supported this project. Thanks are also due to the Robert Burr Endowed Chair of the UCLA History Department for its support.

We are indebted to Brandeis University Press for its willingness to publish this volume: at UPNE Editor in Chief Phyllis Deutsch undertook this project with her usual gusto and discernment. Susan Abel and Lori Miller presided over important details at crucial points in the process. Will Hively proved to be an attentive copy editor whose work has made this a better volume. Martin White completed the index for the book with great dispatch and efficiency.

Financial assistance for the index came from the Tauber Institute for the Study of European Jewry of Brandeis University. The institute's executive director, Sylvia Fuks Fried, has been a source of ongoing encouragement and wise counsel. We thank her for arranging for a key piece of translation for the volume from Golan Moskowitz.

The editors are indebted to a number of research assistants, all UCLA Ph.D. candidates, who worked on the volume. Talia Graff and Nadav Molchadsky provided key assistance at various stages of the project. With her keen editorial eye and uncommon competence, Lindsay King saw this volume through to completion as style editor and researcher.

This volume benefited greatly from the diligence of the research librarians at the Jewish Theological Seminary Library, who pointed the way to some valuable early material, and at the Columbia University Library University Archives where Yosef Yerushalmi's papers are kept. Michelle Chesner, the Norman E. Alexander Librarian for Jewish Studies at Columbia, and Carrie Hintz, head of Archival Processing, were particularly helpful in tracking down and making available papers and photos that were indispensable for this volume. Professor David Berger of Yeshiva University and Diana Benmergui, the interim university registrar, provided important assistance, particularly in finding Yerushalmi's undergraduate transcript. We also thank Eric Vigne, Yosef Yerushalmi's close friend in Paris, who generously shared Yerushalmi's original English texts, upon which he relied in his excellent French translations.

Finally, the editors would like to extend their deep thanks to Ophra Yerushalmi, the gifted pianist to whom Yosef Yerushalmi was married for half a century before his death in 2009. Ophra Yerushalmi offered unfailing support for this volume and kindly agreed to provide access to papers in her own home, as well as permission to republish a number of essays that had already appeared in print.

INTRODUCTION

YOSEF HAYIM YERUSHALMI "IN THE MIDST OF HISTORY"

Yosef Hayim Yerushalmi (1932–2009) was one of the most eminent Jewish historians of the twentieth century. Yerushalmi possessed a stunning range of erudition in all eras of Jewish history, as well as in world history, classical literature, and European culture. The sweep of his knowledge was perhaps matched only by Amos Funkenstein (1937–1995), his slightly younger Israeli colleague and friend who offered a key response to Yerushalmi's most renowned book, *Zakhor* (1982).[1] What Yerushalmi also brought to his craft was a brilliant literary style, honed by his own voracious reading from early youth and his formative undergraduate studies of English and other literatures. In fact, Yerushalmi's final publication marked his debut, posthumously, as a fiction writer—a short story that appeared in the *New Yorker* in August 2011.

Yerushalmi's significance derives from his far-reaching impact on the discipline of Jewish history and beyond. He trained several generations of students at Harvard and Columbia who hold positions in universities around the world, was a well-known figure in Jewish studies circles in Israel, and interacted with leading intellectuals outside the field in

1. See Amos Funkenstein, "Collective Memory and Historical Consciousness," *History and Memory* 1 (1989), 5–26. Also see Yerushalmi's brief discussion of Funkenstein in an excellent new autobiographical source—Sylvie Anne Goldberg's interviews collected now in *Transmettre l'histoire juive: Entretiens avec Sylvie Anne Goldberg* (Paris: Albin Michel, 2012), 17. Yosef Kaplan and Shulamit Volkov also conducted an in-depth interview with Yerushalmi about his work that appeared in the journal of the Historical Society of Israel: *Historyah* 16 (2005), 5–19. Meanwhile, for a narrative overview of Yerushalmi's career, see David N. Myers, "Of Marranos and Memory: Yosef Hayim Yerushalmi and the Writing of Jewish History," in Elisheva Carlebach, John M. Efron, and David N. Myers, eds., *Jewish History and Jewish Memory: Essays in Honor of Yosef Hayim Yerushalmi* (Hanover, NH: Brandeis University Press, 1998), 1–21. See also the contributions on various aspects of Yerushalmi's work based on a conference in Paris in Sylvie Anne Goldberg, ed., *L'histoire et la mémoire de l'histoire: Hommage à Yosef Hayim Yerushalmi* (Paris: Albin Michel, 2012). In addition, one may consult the bibliographies of Yerushalmi's publications in *L'histoire et la mémoire de l'histoire*, 179–185, as well as in the Yerushalmi Festschrift, *Jewish History and Jewish Memory: Essays in Honor of Yosef Hayim Yerushalmi*, 457–460.

France and Germany.[2] Indeed, uniquely among Jewish studies scholars in his day, Yerushalmi gained considerable renown beyond the precincts of Jewish history. He counted as friends and admirers a noteworthy array of artists, intellectuals, and scholars in Europe and the United States including Avigdor Arikha, Harold Bloom, Jacques Derrida, Carlo Ginzburg, Jürgen Habermas, Pierre Nora, Pierre Vidal-Naquet, and Cynthia Ozick.

Yerushalmi's eminence, it must be noted, was not a result of the volume of his writing. In striking contrast to his doctoral mentor at Columbia University, Salo Baron, whose scholarly output was overwhelming, Yerushalmi was not an especially prolific writer. He was a careful guardian of quality control, a slow and meticulous craftsman, at times burdened by writer's block and perhaps the anxiety of having the massively prolific Baron as his teacher. After producing a masterful monograph for his first book, Yerushalmi moved away from that genre, preferring relatively brief books, often first delivered in oral fashion. *Zakhor*, based on the Stroum Lectures at the University of Washington, was the most famous example. This was no coincidence, for it must be noted that, alongside his excellence as a researcher, Yerushalmi was an exceptionally gifted orator. His lectures, whether in the classroom or beyond the university campus, were spellbinding, rich in colorful biographical and historical detail, probing in philosophical reflection, and stimulating to neophyte and expert alike.[3]

This collection seeks to capture the scholarly spirit of one of the great Jewish historians of our time. At the same time, the essays included in it offer a glimpse into the atelier of the historian as he goes about sifting evidence, weighing hypotheses, offering synthetic conclusions, and telling a compelling story. Each of the pieces introduces its readers — from first-year college students to advanced scholars — to a carefully reconstructed historical world, as well as to the methods of the historical discipline at its very best. It is thus our hope and expectation that this volume will be of interest not only to researchers in Jewish history but to those interested in historical writing of the highest order.

2. See, for example, Nancy L. Green, "Un Américain à Paris: Yosef Yerushalmi à l'École des Hautes Études en Sciences Sociales," 99–106, and Michael Brenner, "Yerushalmi en Allemagne — l'Allemagne en Yerushalmi," 107–115, in Goldberg, *L'histoire et la mémoire de l'histoire*.

3. See the discussion of Yerushalmi's teaching style in John Efron, "Yosef Hayim Yerushalmi: The Teacher," in *Jewish History and Jewish Memory: Essays in Honor of Yosef Hayim Yerushalmi*, 453–456.

A large majority of the essays here originated as lectures, and a good measure of Yosef Yerushalmi's oral virtuosity is thus preserved. Most of them are unknown to the general public, and some appear here in English (or at all) for the first time. A smaller number of essays—for example, Yerushalmi's Spinoza or Leo Baeck lectures—are regarded as minor classics among specialists. The aim of the editors was not to be systematic in assembling all of Yerushalmi's key papers. Rather, it was to produce a selection of essays that reveal Yerushalmi's historical mastery and stylistic verve, as well as his sweeping range and intellectual arc. To the extent that all history, as Croce famously quipped, is "contemporary history," the book will also show the important, though often muted, interplay between Yerushalmi's personal background and his professional voice.

In order to make that link more visible, the next section will present an overview of Yerushalmi's upbringing, intellectual formation, and professional career. Thereafter, in the following section, a brief road map of the current volume will be offered, noting the key scholarly stations at which Yerushalmi chose to stop in his forty-year career. This road map complements the short introductions that precede each essay in the collection.

THE MAKING OF A JEWISH HISTORIAN

One of Yerushalmi's recurrent interests, as we shall later see, was the history of Jewish historical writing. He offered important insight into the lives, motivations, and intellectual interests of his predecessors, from the sixteenth-century Solomon ibn Verga to the nineteenth-century avatars of *Wissenschaft des Judentums*. And yet, for all his learned excavation of this historiographical terrain, Yerushalmi only rarely elaborated on his own life or motivations. One important exception is the introduction to the Russian translation of *Zakhor*, which appears here in English for the first time. Another important exception—and an extremely valuable source—is the recently published volume of interviews conducted by the French scholar of Jewish history Sylvie Anne Goldberg with Yerushalmi over a number of years.[4] The Goldberg volume covers many aspects of his life and career, and opens up the path toward a fuller biography of Yerushalmi that, with the cataloging of his papers in the Columbia University archive, is now possible.

To return to the matter at hand, let us begin at the beginning of our story. Yosef Yerushalmi was born on May 20, 1932, in the Bronx, New

4. See *Transmettre l'histoire juive*, 11–12.

York, to Yehuda and Hava (née Eva Kaplan). His parents were immigrants from the Russian Empire, his mother from Pinsk and his father from Goloskov, and both spoke Russian to one another. Yerushalmi fils maintained a lifelong fascination, as he admits in the revealing preface to the Russian *Zakhor*, with Russian literature and culture. Although he never learned to speak the language, he did learn Russian songs as a young child to the point that he averred that "Russian music entered deep into my soul, moving me as no other can."[5] From his teenage years, he also became a passionate reader of Russian prose and poetry. In fact, there was in Yerushalmi's personality something of the Russian spirit—grand, heavy, fatalistic.

Although Russian was the language his parents spoke to each other, it was not the language in which they communicated to their son. Yerushalmi's mother spoke to him in Yiddish—the high literary Yiddish of Vilna, he noted—and his father addressed him exclusively in Hebrew, dedicated Hebraist that he was. As a result, when Yosef was sent to public school in the Bronx at age five, he did not know how to speak English. To assist his acquisition of that language, his parents engaged a tutor from England, which Yerushalmi understood to be the reason for his unusual accent, "not really British nor American," he admitted—what some have called "Bronxford."[6]

The world in which Yerushalmi grew up in the Bronx in the 1930s was a colorful one, similar to urban settings in Vilna, Paris, or Berlin a decade earlier. "The entire neighborhood," he reported, "was Jewish, not necessarily orthodox, but Jewish to the core, mostly from Eastern Europe, traditionalists and secularists, Zionists, Bundists and Communists, all perpetually and passionately debating, but friends nonetheless."[7] The Yerushalmi home was permeated with Jewish culture but not stringently observant. Candles were lit on the Sabbath and kiddush offered, though Yerushalmi's father indulged in the "oneg" (pleasure) of the Sabbath with a cigarette. Despite not being Orthodox, his parents decided to send Yosef to the Rabbi Israel Salanter yeshivah to receive a proper Hebrew and Jewish education. In making this decision, Yerushalmi's father explained to

5. The Russian version of *Zakhor* appeared in 2004. The preface appears in this volume (chapter 1) in English.

6. *Transmettre l'histoire juive*, 53.

7. See "To the Russian Reader," chapter 1 in this volume. See also *Transmettre l'histoire juive*, 52.

his young son that he was at liberty to choose his own Jewish path.[8] It was there that he received a firm grounding in the classical sources of Judaism—the Bible, Talmud, and rabbinic commentaries—as well as his first sustained exposure to modern Hebrew literature and Jewish history.

Alongside his formal education at the Salanter yeshivah, Yerushalmi was a devoted thespian in various Yiddish theater troupes and an uncommonly voracious reader. Books in various languages were a ubiquitous presence in his parents' household. Yerushalmi remembers one especially fateful book that he received from his parents around the age of ten: an illustrated Yiddish book that was part of the *Kinderbibliotek* series and was devoted to the renowned fifteenth-century Jewish courtier, leader, and scholar Isaac Abravanel (1437–1508).[9] While reading this book, Yerushalmi for the first time encountered crypto-Jews or Marranos, those Spanish Jews who had been forcibly converted to Catholicism but lived secret Jewish lives in the privacy of their homes. The phenomenon of Marranism, both in its original Iberian context and in a more figurative sense (as a reflection of the modern Jewish condition), would remain a recurrent concern of Yerushalmi's throughout his professional career.

That said, despite the intensity of his Jewish world as an adolescent—yeshivah, youth movements, summer camps, and native Hebrew and Yiddish—it was not a foregone conclusion that Yosef Yerushalmi would become a Jewish studies scholar. At the end of his high school years, he was seriously contemplating law as his chosen path of study, even spinning out the fantasy that he would work one day as a lawyer for the Israeli Foreign Ministry. Yerushalmi harbored, from youth, deep bonds of connection to Zionism and the State of Israel, much of which he inherited from his father, who had moved from Russia to Palestine in 1920 but left for New York after contracting malaria in 1928.[10] Like his father, Yosef felt continually drawn to Israel, especially but not exclusively because of his flawless Hebrew. He considered immigrating there at the age of seventeen in 1948 and later expressed regret that he did not have the opportunity to assume a teaching position at the Hebrew University.[11]

8. *Transmettre l'histoire juive*, 51, 55.

9. Ibid., 42.

10. *Transmettre l'histoire juive*, 48, 50.

11. Yerushalmi often told the story to students that he *was* offered a position in Jewish history at the Hebrew University. The rector proposed that he teach the period between the advent of the false messiah Sabbetai Zevi and the French Revolution.

In any event, Yerushalmi neither immigrated to Israel nor took up the study of law. After high school, he simply headed south from the Bronx into Washington Heights in Manhattan to commence his higher education at Yeshiva College. Given the fact that he did not come from an Orthodox home and described himself as caught in the throes of an identity crisis about his Jewishness at that time,[12] it is somewhat surprising that he decided to study at the flagship Orthodox institution. He began at Yeshiva College in February 1950. He took a wide range of courses in English, comparative literature, history, political science, French, and German over three years, graduating summa cum laude as an English major in 1953 (and ranking seventh in his class of 103). While in college, he served as president of the French Club and as a member of the college's debating society, which provided training to develop his formidable oratorical skills.[13] Meanwhile, his transcript from Yeshiva College indicates that he underwent in this period a slight name change from Joseph (known as Josephy) Hyman Erushalmy to Yosef Hayim Yerushalmi, perhaps inspired by the great Hebrew modernist author Yosef Hayim Brenner, whom he would surely have known through his reading of modern Hebrew literature.[14]

Yerushalmi, then a tenured professor at Harvard, demurred. Ibid., 232–235. A recent book suggests that Yerushalmi's proposed appointment to the Hebrew University was blocked by the Hispanist Haim Beinart. See Jacob Barnai, *Shemu'el Ettinger: Historiyon, moreh ve-ish tsibur* (Jerusalem: Merkaz Zalman Shazar, 2011), 233.

12. Yerushalmi was involved in a number of Jewish youth groups, the last of which was the modern Orthodox Bnei Akiva, which he remembers as a movement "animated by remarkable people, devoid of any fanaticism." Ibid., 43, 56.

13. Although he graduated summa cum laude in 1953, Yerushalmi was included in the Yeshiva College yearbook, *Masmid*, of 1952. The description next to his picture, clearly not written by him, offers a few intriguing details about his personality and reputation in college: "Sad-eyed Joe, otherwise known as Josephy, has claimed, at different times, to stem from such varied backgrounds as Turkey, Tagikistan, and Oxford. Actually he was born in a Cambridge-tinged area of the Bronx. Upon entering the college, Joe quickly distinguished himself as president of Le Cercle Francais and as a master debater. An English major, he may be found quite frequently quaffing a cup of coffee with Doc. His interests tend to the classical, from literature to music. Beside these and other sundry artistic interests, Joe finds time to guide Ehrman in the ways of true 'scholarship.' His verbosity combined with a natural belligerence in argument make him a good bet for the law profession." *Masmid* (1952), 21, accessed on 22 November 2012 at http://archive.org/details/masmid1952.

14. Yerushalmi's Yeshiva College transcript covers the period from February 1950 to the end of spring semester 1953. It notes that Yerushalmi entered Yeshiva College

After completing his B.A. at Yeshiva College, Yerushalmi headed further downtown to the Jewish Theological Seminary (JTS), whose rabbinical program he entered in 1953. The source of attraction to him was not the prospect of becoming a rabbi but the fact it was "the best place in New York to study Judaism from a critical perspective."[15] The assembly of academic talent at JTS in this period was extraordinary and included Saul Lieberman, H. L. Ginsburg, Abraham Joshua Heschel, and Mordecai Kaplan. Yerushalmi's favorite mentor at JTS was the scholar of medieval Hebrew literature Shalom Spiegel, whom he remembered as the mythic "homo universalis" and who is perhaps best known for his multilayered analysis of the biblical story of the binding of Isaac (Genesis 22) in rabbinic literature in *The Last Trial*.[16] The opportunity to work with the likes of Spiegel and Lieberman left an indelible imprint on Yerushalmi and solidified his desire to make the study of history his chosen path. It was at the Seminary that he also encountered as a guest professor a visitor from neighboring Columbia University who would have the most profound impact on Yerushalmi as a scholar: Salo Wittmayer Baron (1895–1989).

Upon receiving rabbinic ordination from JTS in 1957, Yerushalmi spent a number of years as the rabbi at a Conservative synagogue in Larchmont, New York. To his later students, the idea of Yosef Yerushalmi as a congregational rabbi defied credulity. He hardly seemed the type to indulge in the wide range of pastoral functions demanded of the congregational rabbi. That said, a key function of the rabbi—the delivery of a sermon—was clearly one in which he could and did excel.

And yet, it was historical study where his passion lay, and he continued his educational path a few blocks downtown from JTS by entering the doctoral program at Columbia University under the tutelage of Baron. His years at Columbia provided him with the opportunity to study with other leading scholars including Zvi Ankori (Jewish history), Gavin Mattingly (Spanish history), John Mundy (medieval Europe), and Paul Kri-

---

with advanced standing owing to courses taken at City College. He also took a summer course in educational psychology from New York University in the summer of 1952. The transcript is located in the Office of the Registrar, Yeshiva University.

15. *Transmettre l'histoire juive*, 33.

16. Ibid., 35. See Shalom Spiegel, *The Last Trial: On the Legends and Lore of the Command to Abraham to Offer Isaac as a Sacrifice: The Akedah* (New York: Pantheon Books, 1967). Yerushalmi encountered Spiegel's masterful account in Hebrew in "Mi-agadot ha-'akedah," in Saul Lieberman, ed., *Alexander Marx Jubilee Volume* (New York: Jewish Theological Seminary of America, 1950), 471–547.

steller, the great scholar of Renaissance philosophy. But the fulcrum of his Columbia experience was Baron's annual seminar, conducted at his home on Claremont Avenue, where students would present summaries of their research. At the end of each session, after fellow students delivered their comments and critique, Baron would present a wide-ranging summation of the strengths and weaknesses. This was a skill that Yerushalmi inherited from his teacher—the ability to distill the essence of an extended argument, note its strengths, and then home in on its weaker points in a synthesis whose quality almost invariably surpassed the original presentation.[17]

At Columbia, Yerushalmi began to follow a scholarly lead that would culminate in his master's thesis—and later appeared as one of his first published articles.[18] The theme was the Inquisition, not in its Spanish guise, but in its initial appearance in France, where it was introduced by the pope in the thirteenth century. Originally intended to contend with the perceived Albigensian heresy, the Inquisition was redirected against French Jewry in the fourteenth century. Yerushalmi began to familiarize himself with the subject in his first year at Columbia when he wrote a forty-page paper in John Mundy's seminar on "The Rise of the Kabbala in Southern France." This preliminary work paved the way for his master's thesis on "The Papal Inquisition in France and the Jews" in the thirteenth and fourteenth centuries. And it was but a short distance from this topic to the subject of his doctoral dissertation, as Yerushalmi recalled: "It was my interest in the papal inquisition that led me progressively to the study of the Spanish and Portuguese inquisition."[19]

The persecution of those deemed religious deviants had resonated in Yerushalmi since his youthful encounter with crypto-Jews in the Yiddish biography of Isaac Abravanel. He would continue throughout his life to be fascinated not only by the coercive methods of the persecutor but also by the complex psychology of the persecuted, who often possessed radically divergent public and private personae. It was the resulting psychic makeup of the crypto-Jew—and in a different way of the assimilated mod-

17. *Transmettre l'histoire juive*, 37, 38.

18. See "The Inquisition and the Jews of France in the Time of Bernard Gui," *Harvard Theological Review* 63 (1970), 317–376.

19. *Transmettre l'histoire juive*, 41. A copy of Yerushalmi's paper for Mundy (under the name Joseph Erushalmy) is deposited in the Yerushalmi Archive, Box II, Folder 40, Series III; the master's thesis is contained in Box II, folder 37, Series III.

ern Jew—that animated Yerushalmi's constant interest in the manifold and tortured permutations of Jewish identity.

In jumping from the medieval French context to the early modern Spanish setting for his Columbia dissertation, Yerushalmi was consumed by a single book he had first happened upon as an adolescent bibliophile: Isaac Cardoso's apologia *Las excelencias de los Hebreos*. It was this book that opened Yerushalmi's eyes to the Marrano experience in all its complexity, from Cardoso's time as a prominent and well-placed Christian physician in Spain to his "return" to a full Jewish life—and the defense of Judaism—in Italy. Yerushalmi recalled that he approached Baron with trepidation about the prospect of devoting his dissertation to Cardoso, but Baron responded affirmatively. Yerushalmi then undertook an extended research trip to archives in Spain and Portugal in 1961 that laid the documentary foundation for his dissertation—and subsequent work in the field of Sephardic history.[20] For the next four years, he conducted additional research on the life path of Cardoso while also serving as an instructor in Jewish history at Rutgers University in order to support himself and his wife, Ophra, whom he married in New York in 1958.

In 1965, Yerushalmi received word through Salo Baron that Harvard University was opening a position in Jewish history and might be interested in hiring him. But he would be eligible only if he had a Ph.D. in hand. Faced with that deadline, Yerushalmi rushed to complete his dissertation, which he did in 1966. Shortly thereafter, he won the Ansley Dissertation Award at Columbia, which provided funds for publication by the Columbia University Press.[21] In the meantime, he did indeed receive the appointment as an assistant professor at Harvard and began teaching there in 1966. Five years later, he published with Columbia his award-winning first book, *From Spanish Court to Italian Ghetto*, which was an expanded version of his doctoral thesis. *From Spanish Court* was a massively researched, erudite, and vivid study of the peregrinations of a fascinating figure, a well-established scholar and intellectual at home in the court culture of Spain who came to consciousness about his family's Jewish roots and decided to leave behind that world—and the constant threat of the Inquisition—to live an open Jewish life in Italy. More than

20. *Transmettre l'histoire juive*, 68–71.

21. Ibid., 129–130. See Yosef Hayim Yerushalmi, *From Spanish Court to Italian Ghetto: Isaac Cardoso; A Study in Seventeenth-Century Marranism and Jewish Apologetics* (New York: Columbia University Press, 1971).

a simple biography, the book offers an expansive historical portrait of seventeenth-century Spain and Italy, interspersed with rich profiles of crypto-Jewish and Jewish life.

On the basis of this book—and his extraordinary promise—Yerushalmi was granted tenure at Harvard, a process that began and ended, unlike today's drawn-out procedure, with the summary arrival to his home of a letter announcing his promotion.[22] At Harvard, Yerushalmi worked closely with Professor Isadore Twersky, the renowned scholar of Maimonides who also served in his spare time, remarkably enough, as a Hasidic rebbe in Brookline; together, the two, unlikely partners and an eminent pair, trained a cohort of outstanding doctoral students. While at Harvard, Yerushalmi published his handsome large volume *Haggadah and History* (1975) that revealed the dazzling array of Passover ritual manuals produced over centuries. Meanwhile, in 1978, he was selected to be the holder of the Jacob E. Safra Chair in Jewish History and Sephardic Civilization and delivered his inaugural lecture in February 1979 (see chapter 7). During this period, he also served as chair of Harvard's Department of Near Eastern Languages and Civilizations. Later in life, Yerushalmi described his fourteen years at Harvard as stimulating and pleasant, if somewhat confined within the four walls of the university. This sense of claustrophobia, he averred, gave rise to "a sort of undefinable sentiment, of immobility, in this delicious situation."[23]

And thus, Yerushalmi listened attentively in 1980 when the Columbia University History Department offered him a position, the third time that his home institution had sought to entice him back to New York. On this occasion, after consulting with his wife, Yerushalmi agreed to return to

22. In response to a request for an evaluation from Professor Isadore Twersky, then chair of Harvard's Department of Near Eastern Languages and Culture, Salo Baron wrote a short, but powerful, letter on June 6, 1969: "Professor Yerushalmi was one of my best students during almost half a century of my teaching career. Even outwardly this was documented by the marks *Excellent* he received by the unanimous vote of the committees that examined him at his orals as well as at his defense of the dissertation. . . . He has not only the makings of a truly first-rate scholar, but is also a brilliant teacher." Twersky wrote back to Baron on June 23, 1969, to inform him that the president of Harvard had approved Yerushalmi's advancement to tenure—a mere three years after Yerushalmi was hired as an assistant professor. Baron's letter and Twersky's response are contained in the Salo W. Baron papers (MO 580) in the Department of Special Collections, Stanford University Library, box 97, folder 15.

23. *Transmettre l'histoire juive*, 137.

Columbia and assume a new post: the Salo W. Baron Professor of Jewish History, Culture, and Society. This provided him with the opportunity not only to follow and honor his mentor but also to do so at the first university in the United States to create a position in Jewish history. Columbia became a lively staging ground for Yerushalmi, who quickly assembled an excellent cohort of graduate and undergraduate students and created one of the leading centers of Jewish historical study in the world. He also resettled in New York with gusto, connecting with old friends and developing new ones.

Yerushalmi's first years at Columbia were also a period of considerable intellectual fermentation. In 1980, he was invited to deliver the Stroum Lectures at the University of Washington. He devoted his four lectures in Seattle to his long-standing interest in the relationship between traditional modes of ritualized memory and the modern practice of critical history. He had taken a first stab at this issue, or at least a portion of it, in 1977, when he delivered a lecture in Jerusalem titled "Clio and the Jews: Reflections on Jewish Historiography in the Sixteenth Century." The more fully formed expression of his thinking, based on the Stroum Lectures, was published in 1982 as *Zakhor: Jewish History and Jewish Memory*, a book in which Yerushalmi revealed his masterful command over all periods of Jewish history and for which he would gain his greatest renown.[24] Indeed, it was *Zakhor* that inspired a new and rich discourse within Jewish studies about memory and history, leading to scores of articles, dissertations, and books. It was also this volume that brought Yerushalmi, already a distinguished Hispanist, to the attention of wider circles of scholars, beyond the Iberian Peninsula and beyond Jewish studies.

Yerushalmi's reputation continued to grow as he entered a new terrain of inquiry shortly after arriving in New York: the study of Sigmund Freud. As someone always interested in psychoanalysis (and himself an analysand on two occasions), he was intrigued to hear of a group of thirteen

---

24. *Zakhor: Jewish History and Jewish Memory* (Seattle: University of Washington Press, 1982). The book has attracted a wide range of reviews and comments since its appearance in 1982. See, for example, the six contributions to the quarter-century retrospective in the *Jewish Quarterly Review* 97:4 (2007). The early kernel of Yerushalmi's thinking on Jewish history and memory, "Clio and the Jews," focused on one aspect of that relationship: the proliferation of Jewish historical writing in the sixteenth century. It was published in the *Proceedings of the American Academy for Jewish Research (Jubilee Volume)* 46–47 (1979–80), 607–638. On this essay, see Myers, "Of Marranos and Memory," 9–10.

New York psychoanalysts who had joined together to address the question of whether their chosen field had anything to contribute to an understanding of antisemitism. And thus he readily heeded their invitation to join the group. At that point, Yerushalmi began to read systematically the entirety of Freud's literary output, first in English and then in German.[25]

There was in Freud's own sense of connection to his Jewishness—and the broader societal perception of it—something that evoked the Marrano experience. In a manner similar to his investigation of Isaac Cardoso's path back to Judaism and subsequent defense of the Jews, Yerushalmi came to understand Freud not as the epitome of self-abnegation but as a more knowledgeable and engaged Jew than previous scholars had thought. Specifically, after years of study, he came to grasp Freud's controversial *Moses and Monotheism* (1939) not as a renunciation of Judaism, as many in Freud's day and beyond had read it, but in fact as an attempt to understand and empathize with the transmission of Jewish memory from the time of Moses. It is toward an elucidation of this reading that Yerushalmi aimed his *Freud's Moses: Judaism Terminable or Interminable* from 1993, which bore the same format as *Zakhor*—a small book based on a series of lectures, in this case the Franz Rosenzweig series at Yale.[26]

One must hasten to add that Yerushalmi was no mere reclamationist, seeking to restore Freud, or the Marranos, to the Jewish fold in simpleminded fashion. He was too sophisticated in approach and dedicated to the historians' craft to permit that. Moreover, he earnestly believed that one must labor as much as humanly possible to attain a measure of historical objectivity.[27] That said, he always approached his subjects with considerable empathy. In fact, he often told his students that they

25. *Transmettre l'histoire juive*, 90, 91.

26. Sigmund Freud, *Moses and Monotheism* (New York: A. A. Knopf, 1939). Cf. Yosef Hayim Yerushalmi, *Freud's Moses: Judaism Terminable and Interminable* (New Haven: Yale University Press, 1993).

27. *Transmettre l'histoire juive*, 189. It should be noted that Yerushalmi resisted any attempt to be connected to the contemporary moment of postmodern skepticism about the quest for objectivity. For such an attempt and Yerushalmi's strong response, see David N. Myers, "Selbstreflexion im modernen Erinnerungsdiskurs," in Michael Brenner and David N. Myers, eds., *Jüdische Geschichtsschreibung heute: Themen, Positionen, Kontroversen* (Munich: Beck Verlag, 2002), 55–74, and Yosef Hayim Yerushalmi, "Jüdische Historiographie und Postmodernismus: Eine abweichende Meinung," in ibid., 75–94.

should develop their olfactory senses as historians, learning to sniff out both potential leads for sources and the fullness of the characters they studied.[28] Empathy need not entail an abandonment of the quest for objectivity. Nor did objectivity, he insisted in evocation of historian Thomas Haskell, demand neutrality.[29]

Yerushalmi's awareness of contemporary issues and challenges was an important part of his scholarly personality. For example, his ability to link past and present is evident in one of his early public utterances, an address he delivered to the graduating class of the Hebrew College in Boston in 1970 (and which is presented here) called "A Jewish Historian in the 'Age of Aquarius.'" The title of the talk made reference to the lyrics of one of the most popular songs of the blockbuster Broadway musical *Hair*. Yerushalmi unpacked the present "Aquarian moment" and its apocalyptic sensibility with typical contextualizing acumen and style, and then went on to compare this moment to the messianic worlds of the twelfth-century Joachim da Fiore and the seventeenth-century Sabbetai Zevi.[30] An unusual aspect of the address was that it revealed Yerushalmi's familiarity with popular culture of the day. Yerushalmi knew *Hair* and its songs well, though his typical cultural preferences tended to the more highbrow. Throughout his life, he was an avid consumer of classical music, fine art, and world literature. (He once lamented that his students did not possess this appreciation for culture that earlier generations had possessed, particularly for classical music.)[31]

More important for understanding Yerushalmi's notion of the role of the historian was the proposition that he formulated at the end of his Hebrew College lecture: "It is therefore *in the midst of history* that we must know ourselves as Jews and build a Jewish future, slowly, often painfully. But to do so we must consciously carry a Jewish past within us" (emphasis added).[32]

The young Yerushalmi proceeded to echo Eugen Rosenstock Huessy's well-known image of the historian as a "physician of the soul" whose job it is to heal the wounds of memory. This sentiment reflects a distinctive

28. *Transmettre l'histoire juive*, 32.

29. Ibid., 188. See Thomas Haskell, *Objectivity Is Not Neutrality: Explanatory Schemes in History* (Baltimore: Johns Hopkins University Press), 1998.

30. See "A Jewish Historian in the 'Age of Aquarius,'" chapter 4 in this volume.

31. *Transmettre l'histoire juive*, 144.

32. See chapter 4 in this volume.

facet of Yerushalmi's professional personality—not so much the historian embarked on the ceaseless quest for objectivity as the engaged student of the Jewish past for whom history was a tool of consolation and reconstruction. It also stands in stark contrast to Yerushalmi's tenor in the fourth chapter of the far better-known *Zakhor*, where he famously diagnosed history, in its modern guise, as the "faith of fallen Jews." Indeed, the culmination of Yerushalmi's argument in *Zakhor* is that, unlike premodern rituals and liturgy, "modern Jewish historiography can never substitute for Jewish memory."[33] It is this claim that stands at the center of the guiding juxtaposition in the book's subtitle: Jewish history and Jewish memory.

Yosef Yerushalmi was a complex man, thinker, and scholar. A great deal of his professional life was devoted to studying the manifold varieties, vicissitudes, and problematics of Jewish identity. This preoccupation was hardly born of disinterest; Yerushalmi admitted in his interviews with Sylvie Anne Goldberg that he devoted himself to Jewish history "for very personal existential reasons," even though, he reiterated, this did not impinge on his quest for objectivity.[34] Even in the fourth chapter of *Zakhor*, where the gulf between memory and history seemed to be most pronounced, Yerushalmi declared that the "burden of building a bridge to his people remains with the historian."[35] Sentences such as these and, more generally, Yerushalmi's extraordinary passion for his scholarly work, lend a sense of a person who lived and was engaged "in the midst of history," as we read in the line from his Hebrew College address. It reminds us that Yerushalmi's life and work were inextricably linked. He was not able, and nor did he desire, to remove himself from the living currents of history, which molded him into the scholar and thinker that he was. In this sense, we might wonder whether the "faith" that he imagined the historian to be offering to "fallen Jews" was perhaps more multidimensional than a simple dispassionate skepticism toward the past.

The task of balancing existential fulfillment and the scholar's quest for objectivity, which has been a leitmotif of modern Jewish historians since the early nineteenth century, was an important and animating one for him. It was also related to the tension between competing religious, cultural, and intellectual demands to which Yerushalmi was drawn both

---

33. *Zakhor*, 101.
34. *Transmettre l'histoire juive*, 243.
35. *Zakhor*, 100.

personally and in his study of the modern Jewish condition, beginning with his childhood fascination with the Marrano and running through his professional work from Cardoso to Freud.

Yerushalmi was mindful of the fact that there was a close link between subject and object in his research. "I discovered an array of things [through history]," he observed, "that were, are and will remain important for understanding myself and my situation in this time."[36] But this did not transform him into a public intellectual or political activist in Jewish or other circles. Although he was well known as a scholar in the United States, Europe, and Israel, he did not believe that his historical knowledge bestowed upon him any particular right to speak out on issues of the day with regularity or in forums other than scholarly ones. That said, he did begin to think and write about issues of a political nature in the last fifteen years or so of his life, particularly surrounding the State of Israel. This was rooted in a long-standing interest in the political history of the Jews, which he inherited from his teacher. Already in his doctoral dissertation (actually one of the three he wrote in Vienna), Salo Baron engaged a political historical topic, analyzing the Jewish question at the Congress of Vienna of 1815. Over the course of his extraordinary career, Baron returned again and again to political themes, ranging from his insightful essays on the status of Jews in the Middle Ages to his memorable testimony as an expert historical witness in the trial in Israel of SS Jewish affairs officer Adolf Eichmann.[37]

Yerushalmi, Baron's preeminent disciple and heir, continued that interest by exploring at various points in his career the structural relationship between Jews and the state. In 1976, he published a small monograph devoted to an outbreak of mass violence against Lisbon's New Christian (or crypto-Jewish community) in 1506 in which King Manuel neglected to intervene expeditiously on their behalf. Notwithstanding Manuel's dilatory behavior, the community of Portuguese New Christians continued to harbor the myth of kingly virtue, even though it was Manuel who had forcibly converted them in 1497. Yerushalmi's concern for this

---

36. *Transmettre l'histoire juive*, 243.

37. Baron, *Die Judenfrage auf dem Wiener Kongress* (Vienna and Berlin: R. Lowrit, 1920). See also Baron's essays on the protected status of medieval Jews, "Plenitude of Apostolic Powers and Medieval Jewish Serfdom," and "Medieval Nationalism and Jewish Serfdom," in Baron, *Ancient and Medieval Jewish History* (New Brunswick, NJ: Rutgers University Press, 1972), 284–307 and 308–322.

case extended beyond the tragic details of the massacre itself. It reflected his sustained engagement with the phenomenon of the Jews' royal alliances, as well as with Hannah Arendt, whose views of the destructive consequences of Jewish ties to state power were spelled out with stark clarity in both *The Origins of Totalitarianism* (1951) and *Eichmann in Jerusalem* (1963). Yerushalmi returned to Arendt and the royal alliance in a lecture that he delivered in German in 1993 on the occasion of winning a prize from the Siemens Foundation (and repeated in English at Emory University in 2005, which is included in this volume). He built on Baron's work on the status of medieval Jews as "serfs of the chamber" (*servi camerae*) to reconstruct a Jewish political history up to the twentieth century. Thus, he directly challenged Arendt's assertion in *Origins* that "the Jews had no political tradition or experience."[38] In tracing the *longue durée* of the Jews' royal alliance, he argued contra Arendt that there was nothing in their historical experience to prepare them for the genocidal rage of Nazism.

Yerushalmi was keenly attentive to the fissures of modernity, pointing to them as a defining feature in rending the fabric of memory and allowing for the rise of historicism. Ruptures need not generate negative outcomes, he argued in another lecture in Germany in 2005, this time on the occasion of receiving the Leopold Lucas Prize in Tübingen. He devoted this talk to another key chapter in Jewish political history: the rise of the State of Israel. Here he followed in the path of the other great scholarly influence in his life alongside Salo Baron, the renowned Israeli scholar of Jewish mysticism Gershom Scholem.[39] That is, he asserted that the modern State of Israel marked a decisive rupture from the long tradition of Jewish messianism, whose ingrained passivity mandated that believers live, as Scholem famously declared, a "life lived in deferment." The activist ethos of Zionism dispensed with messianic passivity and enabled a modern political state to come into existence. And yet, Yerushalmi noted, this did not spell the demise of messianism altogether. Both Jews and Christians continued to harbor their own messianic dreams about Israel and the Jews, and largely to deleterious effect.

38. Hannah Arendt, *The Origins of Totalitarianism*, 2nd ed. (New York: Meridian Books, 1958), 23, quoted by Yerushalmi in "'Servants of Kings and Not Servants of Servants,'" chapter 11 of this volume.

39. Gershom G. Scholem, "Toward an Understanding of the Messianic Idea in Judaism," in Scholem, *The Messianic Idea in Judaism and Other Essays on Jewish Spirituality* (New York: Schocken Press, 1971).

In offering his reflections on messianism and the State of Israel, Yerushalmi was actively engaged in a kind of applied history, seeking to marshal the lessons of the past to a richer understanding of contemporary Jewish life. This was part of the bridge building in which he believed the historian can and should engage. In related fashion, Yerushalmi embodied the call of the Englishman R. G. Collingwood, who declared that history is "not a dead past, but a living past, a heritage of past thoughts which by the work of his historical consciousness the historian makes his own."[40] Yerushalmi's decades-long inquiry into the history of historical thought and writing was an extended meditation on the sources of his own historical consciousness. In this regard, we should note that perhaps his most persistent subject of scholarly interest was the sixteenth-century Spanish historian Solomon Ibn Verga, author of the historiographical work *Shevet Yehudah*. Yerushalmi discussed Ibn Verga—and his allegiance to the royal alliance—in his study of the Lisbon massacre, among many other places (including throughout this volume). At the same time, Yerushalmi was deeply intrigued, especially given his interest in the intellectual genealogy of modern history, by Ibn Verga's invocation of the term "natural cause" (*sibah tiv'it*) as a new model of causal explanation for historical events in *Shevet Yehudah*. Having contemplated and studied his Spanish Jewish precursor for forty years, Yerushalmi found it strange that he could not bring to the light of day his own translation and commentary on *Shevet Yehudah*.[41] He continued to work on and fine-tune this project until his last days. It remained the last major—and uncompleted—work in his scholarly oeuvre, a telling reminder of his unstinting and, at times inhibiting, perfectionism.

A ROAD MAP OF THE VOLUME

The aim of this volume is not to provide an exhaustive catalogue of Yosef Yerushalmi's articles. Rather, the editors have attempted, through

40. R. G. Collingwood, *The Idea of History* (Oxford: Oxford University Press, 1956), 170.

41. *Transmettre l'histoire juive*, 163–64. Yerushalmi's lifelong interest in Ibn Verga yielded a translation and commentary on *Shevet Yehudah*, though this important work never saw the light of day. This long-expected volume will soon appear under the editorship of the Tel Aviv medievalist Jeremy Cohen. See Solomon Ibn Verga, *The Scepter of Judah (Shevet Yehudah)*, translated and interpreted by Yosef Hayim Yerushalmi; edited, with an introduction, by Jeremy Cohen (Cambridge, MA, and Tel Aviv: Harvard and Tel Aviv University Presses, forthcoming 2014).

their selection, to offer a glimpse into the trajectory and abiding interests of a great historian at work. In going about this task, we began with the criterion of including a number of pieces that have not yet appeared in English and that shed light on important aspects of Yerushalmi's personality and/or scholarship. These essays open the volume in part I and offer intimate glimpses into Yerushalmi's formation, focusing, in one case, on the impact of Russian culture in his early life and, in another, on his textured relationship to France, French language, culture, and scholarship.

A second criterion was to include early essays that adumbrate in compelling ways some of the recurrent and key themes in Yerushalmi's research. Accordingly, part II features some of the first fruits of Yerushalmi's scholarly pen, beginning with his review of the book on the history of the Jews in Christian Spain written by one of his great forebears in the study of Spanish Jewish history, the Hebrew University historian Yitzhak Fritz Baer. This section also includes the 1970 Hebrew College address that anticipates *Zakhor* and, in a certain sense, is even more forthcoming about the communal mission of the historian than the more renowned work of 1982. Following that essay comes Yerushalmi's lengthy 1970 article from the *Harvard Theological Review*, based on his Columbia University master's thesis. As noted above, it represented his first major research effort and his initial foray into the workings of the Inquisition, though the focus was on France, not on Spain, as it would be in his later work. Yerushalmi manifested an early interest in this article in the Inquisition's focus on alleged Judaizing activity and anti-Christian blasphemy of French Jews, thereby laying the groundwork for his research on Iberia. Meanwhile, the final selection in part II pivots to the Sephardic milieu, offering a critical review written in 1973 by Yerushalmi, then a Harvard professor, of an anthology devoted to Ladino language and culture.

Part III is dedicated more fully to Spanish and Sephardic Jewish history, and rests on the criterion of highlighting the importance of Yerushalmi's scholarly contribution to that field, upon which his reputation as an historian of the first order was initially based. The section opens with Yerushalmi's inaugural 1979 lecture as the Jacob Safra Professor at Harvard in which he presented a majestic panorama of the Spanish Jewish experience and then concluded with an assessment of the resilience and impact of Spanish Jews and former crypto-Jews on international commerce and culture after 1492. The next entry, delivered as the 1980 Feinberg Lecture at the University of Cincinnati, provides Yerushalmi's responses to two questions that he frequently asked about crypto-Jews: first, how did they know what they knew about Judaism (that is, what were their sources of knowledge); and second, what were the challenges—psychological, intellectual, and even physical—faced by crypto-Jews in leaving behind their lives of secrecy in their home countries to live a full Jewish life abroad? This essay is followed by Yerushalmi's well-known attempt at comparative history in the 1982 Leo Baeck Memorial Lecture. There he demonstrated his considerable historical range and dexterity by discussing the introduction of protoracialist laws against New Christians in fifteenth-century Spain as a prelude to the emergence of antisemitic racial standards in late nineteenth- and twentieth-century Germany.

Part IV has the aim of bringing together a significant body of Yerushalmi's work that has hitherto remained dispersed—that is, his writings on the political history of the Jews. With Baron and Arendt constantly in his mind as guides and foils, Yerushalmi regularly addressed, though not always in sustained monographic form, the nature of the relationship between Jews and state power. His essay on Baruch Spinoza that opens this section, delivered as a lecture in Israel in 1977, revolves to a great extent around the Amsterdam philosopher's inaccurate historical account of the relative tolerance of Spain toward New Christians compared with Portugal. This mistake provided Yerushalmi with an opportunity to excavate the sources and aftereffects of Spinoza's famous view that it is Gentile hatred that preserves Jewish identity. In the next essay, a lecture delivered at Emory University in 2005, Yerushalmi recalled Salo Baron's assessment that medieval Jews were "servants," not "serfs," of royal authority, but continued on his own path by explicating with empathy the long history of the Jews' royal alliances, in sharp contrast to the condemning tenor of Hannah Arendt's analysis. The final essay in this section, Yerushalmi's 2005 Lucas Prize address, attempts to understand the State of Israel in light of another long and somewhat competing tradition, messianism, that typically breeds a lack of political realism. The State of Israel, Yerushalmi argued, breaks from this tradition, though some of its critics, Jewish and non-Jewish alike, continue to hold it to an unreasonable, antiquated, and theologically saturated messianic standard. It is in this last essay that Yerushalmi moved most demonstrably from his role as historian to commentator on contemporary affairs who evinces concern over the path and reputation of the State of Israel.

Part V, the final section, includes a number of essays that reflect the main focus of Yosef Yerushalmi's scholarship in the last quarter century of his life: the study of the vagaries, permutations, erosion, and vestiges of Jewish memory. The first essay has a melancholic tone familiar to us from *Zakhor*, but also an ironic one in that its subject is the history of Jewish *hope*. Yerushalmi issued a call for more scholarly attention to the history of hope, within which the more specific, dramatic, and well-researched history of Jewish messianism should be included. The history of hope, he argued, can only emerge out of an inquiry into Jewish despair. The reward for a study of hope and its absence will be the discovery of important clues to the perdurance of Jewish memory over the generations. The next essay treats of Sigmund Freud, one of Yerushalmi's favorite modern purveyors of Jewish memory. The essay, which emerged out of a 1994 conference in London in which Yerushalmi was scheduled to engage with Jacques Derrida, warned against a fetishization of the archive as the repository of truth, especially in the hands of the self-anointed guardians of the Freudian legacy. The third selection also continues the focus on the memory of Freud, making use of a curious piece of photographic evidence—the existence of a kiddush cup on a table in Freud's study—to upend the received notion of Freud as uninterested in, uneducated about, and at odds with his Jewish identity. Concluding this section, and the book at large, is Yerushalmi's first published work of fiction, a short story in the *New Yorker* that appeared in August 2011, a little more than a year and a half after his death. The story's title "Gilgul," the Hebrew term for the kabbalistic notion of the transmigration of the soul, features a main character, Ravitch, who is so desperate to achieve a state of psychic calm and make peace with the past that he seeks out a medium. The story is replete with recognizable Yerushalmi themes, beginning with the appearance of a sixteenth-century Spanish Jewish doctor, Isaac Benveniste, who bears a strong resemblance to the main protagonist of Yerushalmi's first book, Isaac Cardoso, as well as to another contemporaneous Isaac, the great courtier, scholar, and messianist Abravanel. Unlike Cardoso and Abravanel who left Spain for Italy, Benveniste set out after 1492 for Palestine but never succeeded in arriving, dying on the island of Rhodes. The medium tells Ravitch about Benveniste, who induces in him a strong dose of nostalgia. Hovering over the story is a deep yearning for the past, for a living memory that can nurture the present—a motif that courses through the pages of *Zakhor* and indeed one that exerted a persistent and poignant effect on Yosef Hayim Yerushalmi's life and work.

A NOTE ON STYLE

As noted above, each of the essays included in this volume is introduced by a brief preface that identifies its original appearance and explicates its main themes. For the most part, the articles have not been altered from their original form except where necessary to ensure readability. In the case of chapter 10, which initially appeared in Hebrew, we were required to draw on different sources in order to round out the text in English; the same obtained for the critical apparatus accompanying that chapter, as well as for chapter 13. In terms of transliteration, the editors generally followed the Library of Congress style. Yerushalmi himself diverged from that style on multiple occasions. He did not, for example, generally differentiate between alef and 'ayin. In these cases, his original transliteration has been preserved. Finally, to reiterate, the overwhelming majority of the essays were delivered as lectures, and the spoken form has been retained.

PART I *Self-Reflection*

1 : TO THE RUSSIAN READER

Preface to the Russian edition of *Zakhor* (Moscow: Gesharim, 2004).

The following is the English original of the preface to the Russian-language translation of *Zakhor*, published in Moscow in 2004. Although *Zakhor* was translated into eight languages, Yosef Yerushalmi professed a special feeling for the Russian version, even though he could not read it.

He began this brief, but revealing, excerpt by discussing his family's Russian roots and the origins of the family name—Yerusalimski—which was changed to Yerushalmi after his father fled the post-Revolution violence in Russia and immigrated to Palestine. Yerushalmi further recounted the arrival of his parents to the United States, his father from Palestine and his mother from Russia. Then he described the distinctive cultural milieu in which he grew up in the Bronx, a mix of Jewish religious sensibilities, ideologies, and languages.

In reporting on his multilingual upbringing (Hebrew and Yiddish), Yerushalmi admitted to a "lifelong regret" that he never learned Russian, which was his parents' "private language." He confided his great passion for Russian song, which filled his childhood home, as well as for Russian belles lettres. Indeed, it was Russian literature, of all the world literatures that Yerushalmi knew and loved, that spoke to him "most directly and intimately." There was something of the capacity to peer into the human soul, in all its richness and darkness, that drew Yerushalmi to the Russian classics. This capacity informed his own historical labors, most particularly, his attempts to peer into the soul of the crypto-Jew—and of the inquisitor, as well. So too it would seem that the Russian literary ethos, which yielded a deep, at times tortured, introspection, left a profound mark on Yerushalmi as a person.

Since its first publication in English in 1982 *Zakhor* has been translated into eight languages, including Japanese, yet this translation into Russian has for me a special and very personal significance. My parents were both Russian Jews, my mother born Kaplan in Pinsk, my father born Yerusalimski in Goloskov, though he received his Hebrew and Russian education in Odessa and studied at the university prior to the Revolution. I was born Yerushalmi in New York.

As far as I can determine, Yerusalimski was a rather uncommon name among Russian Jews. The family tradition is that in the reign of Tsar Nicholas I, when all Jews were forced to adopt family names, my fore-bear chose Yerusalimski because he hoped one day to live in Jerusalem. It was my father and an older brother who finally took this step. During the Civil War following the Revolution, when another brother had been killed in a pogrom, the two young men managed to flee from Russia and make their way to what was then Palestine. There they lived the life of pioneers and the name changed automatically to its Hebrew form—Yerushalmi. My father joined a kibbutz, working as a guard, in construction, and in the fields. In 1923 his brother returned to Russia intending to bring my grandfather to the Land of Israel. Unfortunately, this was just around the time that the anti-Zionist persecutions had begun. Neither of them got out, and thus I never knew my grandfather, my uncle, or any other members of my father's large family, some of whose members were exiled as Zionists to Siberia and dispersed to other places in Russia. As for my father, in 1928, he was engaged in draining swamps and became severely ill with malaria, an illness that broke his health completely and made further physical work impossible. A friend from Russia who had settled in America invited him to come, recuperate, and then he could go back. He came, and for the rest of his life he was always "going back." But he never had the money to do so, nor any useful profession that would earn him a living there. My mother had come directly to America with my grandmother in 1922 as a girl of sixteen. In 1930, at the beginning of the Great Depression, she met my father in New York, they fell in love, married, and two years later I came into the world.

It is almost impossible for me to describe the culture and society in which I was raised, because that world has disappeared. The entire neighborhood was Jewish, not necessarily Orthodox, but Jewish to the core, mostly from Eastern Europe, traditionalists and secularists, Zionists, Bundists and Communists, all perpetually and passionately debating, but friends nonetheless. Suffice it to say that, although born in New York, my first language was not English. Until the age of five I spoke fluent Hebrew and Yiddish, as I do to this day. The Hebrew came from my father, who spoke only that with me when we were alone. My mother did not speak Hebrew, so the lingua franca when we were together was Yiddish (a very literary "Vilna Yiddish"). However—both my parents, as I heard from their friends, also spoke and wrote a beautiful Russian. This language, to my lifelong regret, they withheld from me. It was their private language, spoken behind closed doors. When I went to university I did not study Russian; there were so many other languages I needed to learn for the historical work I wanted to do.

The one aspect of Russian that they did not keep to themselves was Russian song. Both of them loved to sing, whether in Hebrew, Yiddish or Russian, as did many of their friends. From my earliest childhood, when my mother would sing me to sleep with Russian lullabies, through the years when, on a summer evening, I would stroll through the park facing our home and hear Jews on the benches singing, some with guitars or even balalaikas, Russian music entered deep into my soul, moving me as no other can. It is part of what the French call my *moi profond*.

Perhaps it was from this that I came to Russian culture in the broader sense, of course in translation. In my adolescence I began to discover Gogol, Tolstoy, Dostoevski, Chekhov, whom I have read and reread to this day and to whom I have added many others, from Alexander Herzen to Isaac Babel. Yet although I have read widely in modern Hebrew, Yiddish, English, American, French, German, and Spanish literature, and have many loves in each, somehow Russian literature which, unlike the others, I can only read in translation (I first read Goncharov's *Oblomov* in Yiddish!), speaks to me most directly and intimately.

Only Russian poetry in translation has defied me. I have read Vladimir Nabokov's translation of Pushkin's *Eugene Onegin*, anthologies of Russian poetry, Tsvetaeva, Pasternak, Mandelstam, all with the feeling that I remain outside of what I am reading. I own a two-volume edition of the complete poems of Akhmatova with the Russian and the English on facing pages, and even visually I can feel how much is lost. When I asked a Russian colleague to read me a few poems in the original, I realized what it was. The music of her Russian language could not be transposed. . . .

In light of all I have said, you can imagine how moved I am to find one of my books translated for the first time into Russian. Happily, *Zakhor* is not poetry but prose, and while my style may be difficult to render in Russian, I have been assured that the translation has overcome all obstacles. In the years that have passed since the first edition in English, I have found nothing that would make me change any of the premises of the book. It is now for you, my new readers, to make your own judgments.

As the book goes to press I cannot help but think of my father's family who remained in Russia. I do not know how many survived the Second World War, nor where they or their children or grandchildren may be today. All contact was broken off in the early 1950's. I have never been to Russia. If I go, it will be to see the glories of the Hermitage in St. Petersburg and the Tretyakov in Moscow, and to meet Russian intellectuals,

Jews and non-Jews alike. I do not think I will go to Pinsk, because that will bring me only heartache. The "Great White Synagogue" of which my mother and grandmother spoke is no more; there is nothing left of what they knew and cherished. I would go to Goloskov only if the Jewish cemetery is still in existence, which I doubt. But Russian Jewry, though reduced in number, is still alive and full of creative potential, and the future, as historians should know, remains always unknown and open. This book and this preface are now for you, my dear and unknown Russian reader.

Yosef Hayim Yerushalmi
New York
13 Tammuz, 5764
2 July 2004

2 : WORDS DELIVERED ON THE OCCASION OF RECEIVING AN HONORARY DOCTORATE FROM THE ÉCOLE PRATIQUE DES HAUTES ÉTUDES

The Sorbonne, Paris, January 14, 2002.

This short speech afforded Yosef Yerushalmi the opportunity to reflect on his connection to the language and culture of France. He recalled his first teacher of French as a boy, as well as his wide reading of French literature in college, where he served as president of the Yeshiva College French Club.

Yerushalmi also gave voice to his admiration for the French tradition of Jewish studies and its scholars, for example, I. S. Révah, whose work on Marranos he often quoted in lectures and seminars. Yerushalmi also expressed esteem for notable French historians in fields other than his own, from Marc Bloch to Pierre Nora, whose multivolume *Les lieux de mémoire* appeared in 1984, the same year that *Zakhor* appeared in French (in Éric Vigne's translation). It was in that same period that Yerushalmi began to go to France regularly. During his visit in 1984, he met Nora, and the two discussed the affinities in their respective work on the formation of collective memory, an area of research in which the two scholars would gain international acclaim.

In the second half of his remarks, Yerushalmi reflected on the malleability of history. He noted the irony in the fact that the very city, Paris, in which rabbinic literature was now the subject of serious academic study was where the Talmud was consigned to flame in 1242, on the very site where brutal executions later took place during the Terror. That swing of the historical pendulum reminded Yerushalmi that history, like life, is open.

Yerushalmi followed on that point by addressing the utility of historical knowledge. History served as an antidote to both excessive despair and excessive hope by navigating between the poles of apocalypse and utopia. This realization led Yerushalmi to conclude that history was contingent and open-ended, resulting not in "ultimate knowledge" but rather "unexpected turns and byways"—exactly the stuff of the historian's craft and delight.

This is for me above all an occasion for gratitude and I have many to thank. I had the good fortune to study with great masters in Jewish and other fields, prodigious scholars who guided me while allowing me to become myself. But it seems to me more appropriate today to focus on my relation to France. I will begin with Lillian Krotky, an unforgettable teacher in an obscure Jewish school in New York who never received an "honoris causa," but who, when I was ten years old, introduced us with love and passion to the French language, and taught us to sing the "Marseillaise" as fervently as though we were storming the barricades. Thanks also to the stern teacher in my high school who forced us to memorize a French poem every week (out of all of Baudelaire he chose "L'Albatros," no doubt because he thought this "Fleur" contained no "Mal" that could corrupt us).

In college I read history for pleasure, but my field of study was comparative literature—English, Hebrew, German, and of course—French. My professors, less charismatic than Mlle. Krotky, at least exposed me systematically to texts from the *Chanson de Roland* through Albert Camus. When, still a student in New York, I met the young Israeli pianist who would soon become my wife and fill my life with music, not the least of her attractions was her knowledge of French (our son has by now surpassed both of us), and it was she who revealed to me the profundities of Debussy's *Préludes*, Ravel's *Gaspard de la nuit*, and so much else.

Yet I confess that even now I am not entirely secure in speaking French, and, while I accept that my spoken Portuguese in Lisbon is far from perfect, only in Paris do I feel that if I make a verbal slip I have committed a sin. No one can imagine the anxiety I felt before I taught my first seminar in French at 54 Boulevard Raspail, nor my embarrassment when, after a lecture in Geneva, a Parisian friend said to me: "C'était vraiment beau. Mais—qu'est-ce que c'est les '*zazards*'"? (That was really good. But what is "zazards"?) It took me a moment to realize that at one point I had said "*lesazards*" instead of "le[s] hazards." Other nuances are not grammatical but cultural. Outside of France it is not immediately evident that an École can be both "Normale" and "Supérieure," and only later did I fully appreciate the "Pratique" in L'École Pratique des Hautes Études. For an Anglophone, "Sciences Religieuses" translates into an impossible "Religious Sciences" or "Sciences of Religion" unless, perhaps, if one thinks of the German *Religionswissenschaft*. "Histoire du Judaïsme" becomes in English "The History of Judaism," where "Judaism" can only mean the Jewish religion, whereas the more elastic "Judaïsme" includes both the Jewish religion and the Jewish people, as in *Wissenschaft des Judentums*. I am a historian of the Jewish people, and as such I am inevitably also a historian of its religion. I would not feel at ease in a "Department of Religion" at an American university; I am delighted to be linked to "Sciences Religieuses" at the École Pratique which, in its breadth and scope, remains unique.

If I still lapse occasionally while speaking French, I believe I have been a good reader, and the decades of reading have brought me untold riches. I cannot express fully, in this brief time, what I owe to France and to French culture, and this is so even if I limit myself to scholarship. My debt to French Jewish historians from Isidore Loeb to Isaac Salvador Révah and to the inexhaustible *Revue des Études Juives* is directly reflected in my work and requires no further comment. Less obvious but no less important to me has been the impact of French historical scholarship beyond Jewish historiography per se.

The names come easily but I shall mention only a few. Marc Bloch— not *La société féodale* or even *Apologie pour l'histoire*, but—*Les rois thaumaturges*! Lucien Fèbvre on Rabelais, and his seminal essay "La sensibilité et l'histoire." Philippe Ariès on childhood and on death. Louis Massignon on Al-Hallaj. Marcel Bataillon, *Érasme et l'Espagne*. It is not that I became a disciple of any of these or have necessarily pursued their themes. It is just that when one is young, in one's twenties, an apprentice historian, certain books come like revelations; they stretch the mind and the imagination beyond their prior limits. So *this* is what a historian is capable of writing! Such history is possible! And suddenly other possibilities unfold. . . .

I have reached an age when I ask myself what I have learned beyond what I have read or written. For myself I can say I have learned that life is open, full of the unexpected whether for better or worse, full of surprise. In the long years when I was studying for my doctorate in Jewish history I did not know whether there would even be an academic position available when I finished. I certainly did not dream that I would have the privilege of teaching at the two institutions that were the first secular universities in the Western world to fully integrate postbiblical Jewish studies as part of the patrimony of world civilization (Harvard—Jewish Literature and Philosophy—1925; Columbia—Jewish History—1930). Needless to say, the thought that one day I might be honored here, at the Sorbonne, never crossed my mind.

Yet here I stand, and I am deeply moved. My sincere thanks to Prof. Jean Baubérot, President of the École; to Prof. Claude Langlois, president of the Cinquième Section and to his colleagues; and in particular to Professors Esther Benbassa and Jean-Christophe Attias, who had much to do with this honor, and who continue with distinction the admirable tradition of Études Juives forged by their predecessors at the École—Israel Lévi, Georges Vajda, Charles Touatti, Gérard Nahon.

I take this occasion also to express publicly my gratitude to Éric Vigne, my French editor and translator, my dear friend. Whatever reputation I have in France I ultimately owe to him. For it was he, on his own initiative, who translated and published *Zakhor* in 1984. I arrived in Paris that year to find that the first volumes of Pierre Nora's monumental work, *Les lieux de mémoire*, had just appeared. A new friendship began when Nora and I met, both astonished that, separated by an ocean, unknown to one another, within totally different historical contexts, we had been working along strikingly parallel lines. Another surprise. How to explain it? It has been suggested that there must have been "something in the air," an explanation that turns historiography into meteorology. . . .

If life is open, the same is true of history. Rather than speak abstractly, I choose one specific and for me poignant example that is not, perhaps, without relevance.

The beauties of Paris and the glories of its history have long been celebrated, not least by Americans. But for a historian of the Jews with a long historical memory, Paris has yet another, darker claim to fame. It is the city in which, in 1242, in the Place de Grève which is today the splendid Place de l'Hôtel de Ville, for the first time in history the Talmud was publicly burned.

Not only the Talmud was burned in the Place de Grève. It was also, as you know, the place for burning heretics, for executing criminals, for the first guillotine during the Terror. Certainly the taking of human life is graver than the slaughter of books. Yet the two are related. Those who are prepared to burn books will not stop with books. In Rome the Talmud was burned in 1554 in the Campo de' Fiori. Forty-six years later Giordano Bruno was burned in the same "Champ des Fleurs." Who among those who saw the flames in Paris or Rome could have imagined that centuries later the Talmud would be studied in Paris at an institution such as this? Or, for that matter, that the four-hundredth anniversary of Bruno's death would be commemorated around the world?

I share these thoughts with you not in order to demonstrate progress in history. That illusion is no longer possible. After the horrors we have witnessed, who will dare affirm that the twentieth century was superior to the thirteenth? On the other hand, in the wake of the catastrophe in New York four months ago, shall we already give up hope for the twenty-first? I only insist that history is always open, that there is gain and loss, and that we cannot know in advance what will be gained and what will be lost. Whatever its other uses, historical knowledge should immunize us against all apocalypses and utopias alike, for it is in the nature of such thinking to regard history as closed and determined. How many "ends" are being proclaimed—the end of the book, of reading, of universities, the end of the Jewish people, the end of history, the end of the world itself. And conversely—the rosy, imminent paradises of the global village, of infinite knowledge, of perfect health and eternal youth.

Any of these may indeed occur. But we do not *know* this. Deprived of ultimate knowledge we can only follow our paths to the best of our abilities, as they unfold, through unexpected turns and byways, trusting that the journey itself is worthwhile. By inviting me here today you have helped me feel that my own is not in vain. For that too—I thank you.

PART II *Early Patterns*

3 : BAER'S HISTORY,
TRANSLATED AND REVISITED

Published in *Conservative Judaism* 21:1 (Fall 1966), 73–82.

This review of the English translation of Yitzhak Baer's *History of the Jews in Christian Spain* was published in 1966, the year in which Yerushalmi, then thirty-four years old, completed his Ph.D. and took up a position at Harvard University. The journal in which it appeared, *Conservative Judaism*, was the scholarly organ of the Rabbinical Assembly, the national association of Conservative rabbis affiliated with the Jewish Theological Seminary, where Yerushalmi had been ordained in 1957. Baer was a leading figure in the "Jerusalem School" of historians at the Hebrew University. Born and raised in Germany, Baer studied medieval Spanish history with Heinrich Finke at the University of Freiburg. He immigrated to Palestine in 1930 to become the first professor of Jewish history at the Hebrew University in Jerusalem.

Baer wrote about many aspects of Jewish history from ancient times on but gained his greatest renown for his work on the medieval period, and especially on the history of the Jews of Spain. After visiting the Spanish archives in the 1920s, Baer followed the path of his teacher Finke and published a large collection of primary materials relating to the life of Jews in medieval Spain. The first volume of this documentary collection from 1929 served as the prelude to Baer's most well-known book, *A History of the Jews in Christian Spain*, originally published in Hebrew in 1945 and then in two volumes in English from 1961 to 1966.

Yerushalmi was an ideal person to review this book. The doctoral dissertation that he was wrapping up in this period under Salo Baron at Columbia was rooted in the post-Expulsion history of Sephardic Jews, a period later than that covered in Baer's *History*. But it rested on a deep familiarity with the sources and structures of medieval Spanish Jewish life that stood at the heart of Baer's *History*. Yerushalmi maintained an active interest in Baer's work throughout his life, and some thirty years later would write a preface to the French translation of another of his books, *Galut*.

Because the central themes and argument of Baer's book were known, Yerushalmi assumed, to many of his readers from the Hebrew edition, he used the review to discuss key themes occasioned by the appearance of the new translation. He considered the translation in the context of the growth of Jewish studies in postwar American universities (of which his own position at Harvard was an instance) and noted that English translations of classic texts had become a pedagogic necessity. But his main comments were directed at the self-perception of American Jews. He pointed out that contemporary American Jews often appealed to medieval Spanish Jewry—and particularly to its sense of security and prosperity, its intimate relations with Gentile society, and its enlightened interest in secular knowledge—as a kind of validating historical precedent. But this analogy, Yerushalmi claimed, was based on a false belief that the mythical Spanish "Golden Age"—and the corresponding spirit of *convivencia*—characterized Jewish society in Spain throughout the medieval period. In fact, occasional bursts of creativity and periods of stability notwithstanding, the history of the Jews in Spain was marked by the recurrent hostility of the Gentile population of Spain, both Muslim and Christian. And this pattern was not restricted to Spain. In a line of argument consistent with Baer's own understanding, Yerushalmi argued here that the Expulsion of 1492 was not an aberration but the culmination of a centuries-long process of Christian Europe disgorging its Jews. Accordingly, he declared, in the rather lachrymose tone of the review, that "catastrophic elements were implicit in the development of Spanish Jewry from the very beginning."

Yerushalmi ended his review with a reflection on Jewish historical self-consciousness, an early foray into the field of Jewish historiography that would, of course, be the subject of his *Zakhor* twenty years later. Spanish Jews were too used to thinking about historical causation in terms of divine providence to be able to think analytically about the catastrophes they endured and the factors that had produced them. This led Yerushalmi to conclude that although "sacred history" may have "sustaining qualities," it "has often extracted a heavy price from the Jewish people by inhibiting it from grasping the realities of its struggle to survive in a profane world." Yerushalmi concluded his review by quoting Baer, who acknowledged that one contemporaneous Spanish Jew had a chance to pierce through the veil of sacrality in understanding the past on its own terms. That was Yerushalmi's own recurrent hero, Solomon Ibn Verga. Ultimately, even Ibn Verga was unable to grasp historical reality as it was. The lesson of this invocation of Ibn Verga was clear. Yerushalmi exhorted modern Jews, who, after the nineteenth century, are now "historically oriented," to extend their historical sensibility to an analysis of their own existence. To fail to do so in the aftermath of the Holocaust would be "unpardonable."

It is somewhat unsettling to be invited to "review" a classic. Baer's study of the Jews in Christian Spain has been available to all who read Hebrew for over twenty years,[1] and is a recognized landmark in Jewish historiography. Indeed, perhaps with the exception of England, it is the only authoritative and comprehensive treatment we possess, in any language, of the historical development of an entire medieval European Jewry. Nothing comparable to it exists for medieval France, Provence, Germany or Italy, although to be sure, monographs abound on specific localities and epochs within these countries. Curiously Spain's Iberian neighbor, Portugal, remains virtually terra incognita to Jewish scholarship, at least with regard to developments prior to the late fifteenth century.[2]

However, Baer's work claims a place of honor in our historical library not merely for its scope, but because of the foundations on which it rests. The author had himself prepared the ground with the earlier publication of his two monumental volumes of sources and documents,[3] incorporating the results of his extensive research in the Spanish archives, and materials scattered far and wide in older monographs of both Jewish and gentile scholars, a model of what must be done before we can treat the history of other Jewries in similar depth.

Now at last we have been given a complete English translation of this seminal work, under the aegis of the Jewish Publication Society of America. It is thus made available for the first time not only to Anglo American Jewry, but to the scholarly world at large, which, but for some of the Spanish Hebraists of the *Instituto Arias Montano* in Madrid and Barcelona, had no access to the book in the original. The JPS can well be proud of having sponsored such a project, while the translators are to be congratulated for their achievement in overcoming the many obstacles posed by a work which itself abounds in translations of texts from Aramaic, Spanish and Latin sources. It is a measure of their success that I, for one, was able to discover only one slip: In Vol. II, Aragon sometimes becomes "Aragonia" (e.g., pp. 111, 160), a minor lapse, in which the translator merely transliterated the Hebrew form of the word. The translation as a whole is both accurate and fluent, and without prior knowledge one would scarcely detect that the second volume is the work of several different hands. Moreover, as Baer notes in a special preface, this translation of the second Hebrew edition "should be considered a third edition of the book," and so it is. New materials have been incorporated into the footnotes, bibliographical references have been expanded and brought up to date, and a special appendix has been added.[4] We are confronted with that rare phenomenon, a translation to which even those who know the original will henceforth be obliged to refer.

Despite these novelties, Baer's *History* is sufficiently familiar to the readers of this journal to obviate the need for a technical analysis of its contents two decades after its initial publication. However, the very appearance of the translation is an event with manifold significance of its own, and gives rise to a number of reflections.

A BOON TO STUDENTS

One of the more interesting developments of recent years has been the unprecedented expansion of offerings in Jewish studies at American colleges and universities. Since the teacher can only rarely assume that the undergraduate student possesses a reading facility in Hebrew, or even in the European languages in which Jewish scholarship expressed itself, the dearth of suitable materials in English poses a real problem. This translation, then, is a real boon to those concerned with a new and dynamic educational frontier. Both the JPS and the translators may be gratified to know that already last year Baer's *History* served as the basic textbook for a full undergraduate course in Spanish-Jewish history at Rutgers University.

Still, it would be a pity if the book were to have currency in academic circles alone. Perhaps one may rather be permitted to view this publishing venture as an incipient act of faith in the maturity of the Jewish public in this country, or at least as a sign of expectation that a potential audience can be found for such a work. Coming only shortly after the translation of Tcherikover's study of the Hellenistic period,[5] also under the sponsorship of the JPS, it marks a new concern to bring the rich harvest of serious Israeli scholarship to the attention of American Jews. At a time when adult Jewish education in the United States is still largely guided by the premise that lay audiences cannot bear anything more taxing than what Rosenzweig so accurately labeled lectures on "Judaism and . . . ," this is welcome indeed. With such books increasingly accessible, the challenge now rests with rabbis and educators to make creative use of them in their adult classes.

THE MYTHOS OF THE GOLDEN AGE

It is to be hoped, in particular, that the wider dissemination of Baer's *History* might help put an end to the facile analogies between Spanish Jewry and American Jewry, drawn so often from pulpit and platform. The motives behind such analogies are, of course, sufficiently clear, though not always made manifest. In essence, they stem from the fact that we are caught in a peculiar ambivalence. On the one hand, when we are reminded of the historical pattern of Jewish tragedy in the diaspora, we insist that "America is different." Yet at the very same time, we do not wish to regard ourselves as being *so* different as to constitute a complete *novum* in Jewish history. In our search for that authentication which can come only from a sense of continuity, in our need to be reassured that our situation has its precedents, we should like to find some past Jewish community with which we might identify, or at least empathize. Since neither the medieval Ashkenazic Jewries, nor even the Eastern Europe of our parents and grandparents, will serve the purpose (for the contrasts are too obvious to be ignored), we anchor ourselves to medieval Spain. Amid the many elements which form the popular mythos of the "Golden Age," there are a number which elicit from us a glow of recognition: the size and prosperity of Spanish Jewry, its intimate relations with the gentile society, the passion for secular knowledge, Jewish physicians and scientists, poets and philosophers, courtiers and statesmen. In this attractive historical Midrash it is easy to gloss the synagogues of Toledo as forerunners of our own opulent houses of worship, while Hasdai ibn Shaprut seems an excellent prototype for Ambassador Goldberg. In short, we are avid to see the achievements of Spanish Jewry as paradigms for ourselves, while we reject the tragic features of Spanish Jewish history, or merely ignore them. Even the Expulsion of 1492, a matter of common knowledge, is popularly regarded as the capriciously cruel act of Ferdinand and Isabella, almost a mere expression of personal vindictiveness, rather than as the final resolution of forces set in motion long before.

The fact is that catastrophic elements were implicit in the development of Spanish Jewry from the very beginning. We would do well to remember that the "Golden Age" was not coextensive with Spanish Jewish history, but can perhaps be applied legitimately only to the burst of hyper creativity from the late tenth to the early twelfth centuries under Muslim rule, a period which falls outside the scope of Baer's work. Even then, except for the few decades prior to the disintegration of the Caliphate of Cordoba in 1013, this golden age of culture was one of considerable turmoil for the Jews, just as the Renaissance was an age of war and political anguish for the Italian states. Shemuel Ha-Nagid, that remarkable blend of poet, scholar, warrior and statesman, died in his bed; but in 1066 his son Yehosef, who had succeeded him as vizier of Granada, was slaughtered in a pogrom which engulfed the entire community. The arrival of the Almoravides some twenty years later made of Moses ibn Ezra a wanderer, and the invasion of the fanatical Almohades in 1141 put a decisive end to open Jewish life in Muslim territory.

That Spanish Jewry received a new lease on life in Christian Spain, which enabled it to continue to develop there for another three hundred and fifty years, was due to the peculiar constellation of forces in the Iberian Peninsula. While the rest of Europe was off carrying the war against Islam to the Near East, Christian Spain alone had to fight its crusade against the Muslims at home, over a span of centuries. It was the Christian *Reconquista*, the sporadic drive to reconquer the Muslim South, which opened new possibilities for the Jews, and made them welcome. Their skills, their experience in the Muslim environment and, not least, their ability to contribute to the royal treasuries of the Christian states, made them an important asset in that obsessive war which is the leitmotif of medieval Spanish history. Yet, although even in the thirteenth century the status of the Jews in Christian Spain was markedly superior to that of Jews in other European countries, whatever stability they enjoyed rested on potentially weak foundations. The Christian burghers, the Mendicant Orders, and increasingly the masses, were overtly or tacitly hostile. Jewish security was never broadly based, but was linked directly to royal protection. It is no accident that the frightful pogroms of 1391, when the first great mass conversions occurred, should have erupted during an interregnum in Castile, and while Aragon was governed by a king (John I) who was weak and irresolute. Moreover, in Christian Spain as previously in the Muslim South, the destinies of the Jewish communities were largely in the hands of relatively small aristocracies of privileged courtiers, tax-farmers and financiers. While this structure could be a source of strength when such men used their power and influence in the interests of the community, at other times it led to arbitrary rule and social unrest. The analysis of these internal stresses and strains constitutes one of the most brilliant aspects of Baer's work.

If, despite such chaotic forces, both within and without, Spanish Jewry was able to achieve what it did, it is a tribute to its enormous vitality. On the other hand, that so many thousands of Spanish Jews converted to Christianity in the late fourteenth and early fifteenth centuries, should not surprise us. In no other country of medieval Europe were the Jews subjected to so protracted and relentless a campaign of conversion. Perhaps nowhere else did Christianity possess quite so intense a missionary zeal, as did that Spanish Catholicism which had been forged in the crucible of a "holy war" to drive the infidel out of the homeland. The Jewish communities had barely begun to recover from the cataclysm of 1391, when they were subjected in 1411 to the spiritual avalanche of the Disputation of Tortosa. As one reads Baer's description of these two crucial decades, one begins to wonder, not at the many who converted, but that so many should have remained constant.[6] Yet after each of these enormous crises the Jewish communities, reduced in numbers and strength, undertook the task of rebuilding. Ultimately, of course, it was futile. If the *Reconquista* had originally provided the Jews with a place and a function in the Christian states of Spain, its final completion sealed their doom. With the marriage of Ferdinand and Isabella the crowns of Aragon and Castile were united. The entire policy of the Catholic Monarchs was now devoted to the political and religious unification of the Peninsula. On January 2, 1492, the king and queen triumphantly entered Granada, the last Muslim stronghold. There, on March 31st, they signed the Edict of Expulsion.

This sketch, inadequate as it is, should be sufficient to indicate the gulf which separates American Jewry from that of Spain. No fruitful parallels can be drawn between a community which is essentially a voluntary association, and one which exercised almost total control over its members; between a modern state predicated on individual citizenship, and one which was composed of rigidly defined corporate groups; between assimilatory pressures in a secular society, and those in a religious body-politic. In these and other essential respects we *are* different. Which is not to say that "it can't happen here," but merely that, should it happen, it will be due to very different factors.

The differences are not only sociological and political, but in a profound sense cultural as well. For all the vaunted openness of Spanish Jewry to the surrounding culture, we should not ignore the fact that Jewish creativity in Christian Spain expressed itself largely on its own terms, in organic continuity with the Jewish past, and certainly in its own idiom. To focus only on the latter characteristic, let us note that although the Castilian language was widely diffused among the Jews, the Jewish intelligentsia read and wrote Hebrew. Shem Tob Ardutiel (Santob de Carrión) composed the *Proverbios morales* in Castilian and dedicated them to the Infante Don Pedro, but he was also a Hebrew poet. At the very moment that we hail the translation of Baer's *History* into English (the language of this review as well), we may point out an interesting paradox which can itself be regarded as symbolic: We are eagerly awaiting the completion of the JPS translation of the Bible, for this and similar projects are a necessity *for the Jews*. In fifteenth century Spain, when a Castilian translation of the Bible was prepared by Moses Arragel, it was at the behest of the Grand Master of the chivalric military order of the Knights of Calatrava.[7] These remarks are not aimed at invidious comparisons. They are rather meant to emphasize that loose historical analogies can only obscure from our view the radically altered problems inherent in the development, and present state, of American Jewry.

HISTORY AND SELF-UNDERSTANDING

What then is to be gained by laymen and leaders from the study of such a work as Baer's? Certainly it offers its own rewards. The history of Spanish Jewry is especially colorful and dramatic, and in Professor Baer's account, often extremely moving. But there is something else. When the study of past epochs in Jewish history is undertaken, not for the sake of crude identifications, but in an attempt to understand their dynamics in their specific contexts, it may potentially heighten our own historical sensitivity and awareness.

A reading of Baer's *History* reveals, ironically perhaps, but with terrifying clarity, that Spanish Jewry itself had no such historical self-understanding. That other medieval and modern Jewries were equally unhistorical in their outlook offers no consolation, but only makes the phenomenon more grim. The Spanish Jewish leaders reacted to each crisis in turn, often with prodigious energy, inventiveness and devotion. But they were unable to perceive the historical forces which ran beneath these eruptions. In all the long history of the Jews in Spain, it seems that Yehudah Halevi alone was able to arrive at an intuitive realization that Jewish life was ultimately untenable in both the Muslim and Christian territories; but he remains an isolated figure. Even after the deluge of 1391, all efforts were channeled into the reconstruction of the communities, on the tacit assumption that, now that order had been restored, Jewish existence in Spain was still viable. So again after Tortosa, and even after the establishment of the Inquisition. Despite his vast and intimate experience in the political world of his day, even Isaac Abravanel, the last great leader of Spanish Jewry, did not perceive the impending disaster with sufficient clarity to prepare his brethren. If we may functionally accept Burckhardt's definition of history as "the record of what one age finds worthy of note in another," then certainly for us the tragic lack of historical perspective among the Spanish Jews must appear as noteworthy a phenomenon as the composition of the Zohar.

We cannot, of course, sit in judgment of them. We understand why it was so. So long as a strictly providential view of history gripped the minds of Jews, so long as the vicissitudes of Jewish life were interpreted primarily as evidence of Divine favor or disfavor, it was essentially irrelevant to search for rational causalities in the flux of events. Maimonides characteristically frowned upon the study of secular history as "a waste of time."[8] A measure of the extent to which the ancient theodicies held sway may be seen in the fact that, even after the Expulsion, while Jewry was still reeling from the blow, the moralists sought to explain the catastrophe as punishment for the hubris of the Spanish Jews.[9]

For us, it is otherwise. Heirs, for the most part, of nineteenth-century Western culture, we are in a preeminent sense historically oriented. Unfortunately however, all too often our historical sensibility does not extend to our Jewish existence. Perhaps we have here another instance of the dichotomy which has long afflicted the souls of modern Jews, dividing the Jewish from the generally human. In any case, the same intelligent Jew who will consistently seek an historical approach in any analysis of the current world situation, is somehow reluctant or incapable of apprehending the contemporary Jewish world in similar categories. This is not merely the result of a widespread ignorance of Jewish history. I suspect that most often it is due to an inherited or atavistic tendency, even among the skeptic and agnostic, to regard the Jewish position in semi-mystical or quasi-theological terms. That this may prove as disastrous for the future as it has been in the past, is something we have not yet learned. Whatever its sustaining qualities, "sacred history" has often exacted a heavy price from the Jewish people by inhibiting it from grasping the realities of its struggle to survive in a profane world.[10] The quest for a theology of Jewish history may still be a religious need of our day, perhaps even the most agonizing need, but I doubt that it can be satisfied in our lifetime or that of our children. In any event, it must never again be allowed to overstep its limitations, and thus enable us to evade an objective assessment of mundane realities. To those who insist that they hear the *bat kol*, we must say of history, as Rabbi Joshua once said to Rabbi Eliezer of the Law: "It is not in heaven. . . ." If there is an historical parallel to be sought, I would submit that it is not to the life of Spanish Jewry, but to the generation or two following its extinction. Like world Jewry then, we have witnessed in our time a decisive historical catastrophe of unprecedented dimensions. As the Spanish Expulsion was the culminating exile of the Middle Ages, so is the Nazi holocaust the culminating slaughter. As in the early sixteenth century, so today, the entire geographical orbit of World Jewry has shifted radically, and the spiritual repercussions have yet to unravel themselves. Two decades after the extermination of European Jewry it is sobering to re-read Professor Baer's remarks on "The Expulsion as Viewed by Contemporaries," the last section in his book:

> Among Jews there was one single individual who some thirty years after the event, ventured to discuss the real causes of the Expulsion from Spain in the light of Italian political thought. This was Solomon ibn Verga in his Shebet Yehudah. But . . . he neither probed to the necessary depth nor arrived at any practical conclusions which might conceivably have pointed a way toward the improvement of the political status of his people. In the final analysis, he too failed to penetrate beyond the traditional religious framework common to all ages of Diaspora Jewry.
>
> As for his many contemporaries who had occasion to mention the Expulsion in their books, none forsook the narrow confines of that mythicizing mentality which has been at once the peculiar strength and weakness of the Jewish people since earliest antiquity. Though their accounts of the Expulsion, of the twelve years that preceded it, and the difficult events that followed, are not without interest, their horizons are modest, and they make no serious effort to explore the real issues having to do, whether directly or in a more oblique manner, with the great crisis. . . . An entire world lay in ruins before them and yet—except for the great religious resurgence which led to the temporary renewal of the Jewish community in Palestine—the foundations of the old modes of thought remained unshaken. . . ."[11]

For our fathers this was perhaps inevitable; for us, it shall surely be unpardonable.

NOTES

A History of the Jews in Christian Spain, by Yitzhak Baer. Vol. I, "From the Reconquest to the Fourteenth Century," tr. by Louis Schoffman, vii + 463 pp., Philadelphia, 1961; Vol. II, "From the Fourteenth Century to the Expulsion," tr. by Lotte Levinson, Hillel Halkin and Shulamith Nardi, xi + 537 pp., Philadelphia, 1966.

1. *Toledot ha-Yehudim bi-Sefarad ha-notzrit*, first edition, 2 vols., Tel Aviv, 1945; second edition, revised and enlarged, 1 vol., 1959.

2. The standard guide remains Meyer Kayserling's *Geschichte der Juden in Portugal*, 1867, in which no archival sources were utilized. The first three hundred years of Portuguese Jewish history are dealt with schematically in a bare sixty pages.

3. Fritz (Yitzhak) Baer, *Die Juden im Christlichen Spanien*, Erster Teil: Urkunden

und Regesten. Vol. I, *Aragonien und Navarra*, Berlin, 1929. Vol. II, *Kastillien/Inqui-sitionsakten*, Berlin, 1963. A third projected volume on Judeo-Christian polemics has not appeared.

4. The new appendix is devoted to a rebuttal of the thesis advanced by Américo Castro, and subsequently by Claudio Sánchez Albornoz, that the Spanish Inquisition had its origins in the climate and judicial procedures of the Jewish communities themselves. Baer might also have addressed himself to Castro's allied contention that the statutes of Purity of Blood (*limpieza de sangre*) were a reflection of an alleged preoccupation with such matters among the Spanish Jews. (This has been rejected effectively by Albert Sicroff, *Les controverses des statuts de "pureté de sang" en Espagne*, Paris, 1960, p. 88 n. 98.)

One should note also that Baer fails to make a significant distinction between what Castro and Sánchez have written. While the latter states crudely, that "there is no doubt that the Inquisition was a satanic Hispano-Jewish invention" (cited by Baer, II, 444), Castro was careful to emphasize: "We have already seen how the belief in Santiago was magnified to oppose the faith in Mohammed. *This does not mean that the belief in Santiago was Islamic, or that the Inquisitorial reaction was Jewish, even though we cannot explain these phenomena without keeping in mind the situation of the Moors and the Jews.*" Though Baer is correct in refuting the substantive point, it would be most unfortunate if his appendix would unwittingly deter some from reading Castro's fascinating and provocative work, available in English translation as *The Structure of Spanish History* (Princeton, 1954; the above citation on p. 531, n. 138). The uninitiated may even infer from Baer's appendix that Castro is an anti-Semite, which is emphatically not the case. One of his central themes is the argument that the history of Spain can only be understood as a thorough interaction of Christian, Jewish and Moorish elements. Castro's influential work has stimulated in recent years an intensive research into the Jewish extraction of some of Spain's more illustrious figures, a reappraisal of the profound impact of the *conversos*, and in general, a new appreciation of the Jewish factor in Iberian civilization. Despite its often venturesome and controversial hypotheses, it opens new vistas to the Iberian side of the Judeo-Spanish symbiosis.

5. Victor Tcherikover, *Hellenistic Civilization and the Jews*, Philadelphia, 1961. Parenthetically, I find myself wondering why the JPS has allowed Abraham A. Neuman's *The Jews in Spain* (2 vols., Phila., 1942) to remain out of print. This work, rich in materials on the inner life of the community, is a fine complement to Baer, and should be reissued. [Editors' note: Neuman's volumes were indeed reissued in 1969–70.]

6. Nevertheless, Baer himself tends to make a disparaging contrast between the alleged weakness of the Spanish Jews in 1391, and the constancy of the Ashke-

nazic Jews who chose martyrdom during the Crusades. This approach has been rightly criticized as oversimplified in Isaiah Sonne's incisive review, "On Baer and His Philosophy of History," *Jewish Social Studies*, IX (1947), 61–80, which should be read by any serious student of the book.

7. Significantly, the fifteenth-century translations of Maimonides' *Moreh Nebukim* and Halevi's *Kuzari* seem to have originated in *converso* circles. See Baer, II, 486, n. 8.

8. See the illuminating essay by Salo W. Baron on "The Historical Outlook of Maimonides," now reprinted in a collection of his essays on *History and Jewish Historians*, ed. A. Hertzberg and L. Feldman, Philadelphia, 1964; especially pp. 110 ff. Cf. also his discussion of the profuse apologies offered by the sixteenth century author of *Me'or 'Enayim* for spending too much time on history ("Azariah de' Rossi's Historical Method," ibid., p. 207).

9. See Baer, II, 442 f. Though Baer is certainly not attempting a theodicy of his own, it is interesting that he should himself immediately add: "The simple kept faith," thus, perhaps unintentionally, conveying the impression that the moralists were somehow correct in claiming that it was the rich and educated alone who succumbed to conversion in order to avoid being expelled. The reality was rather more complex. One has but to glance at the Sephardic Diaspora following the Expulsion, to realize that it was not merely the ignorant poor and the humble who were arriving in the ports of Italy and the Near East to continue their lives as Jews. On the other hand, Baer knows better than anyone that in times of stress conversions occurred at all levels, and the ranks of *conversos* were also filled with those of the lower classes of Jews (cf. ibid., 273).

10. In his discussion of "Newer Emphases in Jewish History" (*History and Jewish Historians*, 90–106), Salo Baron stated: "A more balanced view must also be taken by Jewish historians with respect to concerted Jewish political action. In the past, neither the need nor the possibility of such action was fully understood. No crasser illustration need be adduced than the earlier generations' lack of historic appreciation of the few political actions of this type which had taken place in their lifetime." As a vivid example, Baron cites Jewish reactions to the attempted boycott by Ottoman Jewry of papal Ancona after twenty-four Marranos were burned there in 1556 (ibid., p. 97 ff.).

11. Baer, II, 441 f.; cf. also his *Galut* (New York, 1947), pp. 77 f.

4 : A JEWISH HISTORIAN IN THE "AGE OF AQUARIUS"

Originally delivered as the Commencement Address at Hebrew College, Brookline, Massachusetts, June 1970.

This lecture was delivered in 1970 as a commencement address for graduates of Hebrew College in Brookline, Massachusetts, one of the sites of Jewish higher education in the era before the major expansion of Jewish studies into American colleges and universities. The backdrop of the address, whose title echoes the well-known song from the popular American musical *Hair*, was the revolutionary counterculture of the 1960s and '70s. This gave Yerushalmi the opportunity to reflect on the history of apocalyptic messianism, a preoccupation of his from the time of his own doctoral dissertation to his very last year of teaching in 2006–7, in which he delivered an undergraduate lecture on the history of Jewish messianism. The 1970 address also touched on two other kinds of revolutionary culture. The first was the cultural relativism in the academy that treated the conventional subjects and methodology of historical study with suspicion. And the second was the attempt of many Jews in the modern period to break all ties with the past and to assimilate into a universal "Mankind" in which Jewish history would be irrelevant. In this address, then, we once again encounter Yerushalmi's early preoccupation with the problem of the modern Jew's approach to history. It is also one of the earliest adumbrations of his concern with the predicament of the modern Jewish historian that would reach its most mature expression twelve years later in *Zakhor*.

Yerushalmi resisted the assault on historical study by affirming the "existential fact" that "man is an historical being" in whom "the past is always present." Echoing R. G. Collingwood, Yerushalmi insisted that in order to know himself, man must know his past. To illustrate the point, he contextualized the Aquarian urge of the Vietnam era, in which young revolutionaries were ushering in a new cosmic era, by pointing out that similar urges characterized apocalyptic movements throughout history, from Joachim da Fiore, a monk in the twelfth century, to Jakob Frank in the eighteenth century, and beyond. This contextualization, Yerushalmi argued, allows for understanding and precludes rash judgment. At the same time, it "should not"—and here Yerushalmi referred to certain trends in the academy— "as so often happens today, relativize everything." Indeed, Yerushalmi issued a warning that, for all the potential of Aquarian movements past, they have commonly moved from libertarian promise to mystical anarchism to the violence of charismatic dictatorship. The problem is that the apocalyptic revolutionary, mistakenly believing history to be at an end, flees from it by trying to annihilate the past, only to be hurled back into it "more naked, more bereft, more impotent than before."

If "amnesia"—the flight from history—"is not a goal but a disorder," it is a very common disorder among contemporary Jews. In the modern age, most Jews have held on to one form or another of eschatological Aquarianism, be it the emancipatory universalism of the German Maskilim, the revolutionary nationalism of the Zionists, or the great migration to America, fueled by dreams of the millennial *goldene medineh*. But these various flights from history, Yerushalmi maintained, like all others, are ultimately misguided. We are not, as Francis Fukayama famously maintained in a 1992 book, at the end of history, nor at its beginning. Rather, we dwell "in the midst of history"—a statement that lay at the core of Yerushalmi's own guiding historicist credo. The Jewish future can only unfold upon a consciousness of the Jewish past. And so the ancient biblical exhortation to remember—*zakhor*—remains pertinent in the aftermath of the Holocaust. In his closing comments, Yerushalmi tied together Jewish memory and Jewish history. Whereas before the modern period, Jews could find the past in their "learning, liturgy, law and practice," their modern descendants devoted themselves to the study of history, which served as an essential tool in the recovery of their collective memory. In this regard, the modern historian plays an important role as transmitter of memory.

Of course, Yerushalmi would address the relationship between history and memory at greater length in *Zakhor*. This early essay advances a more constructive and, in some sense, optimistic reading of history and the role of the modern historian. *Zakhor* places emphasis on the rupture wrought by modern critical history, which became, in Yerushalmi's well-known turn of phrase, the "faith of fallen Jews." And yet, a thread of continuity can be seen between the earlier and later meditations as, for example, when Yerushalmi asserted at the end of *Zakhor* that "the burden of building a bridge to his people remains with the historian."

Mr. Lown, Dr. Silberschlag, officers, faculty and students of the Hebrew College, ladies and gentlemen:

With uneasy memories of the speakers at my own commencements lingering from over the years I have decided, as an act of compassion, not to offer the proverbial "advice to the graduating class." I would rather, with the indulgence of this captive audience, speak of what is closest to me, and that is Jewish history. And if, in the course of airing some hitherto private thoughts at this public occasion, what is closest to me moves closer to you, why then I shall consider myself the most blessed of commencement speakers in this or any other year.

Of course, to speak of Jewish history is more difficult today than it was in the nineteenth century, or even fifty or thirty years ago. Today all history is increasingly in disrepute, precisely because the present is so disappointing. If the entire past could only spawn the terrifying, agonized world in which we live, of what value can it be? And as for that curious breed of men who style themselves historians, what better comment than that which appeared on the editorial page of the student newspaper at my own university, on May 29th, when the *Harvard Crimson* delivered its verdict on historians in its most Churchillian cadences, as follows: "Never before, have so many scholars, spent so many hours, in so many libraries, to produce so much useless scholarship. . . ."

You will have guessed by now that Dr. Silberschlag's gracious invitation to speak was issued to me before that editorial appeared. And since the Hebrew College did not retract the invitation after May 29th, and since I could not resist so irresistible an honor, I have crawled, my antiquarian heart fluttering, out of the musty bowels of Widener Library, to stand before you, still blinking in the unaccustomed light. So be it. It is done.

But I have not really come here to "defend" history, which requires no defense of mine. Philosophically, the case for history can be stated succinctly. It is the nature of man that he seeks to know all. Because he must know all, he also seeks to know himself. And he cannot fully know himself unless he knows the history of his own past. For man is an historical being, historically conditioned, and in him the past is always present. That is an existential fact. Much depends, however, on whether men choose to recognize this fact and cope with its implications. And that brings me to the substance of this address.

The bizarre title printed in your programs is not fortuitous but deliberate. At the same time, it was not conceived in an effort to appear "au courant" with the younger generation ("au courant" being an older equivalent of "hip," and therefore more suitable to historians). Nor is it my intention to regale you with a satire of the "Age of Aquarius," or to poke fun at it, for I take the "Age of Aquarius" very seriously indeed. And because I do, I have the temerity to choose as a text for historical exegesis at the Hebrew College, not a passage from Bible, or Talmud, or Midrash, but the following famous lyric from the "rock-musical" *Hair*:

> When the moon is in the seventh house
> And Jupiter allies with Mars
> Then peace will guide the planets
> And love will steer the stars.
> This is the dawning of the Age of Aquarius.
>
> Harmony and understanding
> Sympathy and trust abounding,
> No more falsehoods or derisions,
> Golden living dreams of visions
> Mystic crystal revelation
> And the mind's true liberation.
> This is the dawning of the Age of Aquarius.

The aspiration for peace, love, harmony and trust, is a poignant one. But there is more here for him who listens more closely. A new cosmic era is being hailed in this lyric, of an entirely different quality from those of the past, the "Age of Aquarius," about to dawn according to some, it has already dawned according to others. Its climactic aspects are those of an inner redemption—visions vouchsafed to all, revelation, liberation of the mind. Not the least striking, its advent is almost independent of the efforts of man. This radically new age, unlike any that ever existed before, is being ushered in by the astrological conjunction of heavenly bodies. Man, by implication, has but to realize what is happening and open himself to his new, astrally determined, experience.

I urge you, ladies and gentlemen, not to dismiss the "Age of Aquarius" as a mere "song." It is rather to be regarded as a vivid document of a certain temper of our times, and a ubiquitous one at that, which distills its essence in a few lines. And in this respect, whether it be taken literally is not important, for whether literal or symbolic, it has struck a deep responsive chord around the world.

It strikes a chord in the historian as well, but with a different resonance. To his inner ear the Aquarian hymn has a familiar ring, for though the nomenclature changes periodically, he knows that history is strewn with the debris of Aquarian ages and expectations. In short—an historian has a place in the Age of Aquarius, if only because the Age of Aquarius has itself a history which is of some moment. And it is his function, as an historian, to bear witness to what he knows.

The Aquarian mood is essentially an apocalyptic mood and, as such, one which appears and reappears throughout the ages at times of severe historical crisis. When history is particularly cruel, when the cup of suffering seems already full, there have always been those who could envision only a drastic apocalyptic solution: either the sudden end of the world, or an equally abrupt rebirth of the world into a radically new and blessed era. Either the Bomb, or Aquarius.

Sometimes the Aquarian temper remains merely dormant or speculative. More often it erupts into apocalyptic or, if you wish, "Aquarian" movements. At that point, when those who are convinced that the new age has dawned begin to act as though it really had, they generate movements of truly volcanic force, and convulse society to its very foundations. The forms change in time and place, and yet the features remain surprisingly constant. There is hardly an element in the Aquarian phenomena of our time that you will not find, albeit in somewhat different garb, in those of the past.

In the time at our disposal I can only give you a few random examples, chapter headings as it were, to be filled in elsewhere.

Thus in the twelfth century in Southern Italy, Joachim da Fiore, a hermit monk, received a revelation which he then divulged to others. Time, he taught, is divided into three great cosmic ages, or aeons, corresponding to the Trinity, each following the other out of an inner necessity. The first was the age of the "Father," when men were bound to the Old Law of the Jews. This was succeeded by the age of the "Son," when men were freed, but only partially. Now, however, the third and final age was dawning, the aeon of the "Holy Spirit," in which man is to attain complete spiritual freedom. The explosive consequences of this teaching, often beyond what Joachim himself had anticipated, were to send shock-waves throughout Europe for the next two hundred years, as a host of apocalyptic movements arose to put the teaching into practice.

Again, independently, throughout the Middle Ages and early modern times, there arose groups who ecstatically heralded the beginning of the final liberating age. Since ultimate liberation is, by definition, incompatible with restraints or feelings of guilt, these men and women necessarily felt that they had already transcended all laws and moral conventions, for those belonged to the dead past.

— Nothing is sin, except what is thought of as sin.
— I belong to the Liberty of Nature, and all that my nature desires, I satisfy.
— The free man is quite right to do whatever gives him pleasure.

These phrases sound somehow contemporary, do they not? They emanate from the so-called Brethren of the Free Spirit in the fourteenth century.

Yet another fascinating dimension is revealed in those "Aquarian" movements which, in the name of a messianic egalitarianism, became movements of mystical anarchism. The communes of San Francisco, or Cambridge, or New York, are often unwittingly the latter-day reincarnations of the apocalyptic communes of the Middle Ages and the sixteenth century, all of them convinced that they were the vanguard of the New Jerusalem which would soon embrace all of society. Beginning with an apocalyptic abolition of all property, and sometimes progressing to polygamy, one is impressed above all by the ease with which such communes succumbed to the absolute dictatorship of a charismatic leader, and the facility with which love could become violence against those who did not join the elect. The reasons are not hard to find. One who has thoroughly convinced himself that the Aquarian Age has dawned is increasingly impatient to see it objectified in reality, acknowledged by others, and from there it is not a far step to seek to impose the new-found freedom on others, by force if necessary. When, in 1534, the Anabaptists inaugurated their communal Utopia in the Westphalian town of Muenster, they drove out all the inhabitants who were suspected of being unsympathetic, during a bitter snowstorm. Among the banished were old people, invalids, children and pregnant women. By the time the experiment was ended from without, the commune had become a grotesque monarchy, and life in Muenster a nightmare.

Though there is more than enough material available for a full year's course on the History of the Age of Aquarius, it cannot, obviously, be capsuled here. Should you want details, there is an abundant literature. You may turn, for example, to Norman Cohn's provocative study of *The Pursuit of the Millennium* (it's out in paperback) which traces the history of these and other movements, and proposes that there is an actual link between them and the totalitarian movements of our own time. Thus, Cohn argues, it is no accident that Communist dialectic divides time into *three* successive epochs: primitive communism, class society, and a final communism which is to be the realm of freedom after the state has withered away; or that the Nazis proclaimed their final thousand-years reign as a *Third* Reich. Far as each is from the other, both are, at their core, secularized metamorphoses of the vision of Joachim da Fiore.

All this is sufficient to render the Age of Aquarius somewhat suspect. For us the suspicion mounts, when we discover that Aquarian movements in the Middle Ages often lashed out against the Jews along the way to the Millennium. And why not? For if the final aeon is the age of final liberation, why should it not also liberate men to attack the Jews without restraint? In the Age of Aquarius, why not an Aquarian pogrom?

III

Nor has the Jewish people itself been immune to Aquarian tendencies and movements. The first verse of the lyric from *Hair* sounds almost as though it could have been written in twelfth-century Barcelona by Abraham bar Hiyya who, in his *Megillat ha-megalleh*, tried to compute the beginning of the Messianic age by astrological calculations. True, the Talmud states in *Massekhet Shabbat—Eyn mazal le-Yisrael*—which means, not that Jews have no luck, but literally—that "Israel has no constellation," that Jewish history and destiny are not determined by the stars. Maimonides and others fought astrology fiercely. But there were always *meḥashvey kiẓim*, "those who compute the end" by astrological or other means, and the roster includes some very eminent Jews indeed.

Nor do we lack speculations on successive aeons of time, akin to those of Joachim da Fiore, though not dependent on them. In the kabbalistic *Sefer ha-temunah* of the mid-thirteenth century, the aeons are called *shemitot*. In each *shemitah* the Torah reveals itself in a different way. Right now the *shemitah* is that of *midat ha-din*, "judgment," and therefore our present understanding of the Torah sees only commandments and prohibitions, do's and dont's, holy and profane. But in the coming *shemitah*, that of *midat ha-rahamim*, "Mercy," all these distinctions shall become obsolete, for the power of evil shall have ceased, and the same Torah will reveal its meaning to us in a new way.

And surely we have not lacked Aquarian eruptions in the form of apocalyptic movements. There is hardly an age in Jewish history which has not witnessed at least one Jew rising to proclaim: "The End is at hand, and I am the Redeemer" (or, "I am his herald"), with Jews flocking to his banner in varying numbers. I need not remind an audience at the Hebrew College of the most climactic movement of them all, that of Sabbatai Zevi in 1666 (a year, incidentally, which not only Jews, but various Protestant groups, and even the Portuguese, expected to usher in the Aquarian age). Nor need I dwell on that darker climax to Jewish apocalyptic in the eighteenth century, when, in the name of an ultimate liberation, Jakob Frank led his followers into the abyss of nihilism.

Yes, because we are sophisticated, because we now stand at a distance, because historians have done their work well, we do not self-righteously condemn the Aquarian phenomena of the past, whether among the gentiles or among our own people. In any case, such smugness would avail us little. We understand all too well the enormous lure that Aquarian ideas possess; we see it in our own day. We feel the tremendous pathos of the Sabbatian movement, and the intense yearning for redemption which it expressed. Against the background of the history of Jewish mysticism and the plight of eighteenth century Polish Jewry, we can even understand the Frankists. But understanding should not, as so often happens today, relativize everything. In life there are many things we understand but would not advocate for others nor adopt for ourselves. On an emotional level, perhaps, Sabbatai Zevi attracts us more than his arch-opponent Jacob Sasportas. But the hard fact remains. Sasportas was, after all, correct. Sabbatai Zevi was not the Messiah. . . .

IV

Vision chasing vision, promise upon promise, movement after movement, down through the centuries, all announcing with absolute certainty that the final age has arrived. And men still toil and weep under the sun. For all the Aquarians have committed the same fundamental error: they have subjectivized redemption; they have proclaimed redemption in an unredeemed world, on the strength of inner experience alone. In the old Jewish phrase, echoing the Song of Songs, they have "awakened love too soon. . . ."

The Aquarian phenomenon is possible, to begin with, only because the Aquarian flees from history, and this in a double sense. First, he literally attempts to evade the yoke and ambiguity of living within history itself, and so he declares that it is come to an end. His final aeon is not a fulfillment of the past, but rather its annihilation. And because this is so, he rejects the past in toto, with no distinctions, with no attempt to salvage from it what may have been noble, or beautiful, or humane. For him the entire past is not merely irrelevant; it is inimical. "The grain must first rot in the ground," declares Jakob Frank, "before the wheat can sprout forth." Across the entire history of mankind there throbs a perennial struggle between those who would "hasten the end" before its time, and those who would wait and work, in trust, for the fulfillment of time —*ve-ʾafʾal pi she-yitmahmehah*—"and even though he tarry. . . ."

Does this sound reactionary? There are places on earth where I pray a revolution will occur. Where there is no other means to remedy oppression and inhumanity, revolutions are not only necessary; they become moral imperatives. But beware the revolution with Aquarian pretensions, the revolution that offers not merely to rectify concrete social evils, but to transform both man and the world forever, the revolution that would obliterate the entire past and begin from zero, the revolution that claims to be the "final" one. Such revolutions will not hesitate to create a hell and call it paradise.

"Down with the past for the sake of the future" is a slogan we have heard before. "Forget the past, for we, the illumined, have no use for it." We have heard that too. And often we have heeded, and have been swept up into the cry. And each time the vision proved to be an illusion, each time the computation turned out to have been wrong, each time we woke from the revolution to find that the reign of terror had begun, we were left more naked, more bereft, more impotent than before. From the heights of the Aquarian ecstasy we were hurled back into the reality of history, but now with fewer resources at our command with which to bear its burdens.

Amnesia, ladies and gentlemen, is not a goal but a disorder. And historical amnesia can be no less grave than that of the individual. By now the number of Jewish amnesiacs is legion, through no fault of their own. For they are the heirs to a malady whose source lies largely in the Aquarianism of Jews in modern times.

V

The vanguard of Jewry entered the modern era with absolutely Aquarian expectations, and clung to them even when others had already abandoned them. With an eschatological faith in the slogans of the European Enlightenment, the German Maskilim abandoned Hebrew after a brief flirtation, and their disciples rushed headlong to becoming Europeans, believing with messianic fervor, that the era of Man with a capital "M" was dawning, and that the Jewish past was but cumbersome baggage with which to enter into the new society. When the early nineteenth century quickly revealed that "Man" was an abstraction in a Europe of burgeoning nationalisms, other Jews discarded their past in the same way, but now for the sake of an ultimate fusion with the nations, now in order to become, not "Men," but "French-men," "German-men," "Austrian-men." When, in the struggle for emancipation which was to inaugurate the final era of Jewish salvation, it was discovered that age-old Jewish national aspirations might be an impediment, those were sloughed off as well. "Germany is our Zion," cried an Aquarian rabbi, "and Düsseldorf our Jerusalem." After the emancipatory dream was invaded by the cries of the mob in the Paris of Dreyfus' degradation, in the midst of our great national revival a new Aquarian choice was sounded by Berditchevski and others—"to be the last Jews, or the first Hebrews." And when the East European Jewish immigrants flocked to America, their expectations too were nothing if not Aquarian, for America was indeed to be the scene of the Millennium, *die goldene medineh*, where the Jewish past belonged to Russia, Poland or Galicia, and had no place in the Aquarian leap from the tenement to the suburbs.

Yes, again we understand. And we understand also why it is that the memory of so many American Jews extends at best to some vestigial images of a grandmother. We understand the *Kena'anim* in Israel who declared themselves free of the last two thousand years of the Jewish past, and who, because they are the first "Hebrews," call their publication *Aleph*, the first letter of the alphabet, a new beginning.

But the fact is that we are not at *Aleph*, nor can we ever be again. The last "Hebrew" to stand at *Aleph* was our father Abraham. Yet if we are not at *Aleph*, neither, by the same token, are we yet at *Tav*. Not for us the new Age of Aquarius, not twenty-five years after the Holocaust, and with the knowledge that it could happen again. We are, for better or worse, somewhere in between, in the midst of history, where nothing is pure or clear, where good and evil, joy and suffering, hope and despair, coexist and commingle.

It is therefore in the midst of history that we must know ourselves as Jews and build a Jewish future, slowly, often painfully. But to do so we must consciously carry a Jewish past within us. The first *zakhor*—"Remember"—was uttered in the Torah. The latest was uttered on the night of December 7, 1941, in Riga, when the Nazis rounded up the Jews for deportation. As the historian Simon Dubnow, eighty-one years old, was being led to a truck, he moved too slowly and was shot by a Latvian guard. Just before that, he had been heard to cry out: "Brothers, don't forget! Make a record of it all!" From the first *zakhor*, to the last *zakhor*, it is we who are addressed.

The amnesia of a Frenchman, or an Italian, or a Spaniard, is more easily cured than that of a Jew, being only partial to begin with. Their sojourn in their lands has an unbroken continuity. Their history surrounds them physically. The Frenchman can feel his past each time he sees the spires of Notre Dame de Paris. Every layer of the history of Italy is visible in Rome. There are Spanish towns which have not changed in appearance since the Middle Ages.

With us it is different. Our physical monuments in the diaspora have almost all vanished. Even in Eretz Yisrael, even with the remarkable achievements of the archaeologist's pick, only sparse remnants come to view of what once was. In united Jerusalem a Jew sees in the Old City, not David's Jerusalem but a Turkish Jerusalem. The monuments of our past are in the mind and heart; they have no independent existence. From the *Kotel ha-Ma'aravi*, from one wall, we conjure up an entire Temple and all the generations who stood at that wall.

In the past, history as a subject was of little concern to Jews, for history was present in the organic complex of Jewish learning, liturgy, law and practice. Today, after the Aquarian shocks of the last two hundred years, that unity has been rent asunder, and as a consequence history itself becomes vital. The historian, writes Eugen Rosenstock-Huessy, *is the physician of memory. It is his honor to heal wounds, genuine wounds. As a physician must act because his patient is ill, so the historian must act under a moral pressure to restore a nation's memory or that of mankind....*

Someday, perhaps, certainly not in our lifetime, nor, I dare say, even in the lifetime of those "under thirty," history may yet reach its fulfillment and culmination. But then, nothing precious must be lost out of the past. Then the laughter and the tears of all the ages shall be gathered together, history shall become saga, and with a polite bow the historian will yield, then and only then, to the poet....

5 : THE INQUISITION AND THE JEWS OF FRANCE IN THE TIME OF BERNARD GUI

Harvard Theological Review 63:3 (July 1970), 317–376.

This sixty-page article in the prestigious *Harvard Theological Review* was based on Yerushalmi's master's thesis at Columbia under Salo Baron. The paper was originally intended for inclusion in a book to be published in 1964, but the book never appeared. Yerushalmi's article was instead published six years later, in 1970, when he was an assistant professor at Harvard.

This article represents Yerushalmi's first sustained piece of original research to be published. It contains a number of themes that frequently recur in his later research on Iberian Jewry, as well as motifs that would not surface again. The most obvious link between this work and later scholarly writings is the central focus on the Inquisition as an agent of inquiry and punishment against converted Jews. The historical milieu of interest here, though, is not the early modern Sephardic world, for which he would gain such renown, but rather the medieval Ashkenazic world. The young Yerushalmi demonstrated considerable mastery over medieval French history, as well as over the history of French Jews in the thirteenth and fourteenth centuries—the latter a rather scattered affair owing to the frequent edicts of expulsion directed against them (e.g., 1306, 1322, and 1394). In studying this period in French Jewish history, he followed in the path of his teacher, Baron, as well as scholars such as Solomon Reinach, Isidore Loeb, Israel Lévi, Louis Newman, and Adolf Kisch. He noted here that the dearth of primary sources made this era a relatively dark one in terms of historical research. Nonetheless, its potential to shed light on later periods, Yerushalmi insisted, was substantial, especially on the roots of the Spanish Inquisition.

At the center of this article was the Dominican priest and scholar Bernard Gui, who served for sixteen years (1307–1323) as Inquisitor of Toulouse. More importantly for Yerushalmi, Bernard Gui published a five-part inquisitorial manual in 1323–4, *Practica inquisitionis heretice pravitatis*. Yerushalmi set out to analyze those parts of the *Practica* that dealt with Jews (i.e., converts from Judaism) or Jewish-related affairs. He commenced this task by situating Gui and the Jews of France in historical context, noting the tensions that arose between secular and ecclesiastical authorities when dealing with the Jews. Whereas the former sought to extend protections to Jews as a means of safeguarding their own economic interests, ecclesiastical authorities such as Bernard Gui were intent on defending the interests of the Church against heretics. The Inquisition was an important new instrument in this battle, introduced in Toulouse in 1229 to bring to heel a group of perceived heretics known as Albigensians or Cathars. Notwithstanding the fact that both Albigensians and Jews came under inquisitorial scrutiny in Toulouse, Yerushalmi insisted, contra Louis Newman, that there was no evidence whatsoever of links between them, or, more specifically, of Jewish influence on the Albigensians. There were, however, Jews who had converted in the fourteenth century, often under duress, whom the Inquisition subsequently accused of relapse to Judaism.

Yerushalmi examined here the case of one of the "relapsi," as they were known, Baruch, who fell under the jurisdiction of the Inquisitorial Tribunal of Pamiers in 1320. It was on the basis of such cases that Bernard Gui produced his *Practica*—and particularly the "Interrogation Formula" used against "relapsi" that Yerushalmi dissected carefully. On the basis of his evaluation, he concluded that, in both theory and practice, "the Inquisition in France was but the laboratory in which the inquisitorial mechanism was first tested," yielding an instrument that was "already complete in most details" and would be used on a mass scale and to devastating effect in Spain at the end of the fifteenth century.

In the course of this article, Yerushalmi already staked out a position on one of the most contentious issues concerning the Inquisition. As against the well-known view of Benzion Netanyahu in *The Origins of the Inquisition in Fifteenth-Century Spain* (1995) and other writings, Yerushalmi assumed the sincerity of inquisitors such as Gui in believing that there were indeed Judaizing heretics alive and at work in their midst. Concomitantly, Yerushalmi sought in the latter portion of the article to understand the world of the "relapsi," in particular by piecing together evidence from the *Practica* and other sources to argue for a set of distinctive rituals accompanying them on their return to Judaism: for example, the invocation of anti-Christian prayers and a re-Judaizing immersion in water (along with the shaving of hair and cutting of nails).[1] The bathing rite in particular hints at the custom of Christian baptism and, as such, at a set of ritual norms shared by Jews and Christians, declared enemies, in medieval Europe. That link was noticed by Yerushalmi's important precursor in the study of both Spanish and Ashkenazic history, Yitzhak Baer (see chapter 3). It also became the subject of considerable attention and even controversy in the work of the generation of researchers that followed Yerushalmi including Jeremy Cohen, Peter Schäfer, Kenneth Stow, and Israel Yuval.

---

1. For an interesting gloss on Yerushalmi's argument about the rejudaizing immersion ritual, see Joseph Shatzmiller, "Converts and Judaizers in the Fourteenth Century," *Harvard Theological Review* 74 (1981), 63–77. See also Paola Tartakoff, *Between Christian and Jew: Conversion and Inquisition in the Crown of Aragon, 1250–1391* (Philadelphia: University of Pennsylvania Press, 2012), 125–128.

The Papal Inquisition of the thirteenth and fourteenth centuries cannot be assigned so prominent a position in the history of French Jewry as that which the "New" Inquisition later occupied in the destinies of the Jews of Spain. It is perhaps for this reason that the Jewish aspects of the Inquisition in France have attracted little attention from scholars.[1] The paucity of original documents relating to the subject may also have been a contributing factor.[2] Still though it can be understood, this neglect remains unfortunate. In addition to its intrinsic interest for the study of Franco-Jewish history and of Jewish relations with the medieval Church, research into the treatment of the Jews by the French Inquisition can shed much light on the later development in Spain. For all the difference in the historical situations, the Papal Inquisition adumbrated, in its dealings with the Jews, the institution which was to play such a formidable role in the Iberian Peninsula. There is surprisingly little in the theoretical, procedural, and even the practical approach of the Spanish Inquisition to Jewish affairs for which one cannot find the archetype in the earlier Inquisition.

The present study is limited to the years between 1306 and 1322. The period has a natural coherence, opening with the expulsion of the Jews of France by Philip the Fair, and closing with another expulsion, by Charles IV. It is a time when the Inquisition in France was still at its zenith. Above all, these years coincide approximately with the tenure of Bernard Gui as inquisitor in Toulouse.

Bernard Gui (1261?–1331) is of particular interest. After entering the Dominican Order in 1280, he rose rapidly to high position. In 1284 he taught logic at the convent in Brives and then pursued further studies in theology at Limoges and Montpellier. In 1291 he taught at Limoges, and from 1292 until 1297, at Albi. Possessed of great energy and considerable erudition, he now was recognized for his administrative ability as well. He was appointed Prior of the Dominican Convent in Carcassonne, subsequently occupying similar positions in Castres and Limoges. On January 16, 1307, Bernard received from the Provincial of France an appointment as Inquisitor of Toulouse. He served in this capacity for some sixteen years. In 1323 John XXII gave him the bishopric of Tuy in Castile and, a year later, that of Lodève.[3]

During his long and busy career Bernard engaged in an extensive literary activity, writing on Dominican history, as well as chronicles of the popes and of the kings of France. One major document directly related to his inquisitorial office has also fortunately survived. The record of the sentences imposed by Bernard Gui's tribunal was published in the seventeenth century by the Dutch scholar Philip van Limborch.[4] But of all his works, the most valuable for the study of the Papal Inquisition is the great inquisitorial manual known since its publication as *Practica inquisitionis heretice pravitatis*.[5] Completed in 1323–4, and divided into five parts, it was the most extensive and thorough treatise yet written on the subject. In the *Practica* Bernard culled from older inquisitorial compilations and guides, from the archives, and from his personal experience, to provide an elaborate codification of inquisitorial practice as it had crystallized up to his time.[6] He thus furnished the inquisitor with instructions, formulas, and procedures for the many aspects of his work. To make the manual even more useful, he also included expositions of the rites and beliefs of the important heretical groups. With but one exception, the material relating to Jews and Jewish matters is concentrated in Part Two and Part Five of the *Practica*.[7] An analysis of these passages will be undertaken after we first examine the period itself.

I. FRENCH JEWRY AND THE INQUISITION: 1306–22

The sudden expulsion of the Jews from all the territories of the Kingdom of France in 1306 was exclusively an act of the Crown; the Inquisition had no share in the decision.[8] Nor is there any evidence to indicate that the inquisitors had ever advocated in the preceding years that the Jews be expelled.[9] In any case, unlike the later Spanish Inquisition, the Inquisition of France was an arm of the Papacy and not of the State. Relations between Philip the Fair and the Inquisition were characterized by tension throughout almost all his reign.[10] The king cooperated with the inquisitors when it suited him or, as in his suppression of the Templars, when he needed them. However, when he felt that his own interests were in jeopardy, Philip did not hesitate to assert himself and to curb the inquisitors' activities. Because "his" Jews were a significant source of income, the king jealously guarded his rights over them, and for this reason he restrained the inquisitors on several occasions from intervening in Jewish affairs.[11] Anything which might diminish the number of *juifs-du-roi* or undermine their ability to pay taxes was of concern to the royal treasury. A Jew arrested or fined by the Inquisition thus represented a real or potential loss of income. Economic motives were paramount when Philip protected Jews from the inquisitors, and certainly in the Expulsion itself.

Between 1306 and 1315 Jewish residence in France was forbidden by law. A small number of Jews were permitted to remain or return after 1306 in order to help pursue, largely to the king's profit, debts due those who had been banished. However, even this remnant was expelled by a royal decree of August 22, 1311.[12] During these years there were, of course, Jewish converts resident in France. Definite information on inquisitorial proceedings against relapsed Jewish converts comes to us first from Paris.

In 1307 Prote, a baptized Jew, declared to the inquisitors that his brother had seduced him back to Judaism. Then he retracted the story, saying that he had only wanted to implicate his brother because the latter owed him money. His judges decided, nevertheless, to believe the account, and he was sentenced to imprisonment for life. In prison he was allegedly heard to say that he was a Jew named Samuel, that Christians eat their God, and similar blasphemies. He was, without an additional trial, relaxed to the secular authorities and burned at the stake.[13] In the same year, and again in Paris, Jean, another convert, confessed to the Inquisition that he had said publicly in front of the Chatelet that he was really a Jew named Mutlot (*sic*), and that he wished to purge by fire the sin he had committed by water. Soon, however, he withdrew his confession and declared it was only melancholy and "lightness of head" which had prompted him to say these things. We are informed by the chronicler that a "salutary penance" was imposed.[14] Finally, the same source relates that in Paris in 1310 a baptized Jew was burned in the Place de la Grève on the same day that a female heretic was executed there in a similar manner. He had been condemned for spitting at an image of the Virgin, and now passed "from the temporal into the eternal fires."[15]

One would like to know how many other prosecutions of relapsi by the Inquisition occurred in this period. Unfortunately, the facts recorded for those condemned in Paris are too meager to permit any definite conclusion. In the third case we are told specifically that the Jew had been converted to the Catholic Faith, but no such information is given for the other two. It is possible that they had submitted to baptism in 1306 in order to remain in Paris, but this is at best a reasonable conjecture. One chronicler, Jean de Saint-Victor, states that few Jews accepted conversion to avoid being banished.[16] Perhaps there took place an intensified search for relapsi following the Expulsion of 1306, especially in the capital. Indirect evidence of "marranism" among French Jews as a result of the Expulsion can be found in documents from Aragon. The king, Jaime II, had opened the frontiers to the refugees. After the first wave of exiles had been absorbed by the Aragonese Jewish communities, other Jews who had accepted baptism during the Expulsion continued to cross the border in order to return openly to Judaism. In 1311 the inquisitors of Aragon began a series of investigations of aid being extended to relapsi, some of them from France, in the course of which several Jewish communities were endangered.[17]

Gui began his duties as inquisitor in 1308. His first ventures into an area relating to Jews occurred in 1310, and were concerned, not with Judaizers, but with Jewish books. On January 4th of that year he ordered the confiscation of all Jewish books, especially the Talmud, in the séné-chaussées of Toulouse, Rodez and Agen. The books were to be delivered for examination and burning, and failure to comply would incur a penalty of excommunication. Of the three letters issued on this occasion, one was addressed to Jean de Crépy, in charge of Jewish affairs in Toulouse and Rodez; another to the Sénéchal of Agen; and a third to the Dominicans of the latter town.[18] Eight days later, on January 12th, Bernard wrote to the rectors of all churches ordering them to announce a ban of excommunication against all those who held back or hid Jewish books.[19]

It is hard to believe that the copies of the Talmud and other books in question were in the hands of the few Jews who were still to be found at this time in the aforementioned areas. We should rather conclude that many Jewish books must have fallen into the hands of royal officials and even ordinary burghers during the extensive confiscations of Jewish property which followed the Expulsion and which, in 1310, were still not completed. Furthermore, it would appear that Bernard Gui was not acting solely on his own initiative. A month earlier three wagonloads of Jewish books had been burned in Paris.[20] One is left with the impression that Bernard's action may have been part of a general drive to collect and destroy Jewish books in various parts of the realm.

On July 28, 1315, Louis X formally permitted the return of the Jews to France.[21] The edict brought Jews once more into the country, but could not restore the Jewish community to its former estate. In their absence, houses, synagogues, and other properties had been confiscated, sold, and sometimes destroyed. Of those debts which the Jews were now allowed to recover, two-thirds had to go to the Crown. The terms of the recall specified a limited period of twelve years for their sojourn, with the concession that they would not be expelled again without a year's prior notice. Thus it was impressed upon them that their stay was a temporary one, though conceivably it could be renewed and extended.[22]

If the record of sentences from Bernard Gui's tribunal is an adequate reflection of his activities, he apparently proceeded only twice in cases of Judaizing. Both cases occurred in 1317. The first involved the posthumous condemnation of a relapsed Jewish convert. Johannes, formerly a Jew named Josse, had relapsed after baptism, declaring that he wanted to live and die as a Jew. He persisted in his intention despite repeated exhortations. One must infer that he died before he could be tried and sentenced by the Inquisition. Now, in accordance with standard inquisitorial procedure, Bernard ordered his body exhumed and burned.[23]

The second case concerned Johannes de Bretz, the converted son of the Jew Jacob de Serinhaco in the diocese of Toulouse. After being baptized in Bretz, Johannes remained a practicing Christian for some three years. Then he fled to Lerida in Aragon where he reverted to Judaism. He lived as a Jew in Lerida for another three years, until he came to the attention of the inquisitors. Brought to Toulouse for trial, he was sentenced to life imprisonment by Bernard Gui.[24] In addition to furnishing some interesting details on an alleged rejudaizing ceremony which we shall examine later in connection with the *Practica inquisitionis*, the case is important as a concrete example of the return to Judaism of French converts in Aragon to which we have already alluded. We see also that on occasion the inquisitors in France could have a prisoner extradited from Aragon in order to be tried by their own tribunals.[25]

Bernard Gui's interest in Judaizers was only sporadic. He was much more attentive to the investigation and condemnation of Jewish books and his inquests in 1310 by no means exhausted his concern in the matter. The decree of Louis X permitting the return of the Jews to France had stipulated that while other books were to be restored to them, they were forbidden to possess the Talmud.[26] In the next few years this clause may have been ignored or perhaps indifferently enforced, and this time Bernard took matters into his own hands. Having collected all the copies of the Talmud that he could find, he ordered them burned publicly in Toulouse. The burning was carried out with great fanfare. On November 28, 1319, two wagons filled with volumes of the Talmud rolled through the streets of Toulouse preceded by royal officials and criers who proclaimed the blasphemies contained therein. The books were then consigned to the flames.[27]

Less than a year later, and perhaps influenced by the example of Bernard Gui, the pope himself took decisive action against the Talmud. In the bull *Dudum felicis recordationis*, sent on September 20, 1320. to the Archbishop of Bourges, John XXII demanded that the Talmud "and all other books with their additions and commentaries" be confiscated and handed over to the Franciscans and Dominicans for examination. In order that the Jews might have no opportunity to hide their books, he specified that the search must be both sudden and coordinated. After examination for blasphemy and heresy the books were to be burned and, if necessary, the assistance of the secular authorities should be enlisted.[28] According to Raynaldus the bull was also sent to the Archbishop of Toulouse and to the Bishop of Paris.[29]

John's bull did not remain unheeded. In 1321 the Talmud was burned in Pamiers by the bishop, Jacques Fournier.[30] In the same year, during Lent, it was burned in Paris.[31]

The attacks against the Talmud which had come in such rapid succession must have been disquieting enough to the Jews of the time.[32] But the efforts of the inquisitors were not confined to books alone. Not content with matters legally within its competence, the Inquisition sometimes vexed entire Jewish communities. Thus, in Marseilles, on March 10, 1320, a statute was passed at the instigation of the inquisitor Michel le Moine, ordering every Jew who lived outside the Jewish quarter to move into it within ten days. Previously the *juiverie* of Marseilles had been merely a section of the city where Jews had concentrated voluntarily. Apparently the inquisitor wanted to turn it into a ghetto. The extent to which the statute was enforced is not clear. We hear only that the very next day (March 11) the inquisitor authorized the Jew Abraham of Narbonne to live as before, *prope fontem judaycam*, and to conduct business as usual, *prope Jusateriam*.[33]

In the same year (1320), the Jews of Southern France were suddenly exposed to the massacres and pillage of the Shepherds. Assembling at Agen, the bands of Pastoureoux swept through Southern France and thence into Aragon and Navarre.[34] From these harrowing times a document of great value has survived: the trial of a relapsed Jewish convert by the inquisitorial tribunal of Pamiers.[35]

Baruch was a German Jew residing in Toulouse in 1320. On June 15th, Alodet, the Subvicar of Toulouse, brought to the city twenty-four cartloads of Pastoureaux who had been apprehended for killing one hundred and fifty Jews at Castel Sarassin. As they were being led into the Narbonne Fort in Toulouse, the crowd of bystanders released them. Together the Pastoureaux and the mob made their way into the Jewish quarter. Baruch was studying in his room when a group of men broke in, shouting that he must either be baptized or killed. Faced with the choice Baruch consented and was immediately led to the Cathedral of Saint Etienne.

There he tried in various ways to delay the inevitable, but in the end his ingenuity was exhausted and he submitted to baptism.

He later noted at his trial that he had been instructed to declare to the chaplain that he accepted baptism willingly, for otherwise he would be killed. Eventually a Christian friend advised Baruch to leave Toulouse. He went first to Montgiscard where he spent a day in a Jewish home, then to Mazères, and finally arrived in Pamiers.[36] Not long after his arrival he was arrested by order of the Inquisition, and although he had been baptized in Toulouse, he was not extradited. On July 13th he was brought out of prison to stand trial on a charge of relapse. At a preliminary hearing he entered a deposition relating the circumstances of his conversion.

The first phase of the trial, which began the next day, revolved around the question of the validity of his baptism. Baruch tried desperately to convince the court that forced baptism is invalid under any circumstances. But whatever hopes he may have entertained on this score were shattered by the presiding judge Jacques Fournier, serving in his dual capacity of Bishop and head of the Inquisitorial Tribunal of Pamiers.[37] This man who, as we have noted, was to have the Talmud burned in Pamiers in 1321, and who later became Pope Benedict XII, was not concerned with Baruch's inner intentions at the baptismal font. Well versed in Canon Law, he merely asked the accused whether in the midst of the ceremony itself he had "protested by word or deed or shown a contrary will by resisting, that he did not want to be baptized."[38] Baruch replied that he had done none of these things, simply because he had been told that to protest meant certain death. Jacques Fournier was not impressed. Basing himself on ample canonical precedent, he regarded such a baptism as irrevocable. The bishop declared that since the baptism was not received under "absolute coercion," Baruch was bound to hold the Christian faith, and that should he continue to be obstinate, the court would proceed against him as a heretic.[39]

At this point the proceedings took a novel and dramatic turn. Baruch announced that since he knew only what Jews believe, having read the Law and the Prophets as a teacher for twenty-five years, he would not accept the Christian faith unless it be demonstrated to him out of Jewish Scripture. On the contrary, he would rather die than leave Judaism "since he was of no small authority among the Jews of these parts." Baruch could not have been so naive as to think that he would be allowed to emerge the victor in a theological disputation with the bishop. He may again have been stalling for time, hoping that some of his gentile acquaintances in

Toulouse would intervene on his behalf. At any rate, Jacques Fournier accepted the challenge to prove the truth of Christianity to Baruch. That he did not delegate this task to some underling may perhaps support Baruch's claim to be a person of some stature in the Jewish community. The remainder of the record is mostly concerned with the disputation itself. We are informed that first there was a discussion of the Trinity which lasted fifteen days, after which, for eight days, the Bishop proved that the Messiah promised in Hebrew Scripture had to be both God and man. The argument then proceeded to a demonstration that the Messiah promised in the Law had already come. The notary adds that this phase was more difficult than the others, and therefore it continued for three weeks until Baruch was finally convinced. Even if the debate was not conducted daily or consecutively, one can imagine Baruch's mental and emotional state during the prolonged barrage to which he was subjected. He was debating, not as an equal, but as a prisoner of his adversary. If he had hopes of receiving aid from outside, they must by now have faded. At this juncture Baruch yielded and declared he would be a Christian. Still, he requested and received permission to isolate himself with a Hebrew Bible, stating that he wished to convince himself more fully of the truth of the Bishop's arguments through his own reading. After fifteen days had elapsed, Jacques Fournier was informed that Baruch was again wavering in his new-found faith, and he therefore gave him further instruction, resolving the doubts which had arisen.

On August 16th Baruch was brought again before the tribunal in the episcopal chamber of Pamiers.[40] He was asked if the Bishop had proved the truth of the Christian faith from the Old Testament. He replied that this was so, but that subsequently he had found further objections through his own reading. With a final show of tenacity he cited various scriptural verses which seemed to him to controvert the doctrine of the Trinity. Asked if he had cited these verses during his discussions with the Bishop, he said that the latter had solved the difficulties at the time, but he did not remember the solutions. Here the record breaks off rather suddenly and awkwardly. The notary does not record which measures were employed in the next nine days to put an end to Baruch's vacillations.[41]

On September 25th Baruch stood once more in the bishop's palace for the final stage of his trial. It was conducted with great solemnity, and a large number of notables were present.[42] Baruch's deposition was read to him, and he declared it to be correct. Asked if he now believed the teachings of the Roman Church to be true, he answered in the affirmative, adding that he believed the persecution because of which he had been baptized came to him for the good of his soul, and that he was brought to the Catholic Faith not by fear, torture, or promises, but by the exposition of Scripture. After this Baruch formally abjured Judaism.

Some nine weeks later, on December 3rd, he came before Jacques Fournier and Gaillard de Pomies, the latter's inquisitorial associate, for sentencing. "Seeking not justice but mercy, he beseeched the said lords to act mercifully." The sentence is not recorded, since sentences were written down in a separate collection which has been lost. Technically, Baruch was still liable to imprisonment despite his abjuration for according to inquisitorial theory imprisonment was a penance. In fact, imprisonment applied *only* to one who had already abjured his heresy, the obstinate heretic being relaxed for burning to the secular arm. In principle, imprisonment obtained for all penitent heretics unless special circumstances justified the indulgence of the judges.[43]

The trial of Baruch offers vivid glimpses into the actual proceedings of an inquisitorial court against a relapsed Jewish convert in France. We shall probably never know how many other "Baruchs" there were during the Shepherd Massacres. It was, in general, a time of travail for French Jewry. One calamity succeeded another to shatter the already precarious existence of the Jewish communities. John XXII, who tried consistently, though ineffectively, to protect the Jews from the Pastoureaux in the summer of 1320, followed in September with the bulls against the Talmud to which we have referred. Now, sometime before February 1321, the Pope expelled the Jews from the Comtat Venaissin.[44] A few months later came the widespread accusation that the Jews of France had conspired with the lepers to poison the wells.[45]

Finally, on June 24, 1322, King Charles IV banished the Jews from the Kingdom of France.[46] The expulsion came as abruptly as that of 1306; the year's warning which had been promised by Louis X was not given. Again, some Jews may have converted in order to remain. Less than a month after the expulsion, on July 3rd, John XXII issued the bull *Ex parte vestra*[47] refusing the right of asylum in churches to converted Jews suspected of relapse, and ordering the inquisitors of France to pursue them even into their places of refuge. The bishops and archbishops of France were enjoined to cooperate, and not to hinder the inquisitors, in terms which suggest that jurisdictional quarrels were still quite common.[48]

Between 1322 and 1359 there was no legal Jewish residence in royal France.[49] The expulsion seems to have been thorough. Once more the Inquisition apparently had no direct influence on the decision. In general the Inquisition could play a decisive role in Jewish history only where, either through persecution or by choice, a really substantial part of the Jewish community had accepted baptism. France in the thirteenth and fourteenth centuries had its Jewish converts whose Christian orthodoxy may have left much to be desired. But even in times of persecution or expulsion there was never a large-scale conversion of the dimensions of those which took place in Spain in 1391 or in Portugal in 1497. Conversion in France was mostly an individual rather than a mass phenomenon, and Jewish converts were never numerous enough to constitute a distinct social class. Since, a priori, inquisitors had no legal jurisdiction over professing Jews unless they in some way attacked the Christian faith, the impact of the Inquisition on French Jewry was necessarily limited. However, no such reservation applies to the realm of inquisitorial precedent, theory, and procedure. If, from the vantage point of Jewish history, the Inquisition in France was but the laboratory in which the inquisitorial mechanism was first tested, the instrument which emerged was already complete in most details. Only a particular confluence of historical circumstances was necessary to enable it to reap its full and bitter harvest.

II. TOWARD AN EVALUATION OF THE JEWISH MATERIAL IN THE *PRACTICA INQUISITIONIS*

1. *General remarks*

Before proceeding to a detailed analysis it may be useful to survey the sections of the *Practica* relating to Jews, under the rubrics and in the order in which they appear:

Secunda Pars

no. 1: Forma relaxandi aliquem Judeum de muro ad quem fuerat pro commissis contra fidem per sententiam deputatis (ed. Douais, p. 35 f.).

(The Jew had originally been convicted for aiding a convert to relapse.) No names appear in the form. Undated.

no. 4: Forma relaxandi. . . . . (ibid., p. 39 f.).

(Identical with no. 1.)

no. 13: Forma littere ad imponendum penitentiam arbitrariam extra sermonem alicui Judeo pro hiis que commisit receptando aliquem vel aliquos baptizatos apostatas, vel alias favorem aliquem impendendo (ibid., p. 49 f.).

(The Jew had knowingly had contact with a relapsed convert.) No
   names given. Undated.
no. 48: Forma requisitionis librorum Talmutorum sub pena
   excommunicationis (ibid., p. 67 f.).
(Addressed by Bernard Gui to Jean de Crépy, "superintendenti
   negocio Judeorum in senescallia Tholosana et Ruthenensi per
   dominum nostrum regem deputatio.") Dated: Toulouse, "pridie
   nonas januarii, sub anno Domini MCCCIX" (= January 4, 1310
   n. st.).
no. 49: Forma mitigationis circa penam sententie
   excommunicationis ex causa (ibid., p. 68).
(Bernard Gui to Jean de Crépy.) Dated: Toulouse "in festo sancte
   Agnetis virginis et martiris, anno Domini MCCCIX" (= January 21,
   1310 n. st.).
no. 50: Sententia excommunicationis contra detentores et celatores
   librorum Judeorum (ibid., p. 69).
(Bernard Gui to "universis et singulis rectoribus ecclesiarum vel
   eorum loca tenentibus." Dated: Toulouse; "pridie ydus januarii,
   anno Domini MCCCIX" (= January 12, 1310 n. st.).
no. 51: Requisitio senescalli Agenesi super libris Judeorum (ibid.,
   p. 69f).
(Bernard Gui to the Sénéchal of Agen.) Dated: Agen, "pridie nonas
   januarii anno Domini MCCCIX" (= January 4, 1310 n. st.).
no. 52: Commissio facta priori Fratrum Praedicatorum Agenni super
   libris Judeorum inquirendis (ibid., p. 70f).
(Bernard Gui to the Prior of the Dominicans in Agen.) Dated:
   Toulouse, "pridie nonas januarii, anno Domini MCCCIX"
   (= January 4, 1310 n. st.).
no. 53: Sententia excommunicationis contra detentores et celatores
   librorum Judeorum in senescallia Agenni (ibid., p. 71).
(Bernard Gui to "universis et singulis rectoribus ecclesiarum vel
   eorum loca tenentibus.") Beginning of a formula, to be completed
   by no. 50, supra.

Tertia Pars
no. 47: Forma seu modus pronunciandi super libris Judeorum
   qui Talmuti vulgariter appellantur et super aliis in quibus
   continentur blasfemie, falsitates seu errores aut ignominie contra

Dominum Jhesum Christum aut ejus sanctissimam genitricem in opprobrium fidei christiane (ibid., p. 170 f.).

(No names given. Undated. However, since the bull of John XXII is mentioned, the document must have been redacted in its present form after September, 1320.)

Quinta Pars

v:1 — Sequitur de perfidia Judeorum contra fidem christianorum (ed. Douais, p. 288; ed. Mollat, II, p. 6).

v:2 — De modo seu ritu quo Judei in rejudaysando conversos observant (ed. Douais, p. 288 f.; ed. Mollat, pp. 6, 8).

v:3 — Interrogatoria specialia ad Judeos et rejudaysatos (ed. Douais, pp. 289 f.; ed. Mollat, pp. 10, 12, 18).

v:4 — De intolerabili blasfemia contra Christum et fidem ejus et populum christianum (ed. Douais, pp. 290–92; ed. Mollat, p. 12 ff.).

vii:9 — Modus abjurandi Judeorum qui deprehensi sunt et confessi se contra fidem enormiter deliquisse (ed. Douais, p. 299 f.; ed. Mollat, pp. 46, 48).

(Abjuration of a Jew who has induced converts to return to Judaism or has had contact with relapsi.)

vii:10 — Modus abjurandi illorum qui conversi a perfidia Judeorum ad fidem baptismi redierunt ad vomitum Judaysmi (ed. Douais, p. 300; ed. Mollat, pp. 48, 50).

(Abjuration of a relapsed convert.)

Several characteristics can be discerned immediately. All the procedural forms which bear a date are concerned with the prosecution of Jewish books (Part II; nos. 48 through 52) and refer to Bernard Gui's confiscations in 1310. In the other forms the names and dates are to be inserted as the occasion requires. The sections themselves may be grouped in the following categories: (a) Procedural forms for the prosecution of Jewish books (Part II; nos. 48, 49, 50, 51, 52, 53; Part III: no. 47). (b) Forms concerned with professing Jews (Part II: nos. 1, 4, 13; Part V: nos. v:3 and vii:9). (c) Forms concerned with relapsed converts (Part V: nos. v:3 and vii:10). (d) A general statement on inquisitorial jurisdiction over Judaizers and their fautors (Part V: v:1). (e) Information for the Inquisitor on various Jewish doctrines and practices offensive to the Church (Part V: v:2, 3, 4).

Thus the greater part of the material deals with Jewish literature, a reflection of Bernard's own interest in this aspect of inquisitorial activity.

It can also be readily seen that most of the sections are of a practical rather than theoretical nature. One will look in vain for a systematic presentation of the various causes for which even Jews who had never been baptized could and did come within the competence of the inquisitors. Only the central crimes of blasphemy in Jewish liturgy and literature, and relapse after conversion to Christianity, are treated directly. Perhaps Bernard felt that the other crimes for which a Jew could be prosecuted by the Inquisition were of a general nature and did not have to be treated under a specifically Jewish rubric. If, for example, a Jew were accused of practicing certain forms of magic, the inquisitor could simply find the appropriate forms in the sections devoted to sorcery.[50]

One is initially surprised to find, apart from the Formula of Interrogation, only one form (the Oath of Abjuration in V: vii: 10) for a relapsed Jewish convert, while there are four forms (II: 1, 4, 13; V:vii:9) which apply to an unbaptized Jew. Here again the reason may be the same. Since the relapsed Jewish convert was, in essence, an apostate Christian in the view of the Church, most of the general formulas for cases of Christian heresy could easily be applied to him. This would include the general forms for sentencing to imprisonment, penances, relaxation to the secular arm, confiscation, etc.[51]

There is, to be sure, an overall impression of a certain arbitrary quality in Bernard Gui's choice and presentation of materials on Jewish matters. (The repetition of the identical form for releasing a Jew from prison is a case in point.) But obviously one should not expect a greater coherence in the *Practica* than was perhaps intended. Though it marked a great advance toward systematization and thoroughness over its predecessors, Bernard's manual does not have the thorough and elaborate character of the bulky treatises which followed in succeeding centuries. Perhaps, also, if Bernard had simply set out to write an original exposition from beginning to end, the presentation might have been more systematic. We shall see, however, that he seems largely to have utilized older materials scattered through the inquisitorial archives. Much of the *Practica* is really a compilation of sources which Bernard had at his disposal. If the result sometimes has an inevitably random quality, it is because he took what was available and made the best use he could find for it.

2. The Jewish "Perfidy"

In only one place does Bernard Gui present a statement on the juridical basis for the competence of the Inquisition in Jewish affairs. This is the section which serves to introduce the material on Jewish rites in Part V. He begins with a declaration that Jews attempt, whenever possible, to bring Christians to Judaism. They are particularly active in this respect among former Jews who have accepted baptism, and most especially among those converts who are related to them.[52]

The passage which immediately follows is a direct quotation from the Decretals of Boniface VIII. Christians who are converted or return to the Jewish faith (i.e. proselytes or relapsi), even if they were baptized in infancy or because of fear of death, provided there was no "absolute" compulsion, are to be treated as heretics. One should also proceed against those who aid, receive, or defend them, in the same manner as against fautors of heretics.[53]

There is no allusion in the *Practica* to the papal bulls, beginning with Clement IV's *Turbato corde* (1267), which had first equated Judaizing with heresy and had placed proselytes and relapsed converts within the jurisdiction of the inquisitors.[54] The decretal of Boniface VIII fixed the canon law on the subject and rendered superfluous the citation of earlier papal pronouncements.

Of course the crucial question remained as to what precisely constitutes "absolute compulsion." The Church itself had consistently stated its official opposition to forced baptism as a means of gaining converts from Judaism.[55] In time, however, the definition of force was severely restricted. The problem had already been dealt with by Innocent III in the bull *Maiores ecclesiae*, sent in 1201 to the Archbishop of Arles.[56] Basing himself on precedents of the Fourth Council of Toledo, Innocent declared that so long as baptism is accepted, even though as a result of violence, fear, or torture, the baptism is valid and the convert is to be compelled to remain a Christian.[57] In effect the meaning of "absolute compulsion," which alone might invalidate baptism, was taken to mean that the person protested aloud and resisted actively during the actual administration of the sacrament. Patently, few who so protested might hope to tell the tale.

The distinction between different kinds of compulsion, subtle though it might seem, was by no means academic. It was to be applied time and time again with most serious consequences. In its simplest terms it meant that Jews converted out of fear during a pogrom could not plead that they had been converted forcibly. We have seen a concrete example in the trial of Baruch at Pamiers, where the case against him rested precisely on this foundation. It was not sufficient for Baruch to show that the Pastoureaux had threatened to kill him, that when he arrived at the Cathedral of Saint Etienne he was shown the bodies of two dead Jews lying in the street, and that during the ceremony it was not his intention to be baptized. Jacques Fournier wanted to know if he had openly protested. The absence of such a protest meant that the coercion had not been absolute; Baruch had, after all, the choice of martyrdom. Hence his baptism was indelible, and his reversion to Judaism an act of apostasy subject to inquisition.[58]

One other aspect of this section in the *Practica* deserves mention. It is noteworthy that in characterizing the perfidy of the Jews Bernard Gui singles out their proselytizing alone, especially in seducing baptized Jews to relapse. Elsewhere only Jewish blasphemy is mentioned. Of a connection between the Jews and the so-called Albigensian heretics who were the prime targets of the Papal Inquisition, we hear nothing. This silence is eloquent. A number of intriguing conjectures have been made by various scholars as to the possibility of some reciprocal ideological influence between the Jews of Southern France and the Christian heretics of the twelfth and thirteenth centuries.[59] Accepting this hypothesis as a demonstrable fact, Louis I. Newman has argued that the involvement of the Inquisition in Jewish affairs was largely motivated by the suspicion that Jewish influence was a major factor in the prevalence of heresy among Christians.

It should be emphasized that there is absolutely no evidence in the sources to support such a thesis. The very existence of a Jewish influence on the heretics is, of course, still far from established.[60] But even if it were present, the fact remains that neither the contemporary church legislation, nor secular legislation, nor the available inquisitorial documents, show any awareness of its existence.[61] One may be quite certain that Bernard Gui himself, intensely and personally involved in the extirpation of heresy in Languedoc, would not have overlooked such a connection if he had in the slightest degree suspected its presence.

3. Procedural aspects

Twice in the *Practica* (II:13 and II:48), in forms dealing with Jewish matters, the inquisitor describes himself as "inquisitor heretice pravitatis *ac perfidie Judeorum* in regno Francie per sedem apostolicam deputatis."[62] Another such form (II:51) gives the full title, but with the omission of the phrase on Jewish perfidy. The question arises whether, in addition to their regular appointments to proceed against heresy, the inquisitors may not also have held special commissions to investigate Jewish affairs. The facts are not at all clear. If Bernard held such a specific mandate, he certainly did not always refer to it in his title. It is also difficult to understand why a special commission would be necessary once Judaizing had been canonically equated with ordinary heresy. Still, other inquisitors are occasionally described in the same way. The earliest definite example of such usage occurs in a decree of Philip III dated February 25, 1284, in which he ordered all officials in Champagne and Brie to assist the inquisitor Guillaume d'Auxerre.[63] The popes themselves did not actually employ the phrase in addressing letters to the inquisitors, even when they were dealing with Jewish matters. There is, however, one example of what may be regarded as a special commission to an inquisitor to pursue relapsed Jewish converts. On September 30, 1359, Innocent VI gave to Bernard Dupuy full powers to apprehend these converts no matter where they might be found.[64] However, in this instance the relapsi had fled outside the province, and perhaps such a special commission was necessary to enable the inquisitor to proceed beyond the territorial limits of his original jurisdiction.

The pursuit of fugitive relapsi and their arrest was handled in the same way as the apprehension of ordinary heretics. Bernard Gui singles out only those procedural elements involving Jews and converts which betrayed special features.

The Interrogation Formula for Jews and relapsi (V:v:3) is most interesting. Bernard offers a total of more than twenty-five model questions which the inquisitor may pose to the suspect.[65] There is good evidence that Bernard did not himself formulate the Interrogation, but rather adopted, with some modifications, a form which had been standardized earlier.[66] The great importance attached to inquisitorial interrogations is self-evident. They were calculated not only to examine the suspect himself, but also to elicit information which might be of use in future investigations.[67] The questions recorded in the *Practica* are listed in no apparent order, but they may be grouped as follows: questions concerning the accused; questions concerning his family; questions designed to implicate others; questions about Jewish rites and beliefs. Of these categories the latter two are the most intriguing. The accused is asked if others were baptized at the same time as he, whether they have subsequently relapsed, when and where they did so, and which persons were present at the ceremony. In addition he is asked to state who influenced him to return to Judaism, whether he had himself induced anyone to "Judaize" or "rejudaize," and whether he is personally acquainted with any proselytes or relapsi. The inquiries about Jewish practices are aimed mainly at obtaining data on blasphemies and on the manner in which baptized Jews are received back into the Jewish community. We shall have occasion to examine the alleged blasphemies and rejudaizing rites in detail. For the moment we shall dwell only on procedural elements.

Two questions in the Interrogation deal with Jewish oaths: Do the Jews consider themselves bound by an oath taken *super legem Moysi et per vocem Dei et rotulum*, and what is the punishment for perjury? The doubt cast on the oath of a Jew was no novelty.[68] The description of the oath itself—on the Law of Moses, the word of God, and the Scroll (of the Torah)—must mirror the actual form of the oath taken by Jews who were summoned before inquisitorial tribunals.[69] It is corroborated by the record of the trial of Baruch, in which we read: "The Bishop interrogated Baruch about the above matters, Baruch having first taken an oath on the Law of Moses that he would tell the whole and pure truth both about himself as principal and about others as witnesses."[70] Neither in the *Practica* nor in Baruch's trial is there an indication that the oath was accompanied by a degrading ceremonial. The actual wording of the oath is not preserved.[71]

The Interrogation Formula provides only a framework of questions intended to serve as a guide. In an actual trial, of course, many other questions would be asked spontaneously. If the accused heretic remained obstinate throughout, he was eventually relaxed to the secular arm for burning at the stake. If, as in most cases, he confessed and desired to be reconciled to the Church, he was required formally to abjure his heresy.

Among the various Abjuration Formulas given by Bernard Gui, two relate to the Jews. The first is a special form for professing Jews "who have committed enormous offenses against the Catholic Faith" (V:vii:9). The crimes at issue are those of proselytizing, inducing converts to relapse, receiving or aiding them. Any of these crimes was sufficient to warrant the grave charge of being a fautor of heresy. The Oath of Abjuration is taken *super legem Moysi coram me positam et manu mea tactam et osculatam*. The Jew swears he will henceforth commit none of the aforementioned crimes, that should he hear of any proselytes or relapsi he will denounce them to the inquisitors and aid in their apprehension. Finally, he promises to abstain from blaspheming against Jesus Christ, his Mother, and the Christian faith.

This is followed by the Abjuration Formula for baptized Jews convicted of relapse (V:vii:10). Since his baptism was indelible to begin with, and as he is now in the process of reconciliation with the Church, the prisoner swears as a Christian, that is, on the Gospels. Some of the terminology employed is identical with the general formula of abjuration for Christian heretics (V:vii:1), but the specific details concern only Judaizing. Thus he states: "I abjure entirely all heresy of any condemned sect," but specifies, "especially and expressly I abjure the rite of the Jewish perfidy. . . ." Or again: "I abjure all belief, participation, favor, reception, and defence of the heretics of any condemned sect," and continues "and especially and expressly those apostates who depart from the Christian faith, or baptized converts who return to the rite or vomit of Judaism. . . ." He promises to denounce to the inquisitors the heretics of any condemned sect, but "specifically . . . those apostate Christians who have gone over to the Jewish rite and those baptized Jews who return to the rite and vomit of Judaism, their believers, fautors, (etc.)." Finally, he swears to uphold the Catholic Faith.[72] This last clause is not given directly; Bernard simply refers to the conclusion of the standard abjuration formula for heretics. In general we may regard the abjuration of relapsed Jewish converts as a variation of the latter.[73]

There is no discussion in the *Practica* of the penalties to be imposed on proselytes, relapsi, and blasphemers. One must conclude that just as judaizing was equated with ordinary heresy so the penalties too were the same for the various degrees of offense, whether by relaxation to be burned at the stake, or by imprisonment. Like an ordinary heretic too, the body of a relapsed convert who had died would be exhumed and burned, and his property confiscated. We have seen that this penalty was applied by Bernard Gui himself on at least one occasion.

Special problems arose only in connection with the penalties to be meted out to professing Jews who had never converted. Information on this matter can be gleaned from two forms:

In II:1 (repeated II:4) we have the "Form for releasing any Jew from prison to which he has been sentenced for acts committed against the Faith." The act for which the Jew had been imprisoned was that of influencing a Jewish convert to relapse and of actually receiving him back into Judaism. We see immediately that the basic punishment for Jews convicted of such a crime was imprisonment but apparently the prison term in these cases was not for life. The form reveals only that he had "long been confined." The Jew is admonished not to repeat such offenses, and he is enjoined henceforth to aid the inquisitors in their pursuits. All these things the Jew promises by an oath *super legem Moysi*.

His release, however, terminates neither his punishment nor the interest of the inquisitors in his person. Ordinarily, even after one had completed his prison term, the inquisitors prescribed further penances. For a Christian these took the form of "pious observances." To a professing Jew such penances could not logically be applied. In the Form of Release Bernard states the dilemma: "It is true that to wear crosses of cloth, to construct basilicas, to visit holy places, or to do the other pious works which are customarily imposed upon guilty persons and penitents for the crime of heretical depravity we do not wish to impose upon the aforementioned Jews, enemies of the Cross of Christ." The solution was not difficult to find: "Upon the counsel of good men[74] we impose some money penalty, to be expended for the investigation and capture of heretics, fugitives, and apostates, or for some other pious use which seems advisable to us."[75] The form ends with a declaration that the inquisitor reserves the right for himself and his successors to increase or diminish this fine, and also to return the Jews to prison at anytime, even without new charges.

It seems that a distinction was observed between the punishment of a Jew who actually received a convert back into the Jewish faith, and one who merely had contact with a convert who had already relapsed, but did not denounce him to the Inquisition. In II:13 Bernard presents a "form of a letter imposing arbitrary penance without (public) notice on any Jew for that which he has committed by receiving any or other baptized apostates, or by otherwise showing favor to them." Specifically, the Jew had known a relapsed convert, and with him "has participated in eating and drinking, listening to the lesson in the synagogue or school, observing other Jewish rites, ministering to him from his goods" (etc.). Again we are told that ordinary penances cannot be imposed and that therefore monetary compensation is required. While the previous form had not mentioned an actual sum, here it is fixed at one hundred *livres tournois*, a sizeable sum indeed. It appears from this form that, unlike the punishment for actively abetting the relapse of a convert, mere contact with the relapsed did not automatically incur a prison sentence. However this was so only for the first offense, since the form ends with a threat of imprisonment should the offense be repeated.

4. *The prosecution of Rabbinic literature*

The Inquisition had become involved in the investigation and con-demnation of Jewish books quite some time before it was called upon in 1267 to proceed against Judaizers. From the evidence available, however, it did not intrude into the domain of Jewish literature on its own initia-tive. Ironically, the first inquisition of Jewish writings is alleged to have been made at the behest of the Jews themselves. It is claimed that in 1233, in the heat of the internal Jewish conflict over the philosophical writings of Maimonides, the Anti-Maimunists of Montpellier brought the *Guide for the Perplexed* and the *Book of Knowledge* to the local friars charged with the investigation of heresy, and succeeded in having these books burned.[76] Again, in 1239, it was not the inquisitors but the apostate Jew Nicholas Donin who incited Gregory IX to issue a call for the confisca-tion and examination of the Talmud. The so-called "Disputation of Paris" which preceded the burning of the Talmud (1242? and again in 1248) was in reality an actual inquisition of the work.[77] Once such precedents were established the attacks against the Talmud became ever more frequent and unrelenting, and there is good reason to believe that in the ensuing years surveillance over Jewish literature was largely concentrated in the hands of the inquisitors.

We have already reviewed Bernard Gui's own prosecutions of Jewish books, culminating with the burning of the Talmud in Toulouse in 1319. The *Practica* itself contains no less than seven forms related to this sub-ject. In six of these Bernard's name appears and the documents are dated 1310. It is probable that similar documents had already been long in use in the preceding decades. That Bernard was himself adapting older for-mulas is likely, but cannot definitely be proven.[78]

The charges against the Talmud repeated in most of these forms are of little interest, for they simply parrot the stereotyped accusations found in the papal bulls since the time of Gregory IX. The forms are more valu-able for the information they yield about the power of the inquisitor to marshal an imposing array of forces in the course of his investigations. He could enjoin the cooperation of the superintendent over Jewish af-fairs in the district (II:48, 49), of the Sénéchal (II:51), and of course of the Prior of the Dominicans (II:52) and the rectors of churches (II:50). More-over, though we have noted that in other matters affecting Jews or Juda-izers the inquisitors were sometimes thwarted by the royal power, in the prosecution of Jewish books they appear always to have been assured of the unanimity of king and pope. When Bernard Gui speaks in the name of both he is not using empty phrases. Louis IX, Philip III and Philip IV, all supported the campaign against the Talmud.[79]

Not only the Talmud was condemned. The forms usually speak of the Talmud "and its glosses and expositions," or sometimes of the Talmud "and any other books containing blasphemies against the name of our Lord Jesus Christ." Though these are not mentioned by name in the forms themselves, we learn from a later section of the *Practica* the titles of at least three Jewish works which were under attack. In the discussion of Jewish blasphemy in Part V, Bernard declares that the Jews greatly esteem a work written by "Solomon" entitled *Glosa super textum legis*. These glosses contain false opinions taken from the Talmud as well as blasphemies against Christ, and the work has been condemned in the same manner as the Talmud itself.[80] The glosses in question are of course the famous commentaries of Rashi. Indeed, they had already been attacked along with the Talmud in Paris in 1240.[81] The second work cited is described as called by the Jews *Glosas Moysi de Egypto*, and entitled by its author, *Declarationem et reformationem legis*. It too contains the falsehoods of the Talmud and blasphemes against the Christian faith. In fact, it asserts that Jesus erred even more than Muhammad, since he made a great part of the world believe in a God who is not One, and because he abolished the law which God gave.[82] Undoubtedly, the work to which Bernard refers is the *Mishne Torah*, Maimonides' great Code of Jewish law.[83] Finally, Bernard mentions the *Glosa David hyspani* which, he states, are glosses to the Psalter, and which contain much against Christ and Christians. The allusion is probably to the Commentary of David Kimḥi (RaDaK) on the Book of Psalms.[84]

5. *Blasphemy in Jewish prayers*

Apart from the brief passages on Rashi, Maimonides, and Kimḥi, the section on alleged Jewish blasphemies (V:vii:4) focuses mainly on the Jewish liturgy. (We shall later examine Bernard's curious description of certain Jewish rituals.) While Bernard Gui's thorough knowledge of the workings of the Inquisition is undeniable, a serious doubt naturally arises as to his information on Jewish life. How much credibility can be attributed to Bernard's data on Jewish belief and practices? What were his sources of information? Should we not assume that his own bias precludes any accurate presentation of the true facts?

Before we approach the actual material, some general observations must be made. It is important that we understand clearly the nature of the *Practica* itself. Bernard Gui's treatise is not a polemic against heretics or against Jews. Nor is it a propaganda tract meant to be circulated among a wide audience. It is solely and exclusively a guide for inquisitors, meant to be used by them as a reference work in the course of their official duties, and destined for their eyes alone. As such it must necessarily aim at the greatest possible degree of accuracy. *Conscious* invention or distortion of information would only mislead the inquisitorial tribunals and thus defeat the very purpose of the work. We must, therefore, begin with the assumption that Bernard Gui recorded what he believed to be the actual facts. Certainly it is possible that Bernard's own sources sometimes contained faulty information, or that in the process of transmission facts may have been distorted. But it would be a serious methodological error to reject information on Jewish matters merely because it comes to us from the pen of an inquisitor.

Data on Judaism must have been slowly accumulating in the inquisitorial archives at least since the investigation of the Talmud in 1240. The Inquisition itself had various means of access to Jewish information. As we have noted, the interrogations contained questions on Jewish rites and beliefs, and one can be certain that the replies were recorded for future use. Jewish converts to Christianity must have served as a major source of knowledge on Jewish affairs. Thus Nicholas Donin was the "Jewish expert" in the inquisition of the Talmud in Paris. Sometimes the Dominicans were fortunate to acquire a convert as a member of their order, as in the case of Pablo Christiani, who disputed with Nahmanides at Barcelona and was active in the prosecution of Jewish literature in Aragon and Southern France in the sixties of the thirteenth century.

Some of the papal bulls and the inquisitorial documents in the *Practica* mention experts in Hebrew who examined Jewish books, without specifying whether or not they were converts from Judaism.[85] Within the Dominican Order itself some recognition of the importance of the study of Hebrew began to manifest itself in the latter part of the thirteenth century, especially in Spain. A *studium arabicum* with eight students had been established at Barcelona in 1250, and in 1291 Hebrew was officially added to the curriculum. The fact that after 1316 Dominican students from Southern France are mentioned as travelling to study at Barcelona may indicate that they went there to study Hebrew; since for theology they had traditionally gone to Montpellier and Paris, and for law to Bologna.[86] Indeed, in 1312, largely through the efforts of Raymond Lull, the

Council of Vienne called for the establishment of chairs in Hebrew, Arabic, and Chaldaic at the universities of Paris, Oxford, Bologna, and Salamanca. The avowed purpose was missionary, and included plans to translate works from these languages into Latin.[87]

Of course one must not exaggerate the importance of these beginnings. What little evidence is available would indicate that the canon of the Council of Vienne yielded only indifferent results.[88] As for the Dominicans, the number of Friars attracted to Hebrew must have been extremely small. Here and there an individual may really have acquired a more-than-superficial knowledge of the Hebrew language and Jewish literature. The outstanding example is Raymund Martini, author of the *Pugio Fidei*.[89] But otherwise it must have been mostly the converted Jew who was relied upon. It is significant that in 1319 the teacher of Hebrew and Chaldaic at Paris was a convert, Johannes Salvati.[90]

In any event, whatever the sources from which the information on Judaism ultimately derived, it deserves careful and serious attention. With this in mind, let us examine the section on Jewish prayers in the *Practica*.

The accusation that Jews blaspheme against Christ and Christians in their prayers was voiced more than once in ancient times by the Church Fathers.[91] With the exception of Agobard of Lyons (who cites St. Jerome), nothing further was heard of the accusation in Western Europe until the thirteenth century. It reappears in conjunction with the accusations against the Talmud in 1240. Of the thirty-five articles drawn up for that occasion, one dealt specifically with Jewish prayer against Christians, and we shall have an opportunity to refer to it presently. Subsequently, the charge begins to appear in papal bulls. It is mentioned by Clement IV on July 15, 1267, in a bull to Jaime I of Aragon calling for the destruction of the Talmud[92] and by Honorius IV in a bull of 1268 to the Archbishop of Canterbury.[93] The Interrogation Formula, which we have traced to an older form from the late thirteenth-century, asks: *Quomodo Judei orant contra goyim et contra clerum Romanae ecclesiae?*

Bernard Gui seeks to furnish the answer.

(a) He begins the section with a Latin translation of a benediction which is immediately recognizable: "Benedictus tu, Deus Dominus noster, rex in seculum, qui non fecisti me christianum vel gentilem."

With the exception of the word *christianum*, we have here an accurate translation of the benediction from the *birkot ha-shaḥar* (Morning Benedictions) which concludes "who hast not made me a gentile."[94] While it is entirely possible that when a medieval Jew said "gentile" he associated the term with "Christian," the latter word was probably added by Bernard Gui or by his source in order to make the meaning explicit.

(b) The next prayer to be offered in Latin is the so-called *birkat ha-minim* (Prayer against the heretics), the twelfth benediction of the daily *Amida*:[95] "Destructis (seu conversis ad fidem Christi) nulla sit spes et omnibus hereticis vel non credentibus, accusatoribus vel bilinguis, (id est traditoribus omnibus), illud momentum sit, (id est in momento sint perditi), et omnes inimici populi tui Israel velociter occisi sint et regnum iniquitatis velociter sit amens, (id est confractum et fractissimum ad de-clinandum vel plus quam ad declinandum) cito vel velociter in diebus nostris. Benedictus tu, Deus, conterens inimicos et declinans perversos."

As in the case of the word *christianum* in the translation of the morning benediction, the phrases we have placed in parentheses are explanatory glosses added to the text. In fact, later on Bernard himself states: "The prayer which they recite three times a day contains many maledictions and imprecations against Christians and against the Roman faith, which they call a damned and depraved kingdom. They pray that God destroy it and all Christians, although they do not expressly use the word 'Christians,' but by all the words they make it understood that this is what they mean, as is clear from this word '*minim*,' which means 'heretics.'"[96] The *birkat ha-minim* had already been singled out for condemnation in the Thirty-Five Articles against the Talmud in 1240. In the *Extractiones de Talmud* published by Loeb, the articles appear with a commentary, in which a Latin translation of the prayer is given, differing somewhat from that in the *Practica*. The commentary also gives ample details, with references to the Talmud, on the origin and meaning of the prayer.[97] The Hebrew text of the *birkat ha-minim* has been altered so many times as to make it virtually impossible to reconstruct the original. In modern prayer books it begins with the word *ve-lamalshinim*, and refers to informers. Bernard Gui's version refers to apostates, and this was generally the reading in the Middle Ages (i.e. *ve-lameshumadim*). Indeed, some Hebrew texts are really quite close to that of the *Practica*.[98] There can be no doubt that Bernard Gui has incorporated a fairly accurate translation of one of the recensions of the *birkat ha-minim* in use among medieval Jewry.[99]

(c) We come next to a Latin translation of the old text of the famous *Alenu* prayer, with interpolated comments. As with some of the other prayers, we are informed that it was translated directly from the He-brew (*hec exemplata sunt ex hebreo*). This version contains the phrase, later deleted from the Ashkenazic rite, "for they prostrate themselves before vanity and emptiness, and pray to a god who cannot save" (*qui illi inclinantes ad vanitates vanitatum et adorant ad Deum non valentem vel salvantem.*)[100] After the words "to cause the idols to pass away from the earth"[101] Bernard adds in explanation: *id est ymagines quas christiani de terra adorant ad honorem Christi.*

Again Bernard Gui cautions: "it is to be noted that in the aforesaid words the Jews intend to curse Christians, although they do not expressly name Christians, but in the circumlocutions they employ, the Christian people is expressly intended and comprehended."[102]

(d) Thus far we have encountered prayers translated in the *Practica* whose authenticity is unimpeachable. Much more problematic is the final prayer to which Bernard Gui alludes. We are told that on the "holiday of propitiation in September" (which can only refer to Yom Kippur, the Day of Atonement) the Jews recite a special prayer called *cematha*, "that is to say—anathema, or separation, or malediction. By certain circumlocutions they make of Christ an illegitimate son of a prostitute, of Mary a woman of voluptuousness and luxury, and they curse both of them together with the Roman faith and its adherents."[103]

None of the scholars who has dealt with this passage, has found a real basis for the allegation.[104] However, I believe we can produce strong evidence that this passage in the *Practica* is substantially correct, and that an anti-Christian prayer was indeed recited by French Jews on the Day of Atonement.

Let us first examine the term used in the *Practica*. Bernard refers to the prayer as a *cematha*. The word is clearly a latinized form of the Aramaic *shamta* used often in the Talmud in the sense of ban, excommunication, or curse.

In 1941, A. H. Freimann published the text of a liturgical poem entitled *Titnem le-ḥerpah* ("Put them to shame").[105] The entire poem, which consists of twenty-two couplets, is a long series of maledictions in which the wrath of God is invoked against both Edom and Ishmael (i.e. Christians and Muslims) in the most dire terms. *Titnem le-ḥerpah* is mentioned in the Responsa of Solomon Luria (Poland, 16th Century) in a section on literary history which draws on older sources. Luria explicitly refers to the prayer as a *shamta* and attributes its authorship to Rashi.[106] Moreover, from the *Sefer Maḥkim* of Nathan b. Judah we learn that it was recited in the Afternoon Service (Minḥa) of the Day of Atonement in French synagogues.[107] Zunz places it in twelfth-century France.[108] It was probably composed sometime after the First Crusade, and expresses the bitter mood of Jewry in that era.

Even the evidence considered thus far is sufficient to substantiate the core of Bernard Gui's statement. We have established that a malediction against the enemies of Israel was recited on the Day of Atonement in France. In fact, we have even a striking corroboration of the use of the term *shamta* applied to the prayer itself. It is true that *Titnem le-ḥerpah* contains no reference, veiled or otherwise, to Jesus or Mary. But we do not claim that this is the *specific* prayer which Bernard Gui had in mind; only that prayers of this genre existed and that they were included in the Yom Kippur liturgy.

However, we can cite another such prayer, also recited on the Day of Atonement, which leaves no doubt as to its anti-Christian character.

The same manuscript which contains the *Extractiones de Talmud* also has a section entitled *De Krubot*. It is a selection of Jewish prayers translated into Latin, which appeared to contain blasphemous allusions.[109] These prayers, too, were collected in conjunction with the inquisition of the Talmud in 1240. One of the prayers cited in the section *De Krubot* begins each verse with the word *goyim*, and appears to be composed of two parts.[110] The Hebrew originals (each a complete alphabetical acrostic after the word *ha-goyim*) have survived:

(a) The first begins: "The nations (*ha-goyim*) are as nothingness and emptiness before Thee." Each verse contrasts the nations and their vain beliefs with the Jewish people and their faith in the true God.[111]

(b) The second begins: "The nations are Emim, Zamzummim, Kedar and Edomites." In each verse the nations are equated with one of the real or mythical peoples mentioned in the Bible, and God is called upon to destroy them utterly.[112]

Both these sections were once part of the piyyut "Indeed who shall not fear Thee, O King of Nations," from the Morning Service (*Shaḥarit*) of the Day of Atonement. In fact, they were included in the Yom Kippur liturgy as late as the sixteenth-century.[113]

In terms of the charges in the *Practica*, (a) is particularly interesting, for it contains obvious references not only to image-worship, but to Mary as well. For example: "The nations link Thy holiness to the yoke of promiscuity, (but) Thy betrothed revile the relation to the promiscuous woman."[114]

As with *Titnem le-ḥerpah*, so here, it is not necessary to argue that this was the specific prayer which Bernard Gui had in mind. Obviously there were a number of such prayers in circulation which have since been lost through censorship, both external and self-imposed. The important fact remains that if we take all three prayers into account, there is not a single element in Bernard's description of anti-Christian prayers on the Day of Atonement which is not credible.

Such prayers existed, the fruit of oppression by the Christian majority. Hatred of the persecutor here became hatred of the religion and the symbol in whose name the persecutions were unleashed. Jewry, which did not have the means or power to strike back in reality, could vent its rage only in prayers calling for vengeance from its God. The loathing that could not be expressed in the street was sometimes released in the liturgy of the synagogue.

6. *The "rejudaization" rite*

Bernard Gui's information on Judaism appears especially problematic when he reports the manner in which apostates were received back into the Jewish community. In V:v:2 he offers a description of a ritual allegedly employed to "rejudaize" converts who return to Judaism (*De modo seu ritu quo Judei in rejudaysando conversos observant*):

> "The rite or mode of the Jews in rejudaizing baptized converts who return to the vomit of Judaism is as follows: He who is to be rejudaized is summoned and asked by one of the Jews present whether he wishes to submit to what is called *tymla* (=*tebila*) in Hebrew, which in Latin means whether he wishes to take a bath or washing in running water, in order to become a Jew. He replies that he does. Then the Jew who presided says to him in Hebrew *Baaltussuna* (=*baal-teshuba*) which means in Latin, "you are reverting from the state of sin."
>
> After this he is stripped of his garments and is sometimes bathed in warm water. The Jews then rub him energetically with sand over his entire body, but especially on his forehead, chest and arms, that is, on the places which, during baptism, received the holy chrism. Then they cut the nails of his hands and feet until they bleed.
>
> They shave his head, and afterwards put him in the waters of a flowing stream, and plunge his head in the water three times. After this immersion they recite the following prayer: "Blessed be God, the

Lord eternal, who has commanded us to sanctify ourselves in this water or bath which is called *tymla* (*sic*) in Hebrew."

This done, he emerges from the water, dons a new shirt and breeches, and all the attending Jews kiss him and give him a name, which is usually the name he had before baptism.

He who is thus rejudaized is required to confess his belief in the Law of Moses, to promise to keep and observe it, and to live henceforth according to it. Similarly, that he renounces baptism and the Christian faith, and that henceforth he will neither keep nor serve it. And he promises to observe the Law and repudiates baptism and the Christian faith. Afterwards they give him a certificate or testimonial letter to all other Jews so that they may receive him, trust him, and assist him. From then on he lives and acts as a Jew and attends the School, or Synagogue, of the Jews.

The issue raised here is of more than academic interest. It has implications for an understanding of the medieval attitude toward apostates and even, on another level, of Jewish-Christian polemics.

According to the doctrine of the Church, a Jew who was baptized definitely ceased to be a Jew. In receiving the sacrament of baptism he was given a sign of an indelible character which could not be effaced. He passed completely from one community into another, losing all ties with the former.

The attitude of medieval Judaism to the apostate, and his status in Jewish law, constitute a more complex problem. The fact is that medieval Jewry, regulating its life on a foundation of Talmudic law, had to cope with a type of apostasy which had not been fully anticipated in the Talmudic period.[115] Talmudic law, developed largely in the midst of a pagan world, did not really have to deal with an apostate who, by a decisive rite of conversion to another religion, simultaneously broke all his ties with the Jewish community. The Talmud knows, as it were, only "partial" apostates, and can even distinguish among specific gradations and types of apostasy. The *mumar* is an apostate relative to individual laws and commandments (e.g. the Sabbath, circumcision, the dietary prohibitions, etc.) or even with regard to the entire Torah.[116] And yet the social reality was such that, even in these circumstances, it is taken for granted by the Talmudic rabbis that the *mumar* has not passed into another community of faith and ceased to be a Jew. Though certain privileges may be denied him (e.g. his testimony is not accepted), he is still by legal definition a Jew. That his betrothal to a Jewess is valid is assumed as a matter of course.[117] There is consequently no question of a "rejudaization ceremony" in the Talmud. Never having ceased to be a Jew, the *mumar* who repented had no need to undergo a special ceremony in order to be "readmitted" into the Jewish community.[118]

The realities of medieval Jewish life were very different. The convert to Christianity or to Islam was not merely abandoning Jewish practices. Both religions took over the exclusive claim of Judaism itself. Just as the Synagogue had considered the proselyte to Judaism as "a child who is newly born," so now the Church and the Mosque regarded the convert as having totally abandoned his former allegiance. Indeed, de facto, such was the case. The apostate in the Middle Ages left not only the Jewish faith, but the Jewish quarter, his family, his friends. Whatever the theoretical attitude that might be taken toward him in theology and jurisprudence, considered from a *sociological* point of view his rupture with the Jewish community was generally complete.

Nevertheless, the jurisprudence of many medieval rabbis did not follow these "facts of life." A tendency emerged to define the convert in law as still being a Jew. Three factors may have combined to impel the rabbis to take such a stand. First, the Talmudic tradition itself obviously carried enormous authority and could not lightly be glossed over. Secondly, there was a refusal to admit the claims of the Church on the efficacy of baptism. Finally, by regarding the apostate as a Jew, the Synagogue held the door open for his return, and indeed made it clear that it was his duty to do so. Rashi was apparently the first to employ as a legal principle the dictum "Even though he sins he remains a Jew" in dealing with the apostate.[119] If this principle were to be applied consistently, then even in the Middle Ages a "rejudaizing ceremony" would not be necessary.

There can be little doubt, however, that Rashi's view flew in the face of the popular attitude. Great hostility toward the apostate, and the sober realization that in most cases his conversion to Christianity was final, combined to make the masses regard him as really no longer a Jew.[120]

It is against this background that we should view the rejudaizing rite recorded by Bernard Gui. The issue is fairly clear: According to the conception of the apostate as still technically a Jew, no special rite would be required by law for his return to the Jewish community. On the other hand, given the fact that this tradition was not universally accepted, and considering the popular attitude toward the apostate, it is by no means unreasonable to expect that in some places it may have been the custom to require of him a formal ritual, including immersion, similar in some respects to the rites of admitting a proselyte.

Let us turn now to the available evidence.

The rite described theoretically in the *Practica* appears in all its essentials in the actual case of a relapsed convert tried by Bernard Gui. The sentence of Johannes de Bretz in 1317, which we discussed earlier, related the manner of his return to Judaism in Lerida. We are told that his head was shaved, that the nails of his hands and feet were cut until they bled, and that he was given a ritual bath during which his head was immersed in flowing water.[121] It is possible, of course, that Bernard derived his information exclusively from this case. Had we no other mention of the rite we might conclude that Bernard had been misinformed, or that the example was an isolated one, and nothing should be deduced from it. However, the same information on a rejudaizing rite does appear elsewhere.

In Baruch's trial at Pamiers in 1320, he must have been asked about the rite: "He said, however, that the baptized who return to Judaism return in the following way according to the teaching of the Talmud: the nails of the hands and feet are cut, and the hair of the head is shaved, and then the entire body is washed in running water in the way that a foreign woman was purified according to the Law when she was to be married to a Jew, for they think baptism pollutes those who receive it."[122]

The comparison of the rite to the Biblical law concerning the foreign woman captured in war is interesting, and we shall come back to it.[123] An even more significant observation occurs with regard to Baruch's own reversion to Judaism: "Asked whether, in Pamiers or elsewhere, he had become rejudaized according to the aforesaid form and manner of rejudaizing, he answered that he had not, because, according to the doctrine of the Talmud, (only) if anyone is perfectly and voluntarily baptized and wishes to return to Judaism, since they think him polluted, do they have his rejudaizing as described above; but when he has not been perfectly baptized, but has been compelled to receive baptism, he is not rejudaized in the aforesaid manner, since they believe that such baptism was nothing."[124]

The testimony of Baruch as summarized by the notary is very much in accord with the information given by Bernard Gui in the case of Johannes de Bretz and in the *Practica*, and in two respects amplifies it. Since the *Practica* was completed some three years after Baruch's trial, and six years after Johannes' capture, it is likely that the alleged ritual was already commonly noted by the Inquisition. In fact, if we are correct in viewing the Interrogation Formula as based on an earlier form, the question concerning the rejudaizing rite may already have been asked in the later thirteenth century.

Though I have not found any further references to the rite in inquisitorial sources from France, the ritual immersion of relapsed Jewish converts is mentioned in a document of the Inquisition in Southern Italy. On April 12, 1292, the inquisitor Bartolomeo de Aquila reported to Charles II that several recent converts had returned to Judaism in the synagogue of Salerno, one of them taking a ritual bath to annul his baptism.[125]

Bernard's description of the rejudaizing rite was repeated almost verbatim in the *Directorium Inquisitorum* composed in 1376 by the Aragonese inquisitor Nicolas Eymeric.[126] Through Eymeric the information was channeled into the later Spanish Inquisition. While it is not my purpose to deal with the Spanish Inquisition per se, the record of one case of proselytizing and relapse from the fifteenth century is replete with details which have an important bearing on our problem.

In 1465 several conversos and descendents of converso families were received back into Judaism in Huesca. The most important of them, Juan de Ciudad and his son, were circumcised, and shortly thereafter left for Palestine. Some twenty-five years later, in 1489–90, the Inquisition in Huesca opened a major trial of all those who had participated in the ceremony, with the result that several leaders of the Jewish community were burned at the stake.[127] During the trial one of the witnesses deposed that before his circumcision Juan de Ciudad had to undergo a ceremony of leaving Christianity and purifying himself of it. Thus they washed his head, shaved it with a razor, and then vigorously rubbed his head and forehead. Another witness testified that his nails were cut, his arms and legs were bathed up to the elbows and knees, his head was washed, and then they rubbed him.[128] All these elements cropped up most significantly in the case against one of the accused, Abram Alitienz. The prosecutor delivered a speech in which he castigated Alitienz for causing Christians to become Jews, heretics, and apostates. Jews, he charged, are duty bound to pervert Christians to the Jewish law. And, after inducing Christians to become pigs, the Jews "debaptize" them, bathing them in running water, scraping off the chrism, cutting the nails, etc.[129]

The defense counsel replied at length to these charges with arguments supplied to him by the accused. Alitienz, whose general strategy was to refuse to admit any involvement in the alleged crimes, also categorically denied the existence of a special ceremony of debaptizing Christians. We shall cite only some of the arguments which are germane to our discussion of the rejudaizing rite. The defense contended that ritual immersion in running water was required of any proselyte throughout the ages, whatever his origin, and therefore it cannot be intended specifically for Christians, since it applies also to those who have never received baptism or the chrism.[130] Furthermore, the bathing must be of the entire body. The Talmud says nothing of cutting the nails or of shaving the hair from the head, and least of all, rubbing the body. If there are references to such elements, the purpose is simply to allow the water of the ritual bath to reach every part of the skin without impediment. This is often the practice of Jewish women when they go to the ritual bath for menstrual purification, and has nothing to do with Christians.

Equally significant is the next argument. The defense stated that the same ritual which is alleged to "debaptize" was decreed in the Bible for the woman captured in time of war, where her captor is commanded to bring her into his house, and she is to cut her hair and her nails.[131] Here is a sure proof that such are not intended for "dechristianizing" (*descristianar*). This can take place only in the heart, and the rest is superfluous; just as in order to be converted to Christianity a Jew need not be "dejudaized." Otherwise it would mean that no Jew could ever be converted, because it would be necessary for him to be "decircumcized." Finally, a Jew who is converted to any religion, and wishes to return, needs neither ritual bath nor anything else. Contrition alone is sufficient. Nor can the Christian really believe that the chrism can be removed by scraping, or rubbing, or bathing, for most Christians scrub and bathe daily, yet they remain Christians!

Alitienz offered an ingenious and well-reasoned argument, bolstered by references to the standard halakhic codes. It was probably as effective a rebuttal of the rejudaizing rite as could be mustered. Yet for all the intensity of his protest, nothing that was said in his defense precludes the possibility that, even if not actually mandatory in Jewish law, it may still have been the custom to employ some such rituals.[132] Not every medieval Jewish custom or folkway found its way into official codes. Furthermore, Alitienz was on trial for his life, and his whole line of defense was to deny every charge from beginning to end. He would hardly have admitted the existence of a practice which, at the very least, would leave him open to a charge of blasphemy against the Christian faith.

Thus far, however, we have surveyed only the information furnished in inquisitorial documents. We have now to inquire whether there are any clues in Jewish sources which might cast some light on the issue. Turning, then, to Jewish halakhic sources, we are confronted with an interesting phenomenon. On the one hand, the standard medieval codes are fairly agreed that according to Jewish law an apostate who wishes to return to Judaism does not have to undergo a ceremony of ritual immersion.[133] On the other hand, there are enough scattered references in the literature to make it almost certain that, at least in the realm of custom, rites of readmitting apostates were widely practiced.

The ritual immersion of returning apostates is mentioned as early as the thirteenth century by the German halakhist Mordecai b. Hillel.[134] It is explicitly prescribed as a rabbinic ordinance by the Spanish Talmudist Joseph ibn Habib.[135] This decision is accepted by Moses Isserles.[136]

Along with the ritual bath for the penitent apostate, the shaving of the hair and paring of the nails were also observed. Solomon Luria asserts that it was still the custom in his day, and that he himself saw it ordered as a matter of practical law.[137] Isserles alludes to it indirectly, stating that a Jew who has been converted and then has repented is permitted to shave even if it is a holiday.[138] Joel Sirkes cites both the opinion of Joseph ibn Habib on the need for a ritual bath, and of Luria on the shaving of the hair.[139]

It is also important to hear some of the reasons adduced for these practices. Shaving the hair and paring the nails were, of course, widely required for the proselyte in conjunction with his ritual bath. Commenting on this, Sabbatai b. Meir ha-Kohen declares that the reason is not merely because of a possible obstruction to the penetration of the water, but rather because the proselyte is now entering Judaism. Even if he first washes his hair and combs or trims it, he must still shave it, and this is also the rite for the penitent apostate.[140] In other words, the reason for the shaving is not merely physical, but *symbolic*. (We will recall that Alitienz argued that the purpose was solely to remove impediments to the water). Similarly, explaining the permission for the returning convert to shave on a holiday, Abraham Gumbiner stated that "we do not allow him to participate in anything holy until he shaves."[141] And David b. Samuel Halevi adds: "Because the idolater is similar to a corpse and to a leper who must be shaven of his hair."[142]

The testimonial document for the returning convert referred to by Bernard Gui is not mentioned in the Jewish sources. However, the codes recognize a problem which is somewhat similar. They prescribe that a gentile who states that he has become a proselyte in another place is not accepted into the community until he brings witnesses.[143] Some authorities were apparently willing to accept a written document signed by two Jewish witnesses.[144]

We are now in a position to summarize our material:

From the sources available to us, both inquisitorial and Jewish, we cannot prove with finality that the rejudaizing rite as described by Bernard Gui is authentic. We can assert, however, that most of the elements appear highly plausible. The custom of requiring a ritual bath of the penitent apostate definitely existed, as did the shaving of the hair and paring of the nails.[145]

The benediction over the immersion is accurate. The testimonial letter may have been necessary in certain cases. It is also quite conceivable that Baruch's distinction between forced and voluntary converts really applied, and that these rites were administered only to those in the latter category. The only truly alien feature of the rite in the *Practica* is the scraping and rubbing of sand on those parts of the body which received the chrism. But then, it is hardly likely that one would find such an explicitly anti-Christian rite openly revealed by Jewish codifiers and commentators, even if they were aware of it. The peril was too great.

Similarly, when one finds the bathing and shaving of the apostate discussed in Jewish legal literature, one should not be surprised that the reasons given are not those mentioned in the inquisitorial sources. It is enough that such practices existed. Perhaps the rabbis did not consider these rites as literally signifying a "rejudaizing" or "dechristianizing," although even this is not certain. But even then, it would not mean that these rituals were not considered rites of rejudaization in the eyes of the masses. It is in the nature of custom and ritual to be interpreted simultaneously on several different levels.

7. *Special circumcision of proselytes*

One practice alleged by Bernard Gui remains to be discussed. In the Interrogation Formula the accused is asked: "How do the Jews circumcise the children of Christians differently from their own?"[146] The question is followed by these observations:

It should be noted here that the Jews circumcise their children differently from Christians, whether children or adults; for when circumcising Christians, adults or minors, they cut their (fore) skins only partially (*semiplene*) and not, as they do with their Jewish children, completely around.

Also, when Christians become Jews or Jewesses, they are given a certificate of "Judaization" which they must always carry with them. Otherwise the Jews would neither drink nor eat with them. And it must contain the names of each of the masters who debaptize them.[147]

This information did not originate with Bernard Gui. He quoted it from a notice which appeared already in compilations of inquisitorial materials from the late thirteenth century.[148] There is apparently no further independent reference to such a practice in any other documents or treatises of the Inquisition. Eymeric merely repeats the same paragraph.[149]

Nor can one find a mention of special circumcision for proselytes in the Jewish sources. The halakhic literature is unanimous in asserting the need for regular circumcision of any Gentile proselytes of whatever age. Only for the certificate allegedly given to the proselyte can we find an echo in Jewish literature.[150] We are thus confronted with an allegation in the *Practica* whose single source is known to us but which is unattested elsewhere. In the absence of any outside information we can only speculate on its authenticity.

There can be little doubt that a circumcision *semiplene* would not have been considered valid by medieval Jews. Even if one were to accept the allegation at face value, one could at most conceive that such an operation took place in some isolated case, and that it was then reported to the Inquisition. It may be that an inadequate circumcision was occasionally performed. Possibly, considering the enormous danger both to the proselyte and to those who accepted him, some Jews may have been content merely to make an incision and draw a drop of blood (*hatafat-dam*). The fact is that the original source which Bernard Gui quoted spoke only of adult Christians who are circumcised in this way.[151] If this really occurred in the Middle Ages the information would be startling indeed. It is well known that in the Graeco-Roman world there was still some question as to the very necessity of circumcision for adult male proselytes.[152] The halakha finally adopted made circumcision absolutely mandatory, and this law remained normative through the ages. Were there some medieval Jews, perhaps of doubtful orthodoxy, who performed a less rigorous circumcision in order to facilitate conversion to Judaism? Or do we have here an anti-Jewish invention? The question must remain open.

This essay was completed in 1964 for inclusion in a collaborative volume of Jewish studies which, regrettably, was never published. For technical reasons it is published now in its original form, with no attempt to bring the bibliography up to date. Some new documents and studies concerning the Papal Inquisition have, indeed, appeared since. None, so far as I know, deal with specifically Jewish aspects.

1. A public lecture by Solomon Reinach on "L'inquisition et les Juifs" was published in *Revue des études juives*, XL (1900), conférences, pp. xlix–lxiv. No comprehensive monograph on the subject has appeared. The only attempt to examine the relations between the Papal Inquisition and the Jews in some detail will be found in Louis I. Newman's *Jewish Influence on Christian Reform Movements* (Columbia University Oriental Studies no. 23; New York, 1923). Important facts and references are assembled by Newman in the section devoted to the Inquisition, and this is the chief merit of the work. The analysis itself is disappointing. Much material is included which proves either irrelevant or misleading. The value of Newman's treatment of the Inquisition is further diminished by his insistent use of the texts as props for his extravagant claims of a major Jewish influence on the Albigensian heresies. For an incisive review of the entire book see Salo Baron, "Jewish Influence on Christian Reform Movements," *Jewish Quarterly Review* (N.S.), XXIII (1932), pp. 405–410.

2. Only a fraction of the original records of the Inquisition in France has survived. Since documents pertaining to the Jews were in the minority to begin with, the loss in this area is even more grave. For surveys of inquisitorial sources see Charles Molinier, *L'Inquisition dans le midi de la France au XIIIe et au XIVe siècle: étude sur les sources de son histoire* (Paris, 1880); idem, "Rapport à M. le Ministre de l'Instruction Publique sur une mission exécutée en Italie," *Archives des missions scientifiques et littéraires*, sér. 3, XIV (1888), pp. 133–336; Célestin Douais, *Documents pour servir à l'histoire de l'Inquisition dans le Languedoc* (2 vols.; Paris, 1900). More recent literature is discussed by Arno Borst, *Die Katharer* (Schriften der Monumenta Germaniae Historica no. 12; Stuttgart, 1953), pp. 1–58.

3. A full discussion of Bernard Gui's life and work will be found in Léopold Delisle, "Notice sur les manuscrits de Bernard Gui," *Notices et extraits des manuscrits de la Bibliothèque Nationale*, XXVII (1879), Pt. 2, pp. 169–454. Cf. A. Thomas "Bernard Gui, frère Prêcheur," *Histoire littéraire de la France*, XXXV (Paris, 1921), pp. 139–232.

4. *Liber sententiarum inquisitionis Tholosonae*, in Philip van Limborch, *Historia inquisitionis* (Amsterdam, 1692). The manuscript which Limborch published is no longer extant. The record of the trial proceedings had been lost earlier and was unavailable to him.

5. First published by C. Douais with the title *Practica inquisitionis heretice pravitatis* (Paris, 1886). Cited hereafter as Gui, *Practica*. Later Part V was edited separately and published with a French translation by G. Mollat as *Manuel de l'inquisiteur* (Les classiques de l'histoire de France au moyen âge, nos. 8–9, 2 vols.; Paris, 1926–7). Cited as: Gui, *Manuel*.

6. A careful survey and analysis of the older inquisitorial compilations, most of them still in manuscript, is provided by Antoine Dondaine in his study of "Le manuel de l'inquisiteur (1230–1330)," *Archivum Fratrum Praedicatorum*, XVII (1947), pp. 85–194.

7. The importance of this material was already recognized by Israel Lévi when he excerpted the Jewish sections of the *Practica* in a small pamphlet entitled *Les Juifs et l'Inquisition dans la France méridionale; extraits de la Practica de Barnard Gui* (Paris, 1891). Curiously, Lévi stated in his introduction that the *Practica* was as yet unedited. He was apparently unaware of Douais' edition of the entire work five years earlier, which was based on MS. 387 in the municipal library of Toulouse. Lévi, therefore, had recourse to the copy of the *Practica* in vols. XXIX–XXX of the Doat Collection in the Bibliothèque Nationale, though in several places he refers to MS. 267 in Tolouse. (Douais and Mollat mention only two Toulousan MSS., numbered 387 and 388.) The Doat copy has been characterized as "assez incorrecte" by Delisle, op. cit., p. 354.

Lévi's extracts were accompanied by sparse notes. Since then only Newman has dealt with the Jewish material in the *Practica* (Newman, op. cit., pp. 263 f., 304, 312, 321 ff. and especially 382–390). His approach is more descriptive than analytic, and adds little to Lévi's rudimentary comments.

8. On the expulsion of 1306 see H. Graetz, *Geschichte der Juden*, VII, pp. 243–249; Gustave Saige, *Les Juifs du Languedoc antérieurement au XIVe siècle* (Paris, 1881), pp. 92 ff. For this as well as the subsequent expulsions from France, see Isidore Loeb, "Les expulsions des Juifs de France au XIVe siècle," in *Jubelschrift zum Siebzigsten Geburtstage des Prof. Dr. H. Graetz* (Breslau, 1887), pp. 38–56.

9. The inquisitors in France had been given jurisdiction over Judaizers ever since Clement IV's famous bull *Turbato corde*, issued on July 26, 1267 (Potthast, *Regesta Pontificum Romanorum*, no. 20095). On this bull see infra, note 54.

10. For a general account of Philip's relations with the Inquisition see Henry Charles Lea, *A History of the Inquisition in the Middle Ages* (New York, 1888; Reprint, 1955), II, p. 57 ff.

11. For example, on May 17, 1288, some three weeks after thirteen Jews of Troyes were burned on a charge of ritual murder, Philip issued a decree forbidding the members of any order to pursue Jews in the Kingdom of France without informing the baillis and sénéchaux of the facts (E. J. de Laurière, *Ordonnances*

des roys de France de la troisième race, I (Paris, 1723), p. 317. On the events see Arsène Darmesteter, "L'auto-da-fé de Troyes," *REJ*, II (1881), pp. 199–247). In September of 1293 the king sent a long letter to Simon Briseteste, Sénéchal of Carcassonne and Beziers, enclosing copies of the bull *Turbato corde* and of his own edict of 1288. He commanded that while the bull was to be obeyed, no Jew was to be arrested for any cause not specified therein (Saige, op. cit., Preuves, xliii no. 18, pp. 231–4).

If, in 1299, Philip issued a new edict (ibid., p. 235 f.) accusing the Jews of blasphemy and other crimes, condemning the Talmud, and ordering the royal officials to obey the inquisitors, it was probably a conciliatory measure in his temporary truce with Boniface VIII. Their quarrel erupted anew in 1301 over the affair of Bernard Saisset, and in that year Philip sent royal "reformers" to Languedoc to curb the excesses of the Inquisitor of Toulouse, Foulques de St.-George, with the result that he was dismissed. The next year all the reforms were embodied in a general decree, and the legislation of 1293, protecting the Jews from the inquisitors, was repeated (Lea, op. cit., II, p. 81). Shortly afterwards the king also forbade the Inquisition to take cognizance of usury, sorcery, and other alleged offenses of the Jews.

Quite often the dealings between Philip and his vassals on questions of inquisitorial jurisdiction over Jews assumed the bland character of a business transaction. On November 4, 1292, he commanded his officials to restore to the Viscount of Narbonne, Aimeri V, property which the inquisitors had confiscated from some of the latter's Jewish subjects, since those condemned were the Viscount's "own" Jews. See Jean Regné, *Étude sur la condition des Juifs de Narbonne* (Narbonne, 1911), Preuves, X, p. 235.

12. *Ordonnances*, I, p. 488 f.

13. *Continuationis Chronici Guillelmi de Nangiaco*, ed. H. Geraud (Publications de la Société de l'Histoire de France, no. 43; Paris, 1843) I, p. 363.

14. Ibid., p. 363 f.

15. Ibid., p. 380.

16. "Hoc etiam anno (1306) in augusto et septembri, omnes Judei, nisi forte pauci qui baptizari voluerunt, de regno Francie sunt expulsi . . ." S. Baluze, *Vitae Paparum Avenionensium*, ed. G. Mollat (Paris, 1914) I, p. 5.

17. On the French exiles in Aragon and the return of converts to Judaism, see Yitzhak Baer, *Toledot ha-Yehudim bi-Sefarad ha-noṣrit* (Tel-Aviv, 1945), I, p. 256 ff.

18. Gui, *Practica*, Part II, nos. 48, 51, 52, pp. 67–71. The date 1309 given by Newman, *Jewish Influence* p. 322, is an error. In dating his documents Bernard Gui began the year on March 25th. (See A. Giry, *Manuel de diplomatique*, p. 123.) Thus the documents in the *Practica* dated January 1309 were actually issued in January

1310 according to our reckoning. Cf. Delisle, *MSS. de Bernard Gui*, pp. 382, 384. On Jean de Crépy's role in the confiscations of Jewish property in Toulouse, see Saige, *Languedoc*, p. 95.

19. Gui, *Practica*, no. 50, p. 69.

20. ". . . nota quod anno Domini mccc nono tres plenae magnae quadrigae librorum Judaeorum fuerunt combusti Parisius ante festum Nativitatis Domini, in crastinum (December 7) festi sancti Nicolai hyemalis, quos Judaei compilaverunt et facerant" (M. Bouquet, *Recueil des historiens de Gaules et de la France*, XXI, p. 813).

21. *Ordonnances*, I, pp. 595–7. For Bernard Gui's curt notice of the return of the Jews to France see Bouquet, *Recueil*, XXI, p. 725.

22. About a decade earlier, of course, the papacy had been transferred to Avignon. Clement V, first of the Avignonese popes, died on April 14, 1314, and until the election of John XXII on August 7, 1316, the papal throne was vacant. However, the Doat Collection (vol. XXXVII, fol. 255r–257r) contains a copy of a bull issued in the name of Clement V and dated February 13, 1315, annulling an earlier bull which had exempted the Jews of Narbonne and Toulouse from the jurisdiction of the inquisitors, and had transferred cases then pending to the ordinary episcopal courts. Now they were once again to be called before inquisitorial tribunals. The text of the earlier bull is quoted without a date. Since it presupposes the existence of a regular Jewish community in Narbonne and Toulouse, it can only have been issued prior to the expulsion of 1306, in the first year of Clement's pontificate. Added weight is given such an assumption when we consider that around that time Clement also responded favorably to complaints of the citizens of Albi and Carcassonne against the inquisitors. (See his bull, dated March 13, 1306, in Jean-Marie Vidal, *Bullaire de l'Inquisition française au XIVe siècle* (Paris, 1913), no. 3, pp. 9–11.)

Neither Clement's first bull in favor of the Jews, nor the bull which revokes the concession are to be found outside the Doat Collection. They are cited neither in the Benedictine *Regestum Clementis Papae V*, nor in Vidal's *Bullaire*. The earlier bull appears to be authentic. It is repeated almost verbatim in a bull of Clement VII granting the same privileges in 1383 to the Jews of Sens, Rouen, Reims and Lyon (Vidal, op. cit., no. 318, p. 450 f.).

However, the date of Clement V's alleged revocation arouses suspicion, since actually he died almost a year before. I confess I have been unable to ascertain whether, during the papal interregnum, it was the practice to issue documents in the name and according to the year of the deceased pope. If the bull is not a forgery, it would mean that the inquisitors had succeeded somehow in obtaining from the papal chancery in Avignon a restoration of jurisdiction which had earlier been taken from them. In that event, it must have been done in anticipation of the return of the Jews. I propose this view with considerable diffidence in the absence of more substantive information.

23. Under the heading "Sentencia defunctorum in heresi," we read: "Item quod Johannes conversus de judaysmo, qui dum erat Judeus vocabatur Josse, et consuevit morari in florencia dyocesis auxitane post sacramentum fidei a se susceptum fidem Christianam abnegando et blasfemando deseruit asserens se velle vivere et mori in fide seu magis perfidia Judeorum, nec admonitus et ortatus sepius per multos bonos viros ab illa perfidia voluit resilire, tandemque requisitus judicialiter et canonice quod fidem Christianam quam susceperat et baptismum teneret et servaret et ore confiteretur noluit resipisci, sicque predictus Johannes conversus postmodum vero perversus et adversus a fide catholica reversusque ad vomitum judeismi in tali perfidia continue perseverans dampnabiliter in eadem" (*Liber sententiarum inquisitionis Tholosonae*, p. 167). On the burning of the remains of deceased heretics see L. Tanon, *Histoire des tribunaux de l'Inquisition en France* (Paris, 1893), pp. 407–413.

24. "Johannes de bretz filius quondam Jacob de serinhaco prope bellum montem dyocesis Tholosane conversus de judaysmo ad baptismum, sicut per ipsius confessionem factam in judicio XVIII Kalendas Julii, anno Domini MCCCXVII legitime nobis constat, dudum conversus fuit de judaysmo ad fidem Domini nostri Jesu Christi, fuitque baptisatus in villa que vocatur bretz prope insulam dyocesis Tholosane, perseveravitque sicut Christianus in fide Christi et baptismi annis tribus vel circa. Postmodum vero reversus est ad judaysmum, fuitque rejudaysatus secundum modum et ritum rejudaysacionis a Judeis in talibus fieri consuetum apud Ylerdam . . . et permansit vivendo judayce per tres annos servando vitam et ritum et fidem Judeorum, derelicta fide Christi et baptismi, et credidit se posse salvari in fide et vita et ritu et observancia Judeorum, et fuit in dicta credencia per tres annos, nec venit ad confitendum de predictis donec fuit adductus captus" (*Lib. sent. inq. Thol.*, p. 230).

It was undoubtedly activities such as these which finally involved the Jewish community of Lerida itself with the Inquisition. In 1323 Jaime II of Aragon upbraided the inquisitor Bernard de Podio Certoso for instituting an inquisition against the Jews of Lerida without first informing him. See the letter in Heinrich Finke, *Acta Aragonensia* (Berlin-Leipzig, 1908), II, no. 540, p. 859 f.

25. Other examples of extradition from Aragon to France can be found, but it was probably not automatic. On July 10, 1321, Jaime II wrote to Bishop Raimund of Urgel that the Pope wanted him to hand over an imprisoned heretic to the Inquisitor of Carcassonne "qui pro eius capcione diu et longo tempore laboravit." Finke, op. cit., II, no. 538 p. 857.

26. "Les livres de leur loy, qui encore sont pardevers nous, qui n'ont esté vendus, leur seront rendus, exceptés les Talameus (*sic*) condamnés" (*Ordonnances*, I, p. 596). The reference to books which have been sold tends to confirm my impression that the confiscation of 1310 was largely of Jewish books in Gentile hands.

27. "In nomine Domini amen. Anno ejusdem Domini MCCCXIX IIII Kalendas Decembris. Ad requisicionem et mandatum ac judicium et ordinacionem religiosi viri fratris Bernard Guidonis inquisitoris heretice pravitatis in regno Francie et specialiter in partibus Tholosanis per sedem apostolicam deputati, fuerunt libri Judeorum qui apellantur Talmut, quotquot apud Judeos portuerunt inveniri, conbusti et tracti prius per publicas carrerias Tholose in duabus quadrigis cum servientibus et ministris curie regalis cum voce preconia proclamante, propter errores et blasfemias contra Dominum Jesum Christum et ejus sanctissimam genitricem Virginem Mariam et nominis Christiani, qui errores et que blasfemie in eisdem libris inveniebantur contineri per juratos examinatores peritos in hebrayca linga, habito prius consilio maturo per eundem dominum inquisitorem cum peritis in utroque jure et religiosis et aliis multis discretis viris in aula veteri domini regis Tholose. Predicti autem libri prius diu antea fuerant cum multa sollicitudine et diligencia per manum regalium ad mandatum prefati domini inquisitoris habiti a Judeis et postmodum diligenter examinati" (*Lib. sent. inq. Thol.*, p. 273 f.).

28. G. Mollat, *Lettres communes de Jean XXII*, no. 12238; T. Ripoll, *Bullarium ordinis FF. Praedicatorum*, II, no. 28, p. 149; Solomon Grayzel, "Jews in the Correspondence of John XXII," *Hebrew Union College Annual*, XXIII (1950–51), pp. 54–58.

29. O. Raynaldus, *Annales ecclesiastici*, ann. 1320, no. 24 ff.; cf. Mollat, *Lettres communes*, no. 14131.

In the *Practica* of Bernard Gui (Pt. III no. 47, p. 170 f.) there is an undated formula for the condemnation of the Talmud which refers to the bull of John XXII and, hence, must have followed it.

30. J.-M. Vidal, *Le tribunal d'inquisition de Pamiers* (Toulouse, 1906), p. 80 n. 3.

31. "Et en cest an, au temps de Karesme, furent condampnez les mauvais livrez de juifz, en la maistresse église Notre Dame de Paris" ("Chronique Parisienne anonyme," in *Mémoires de la Société de l'histoire de Paris et de l'Ile-de-France*, XI (1884), p. 56).

32. It is possible that the lament of Kalonymos b. Kalonymos, תורת ה' תמימה נקדשה ביום חתונתה והיתה לבער, refers to one of these burnings. (See his *Eben Boḥan*, ed. A. M. Habermann (Tel-Aviv, 1956), p. 161.)

33. On the events in Marseilles see Adolphe Crémieux, "Les Juifs de Marseille au moyen âge," *REJ*, XLVI (1903), p. 29. Michel le Moine, a Franciscan, served as inquisitor in Provence, 1312–1328. He was particularly zealous in the persecution

of the Spirituals. In 1312 he was summoned before Clement V to answer chargers of misconduct and maltreatment. The charges were serious enough for the Pope to order his removal from his post, but this measure was apparently not carried out. For these and other details see Vidal, *Bullaire*, p. 38 no. 2.

34. On the massacres of the Pastoureaux see Graetz, *Geschichte*, VII, pp. 255–7.

35. "Confessio Baruc (teutonici) olim judei, modo baptizati, et postmodum conversi ad judaismum." The full Latin text was first published by J.-M. Vidal in his "l'Emeute des Pastoureaux en 1320; Déposition du Juif Baruc devant l'Inquisition de Pamiers," *Annales de Saint Louis des Français*, III (1898–99), pp. 154–174. (Cited hereafter as: *Confessio Baruc*). The text was translated into English with introduction and notes by Solomon Grayzel, "The Confession of a Medieval Jewish Convert," *Historia Judaica*, XVII (1955), pp. 89–120.

36. Two documents in the Doat Collection dated March 1297 (=March 1298 n. st.) led Lea to conclude that by then the Jewish community in Pamiers was under the jurisdiction of the Inquisition. In these documents the inquisitor Arnaud Déjean authorized certain Jews to visit him at will on matters pertaining to his office, and also confirmed the Jews of Pamiers in the privileges they had long enjoyed according to the usages of the province of Narbonne, promising not to impose any new burdens (Bibliothèque Nationale, *Fonds Doat*, XXXVII, fol. 160 f.). However, in an earlier document dated 1279 (ibid., fol. 156), Bernard, Abbot of St. Antonin in Pamiers, approved the sumptuary laws the Jews had drawn up for themselves. Lea assumed therefore that sometime between 1279 and 1297 the Jews "had passed into the hands of the Inquisition" (Lea, *Inquisition*, II, p. 96n). This conclusion is unwarranted. Bernard Saisset, who had been the abbot of St. Antonin since 1267, became Bishop of Pamiers in 1295 when the diocese of Pamiers was created for him. It is hardly conceivable that he relinquished his authority over the Jews of the town after he became bishop. Arnaud Déjean was appointed inquisitor by Boniface VIII in December, 1295. Saisset, totally indifferent to the pursuit of heresy, and much preoccupied with his own affairs, had the fullest confidence in Déjean, and on one occasion even sent him as his envoy to Paris. (See on this J.-M. Vidal, *Bernard Saisset, Évêque de Pamiers* (Toulouse-Paris, 1926), pp. 61, 106.) There can be no question of a conflict of jurisdiction between the two. The documents of 1297 are merely an assurance from the inquisitor, probably solicited by the Jews themselves, that he will not meddle in their internal affairs.

37. In his study of the trial Grayzel states (op. cit., p. 95): "It is to be noted . . . from the case of Baruch that there were bishops who took the initiative in arresting and interrogating relapsed converts. Of course, Jacques Fournier was not the ordinary bishop. He was known for his zeal in discovering and punishing heretics. To be sure, he had an inquisitor as a member of the court which examined

Baruc, but the Bishop conducted the examination. One may well assume that men in Baruc's position preferred it so. For the Inquisition was clearly police-minded and saw its task in terms of eliciting confessions and inflicting punishment. An episcopal court was much more likely to be interested in discussion and instruction."

This is somewhat oversimplified. Though headed by the Bishop, the tribunal which judged Baruch was not an ordinary episcopal court, but rather an inquisitorial tribunal of a very special nature. Jacques Fournier became Bishop of Pamiers in 1317. The pursuit of heresy in the diocese was from the first one of his major concerns. In 1312 the Council of Vienne had given the bishops powers fairly equal to those of the inquisitors in matters of heresy (*Clementin.* Lib. V, tit. III, cap. 1. *Corpus Iuris Canonici*, ed. Friedberg, II, c. 1181–2). With this power in mind, Jacques Fournier turned to the Inquisitor of Carcassonne, Jean de Beaune, for aid in establishing a joint tribunal in Pamiers. The latter designated Gaillard de Pomies, a Dominican of Pamiers, to serve with the Bishop, beginning in December of 1318.

The result was perhaps the only successful example of an inquisitorial tribunal of mixed character, in which both bishop and inquisitor were intimately associated. For further details see J.-M. Vidal, *Le tribunal d'inquisition de Pamiers*, pp. 71–75.

As for Grayzel's intimation that a suspect might prefer to be judged by Fournier, one has only to note the comments of those who actually appeared before him, e.g.: "Everything is lost with this bishop. It matters little whether one is a heretic or a good Catholic. By his interrogations he transforms faithful Christians into avowed heretics" (Vidal, loc. cit., p. 76. For the extraordinary activity of the Pamiers Inquisition in its seven years under Fournier, see the statistics ibid., pp. 115–120).

38. "Interrogatus per dictum dominum episcopum, si quando stetit ante dictum capellanum et dictus capellanus procedebat in officio baptismi, vel etiam quando fuit positus in fontibus baptismalibus et in actu ipsius baptismi, reclamavit verbo vel facto, vel ostendit voluntatem contrariam, resistendo, quod nollet baptizari" (*Confessio Baruc*, p. 164).

39. "Et incontinenti dictus dominus episcopus hortatus fuit dictum magistrum Baruc et monuit quod, cum baptismus taliter susceptus per eum, ut dictum est, quia susceptus fuerat per eum, non vi vel coactione absoluta, obligabat eum secundum iura et racionem ad tenendam et credendam fidem christianam, quia illa necessitas que impulit eum ad fidem, non ad deterius sed ad melius ipsum traxit, quod de cetero fidem christianam crederet et teneret, alioquin sciret pro certo quod, si permaneret in iudaismo obstinatus, quod procederetur contra eum, secundum iura, sicut contra hereticum obstinatum" (ibid., p. 165 f.).

40. If the lengths of time for the disputations recorded by the notary are correct, the date August 16 given here must be an error, and September 16 would be more reasonable. The disputations began on July 14 or shortly thereafter. If we add the number of days given for each disputation, plus the fifteen days in which Baruch read the Bible, we have a total of at least fifty-nine days, whereas the period July 14–August 16 yields only thirty-three. On the other hand, it is possible that the length of the disputations was exaggerated deliberately to emphasize the patience with which the Bishop persuaded Baruch of the truth of Christianity.

41. I am assuming the date on which the trial resumed was September 16, and not August 16. If the latter date were indeed correct, the silence of the record would be even more startling. It would mean that at this point Baruch was so intransigent that it took more than a month (August 16–September 25) to bring about his final abjuration. Cf. Grayzel, *Confession*, p. 119 n. 66.

42. "Postque anno quo supra, die XXVa mensis septembris, constitutus in iudicio dictus Johannes in camera Sedis episcopalis Appamiarum coram dicto domino episcopo, assistente sibi dicto fratre Gaulhardo de Pomeriis, presentibus Archidiacono Maioricen., et canonico Narbonen., Germano de Castronovo, archidiacono Appamiarum . . . Hugone Artaudi priore de Praderiis, et multis aliis canonicis dicte ecclesie Appamiarum et religiosis viris prioribus beate Marie de Carmelo . . . et Augustinorum et subpriore Predicatorum . . . consulibus Appamiarum et multis aliis burgensibus dicte civitatis . . ." (etc.) (*Confessio Baruc*, p. 172).

43. On the nature and types of imprisonment by the Inquisition, see Tanon, *Tribunaux*, pp. 479–490.

44. The time of the expulsion and the motivation behind it have been disputed. While a date in 1322 has been generally assumed, Grayzel (*John XXII*, p. 61 f. n. 1, 2) has demonstrated that it must have occurred in 1321, thus excluding a possible connection with the anti-Jewish agitation during the Leper Persecution. Grayzel's strictures on the various interpretations of the expulsion are well taken. His own suggestion is that "it was due to the existence of converts to Christianity at the height of the Shepherd Persecution, who, having found a refuge in the Comtat, now reverted to Judaism. The inquisitors, especially Bernard Gui, thereupon stirred the Pope to action." This is hardly likely. Faced with a considerable number of relapsi, the inquisitors would have characteristically urged prosecution, rather than an expulsion which would only infect other territories. As for Bernard Gui himself, I know of no evidence that he exerted any influence on the Pope in this matter. In his chronicle of the pontificate of John XXII (Baluze, *Vit. Pap Aven.*, p. 152 ff.), there is an account of the pogroms of the Pastoureaux against the Jews, but no mention at all of the expulsion.

45. Graetz, *Geschichte*, VII, p. 258 f.

46. On the expulsion by Charles IV see Loeb, *Expulsions*, p. 49 ff. Loeb sees no necessary connection between this expulsion and the accusation, a year earlier, that the Jews had participated in the Leper's Plot.

47. L. Wadding, *Annales Minorum*, ann. 1322 no. lxix; Vidal, *Bullaire*, no. 38 p. 69 f.; Grayzel, *John XXII*, p. 64 ff. The bull was first issued in 1281 by Martin IV (Potthast, *Regesta*, no. 21806).

The date given for John's bull by Cherubini (*Bullarium Romanum*, I, p. 216) and Coquelines (*Bull. Rom.* III, Pt. 2, p. 154) is August 13, 1317. Grayzel points out that both dates may be correct. If the bull was first issued by John in 1317, it came shortly after the return of Jews to France, when some converts may have been emboldened to revert to Judaism.

48. At times conflicts of jurisdiction between bishops and inquisitors arose because of financial considerations. One such clash during the pontificate of John XXII occurred in Italy. On January 26, 1328, the Pope wrote to the inquisitors of Apulia ordering them not to proceed against Jews or relapsed converts unless requested to do so by the Bishop of Trani. The Bishop had complained that although the Church had derived considerable income from the Jews of the city, they now had become so impoverished, because of the extortions of the inquisitors, that this source of revenue was exhausted. See the bull in Grayzel, *John XXII*, no. 33 p. 73 f.

49. Loeb, *Expulsion*, p. 51.

50. Jews were also liable to inquisitorial prosecution for usury, but this category is missing entirely in the *Practica*. Just as in other areas, so here too the Inquisition was theoretically concerned solely with matters of belief. Specific acts were important, not in themselves, but as manifestations of the beliefs which motivated them. Thus in theory usury was not subject to the Inquisition by its practice, but rather by the implicit assertion that it is not a sin. In a summary of heretical errors from the archives of the Inquisition of Carcassonne we read: "Dicunt quod tradere ad usuram, ratione termine, non est peccatum aliquod" (de Vic-Vaissète, *Histoire générale de Languedoc* (Toulouse, 1872–92), VIII, Preuves, 983).

51. Such general forms usually contain instructions in the appropriate places for the insertion of the details of the specific heresy involved, e.g., "quod tu talis N. de tali loco commissisti, seu fecisti hoc et hoc" (Gui, *Practica*, III:16). Still, in addition to forms which can be applied to different sects, the *Practica* does contain specific forms for sentencing "Manicheans" (III:32), Waldenses (III:34) and Beguins (III:37). There is no comparable formula for the sentencing of relapsed Jewish converts.

52. "Judei perfidi conantur, quando et ubi possunt, occulte pervertere chris-

tianos et trahere ad perfidiam judaycam, maxime illos qui prius fuerunt Judei et conversi sunt et receperunt baptismum et fidem Christi, presertim illos qui sibi attinent aut sunt afinitate vel consanguinitate juncti" (Gui, *Practica*, V:v:1; *Manuel*, p. 6).

53. "Statutum est autem ut contra christianos qui ad ritum transierent vel redierint Jueorum, etiamsi hujusmodi redeuntes dum erant infantes, aut mortis metu, non tamen absolute seu precise coacti, baptizati fuerint, est tanquam contra hereticos, si fuerint de hoc confessi, aut per christianos seu Judeos convicti, et sicut contra fautores, receptatores et defensores hereticorum, contra fautores, receptatores et defensores talium procedendum" (ibid.).

Cf. *Sexti Decret.* Lib. V, tit. II "De haereticos," cap. xiii "Contra christianos" (*Corpus Iuris Canonici*, ed. Friedberg, II, c. 1075).

54. The bull *Turbato corde* as issued by Clement IV mentions only proselytes explicitly: ". . . quod quamplurimi christiani veritatem catholicae fidei abnegantes, se ad ritum iudaeorum damnabiliter transtulerunt" (*Bullarium Romanum Taurinensis*, III no. 24, p. 785). Joshua Starr maintained therefore that authority to proceed against relapsi was not given until the renewal of the bull by Nicholas IV in 1288. See his "Mass Conversion of the Jews of Southern Italy (1290-1293)," *Speculum*, XXI (1946), p. 205 n. 15. However Guido Kisch is essentially correct in stating that "from the point of view of canon law there can be no doubt that the equation of reversion to Judaism with ordinary heresy was first expressly stated in Clement IV's bull *Turbato corde*" (*The Jews of Medieval Germany* (Chicago, 1949), p. 164 n. 101). Though it was not "expressly" stated by Clement, the bull certainly had equal implications for relapsi, since they were already Christians by baptism. Even in the decretal cited above, relapsi are not named as such, but are called "Christians who return to the Jewish rite."

Specific mention of relapsed Jewish converts in the bull was first made, not by Nicholas IV, but by Gregory X in his recension of March 1, 1274 (Potthast, *Regesta*, no. 20798).

55. The basic position had already been established by Gregory the Great. Opposition to forced baptism was expressed also in the *Constitutio pro Judaeis* first issued by Calixtus II and renewed by almost every subsequent pope in the Middle Ages. See Salo W. Baron, *A Social and Religious History of the Jews* (2nd rev. ed.; New York, 1957) IV, pp. 7 f., 235 f.

56. Potthast no. 1479; Solomon Grayzel, *The Church and the Jews in the Thirteenth Century* (Philadelphia, 1933), no. 12 p. 100 ff. The bull was incorporated into the Decretals of Gregory IX (*Decret. Greg IX* Lib. III, tit. XLII, cap. iii).

57. "Verum id est Religioni Christiane contrarium ut semper invitus et penitus contradicens ad recipiendam et servandam Christianitatem aliquis compellatur.

Propter quod inter invitum et invitum, coactum et coactum, alii non absurde distinguunt, quod is qui terroribus atque suppliciis violenter attrahitur, et ne detrimentum incurrat, Baptismi suscipit sacramentum, talis (sicut et is qui ficte ad Baptismum accedit) characterem suscipit Chrisianitatis impressum, et ipse tanquam conditionaliter volens, licet absolute non velit, cogendus est ad observantiam Fidei Christiane . . ." (ibid.).

58. Similarly on May 7, 1277, Nicholas III responded in the bull *Sicut nobis significare* that certain Jews, converted out of fear of death during a persecution in the county of La Marche, must be punished by the inquisitors for relapse into Judaism (*Fonds Doat*, XXXVII, fol. 191 ff.). Cf. Grayzel, *Confession*, p. 92 n. 11.

Nicholas specifically based his judgment on the fact that the baptism had been "non tamen absolute seu precise coacti." That the inquisitors did not yet know what to do in such a case, and turned to the Pope for advice, indicated that up to 1277 precedent had not yet been firmly established. It was probably Nicholas's bill which fixed the papal policy on the matter, and it is from this that Boniface VIII borrowed the phrase for his decretal.

59. So, for example, Charles Schmidt, *Histoire et doctrine de la secte des Cathares ou Albigeois* (Paris, 1849), II, p. 13; Saige, *Languedoc*, p. 19 n. 3; M. Guedemann, *Ha-Torah ve-ha-hayyim bi-yeme ha-benayim* (Warsaw, 1896–9), Pt. I, pp. 179–182; Newman, *Jewish Influence*, pp. 131–302. See especially, Gershom Scholem, *Reshit ha-kabbalah* (Jerusalem-Tel Aviv, 1948), pp. 86–91, and more recently his *Ursprung und Anfänge der Kabbala* (Studia Judaica III; Berlin, 1962).

60. Scholem, *Ursprung*, pp. 206–9, reviews anew the suggestions on the relations between the nascent Kabbala in Provence and the doctrines of the Cathari which he made earlier in his Hebrew work. While adding some isolated points and modifying others, he is forced to conclude that "Dies sind aber nur lose Details und betreffen nebensächliche Punkte. In der Grundauffassung konnte ja zwischen den beiden Bewegungen keine sachliche Berührung bestehen . . ." (p. 208).

61. As I have stated above, there is no suggestion in the *Practica* of a Jewish link with the Albigensian heresies. In the Interrogation Formula for Jews and relapsed Jewish converts (V:v:3) the accused is never asked if he has information concerning Christian heretics and their beliefs, although these questions were posed to Christian prisoners at every opportunity. In the Abjuration Formula for Jews (V:v:9) there is again no mention of Christian heretical opinions.

Newman has claimed also that Jewish aid to the heretics themselves was a matter of concern to the Inquisition. He speaks of "numerous references in the *Practica* of Bernard Gui calling upon Jews to inform the inquisitors if they know or have heard of any heretics" (Newman, op. cit., p. 312). The fact is that none of these passages deals with Christian heretics. In every instance the Jew is asked to inform the inquisitors about proselytes, relapsi, and their fautors.

Only in the Abjuration Formula for *relapsi* (V:v:10) is there a reference to Christian sectarians: "Et abjuro omnem credentiam et participationem et favorem et receptationem et defensionem hereticorum *cujuscumque secte dampnate. . . .*" It should be emphasized, however, that here the person is abjuring not as a Jew but as a reconciled Christian, and nevertheless the formula immediately continues: ". . . et specialiter et expresse *apostatantium a fide christianorum transeuntium aut conversorum baptizatorum redeuntium ad ritum seu ad vomitum judaysmi. . . .*"

An analysis of the thirteenth- and fourteenth-century papal bulls, conciliar canons, royal decrees, etc. would yield the same conclusions. Many and various charges are hurled against the Jews. Nowhere are they accused of influencing or aiding the heretics. The Church seems to have understood the gulf which separated them. In 1205, when the heretic movements were still at the height of their influence, Innocent III made this significant contrast in a letter to the heretics of Viterbo: "The Jews at least believe in only One God, the author of all things visible and invisible, but most of you believe that the earth and material nature are the works of Satan . . ." (A. Luchaire, *Rome et l'Italie* (Paris 1905), pp. 93–4, cited by Grayzel, *Church and the Jews*, p. 25 n. 19).

62. The Inquisitors of Toulouse regularly spoke of themselves as inquisitors *in regno Francie*, sometimes adding *Tholose residens*. See Vidal, *Bullaire*, p. vii.

All inquisitors were directly responsible to the Pope. In theory it was he who commissioned them, even though the actual function of choosing the inquisitors had been delegated since Gregory IX to the provincials of the Dominican and Franciscan orders. See Tanon, *Tribunaux*, pp. 184–7.

63. ". . . Guillelmo Altissiodorensi ordinis fratrum praedicatorum praesentium exhibitori domini Papae inquisitori haereticorum *ac perfidorum Judeorum* in regno Francie . . ." (Lea, *Inquisition*, II, p. 575). Ten years earlier Bertrand de la Roche is described as inquisitor in Provence "against heretics and wicked Christians who embrace Judaism" (ibid., p. 63).

64. See the bull *Anxia nimis* in Vidal, *Bullaire*, no. 229 p. 342.

65. The Interrogation has been translated by Newman, *Jewish Influence*, p. 383 f.

66. A formula of interrogation, similar in almost all respects to the one given by Bernard Gui and clearly related to it, is found among documents from the archives of the Inquisition in Carcassonne (*Doat*, XXXVII, fol. 262r–263v; *Hist. gén. de Languedoc*, VIII, col. 988). It appears also in a collection of miscellaneous materials of the Inquisition in a Vatican manuscript (MS. lat. 3978; see Dondaine, *Manuel*, p. 149), and in a manuscript of the Bibliothèque Mazarine (MS. 2015; see

Mollat's remarks in Gui, *Manuel*, p. 10 f. n. 1; cf. A. Molinier, *Catalogue des manuscrits de la Bibliothèque Mazarine* (Paris, 1886), II, pp. 323–5). In his edition of the *Practica*, Mollat italicizes all the words in the Interrogation which are identical with the text in the Mazarine MS.

The formula does not bear a date in any of the three MSS. Both C. Molinier (*Rapport*, p. 184) and Mollat (loc. cit.) date the compilation in the Mazarine MS in the thirteenth century.

However, we do not have to rely on this alone. A comparison of the Interrogation in the *Practica* with that contained in *Doat* XXXVII reveals several differences which, I believe, point to an earlier date for the latter text:

(a) One would expect the later redaction to be the more systematic. Comparing the two recensions, we do indeed find one such feature. While all the questions in the *Practica* are consistently phrased in the third person, the first six questions in *Doat* XXXVII are addressed directly to the second person. One observes also that at times a single question in the *Practica* is really a synthesis of two or more scattered questions in *Doat*.

(b) In the evolution of inquisitorial collections and manuals there is a marked tendency at each stage to amplify the older materials which are incorporated. (See Dondaine, op. cit., p. 95). It is to be observed that the *Practica* contains one question ("Quis induxit eum ut redirit ad judaysmum") which is missing entirely in *Doat*. The other questions are the same in both, though sometimes listed in a different order. But, significantly, the phrasing of each individual question is often more ample and precise in Bernard Gui's version. For example:

DOAT XXXVII	PRACTICA
Si es Judaeus vel Christianus?	Item, utrum ipse sit Judeus vel christianus baptizatus.
Quot annis fuit in christianismo. Si fuit confessus vel communicatus.	Item, quot annis fuit aut stetit in christianissimo et in fide baptismi et si tunc fuit aliquando confessus peccata sua sacramen, taliter alicui sacerdoti et si communicavit sicut faciunt alii christiani.
Si scit aliquem Christianum judaizantem et ubi.	Item, si scit aliquem christianum judayzantem vel judayzantum vel aliquem baptizatum apostatam seu rejudayzatum et ubi.
Si ad hoc induxit aliquem christianum.	Item si ipse induxit aliquem christianum ad judayzandum vel aliquem conversum ad rejudayzandum.

(c) Not only the mere fact that questions in the *Practica* are more elaborate, but the very nature of some of the elaborations is important. From the examples above, one can easily discern a major difference. While the Interrogation in *Doat* is content to employ the term *christianus* to cover both the proselyte and the relapsed convert, the corresponding questions in the *Practica* are careful to add distinguishing phrases such as *christianus baptizatus*, or *baptizatum apostatam* or *conversum*. The same care is employed in the *Practica* to distinguish between "Judaizing" and "rejudaizing." All this parallels the terminological development in the papal bulls themselves. In the bull *Turbato corde* as issued first by Clement IV in 1267, mention was made only of "Christians who pass over to Judaism." Only in latter recensions was a clause added on relapsed converts. See supra, note 55.

67. On inquisitorial interrogation in general, see Tanon, *Tribunaux*, pp. 347–358.

68. The reliability of a Jew's oath was under attack in two of the thirty-five articles prepared against the Talmud in Paris in 1240: Article 12—"Et quicumque iuramento aliquot vult non teneri, in anni principio protestetur quod vota et iuramenta eius non valeant que faciet illo anno." Article 14—"Tres quoque Iudei, quicunque sint, possunt absolvere quencunque ab omni iuramento." See *REJ*, II (1881), pp. 267–9.

69. That a comprehensive study of the oath *more judaico* is still a desideratum has been expressed repeatedly by scholars. For the available literature, see Salo W. Baron, *The Jewish Community* (Philadelphia, 1942), II, p. 181 f.; cf. Guido Kisch, "Studien zur Geschichte des Judeneides im Mittelalter," *HUCA*, XIV (1939), pp. 431–456. I know of no study of the Jewish oath in France.

70. ". . . accepto prius ab eo corporali iuramento super legem Moisi de veritate mere et plene dicenda, tam de se ut principalis, quam de aliis ut testis" (*Confessio Baruc*, p. 154).

71. Some indication of the form of the oath before a tribunal of the Inquisition may be inferred from the beginning of an oath preserved in a manuscript compilation of inquisitorial material (Trinity College, Dublin, MS. 268): "Iudee tu iurabis per Patrem omnipotentem Adonay. Et ipse respondit debite 'iuro.' Item iurabis per Patrem omnipotentum qui dixit *ego sum ille qui sum*. Et ipse respondit 'iuro.' Item iurabis per Deum qui se manifestante Moyesi in visione . . . etc." (Cited by M. Esposito, "Sur quelques écrits concernant les hérésies et les hérétiques au XIIe et XIIIe siècles," *Revue d'histoire ecclésiastique*, XXXVI (1940), p. 153.) The same formula is found in Vatican MS. lat. 3978. See Dondaine, *Manuel*, p. 148 f.

72. These are essentially the terms of Baruch's abjuration. See *Confessio Baruc*, p. 173: "Propter que, sponte abiuravit perfidiam iudaicam et supersitionem ac

cerimonias Legis iudaice et omnem aliam heresim. Juravit etiam (quod) omnes illos qui baptismum receperunt et postmodum reversi ad iudaismum, hereticos, eorum credentes, fautores, receptores, nuncios, ac amicos eorum, ac pro heresi fugitivos, per se et per alios, persequetur et investigabit, capiet, revelabit et ad dictum dominum episcopum, vel ad inquisitores heretice pravitatis, adducet, seu adduci et reddi secundum posse suum, per se et per alium procurabit. Juravit etiam insuper, stare et parere mandatis Ecclesie et dicti domini episcopi, seu eius successorum et omnem penitentiam, penam, satisfactionem, aut honus, quas et quod ipse dominus episcopus, seu eius successor, eidem Johanni, in persona propria vel in aliena, in bonis ipsius, duxerit iniungendam, vel imponendam, faciet et complebit." (Cf. the short form of abjuration in *Practica* V:vii:4).

73. Notandum autem quod in abjuratione alicujus specialis secte et heresis quedam specialia convenit exprimere sub vocabulis seu nominibus convenientibus et propriis in modo loquendi" (ibid.).

74. The phrase "de bonorum virorum consilio" refers to a jury, on which see C. Douais, "La formule 'communicatio bonorum virorum consilio' des sentences inquisitorales," *Le moyen âge* (1898), pp. 157–192, 286–311.

75. There was at first considerable discussion as to whether inquisitors, recruited from the Mendicant Orders, might impose monetary fines. In 1244 the Council of Narbonne had ordered inquisitors to refrain from doing so. In 1251 Innocent IV prohibited them entirely from levying fines if any other form of penance could be employed. (See Lea, *Inquisition*, I, p. 472 f.) Eventually, however, the inquisitors won the right to impose pecuniary penances at their discretion, on the theory that the money would be used for pious purposes, which included the expenses of the Inquisiton.

76. On the events in Montpellier see Graetz, *Geschichte*, VII, pp. 34 ff., 53; Joseph Sarachek, *Faith and Reason: the Conflict over the Rationalism of Maimonides* (Williamsport, 1935), pp. 73–88. Serious reservations on the reliability of the reports that the anti-Maimunists had the "Guide" burned were expressed by Baer, *Sefarad ha-noṣrit*, I, pp. 76 f., 318 f.

77. On the "Disputation of Paris" and the burning of the Talmud see Graetz, op. cit., VII, p. 94 ff., and Note 5 (p. 405 ff.); Grayzel, *Church and the Jews*, pp. 29–33, 240 f. (bull of Gregory IX, June 9, 1239), 274 ff. (bull of Innocent IV, Aug. 12, 1247), and Appendix A, p. 339 f. (on Nicholas Donin). For the charges brought against the Talmud see A. Kisch, "Die Anklageartikel gegen den Talmud und ihre Verteidigung durch R. Yechiel b. Joseph vor Ludwig dem Heiligen in Paris," in *Monatsschrift für Geschichte und Wissenschaft des Judentums*, XXIII (1874), and especially Isidore Loeb, "La controverse de 1240 sur le Talmud" *REJ*, I (1880), pp. 247–261, II (1881), pp. 248–270, III (1881), pp. 39–57.

That the disputation of 1240 was in reality a regular inquisition of the Talmud for heresy, in which R. Jehiel of Paris was called as a witness according to the rules of inquisitorial procedure, was shown by Y. Baer in his Hebrew article "Toward a (Critical) Examination of the Disputations of R. Jehiel of Paris and R. Moses b. Nahman," *Tarbiz*, II (1930–31), p. 172 ff.

78. Such forms were probably created during the confiscations of the Talmud at the behest of Gregory IX in 1239 and Innocent IV in 1247, and certainly in the subsequent period.

Five forms relating to the condemnation of Jewish books were listed by Ulysse Robert in his "Catalogue d'actes relatifs au Juifs pendant le moyen âge," *REJ*, III (1881), p. 214 nos. 26–30. The source given is *Doat* XXIX, and they are all dated by Robert ca. 1250. The full texts of four of these forms were printed by Grayzel from the Doat Collection (*Church and the Jews*, Appendix B pp. 341–3).

Apparently neither Robert nor Grayzel took note of the fact that vol. XXIX of *Doat* is not merely a collection of documents, but rather (together with vol. XXX) a copy of the *Practica* of Bernard Gui from the archives of the Inquisition at Carcassonne. The forms on Jewish books correspond as follows:

Practica	Doat XXIX	Robert	Grayzel
II:48	fol. 100 f.	no. 26	no. 2
II:49	fol. 102	. . . . . .	. . . . . .
II:50	fol. 103	. . . . . .	no. 4
II:51	fol. 105	no. 27	no. 1
II:52	fol. 106	no. 28	no. 3
II:53	fol. 107	no. 29	. . . . .
III:47	fol. 287	no. 30	. . . . .

(The attribution by Grayzel of no. 1 to *Doat* vol. 20 appears to be a misprint. His citation in no. 4 of Robert no. 30 is erroneous.)

Unlike the Toulousan manuscript of the *Practica* which Douais edited, the forms in *Doat* XXIX do not carry the name of Bernard Gui, or the date 1310. The question remains as to whether they were really drawn up in the thirteenth century. I do not know on what basis Robert assigned the date ca. 1250. Grayzel accepts it for all but one document (no. 2 = Robert no. 26), which he dates in 1275, apparently because mention is made of King Philip, and he assumes the reference is to Philip III. However, I believe the forms in *Doat* XXIX cited by Robert and Grayzel really originated in 1310, as they appear in the Douais edition, and not in 1250 or even 1275. The tenor of the documents suits the period after the expulsion of 1306. In none of the seven documents are the authorities called upon to search Jewish homes or synagogues. Two of the forms are addressed to the "superintendenti negocio Judeorum." Though no name is given in *Doat*, the office of "supervisor" was created in 1307 when Jean de Crépy was sent to Toulouse and Rodez to oversee the liquidation of confiscated Jewish property. (For the commission see Saige, *Languedoc*, p. 256). Finally, though other details are not given, Robert nos. 27, 28, and 29 all mention Agen. It would be too great a coincidence, if Bernard Gui some sixty years after the forms were allegedly created, had directed his attention to precisely the same place.

In sum, though thirteenth-century forms undoubtedly existed, they have not come down to us directly. The forms in *Doat* XXIX are simply copied from the *Practica*.

79. In 1255 a ban of the Talmud was adopted by the Council of Beziers at Louis' behest (Grayzel, *Church and the Jews*, p. 337 no. XLII). Again, in 1269 he ordered Jews to present their books for examination to the apostate Pablo Christiani (Robert, *Catalogue*, no. 40). Philip III proscribed the Talmud and other books in 1283 and ordered them handed over to the inquisitors (Saige, *Languedoc*, p. 213). Philip IV did the same in 1299 (ibid., p. 236).

80. "Item, in quodam libro cujus actor vocatur Salomon, qui intitulatur apud eos *Glosa super textum Legis*, quem librum omnes Judei maxime tenent et credunt et intendunt dictis ejus, continentur verba et sententie et opiniones false et erronee et abusive Talmuti dampnati in pluribus locis illius libri. Et illas glosas Judei tenent et habent et docent, cum tamen sint dampnate pariter cum Talmuto et sunt expresse contra Christum quem dicunt nullo modo fuisse nec Messiam promissum in Lege . . ." (Gui, *Manuel*, p. 18).

81. Rashi's commentaries figured often in the investigation of the Talmud in 1240. In the Latin manuscript of the *Extractiones de Talmud*, composed shortly after it was burned in Paris, there is a section entitled "De glosis Salomonis Trecensis." See Loeb, *REJ*, I (1880), p. 260. On anti-Christian elements in Rashi see Judah Rosenthal, "Anti-Christian Polemic in Rashi on the Bible," in *Rashi, His Teachings and Personality*, ed. S. Federbush (New York, 1958), Hebrew Section, pp. 45–54.

82. "Item, in quodam libro quem Judei vocant *Glosas Moysi de Egypto* et actor illius libri intitulavit *Declarationem et reformationem legis*, continentur abusiones et falsitates Thalmuti; item, plures errores et blasfemie contra fidem Christi et specialiter quod omnes illi qui tenent viam et fidem Christi vocant et dicunt hereticos, quod est dictum in hebreo 'minim.' Item, Christum Jhesum liber ille dicit errasse et contra Deum fecisse et contra Legem et quod plus erravit Jhesus quam Machometus et quod ipse Jhesus posuit majorem partem mundi in errore colendi alium Deum, qui non est unus Deus, et destruendi legem quam Deus dedit . . ." (Gui, loc. cit.).

83. The statement that Jesus caused most of the world to believe in a non-monotheistic God was made by Maimonides in *Mishne Torah*, Hilkhot Melakhim XII, but was later censored. See the remarks of Abraham S. Halkin in his editions of *Maimonides' Epistle to Yemen*, Hebrew introduction p. xiv n. 92. For Maimonides' views on Christianity cf. Baron, *Social and Religious History*, V, pp. 118 f., 365.

84. "Item, in alio libro quem Judei vocant *Glosa David hyspani*, qui glosavit psalterium, multa continentur contra Christum et christianos et tenentes fidem Christi" (Gui, loc. cit.). The polemical remarks in Kimḥi's commentary on the Psalms were expunged from most printed editions. They can be found in those parts which have been critically edited from manuscripts. See e.g. Jacob Bosniak's edition of *The Commentary of David Kimhi on the Fifth Book of the Psalms* (New York, 1954), passim.

85. E.g. in the form for pronouncing sentence on the Talmud (III:47) we read: ". . . de mandato Regis . . . fecerunt omnes et singulos libros diligenter inspici et examinari per fideles viros ac fidei zelatores peritosque in linga ebrayca et expertos . . ." (Gui, *Practica*, p. 170 f.).

86. On Dominican interest in Hebraic studies see C. Douais, *Essai sur l'organisation des études dans l'ordre des Frères Prêcheurs au treizième et au quatorzième siècle* (Paris-Toulouse, 1884), pp. 135–140. Cf. B. Altaner, "Die fremdsprachliche Ausbildung der Dominikanermissionäre des 13. und 14. Jahrhunderts," *Zeitschrift für Missionswissenschaft*, XXIII (1933); Peter Browe, *Die Judenmission im Mittelalter und die Päpste* (Rome 1942), p. 271 ff.

Significantly, R. Jehiel of Paris stated in 1240 that many clerics had learned Hebrew from Jews. See *Vikuaḥ R. Yeḥiel mi-Paris* (Thorn, 1873), p. 10.

87. Clement. Lib. V, tit. I, cap. 1 (*Corpus Iuris Canonici*, ed. Friedberg, II, c. 1179). Cf. B. Altaner, "Raymundus Lullus und der Sprachenkanon des Konzils von Vienne," *Historiches Jahrbuch*, LII (1933).

88. On the efficacy of the canon on languages, see B. Altaner, "Die Durchführung des Vienner Konzilsbeschlusses über die Errichtung von Lehrstuhlen für orientalische Sprachen," *Zeitschrift für Kirchengeschichte*, LII (1933).

89. On Raymund Martini see André Berthier, "Un maître orientaliste du XIIIe siècle: Raymond Martin," *Archivum Fratrum Praedicatorum*, VI (1936).

While considering the reliability of Jewish information contained in Christian sources, we might well reflect on the case of the *Pugio Fidei* itself. The authenticity of Martini's quotations from rabbinic literature, long impugned by scholars, was vindicated by the eminent Talmudist, Saul Lieberman. Professor Lieberman demonstrated that, although the *Pugio Fidei* is a polemic, Martini's rabbinic quotations contain authentic passages and variant readings of great value. See his "Raymund Martini and his alleged forgeries," *Historica Judaica*, V (1943), pp. 87–102.

90. Browe, *Judenmission*, p. 274.

91. The question of anti-Christian references in Jewish prayers has never been examined systematically. Some material may be found in S. Seeligmann's brief "Anti Christelijke Gebeden," *De Vrydagavond* (1924), p. 195 f.; Peter Browe, "Die religiöse Duldung der Juden im Mittelalter," *Archiv für Katholisches Kirchenrecht*, CXVIII (1938), pp. 36–41. (For the accusations by the Church Fathers, see ibid., p. 37.)

92. The bull *Dampnabili perfidia Judaeorum*, in Ripoll, *Bullar. Ord FF. Praed.*, I, p. 487 f.

93. *Registres d'Honorius IV*, ed. M. Prou (Paris, 1888), no. 809.

94. ברוך אתה ה׳ אלהנו מלך העולם שלא עשני גוי. *Mahzor Vitry*, ed. S. Hurwitz (Berlin, 1893), p. 57, has שלא עשני נכרי. On the benediction in general see Ismar Elbogen, *Der Jüdische Gottesdienst in seiner geschichtlichen Entwicklung* (Leipzig, 1913), p. 90.

95. On the *birkat ha-minim* see Elbogen, op. cit., pp. 39 ff., 51, 519.

96. "Item, in oratione quam faciunt ter in die sunt multe maledictiones et imprecationes contra christianos et contra romanam fidem quam vocant pravum regnum et dampnatum. Et orant quod Deus destruat ipsum et omnes christianos, quamvis non ponant in expresse vocabulum christianorum, set per omnia vocabula dant intelligere et sic intellegunt et intendunt, videlicet per hoc vocabulum *minim* quod sonat hereticos" (Gui, *Manuel*, p. 16).

97. Article 30 reads: "In singulis diebus ter in oracione quam digniorem asserunt ministris ecclesie, regibus et aliis omnibus, ipsis Iudeis inimicantibus, maledicunt." The commentary goes on to describe the Eighteen Benedictions, their importance and manner of recitation, and then gives this tranlation of the *birkat ha-minim*: "Conversis non sit spes et omnes mynym (infideles) in hora (repente) disperdantur, et omnes inimici gentis tue Israel discindantur, et regnum nequicie eradices et confringas et conteras et declines omnes innimicos nostros velociter in diebus nostris; benedictus tu Deus, frangens inimicos et declinans impios" (Loeb, "La controverse de 1240," *REJ*, III (1881), p. 51f.)

98. For example, in several old mss. and in the Maḥzor of Salonika the text reads: ולמשומדים אל תהי תקוה וכל המינים כרגע יאבדו, וכל אויבי עמך מהרה יכרתו, ומלכות זדון מהרה תעקר ותשבר ותמגר ותכניע כל אויבנו במהרה בימינו, ברוך אתה ה׳ שובר אויבים ומכניע זדים. See S. Baer, *Abodat Yisrael*, p. 93n.

In a text of the Amida found in the Cairo Geniza, and perhaps preserving an old Palestinian reading, we find Christians explicitly mentioned with heretics: למשומדים אל תהי תקוה ומלכות זדון מהרה תעקר בימינו והנצרים והמינים כרגע יאבדו ימחו מספר החיים ועם צדיקים אל יכתבו, ברוך אתה ה׳ מכניע זדים. See Solomon Schechter, "Genizah Specimens," *JQR* (O.S.), X (1897–8), p. 657.

It is also interesting that in medieval Germany some Jews whose sons had converted to Christianity were apparently reluctant to recite the *birkat ha-minim*: וכן מי שבניו משומדים, וכי לא יתפלל ברכת המינים? *Sefer Hasidim*, ed. J. Wistinetzky (Berlin, 1891), no. 1506, p. 363.

99. It should be noted also that in a decree of September 3, 1380, King Juan I of Castile expressly outlawed the use of the prayer: "Primera mente por quanto nos fizieron entender que los judíos en sus libros e en otras escripturas de su talamud les mandan que digan de cada día *la oración de los erejes* que se dize en pie, en que mal dizen a los christianos e a los clérigos e a los finados, mandamos e defendemos firme mente que ninguno dellos non las diga de aquí adelante, nin las tenga escriptas en sus libros nin en otros libros algunos. e los que las tienen escriptas que las tiren e chancellen de los dichos libros, en manera que se non puedan leer . . ." Fritz (Yitzhak) Baer, *Die Juden im Christlichen Spanien*. Erster Teil: Urkunden und Regesten. Vol. II, Kastilien/Inquisitionsakten (Berlin, 1936), no. 227, p. 221.

The censorship called for in this decree had begun even earlier, and was, perhaps, self-imposed. It appears, moreover, that in 1336 Alfonso XI of Castile had already decreed against the *birkat ha-minim*. This seems to be the prayer to which the king alludes in an edict issued at the behest of the apostate Alfonso de Valladolid (Abner of Burgos). The King addressed himself to the Jews: "Volo vos scire, nobis fuisse relatum per magistrum Alfonsum conversum, sacristam maioris ecclesiae Valisoletane vos iti a magnis temporibus inter vos quotidie ab utroque sexu adulte aetatis oratione quadam, in qua maledictiones omnipotentis Dei Christianis ac omnibus ad fidem Christi converis imprecamini, eos censendo hereticos, etiam inimicos capitales, et quod publice Deum exoratis, ut eos destruat atque perdat . . ." Browe, *Religiöse Duldung*, p. 40 n. 2 (citing Alonso de Spina, *Fortalitium fidei*, III. 7).

100. שהם משתחוים להבל וריק ומתפללים אל אל לא יושיע. On the *Alenu* prayer see Elbogen, *Jüdische Gottesdienst*, p. 80 f.

101. להעביר גלולים מן הארץ.

102. I have been unable to find an attack against the alleged blasphemies in the *Alenu* prior to Bernard Gui. Around 1400, a convert denounced the prayer in Germany, claiming that the letters of the word "וריק" ("and emptiness") have the same numerical value as "ישו" (Jesus). The *Alenu* was defended against such attacks by Yom-Tob Lipmann-Mulhausen in his *Sefer Nisaḥon*, but to no avail (Elbogen, op. cit., p. 80).

103. "Item, in festo propitiationum in septembri, habent quamdam specialem orationem quam faciant contra omnes inimicos, quam orationem vocant 'cematha' quod est dictum anathema vel separatio vel maledictio. Et in illla oratione per circumlocutionem verborum vocant Christum spurium filium meretricis et

beatam Mariam Virginem mulierem calefactionis seu luxurie, quod nephandum est loqui et etiam cogitare; et maledicunt utrique et fidem romanam et omnes ejus participes et credentes" (Gui, *Manuel*, p. 16 f.).

104. Lévi states simply "j'ignore sur quoi se fond cette assertion" (*Les Juifs et l'Inq.*, p. 19 n. 2). Mollat (*Manuel*, II, p. 17 n. 4) made the incredible equation of the word *cematha* to the *Shema*, the confession of the Unity of God (Deut. 6:4).

105. A. H. Freimann, "Titnem le-ḥerpah" (Hebrew), *Tarbiz*, XII (1943), pp. 70–74. The text is reproduced by A. M. Habermann in his *Sefer gezerot Ashkenaz ve-Sarefat* (Jerusalem, 1946), p. 105.

106. סד' עליו ‎, לפרט תתנ"ו שנת כלו גזרת נגזרה ובימיו . . . יקר בר יצחק מר' קבל רש"י הנקרא שלמה ורבינו ‎‎מהם א' שכח ולא ולקללה לחרפה 'תתנם המתחילה בשמתא וקללה' נוכל לא צרות 'תנות (Solomon Luria, *She'elot u-teshubot* (Lublin, 1574), no. 29). Habermann rejects Rashi's authorship of the poem. Baron, *Soc. and Rel. Hist.*, VII, p. 179 attributes it to one of Rashi's disciples, but admits the possibility that Rashi himself may have written it (ibid., p. 303 n. 59).

107. Nathan b. Judah, *Sefer mahkim* (Cracow, 1909), p. 42.

108. Leopold Zunz, *Die Ritus des Synagogalen Gottesdienstes* (Berlin, 1859), p. 10.

109. The word "krubot" (=Heb. *Krobot*) was used here as a general designation for the prayer book. On the contents of this section of the manuscript of the *Extractiones*, see Loeb, *REJ*, II (1881), pp. 249–251.

110. Loeb (ibid.) describes it as "un passage où sont énumérés les méfaits religieux des goyim et dont chaque phrase commence par le mot *goyim*. Ce passage, qui paraît être composé de deux morceaux différents, est imprimé dans Eisenmenger. . . ." In excerpting the sections of the Hebrew original, I have followed Eisenmenger's text.

111. I give the opening verses:

הגוים אפס ותהו נגדך חשובים

בחוניך ברורים ועמם לא נחשבים

הגוים געולים מעשה תעתוע והבלים

דבקיך בדולים מסוגדי לעץ בולים

הגוים הכין פסל מבקשים חרשים

ותיקיך בהשכם והערב ייחדך פורשים. . .

Johann Andrea Eisenmenger, *Entdecktes Judenthum* (Königsberg, 1711), I, p. 134. Cf. Israel Davidson, *Osar ha-shirah ve-ha-piyyut* (Thesaurus of Medieval Hebrew Poetry), (New York, 1929), III, p. 124 no. 179.

112. Beginning:

הגוים אימים זמזומים קדר ואדומים

בלעם קלעם גמומים דמומים

הגוים גומר ומגוג אשכנז ותורגמים

דכאם הכאם זעומים מוחרמים

הגוים הגרים קטורים לוד וארמים

הוכחם שכחם מתחת שמים

הגוים זרח נחת מזים ושמים

הרסמם כרסמם שיתם שוממים. . .

(Entdecktes Judenthum, II, p. 142. Davidson, no. 178.)

113. The first part was eliminated from printed prayer books because of the censor, though it was customary to write or print them on detached pages and insert them separately. The second is found in its entirety in the Maḥzor printed in Prague in 1522 and 1533 and in the Cracow edition of 1585. See Davidson's remarks, loc. cit.

114. The Hebrew reads:

הגוים מכנים קדושתך לעול הזימה

נשואיך משקצים יחוס אשת הזימה.

(Entdecktes Judenthum, I, p. 135.)

115. On the status of the apostate Jew in the Middle Ages I follow closely the analysis of Jacob Katz in his Hebrew monograph: "Even Though he has Sinned he Remains a Jew," *Tarbiz*, XXVII (1958), pp. 203–217. See also his *Exclusiveness and Tolerance: Jewish-Gentile Relations in Medieval and Modern Times* (Oxford, 1961; reprint, New York, 1962), Ch. VI.

116. E.g. TB *Sanhedrin* 27b, *Aboda Zara* 26b, *Hullin* 5a.

117. TB *Yebamot* 47b, *Bekhorot* 30b.

118. This was also the official view in Gaonic times. The apostate had to receive stripes for his transgressions (as would any Jew), but ritual immersion was not required: כך ראינו שמלקות ודאי צריך שעבר על כמה עבירות עשה ולא תעשה וכריתות ומיתות בית דין. טבילה לא צריך דלאו גר הוא דצריך טבילה. . . B. M. Lewin, *Oṣar ha-geonim* (Jerusalem, 1936), VII, p. 112.

119. The original statement occurs in the Talmud. It was not offered as a juridical principle, but simply as a homiletic elaboration on the biblical story of Achan. Thus: "*Israel hath sinned* (Josh. 7:11). Rabbi Abba bar Zabda declared: Even though (they have) sinned, (they remain) Israel" (*Sanhedrin*, 44a). In this context the term "Israel" refers to the entire people.

Rashi used the statement as a definition of legal status in three concrete cases concerning the individual apostate and in a fourth instance it is implied. Thus: (a) The betrothal of a convert is binding (*Teshubot Rashi*, ed. I. Elfenbein (New York, 1943) no. 171). (b) A Jewess must obtain ḥaliṣah from a levir who has been converted (ibid., no. 173). (c) Interest may not be taken on loans to an apostate (ibid., no. 175). (d) An apostate's Jewish relatives may inherit his property, and he may inherit theirs (ibid., no. 174).

120. The view that the apostate is in fact lost to Judaism, especially if baptized voluntarily, is reflected in various ways in medieval Jewish sources. For example, in Germany and elsewhere it was the custom for the family of an apostate not to mourn his death. (See *Sefer Ḥasidim* no. 192). The names of apostates were distorted to give them, by a play on words, a derogatory meaning. (Ibid., no. 193.)

121. "Postmodum vero reversus est ad judaysmum, fuitque rejudaysatus secundum modum et ritum rejudaysacionis a Judeis in talibus fieri consuetum apud Ylerdam abraso capite et abscissis capitibus unguium manuum et pedum usque ad sanguinem, et facta inmersione capitis in aqua currenti . . ." (*Lib. Sent. Inq. Thol.*, p. 230).

122. "Dixit tamen, quod baptizati, qui ad iudaismum revertuntur, sic revertuntur, iuxta doctrinam Calmutz (*sic*) quod secantur eis ungues manuum et pedum et raduntur pueri (*sic*) capitis et deinde totum corpus abluitur in aqua currenti, sicut secundum Legem purificabatur mulier alienigena, quando debebat duci a iudeo in uxorem; quia ipsi reputant quod baptismus polluit illos qui recipiunt ipsum" (*Confessio Baruc*, p. 156).

Grayzel (*Confession*, p. 101) states correctly: "If Baruc possessed any learning he would not have ascribed it to the Talmud even while admitting the existence of the ritual. The chances are, however, that the Talmud was brought into the discussions by Baruc's examiners . . . and that the word Talmud was entered into the record by the scribe."

123. Grayzel (ibid., p. 106) translates *mulier alienigena* as "a woman convert," and so misses the association, which is to the law in Deut. 21:10 ff.: "When thou goest forth to battle against thine enemies, and the Lord thy God delivereth them into thy hands and thou carriest them away captive, and seest among the captives a woman of goodly form, and thou hast a desire unto her, and wouldest take her to thee to wife; then thou shalt bring her home to thy house; and she shall shave her head, and pare her nails; and she shall put the raiment of her captivity from off her, and shall remain in thy house, and bewail her father and mother a full month; and after that thou mayest go in unto her, and be her husband, and she shall be thy wife."

124. "Interrogatus si in Appamiis vel alibi fuit reiudaizatus iuxta formam et modum reiudaizationis supradictum; respondit quod non, quia secundum doctri-

nam Colnut (*sic*) [si] aliquis perfecte est baptizatus et voluntarie et vult ad iudaismum reverti, quia reputant eum pollutum, fiunt illam eius reiudaizationem que
supradicta fuit; sed quando non est perfecte baptizatus, vel coactus est ad sus-
cipiendum baptismum, non reiudaizatur modo supradicto, quia credunt quod
talis baptismus nichil sit" (*Confessio, Baruc*, p. 162 f.).

125. ". . . Exposuit Excellencie nostre religiosus vir frater Bartholomeus de
Aquila ordinis fratrum Praedicatorum jnquisitor heretice pravitatis in Regno Sici-
lie per Sedem Apostolicam constitutus quod cum pridem per legitimos testes
sibi plene conscientie quod si sinacoga maiorj Judeorum de Salerno scientibus
et consencientibus Judeis Judayce salernitane ad quos predicta sinacoga specte-
bat plures hereticj apostate a fide Christi receptatj faciant in ea et quidem Christianus nomine Moyses fuerat circonsisus ibidem et quidam alij Judeorum heresim profexi et in puteo vel fonte ipsius sinacoge quidam nomine Azarias a fide
Christi potestate in iniuriam baptismatis per Judeos Judaice predicte fuerat ablu-
tus" (G. M. Monti, "Da Carlo I a Roberto di Angiò," *Archivio storico per le province
Napolitane*, LIX (1934), p. 175).

Joshua Starr (*Speculum*, XXI, p. 207) interprets the circumcision of Moses to
mean a "symbolic" circumcision of a relapsed Jewish convert. If this is so, then we
have here an additional and bizarre rejudaizing custom, unattested elsewhere. I
am inclined to think, however, that the person in question was actually a proselyte, and that the circumcision was real.

126. Nicholas Eymeric, *Directorium Inquisitorum* (Venice, 1607), Pt. II, quaest.
xliv, p. 349.

127. For the events see Baer, *Sefarad ha-noṣrit*, II, pp. 481 f., 534 ff. Extensive
extracts from the record of the trial are published in his *Juden im Christlichen
Spanien*, vol. II, no. 410, pp. 484–509.

128. Baer, *Christlichen Spanien*, II, p. 493.

129. Ibid., p. 499 f.: ". . . e mas tiene en su ley y mandiamento el dicho judío que
apres de haver los induzidos y tornados garines, que quiere dezir de christianos
judíos, los deven desbabtizar e banyar los con agua corriente y raer les la crisma
y cortar las hunyas y quitar les todas aquellas cosas que tienen de ley christiana."

130. Ibid., p. 502: "Así que se sigue de necessario que quando nuestros drechos
faulan de fazer guerin, non significan mas a que las tales personas sean primera
mente christianos o moros o gentiles o de otros linages, mas dizen. qual quiere
que se convierte como se a de regir para entrar en la ley de los judíos, y aquella ley
que dan es egual a todos, y non se fallara otra cosa en ninguna manera, donde se
sigue de necesidat que el banyar {e?} nínguna de las otras cosas que se premiten
en tal casso non son fechas por desbatiar nin tirar crisma, pues aquello mismo se
faze a los que non an recebido baptismo ni crisma. . . ."

131. "Ya puede ser lo fallo aquel doctor en alguna parte thomado de aquel acto que mandava fazer la ley en la muxer fermosa en el tienpo de la guerra, que dixo traher la a su casa y esquile se la cabeça e faga las unyas . . ." (ibid., p. 503).

We have seen (supra note 122) that the same law was mentioned by Baruch in his trial. It is possible that Baruch also intended to use it as part of his defense, to prove that such rites are not intended to "dechristianize," and that the notary garbled his testimony. Yet my impression is that this was not the case, and that there was some connection between the law in Deut. 21 and the return of apostates in the minds of some medieval Jews. In the Talmud, Rabbi Akiba had already interpreted the words (v. 13) "and she shall bewail her father and mother" as a reference to her abandoning idolatry (Yebamot, 48a). Cf. Nahmanides' comments on these verses, accepting the view of Rabbi Akiba, and explaining that the rite is imposed because she is becoming a proselyte against her will.

132. So Baer (ibid., p. 504 n. 1): "Trotz allem scheint es einem Volksbrauch des *discristianar* bei den mittelalterlichen Juden gegeben zu haben." For another allegation of washing off the chrism, see the case of Maria Sanchez (ibid., no. 395 p. 447). The charge is repeated in the early sixteenth century in the Canary Islands. See Lucien Wolf, *Jews in the Canary Islands* (London, 1926), p. 28.

133. See, for example, Jacob b. Asher, *Tur Yoreh De'ah*, no. 267: עבד שמלו רבו וחזר לגיורו ומכרו לעכו"ם וחזר ישראל וקנאו ממנו, כיון שנימול ונטבל לשם עבדות פעם ראשונה והכניסו תחת כנפי השכינה, אע"פ שחזר, אינו חוזר לעבדותו, והרי הוא כישראל מומר שא"צ טבילה אלא מלקות.

134. Mordecai b. Hillel, *Sefer Mordecai* on *Ketubot*, Ch. 11, no. 306. The case concerns the testimony of an apostate Jew from France, about a husband who has disappeared. We are told that his testimony is unacceptable because, even though he has been ritually immersed, he has not truly repented.

Some rite of readmitting apostates may perhaps be implied even earlier, in a passage from *Sefer Ḥasidim* (no. 209): ומי שנשתמד וחזר להיות יהודי וקיבל עליו לעשות תשובה כאשר יורוהו החכמים . . . (Cf. Katz, *Exclusiveness and Tolerance*, p. 73).

135. Joseph ibn Habib (late 14th–early 15th Century), *Nimmukey Yosef* (commentary on the *Halakhot* of Isaac Alfasi), on Yebamot Ch. 4, 47b: וישראל שחטא ועשה תשובה דכ"ע שורת הדין אינו צריך טבילה אלא קבלת חברות בפני ב"ד לכתחילה, ואף על פי כן טובל הוא מדרבנן משום מעלה דומיא דטבילת עבד משוחרר שאין טבילתו אלא מדרבנן.

136. Moses Isserles (ReMA. Poland, 16th Century), gloss to *Shulḥan Arukh* Yoreh De'ah, no. 268:12: ישראל מומר שעשה תשובה אין צריך לטבול ולקבל. רק מדרבנן יש לו לטבול ולקבל עליו דברי חברות בפני ג'. Though this and the references which follow are taken from halakhists of the sixteenth and seventeenth centuries, there can be little doubt that the practices of which they speak did not originate then, but have their roots in the Middle Ages.

137. Solomon Luria (Poland, 16th Century), *Yam Shel Shlomo* on Yebamot, loc. cit.

138. Gloss to *Shulḥan Arukh* Oraḥ ḥayyim, no. 531:7: מי שהעמיר דתו וחזר בתשובה ודרכו לגלח מותר לגלח במועד.

139. Joel b. Samuel Sirkes (Poland, 1561–1640), *Bayit ḥadash* (Commentary on *'Arba Turim* of Jacob b. Asher), Yoreh De'ah, no. 267: כגון ישראל מומר שחזר ליהדות דלא בעי טבילה דאינו אלא ישראל ונלקה על חטאת . . . אבל נ"י בפרק החולץ כתב בישראל מומר שעשה תשובה דטובל הוא מדרבנן משום מעלה (ע"כ). והמרש"ל כתב והמנהג האידנא לטבול המומרים ושיגלחו את כל שערן מקודם, וכן ראיתי מורין הלכה למעשה (עכ"ל)

140. *Siftey Kohen* on ReMA, Yoreh De'ah, no. 268:2: משמע אפילו אין חציצה בשערותיו, כגון שיחוף ויסרוק היטב או יגוז מקצת שערותיו הקשורים וחוצצין, אעפ"כ יגלח כל שערותיו משום שנכנס לכלל יהדות.

141. Abraham Gombiner, *Magen Abraham* on ReMA, Oraḥ ḥayyim, no. 531:7: שהרי אין מצרפין אותו לכל דבר שבקדושה עד שיגלח.

142. *Magen David*, ad loc.: פי' במקום שנוהגין שבעלי תשובה מגלחין דע"ז דמי למת ולמצורע שטען גלוח.

Sirkes (*Bayit ḥadash* on Tur Yoreh De'ah no. 268) finds a basis for the comparison of the idolater to a corpse or a leper in Rashi's comment on Num. 8:7 (the law commanding the Levites to shave the hair from their bodies): ואפשר דנטילת שער בגר הוא ע"פ ר' משה הדרשן שהביא רש"י בר"פ בהעלותך, וכן המנהג במומרים כשחוזרים לדת ישראל. (Rashi stated: מצאתי בדברי ר"מ הדרשן לפי שנתנו כפרה על הבכורות שעבדו ע"א והיא קרויה זבחי מתים והמצורע קרוי מת הזקיקה תגלחת במצורעים.)

143. E.g. *Tur* and *Shulḥan Arukh* Yoreh De'ah, no. 268. The source is *Yebamot* 47a.

144. So Joshua Boaz b. Simon Baruch (d. 1557), *Shiltey ha-gibborim* on Alfasi, Yabamot 47a.

145. I believe we may safely disregard Bernard's statement that the nails must be cut so deep as to draw blood. Perhaps this really happened in one case, and in receiving the information the inquisitor thought it was a necessary part of the ritual. Except for the *Practica* it is mentioned only in the case of Johannes de Bretz. Eymeric merely quotes Bernard Gui's material.

146. "Item, quomodo Judei circumcident pueros christianorum aliter quam suos?" (Gui, *Manuel*, p. 12). In *Doat* XXXVII (fol. 263r) the word "pueros" does not appear.

147. "Ubi notandum est quod Judei aliter circumcidunt pueros suos et aliter christianos, sive pueros sive adultos, quia circumcidendo christianos adultos seu parvos, scindunt eis pellem desuper semiplene et non totum circulum, sicut faciunt in pueris suis judeis.

"Item, christianis, quando fiunt Judei vel Judee, tradunt unam cartam sue ju-daysationis quam debent semper portare secum, aliter Judei non biberent aut comederent cum eisdem, et debet continere nomina singulorum magistrorum qui eos debaptizaverunt" (Gui, *Manuel*, p. 12).

148. The passage occurs in an early inquisitorial manual entitled *De inquisi-tione hereticorum* of which two recensions have come down one shorter than the other. The short recension was published in E. Martène and U. Durand, *Thesaurus novus anecdotorum* (Paris, 1717), V. col. 1777–1794, and contains our passage at the end. The long recension was first published and attributed to the German Franciscan David of Augsburg (d. 1271) by Wilhelm Preger, "Der Tractat des David von Augsburg über Waldesier," *Abhandlungen der Histor. Cl. der Kgl. Bayerischen Akademie der Wissenschaften*, XIV (1879), Pt. II, pp. 183–235. This version does not contain the passage on circumcision.

Preger believed the long recension to be the older, the other being an abridge-ment made later in France. This order has been rejected by M. Esposito (*Rev. d'hist. eccl.*, XXXVI (1940), p. 160 ff.). That the shorter version is older is accepted, though on different grounds, by Dondaine, *Manuel*, pp. 180–183. Cf. also Borst, *Die Katharer*, p. 21 f.

Esposito maintains that the paragraph on special circumcision (*De circumci-sione Christianorum iudaizantium*) is part of the original text of the treatise. Don-daine (p. 133) asserts it is only a fragment appended in the manuscripts, which are generally eclectic compilations. (For the MSS see the list in Dondaine, p. 182.) In either case, the notice on circumcision would be not later than the second half of the thirteenth century.

149. Eymeric, *Directorium Inquisitorum*, Pt. II, quaest. xliv, p. 349.

150. See supra, note 145.

151. "Nota quod Judaei aliter circumcidunt pueros, et aliter christianos nostros adultos quando judaizant . . ." (Martène-Durand, op. cit., V. col. 1794).

152. See, for example, Josephus' story of the conversion of the royal house of Adiabene (*Antt.*, XX, 2.4) in which Ananias is satisfied to receive a proselyte with-out circumcision. Even Palestinian Jewry was not unanimous on the subject. The Talmud records the view of Rabbi Joshua b. Hanania (late 1st–early 2nd cent.), regarding the immersion of a proselyte as being sufficient: "If he performed the immersion but had not been circumcised, R. Joshua said he is a proper proselyte. . . . The sages, however, said, . . . he is not a proper proselyte unless he has been both circumcised and immersed" (*Yebamot* 46a).

6 : IN PRAISE OF LADINO

A review essay, published in *Conservative Judaism* 27:2 (Winter 1973), 56–66.

This essay is a review of an anthology of Ladino and Spanish-Jewish literature that was published in 1972. Its editor was the prolific scholar of Ladino literature Moshe Lazar, who taught at the Hebrew University, founded the School of Visual and Performing Arts at Tel Aviv University, and later taught at the University of Southern California. Yerushalmi was a natural choice to review the anthology. His first book about the experience of crypto-Jews in the seventeenth century, *From Spanish Court to Italian Ghetto*, had been published in 1971. Now well established at Harvard University, Yerushalmi was one of the few American scholars at the time who had both the historical expertise and the linguistic facility to assess a work of this nature.

Prior to the publication of this anthology, no accessible introduction to Ladino literature had been available to an English-speaking audience. Yerushalmi recognized that the book at hand was a pioneering project and hoped it would find a wide audience. Nonetheless, he voiced serious reservations about the book. He criticized the "gross imbalance" of Lazar's selections. Half of the book was dedicated to the unabridged reproduction of a poem and a play whose historical and literary importance did not merit, he believed, such prominence in an anthology. He lamented that there was no mention in the book of Ladino periodicals or of Judeo-Christian polemics in Ladino and that Jewish writing in Portuguese was almost entirely ignored. Furthermore, Lazar's decision to include only "secular" and not "religious" literature was flawed both because it was arbitrary and because the distinction between these two categories was so vague as to be misleading.

However, most of Yerushalmi's criticism was reserved for Lazar's historical introduction. The fact that the book was written for a popular audience, he insisted, did not excuse its inaccuracies. For example, Jews were not expelled from Portugal, as Lazar claimed, but forcibly converted en masse in 1497; the Spanish Inquisition began not in 1391, which was, however, a year in which a new wave of violent assaults against Spanish Jews broke out, but in 1478; and it was not possible, on the whole, to practice openly as a Jew in Latin America or in Antwerp, which were both within the jurisdiction of the Inquisition.

Yerushalmi's most strident critique of Lazar was aimed at his characterization of those Sephardim who migrated from the Iberian Peninsula to the Ottoman Empire as lower class and pious and those Sephardim who settled in the "Christian West" as aristocrats more fully assimilated into Gentile culture. Yerushalmi freely granted that Jewish communities in Western Europe were different from those in the Ottoman Empire. Given what Yerushalmi called the "different array of cultural baggage" of the Jews in each place, this was to be expected. But he insisted that the socioeconomic situation of the Spanish Jews was not the main determinant of their choice of home or level of piety; indeed, Yerushalmi balked at Lazar's anachronistic use of the term "Orthodox." Rather, Jews in the East and the West "all have the same traditional frame of reference." Ultimately, Yerushalmi argued, "the question of where to go was not ideological, but above all, *practical.*"

In the background of this review was a foreshadowing of themes that were developed later in Yerushalmi's scholarly writings. In this piece, he briefly compared the Jews of Inquisition-era Spain to those of Nazi Germany. He would later deepen this comparison in an article comparing early modern Spanish protoracialism and modern racial antisemitism (see chapter 9). Even more significantly, Yerushalmi began and ended this review of a book about Ladino-speaking Jews by pointing to the characteristics they shared with Yiddish-speaking Jews (of which he was one). Yerushalmi had in mind the familiar Jewish experience of exile—another of his scholarly preoccupations—in which "organic cultures" were removed from their "natural soil" to "alien environments." Indeed, as Yerushalmi's later work would demonstrate, the experience of exile continued into the modern period, during which the Jew was no longer exiled only from a physical locale but also from the very soil of Jewish memory itself.

In 1917 Franz Rosenzweig, then in the German army, spent a furlough in Üsküb, Yugoslavia, and came into contact with Sephardic Jews for the first time in his life. His report of this experience to his parents is filled with a sense of wonder and delight:

> I have also seen many Sephardim and paid a visit to the president of the community, a merchant whose manner is very dignified but even more markedly astute; his wife looks not at all Jewish, his daughters very much so. The older one, Oro (Goldschen!), went to a German school in Saloniki, the younger one, Fortuna (Glueckel!), fourteen years old, doesn't know German yet. All of them know French, but among themselves they speak Spanish, which the men write in Hebrew characters and the women in Bulgarian characters; it's rather easy to understand them if one knows Italian, probably because it is old Castilian. . . . All the names are magnificent, e.g. Isaac Calderon. . . .[1]

Attracted to these Jews so markedly remote from those he had known, not entirely uncritical of their way of life, Rosenzweig was yet sensitive enough to pierce the veil of the exotic and to meet them, not in anthropological condescension, but with a direct bond of Jewish empathy. He writes: "Whoever says that the Sephardim are of a different race is a liar. But their destiny has been different." In a sense this experience was an anticipation of his even more decisive discovery of the Hasidic Jews of Warsaw a year later. In both he felt something he had never known in Germany, a Jewishness which was part of a pervasive folk-culture, lived naturally and without self consciousness. It is especially interesting to hear him speak of the Sephardic and Hasidic children in almost parallel terms.

Alas, as some current tensions in Israel can demonstrate, sudden encounters between the various Jewish tribes are not always so happy and productive. I can still remember how, in my youth, our entire family, certified East European Ashkenazim all, descended one summer to rent bungalows in Rockaway, not knowing that all the other residents on the street were Sephardic Jews from Turkey. One of my aunts, a good woman of strong and usually vociferous convictions, articulated the general feeling on the very first day: "Dos zaynen Yidn? M'hert do a Yidish vort? A nekhtiger tog! Zey redn dokh bloiz Terkish!" (These are Jews? Do you hear a Yiddish word here? Not on your life! They only speak Turkish!) Naturally, we were never privy to what our strange neighbors might be saying about us, the *Tudesco* interlopers. Presumably, they were paying us similar compliments—in "Turkish."

They were, of course, speaking Ladino, that "judaized" metamorphosis of the Castilian which their ancestors had carried out of Spain, just as my aunt's Yiddish was the judaized German transported earlier from the Germanic lands, each Jewish vernacular evolving independently away from its point of origin. By now, both Ladino and Yiddish have suffered a radical erosion as spoken languages, due primarily to the vicissitudes of twentieth century migrations and the devastation of the Holocaust. The surviving bearers of the two vernaculars have been dispersed to alien environments where children and grandchildren have assimilated linguistically. Communities which once provided the natural soil out of which organic cultures flourished have been destroyed. The separate historical destinies of which Rosenzweig spoke finally merged in a tragic culmination which he could not foresee. Polish Hasidim and Balkan Sephardim entered the gas chambers of Auschwitz together.

Dying cultures can acquire a second life only in translation. In this respect, Yiddish has been the more fortunate, especially in the English speaking world. From Mendele to Bashevis Singer, the American reader has ready access to a wide variety of translations of the best in Yiddish literature. That literature has even become something of a fad in sophisticated circles, while for those who prefer their Tevye *fargressert un farbessert* there is always *Fiddler on the Roof*. It is otherwise with Ladino. The rich spectrum of Sephardic vernacular culture created through half a millennium remains not only alien but unknown to Ashkenazic Jews generally, and to American Jews in particular.

B'nai B'rith is therefore to be commended for its initiative in commissioning an anthology of Sephardic vernacular literature as part of its series of Heritage Classics. Selected and edited by Moshe Lazar, the texts themselves have been translated by David Herman. The volume is divided into five sections: I. *Romances* (i.e. Ladino ballads); II. the *Poema de Yoçef*, a fifteenth-century poetic recasting of the Joseph story which incorporates both Biblical and Midrashic elements; III. Legends, culled from the Sephardic folklore of Spanish Morocco; IV. Ladino sayings and proverbs; and finally—V. A translation by Mr. Herman and Lawrence Lockwood of the allegorical play *Contra la verdad no hay fuerza* by the seventeenth-century Amsterdam Jewish poet and former Marrano Daniel Levi (Miguel) de Barrios. The latter is the only piece included in the volume which was written, not in Ladino, but in the standard Castilian of the time. No sources have been indicated anywhere in the book. Those translations I have been able to compare with the original texts already known to me have impressed me as generally competent.

Anthologies are a boon to the reading public and the bane of critics. Any anthology must necessarily reflect the personal choice of its editor and the reviewer hesitates lest he be accused of castigating the selection merely on the basis of his own equally subjective tastes. One feels all the more awkward in reviewing a pioneer anthology which marks a "first" in the field. In addition, some will maintain that a book obviously intended for a popular audience should not be subjected to the canons which prevail in the intramural world of academic scholarship. Nevertheless, even with these restraints soberly in mind, one must not abdicate the critical task either. It is precisely out of respect for the project, the editor, and the potential audience, that I must register my serious reservations concerning the result. Even within its stated limits the book falls short of its goal. As for its "popular" character, there is absolutely no reason why popularization should not reflect sound scholarship, especially when, as in this instance, the editor is himself a scholar of repute.

To begin with, the title *The Sephardic Tradition* is as misleading as "The Ashkenazic Tradition" would be, were it affixed to an anthology of Yiddish literature. The vernacular literature may constitute an important part of both traditions, but only a part. The bulk of Sephardic literary creativity in the centuries following the Expulsion expressed itself in the Hebrew language. Yet a person coming to this book with no prior knowledge of the history of Sephardic Jewry would not know this. The title should have provided some enlightenment on the subject. An American Jewish audience, whose access to Jewish information is almost exclusively dependent on translations or works written in English, should have been informed of the different and more limited role which the vernacular played among the Sephardim.

The subtitle, "Ladino and Spanish-Jewish Literature," indicates one of the self-imposed limits of the book, namely, the exclusion of Portuguese-Jewish literature. This omission is entirely within the editor's prerogative, and perhaps justifiable by limitations of space. But again, one would expect that the general introduction would at least make the reader aware of the existence of a large corpus of Jewish literature in Portuguese, and of the vitality of spoken Portuguese in many European Sephardic centers. Only twice does Lazar even mention Portuguese, and this only in passing. Thus he casually observes that "in the Amsterdam and London communities . . . Jews continued to speak Castilian (or Portuguese). . . ." There is not even a reference to so distinguished a contribution to Sephardic vernacular literature as Samuel Usque's *Consoloçam as tribulaçoens de Israel*.[2] The Ladino translations of Baḥya ibn Pakuda's *Ḥovot ha-Levavot* or the *Shulḥan Arukh* are recorded, but not the fact that these, as well as many other texts, were also translated into Portuguese.[3] And why place Portuguese in parentheses? In the Sephardic communities of seventeenth- and eighteenth-century Amsterdam, Hamburg, Leghorn, and other cities, Portuguese not only vied with Spanish, but displaced it in importance.

Yet another basic exclusion is marked by the fact that the anthology is expressly limited to "secular" rather than "religious" literature, though the distinction in the texts is not always clear to me. Why are such *romances* as the so-called "Song of Death," extolling the martyrdom of Hannah and her seven sons, or some of those which deal with Moses, "secular"? For that matter, why is De Barrios' Jewish morality play in the secular category, when it obviously derives from that great form of Spanish religious drama, the *auto sacramental*? Patently, the criterion for what is "secular" or "religious" is at once vague and excessively narrow. In essence, the religious literature which has been omitted has been tacitly defined in terms of traditional Jewish religious *genres*, rather than on the basis of content or feeling. Liturgical prayers, Biblical exegesis, homiletic or ethical works, are excluded as obviously religious; folklore and drama qualify automatically for this secular anthology, no matter what their theme. Though I regard such a distinction as quite arbitrary, I will not contest the editor's right to it. It is when we look at the texts actually chosen within the established guideline that one senses a gross imbalance in the anthology as a whole.

The most successful sections of the book are those which contain the *Romances*, the Legends, and the Proverbs. In the latter, especially, it was a felicitous idea to print the transliterated Ladino original before each aphorism. Even a reader with high-school Spanish will thus savor something of the source, with its occasional incorporation of a Hebrew word (e.g. — "Roba pitas, besa *mesusot*" — "He steals bread and kisses the *mezuzot*"; "El ganar y el perder son *ḥaverim*" — "Winning and losing are close companions").

However, one must approach the two longest texts in the book with mixed feelings. On the one hand, I suppose, the availability for the first time in English of the *Poema de Yoçef* (pp. 77–120) and De Barrios' *Contra la verdad no hay fuerza*[4] (pp. 156–218) is to be welcomed in and of itself. But within the context of an anthology which proposes to offer a representative sampling of the range of Sephardic vernacular literature these two pieces occupy a place beyond all proportion to the whole. Out of a total of 218 pages they constitute fully half the book. In the case of the *Poema de Yoçef* it is perhaps easy to understand Lazar's inclusion of the entire work in the light of a footnote announcing his plan to publish a critical edition of the Ladino text. Still, while every man studies that which is dear to him, it is questionable whether, by indulging his own obvious involvement with the Joseph poem, he has not done a disservice to his anthology. Three hundred and three stanzas of this poem add little to the variety one has the right to expect from such a book, while the literary quality, at least in translation, is not so great as to justify its rather overwhelming presence. Perhaps if footnotes had pointed out the midrashic elaborations of the Biblical story to the reader the result would have been more interesting, but even then, a selection would have sufficed. As for the De Barrios play, the conventions of its style and rhetoric are so alien to the modern reader that I suspect it will prove rough going for even the most dedicated aficionados. De Barrios could have been better represented by some examples of his occasional poems on historical and contemporary Jewish events and personalities. Indeed, the sixty-two pages now devoted to the play could have allowed for the representation of some other Castilian writers besides De Barrios.

If, nevertheless, the texts in the body of the anthology may prove useful and stimulating in various ways, the same cannot be said for the editor's introduction. It is, quite frankly, a disappointment, all the more so when one considers the opportunity that presented itself here for an informative popular survey of Sephardic vernacular literature and culture. Instead, the introduction seems inadequate, even perfunctory, and at times quite erroneous or misleading.

The Jews were not expelled from Portugal in 1496 (p. 13), as Professor Lazar should know. The edict of expulsion was not really carried out, and the majority could not leave. Along with the Spanish exiles who had crossed the border in 1492, the Jews of Portugal were engulfed en masse in the sudden forced conversion of 1497, a datum of central importance to the entire subsequent history of Iberian Marranism and the Sephardic diaspora as well. Again, the "first Inquisition" is dated in 1391 (p. 18) when, in fact, the Spanish Inquisition was established in Castile in 1478, and the earlier Papal Inquisition functioned in Aragon already in the thirteenth century. The *conversos* Anton de Montoro, Fernando de Rojas and Alfonso de Baena are all designated as "crypto-Sephardim" (p. 19), a neologism which manages to skirt the issue of whether "crypto-Jews" is really meant here.[5] I suppose a case could be made for some impact of Jewish origins or consciousness in each, though in varying degrees, and subject to precise and subtle definitions totally absent here. But to include among the "crypto-Sephardim" the name of Alfonso de Zamora is quite outrageous. Not only is the genuine Christian faith of this celebrated Converso Hebraist beyond dispute, but he even wrote a major anti-Jewish polemic entitled *Sefer ḥokhmat Elohim* aimed at the conversion of his former coreligionists.[6] On the same page we are informed, concerning the Marranos, that "throughout the sixteenth and seventeenth centuries" (why not also the eighteenth?) "many of them resolved to end their double existence and return to Judaism by joining the Sephardic communities in Antwerp, Amsterdam, and other cities of Europe as well as Latin America." But this is haphazard geography. Antwerp, being in the Spanish Netherlands, harbored no legally recognized "Sephardic" community where a Marrano fleeing the Peninsula could live openly as a professing Jew. Even there he would have to lead, at best, a "double existence." The same, of course, was true in all of Latin America, except for the brief period of Dutch rule in seventeenth-century Brazil.

These, to be sure, are only matters of factual detail. More serious and at times, downright frustrating, are some of the historical and ideological evaluations expressed.

Lazar is at great pains to explain the differences between the oriental and occidental Sephardic diasporas. Some of the contrasts are surely manifest to begin with. Ladino proper was written in Hebrew characters and spoken generally by the Sephardic Jews of the East, from the Balkans through Asia Minor, Palestine and North Africa. In Western and Central Europe, the Sephardim employed standard contemporary Spanish or Portuguese.[7] Beyond the specifically linguistic variations there were also other obvious differences in culture and outlook. But then, such differences have always existed between Western Jewries living in Christian Europe, and the Near Eastern Jewries of the Muslim orbit. Apparently, this simple fact of the geographical dispersion of the Jewish people is insufficient for Professor Lazar. He offers a construct which both exaggerates the contrasts to unhistorical dimensions and, simultaneously, searches for their alleged roots in the pre-expulsion development of Spanish Jewry. Early in his introduction he writes: "The Jews who left Spain after 1492 tended to resettle not only according to their town of origin in Spain, but also and specifically according to their social rank and cultural heritage. Most of the traditionalists—who were mainly Orthodox—chose the Ottoman Empire; the others, who stemmed from the aristocracy or upper middle class and were more fully assimilated into secular life and their surrounding cultures, selected the countries of the Christian West as their new homes" (p. 13).

Even if we gloss over the obvious anachronism of the term "orthodox" in this context, we are left with a severe distortion of the pattern of Sephardic emigration. The facile equation of assimilation with the upper classes and hence, by implication, of traditionalism with the lower classes, is itself an unwarranted overstatement of Yitzhak Baer's position concerning medieval Spanish Jewry. As applied by Lazar to the generation of the Expulsion, and as used by him to explain where the exiles settled, it is simply false. Rich and poor converted in 1492 in order to remain in Spain; rich and poor remained steadfast and wandered forth into exile. The Abravanels were both aristocrats and fully committed Jews, and their case can be duplicated many times over. Yosef Ya'abez, that most pietistic of homilists in the period of the Expulsion, settled in Italy, surely a part of the "Christian West," as did countless other "traditionalists." Conversely, did none of the "aristocracy or upper middle class" settle in Turkey and other parts of the Ottoman Empire? A glance at the lay and rabbinic leadership of the Turkish Sephardic communities in the extant documents and responsa literature will demonstrate the absurdity of the assumption. Indeed, in cultural efflorescence and economic vitality the Sephardic Jewries of the sixteenth-century Ottoman Empire may justly be regarded as enjoying a second Golden Age.

For the exiles of 1492 the question of where to go was not ideological, but above all, *practical.* As in the Nazi era, so here, Jewish refugees went where they were received and admitted. The objective fact which Lazar fails to mention is that, except for Portugal and certain parts of Italy and Germany, no Spanish Jewish exile who wanted to live as a Jew (and this decision was already implicit in opting for exile over conversion) could "choose" to live in the "Christian West," for by 1492 most of Christian Europe was *Judenrein.* England, France, most of Southern Italy, and the major German cities, had all expelled the Jews and forbidden their return. Navarre and Provence would follow the lead of Spain in a few years. The Portuguese mass conversion extinguished open Jewish life in that country in 1497. Sicily and Sardinia were under Spanish rule anyway, and in the sixteenth century Spain would govern the Low Countries as well. To those parts of Italy where Jewish residence was still legal in 1492, Spanish Jews came, regardless of class or degree of "orthodoxy." In the forbidden Christian territories only converts or Marranos who still retained the mask of Christianity could settle—as Christians. If it is these converts that Lazar has in mind when he speaks of "assimilated" Jews, the basic error remains, for clearly Europe had no monopoly on Marrano immigration. The responsa of sixteenth century Turkish rabbis are replete with cases reflecting the continual influx of Spanish and Portuguese Marranos and the problems posed by their arrival in communities throughout the Ottoman Empire.

Open Sephardic communities in Western and Central Europe emerged only when external conditions made their existence possible, at the end of the sixteenth and in the early seventeenth centuries. To mention only a few of the more famous: the Amsterdam Sephardic community was a consequence of the successful Dutch revolt against Spain. That of Leghorn arose because of the open invitation of the Grand Duke of Tuscany in 1593. The Hamburg community was established as a result of successful negotiations in 1612. These and other occidental Sephardic communities were, like their Near Eastern counterparts, composed of all social classes, and were as traditionally structured and oriented. After all, Uriel da Costa and Barukh Spinoza were excommunicated, not in Constantinople, but in Amsterdam. Sephardim East and West engaged in secular pursuits, each had their share of heretics and dissidents, and each generally preserved the religious tradition intact.

Lazar continues (p. 14):

> . . . the occidental Sephardic civilization, by its nature, character and environment followed a path which diverged more and more from its oriental counterpart. Though derived from common ancestral roots, each of the two cultures developed as early as the fourteenth century its own distinctive fruit and flavor. That common tradition, marked by such illustrious names as Yehuda Halevi, Ibn Gabirol, Moses ibn Ezra and Maimonides, and writings of such enormous impact as the *Kuzari*, Bahya ibn Paquda's *Hovot ha-Levavot* (The Duties of the Heart) and the *Zohar*, found direct, uninterrupted expression in oriental Sephardic civilization. But it was to make its reappearance considerably later in occidental Sephardic culture.

How one can presume to trace to fourteenth-century Spain an occidental-oriental cleavage which is artificial to begin with, is an enigma which I shall not attempt to unravel. For that matter, one is almost equally perplexed to find Halevi and Maimonides blithely lumped together in a "common tradition." As for the "later" appearance of the works enumerated in the western communities, it is difficult to know just what Lazar has in mind. Is he referring to the printing of these books, and if so, does he mean the Hebrew text or the vernacular translations? Patently, printing among the occidental Sephardim appears later because, except for Italy, the European Sephardic communities arose later than those of the East, and not because of a different ideology or tradition.

Again, we read (p. 22): "As mentioned above, the literature written in Ladino is not to be confused with that produced in Spanish or Portuguese by Western Sephardic Jews, mainly in Amsterdam. In contrast with the majority of traditionalist Spanish Jews, exiled to North Africa and the Ottoman Empire, those who left Spain gradually during the sixteenth and even seventeenth centuries to settle in Western Europe maintained direct contact with Spanish civilization. The religious, philosophical, scientific and literary works they created were not written in Ladino, and they express an entirely different spirit. . . ."

Here too we are somewhat stymied by the sweeping implications of "an entirely different spirit." Obviously in the seventeenth century, Amsterdam provided a different cultural ambiance than did Salonika or Smyrna, and European Jews, whether Sephardim or Ashkenazim, had a different array of cultural baggage than did their eastern brothers. The scientific or philosophical works written in Latin by occidental Sephardim, or the secular literary works written in Castilian and Portuguese, naturally reflected contemporary European standards. Their works tended to be fleshed out with Iberian, Dutch, or Italian university learning. The Sephardic literary academies of Amsterdam and Leghorn were simply modeled on the *academias literarias* of Spain, and have no parallel in the Orient. That is partly because in the Low Countries and in Italy, Castillian and Portuguese were living languages, not only among Sephardic Jews, but among the considerable foreign colonies of Spaniards and Portuguese who resided there. While other interesting cultural differences between the occidental and oriental Sephardim could be discussed, the only vital question concerns the religious literature of each. Were they so different in spirit as Lazar would have us believe? For all the trappings of European erudition, are the religious works of a Menasseh ben Israel or an Isaac Aboab da Fonseca less "traditional" (or kabbalistically oriented) than those of their Turkish peers? To read them is to realize that they all have the same traditional frame of reference.

Though not represented in the anthology, two major genres of the Sephardic vernacular heritage could have been discussed, or at least mentioned, in the Introduction. I have in mind the vast sphere of Judeo-Christian polemics, as well as the flourishing Ladino periodical press which played such an important role in the lives of Sephardic Jews in the nineteenth and twentieth centuries.[8] Above all, one receives from Lazar no clear notion of the texture of Sephardic life and culture. He is informative concerning the linguistic features of Ladino and the development of Bible translations. But if the reader desires some insight into the Sephardic character and spirit, he is merely told in a footnote to read Abraham Joshua Heschel's section on "The Two Great Traditions" in *The Earth is the Lord's*. However, that suggestive discussion of Ashkenazim and Sephardim will be, I fear, of little help, since it is concerned with the latter only in the medieval period. It was never Heschel's intention to characterize the post-expulsion Sephardic diaspora, which displays significantly new features. The parallel we drew earlier between the development of Yiddish and Ladino in alien environments does not extend to other spheres. East European Ashkenazic Jewry did not preserve vital memories of the Germanic lands from which its ancestors came. Sephardic Jews, even in the East, preserved not only their Iberian memories but their Hispanic culture, to a degree that has continually amazed the Spaniards themselves. The elegiac nostalgia for Spain which suffuses Sephardic folk culture has no counterpart among the Ashkenazim with regard to the Rhineland. In 1905, when that great advocate of Hispano-Jewish rapprochement, Dr. Angel Pulido, published his book on the Sephardic Jews, he called them *Españoles sin patria*, "Spaniards without a country." Whatever its intrinsic merits or defects, a similar title substituting "Germans" for "Spaniards" and applied to Polish Jews would be totally inconceivable. The fruitful interplay of Iberian language and culture, of the inherited customary and intellectual Jewish traditions of medieval Sefarad, and the overriding common heritage of Rabbinic Judaism which has always united the Sephardim with all other Jews, produced that blend which is so specifically "Sephardic" in the centuries after the Expulsion. To convey something of that flavor to those who have not known it before is, after all, the essential purpose of this anthology.

My strictures at an end, I would still wish the book a wide dissemination. Despite its shortcomings, it will serve Ashkenazim not only as an entrée, but as pleasant and salutary therapy. By all means, dip into it, and discover a world of Jews who sang of knights and ladies, of love sacred and profane, and yet told legends about Maimonides and wrote plays about the idea of martyrdom. And if these Jews do not quite fit the categories that come by way of Berlin, Warsaw or Long Island, remember the words of that wisest of Ashkenazic songs:

Voss mir zaynen zaynen mir
Ober Yidn zaynen mir. . . .

What we are, we are; but we are Jews. From there it is only a short step to the Ladino proverb, itself a paraphrase of a Talmudic saying (*Pesaḥim*, 66a):

Si neviim no somos,
de neviim venimos. . . .

We may not be prophets, but we are descended from them.

NOTES

The Sephardic Tradition: Ladino and Spanish-Jewish Literature, selected by Moshe Lazar, translated by David Herman, New York: A Jewish Heritage Classic, published for B'nai B'rith by W. W. Norton, 1972, 222 pp. $6.50.

1. Nahum Glatzer, *Franz Rosenzweig: His Life and Thought* (New York, 1953), p. 51.

2. Available now in Martin Cohen's English translation, *Samuel Usque's Consolation for the Tribulations of Israel* (Philadelphia, 1965).

3. Samuel ben Isaac Abas' Portuguese translation of Baḥya's work, entitled *Obrigaçam dos coraçoens*, appeared in Amsterdam in 1670. The Ladino and Spanish translations of the *Shulḥan Arukh* were abridgements. Similarly, Manasseh ben Israel's Portuguese digest, *Thesouro dos Dinim* which was published in five parts, Amsterdam, 1645–47. The whole was reprinted in Amsterdam in 1710.

4. The title has been rendered here in English as "Truth Triumphs in the End." A more literal translation, "Against the Truth Force Cannot Prevail," is to be preferred. The "force" De Barrios had in mind was that of the Inquisition.

5. Lazar's cavalier use of terminology is further reflected (pp. 13 f.) in his assertion that after the pogroms of 1391 "the Jewish population of Spain apparently split into three groups: first, the traditionalists, who composed by far the greatest part; second, significant numbers of false converts or Marranos; and third, a small minority of true converts to Christianity or 'New Christians'. . . ."

In reality, the term "New Christian" (Spanish—*cristiano nuevo*; Portuguese—*cristão novo*) was merely a technical designation in the Iberian Peninsula for *any* convert or descendants of converts, regardless of the quality of his Christian faith, and was so employed down to the end of the eighteenth century. Its meaning was essentially racial. Applied generally to any Christian of known Jewish ancestry, it suggested no ideological evaluation of the particular person. All Marranos were ipso facto New Christians, though not all New Christians were Marranos.

6. See the study and translation by Federico Pérez Castor, *El manuscrito apologético de Alfonso de Zamora* (Madrid-Barcelona, 1950).

7. Italy provided a meeting ground for Castilian, Portuguese and Ladino; Jewish works were published there at various times in all three languages.

8. On the latter see Moshe David Gaon's comprehensive bibliography, *Ha-'itonut be-Ladino* (Jerusalem, 1965). American readers might be interested to know that twelve Ladino papers have appeared in New York.

PART III *Iberia and Beyond*

7 : SEPHARDIC JEWRY BETWEEN CROSS AND CRESCENT

Originally delivered at Harvard University as the inaugural lecture for the Jacob E. Safra Professorship of Jewish History and Sephardic Civilization, February 26, 1979.

This lecture, delivered in 1979, was the inaugural lecture of the Jacob E. Safra Chair in Jewish History and Sephardic Civilization at Harvard University, of which Yerushalmi was the first occupant. Jacob Safra was a wealthy Syrian-Jewish businessman who had founded banks and other financial institutions in the Middle East, Europe, and North and South America. The chair was endowed by Safra's son, Edmond, a well-known banker and philanthropist.

Though he could have chosen to speak about his own research in early modern Sephardic history, Yerushalmi instead chose to speak about the entirety of the history of Jews of the Iberian Peninsula, from its oldest extant traces in the third century to the present day. He sketched the fate of Spanish Jews under successive conquerors of the peninsula—Romans, Visigoths, North African Muslims, and Spanish Christians—as well as their varied experiences in dispersion in the Ottoman Empire and Western Europe after the Expulsion of 1492.

He ended the lecture with an assessment of the importance of Sephardic Jews at the cusp of modernity. Marranos, who had openly converted to Christianity but continued to maintain a crypto-Jewish identity, constituted "the pioneers of Jewish colonization and resettlement in modern times" by creating a de facto Jewish presence in Western Europe, from which Jews were still formally excluded. Yerushalmi also pointed to the foundational role of Sephardim in establishing new patterns in international commerce. The far-reaching networks of the global Sephardic Diaspora "cut across all the religious and geopolitical barriers that divided the Christian and the Muslim world, or Protestant from Catholic countries."

Despite the breadth of his subject matter, Yerushalmi succeeded in retaining his customary nuance. No part of his story was either idealized or demonized. In this regard, Yerushalmi sought to part ways from his scholarly forebears in the nineteenth-century *Wissenschaft des Judentums* movement. Thus, on his rendering, the "Golden Age" of Spanish Jewish culture, which produced aristocrats such as the scholar-poet vizier of Granada, Shmuel Ha-Nagid, was also the age of the near-total annihilation of his community only years after his death. Nor, claimed Yerushalmi, could one make a sweeping generalization that the Jews fared better under either Muslims or Christians. Whereas the Muslim invasion of 711 saved the Jews from the persecutions of Christian Visigoths, the Christian monarchy of Castile saved them from the persecutions of the Muslim Almohades in the twelfth century. Then, of course, that same Christian monarchy expelled the Jews about 350 years later.

This lecture epitomized a key historiographical principle of Yerushalmi's, which he inherited from his teacher Salo Baron. Baron had insisted on placing Jewish history into a wider comparative framework. Similarly, Yerushalmi noted that the unique aspects of Spanish Jewry could be understood only by reference to the history of Spain itself. That history was characterized by the complex relationships among large communities of Jews, Christians, and Muslims, "a tangle of understanding and fanaticism, of respect and denigration, of mutual influence and of unrelenting war." The complex "dynamic interplay of forces" was epitomized by the *Reconquista*, the centuries-long Christian conquest of all of Spain. This process protected the Jews as long as it continued, for the conflict between Muslims and Christians consumed much of the others' attention and redirected it away from the Jews. With the completion of the *Reconquista*, however, there was no more tolerance for a Jewish presence in an all-Christian state. It is no coincidence that 1492 was the year both of the expulsion of the Jews from Spain and of the Christian conquest of the last Spanish Muslim stronghold of Granada.

Ladies and Gentlemen:

You will forgive me, I hope, if on this rather festive and ritual occasion I do not take refuge in a narrow furrow of any of the several fields embraced by the newly established Safra professorship. I would, instead, and with your indulgence, attempt to offer you some sense of the sweep and scope of Sephardic civilization in its historical dimensions.

That, of course, is a vast domain. If this evening, I can only try to map its general contours, I trust there will be ample time to add the details in the years to come. In brief—I want to give you some indication of the different stages and rhythms of Sephardic history, to stress certain continuities, and to set into relief certain features of Sephardic Jewry that are the result of historical factors peculiar to itself. I do so fully mindful of the peril in trying to teach the entire Torah while metaphorically standing on one leg. . . .

I

Jews settled very early in the Iberian Peninsula, and the actual beginnings are necessarily obscure. There can be no doubt, however, that in the first centuries of the Common Era there was already an established Jewry, a branch of the vast Jewish diaspora that had spread throughout the Roman Empire.

Quite by chance, one artifact has survived from the beginning of the third century. It is our first concrete document and, in its own way, even a poignant one—a Latin inscription on the tombstone of a little girl, Latin then being the language of Jews in Roman Spain. The child's name, so far as we can reconstruct it, was Annia Salomonula. In Hebrew she would be called Ḥannah bat Shelomoh. She died at the age of one year, four months and a day, and she is described in one Latin word: *Iudaea*—a Jewess. Annia Salomonula (or Ḥannah bat Shelomoh, if you prefer) is the first Spanish Jewess known to us by name, a paradoxical assertion, for "Spain" as we know it had not yet come into being. The Jews, in short, were in Spain not only from the beginning; they were there before the beginning. . . .

In the fifth century the Iberian Peninsula fell to the Visigoths, a group of barbarian Germanic tribes who had received Christianity. Regrettably, we have no Jewish documents or writings from the Visigothic period that would reveal the inner life of the Jews. All we know comes from non-Jewish sources, especially from the detailed legal codes of the Visigothic kings and the decrees of Visigothic church councils. One thing however emerges clearly: From the frequency with which Jews and Jewish matters are discussed, it is obvious that this was already then a very large and influential Jewish population.

We find that until the end of the sixth century the Visigothic kingdom more or less continued the tradition of Roman toleration vis-à-vis the Jews. The change came only after the Visigothic kings passed from their Arian Christianity to Catholicism and pressed toward a new fusion of church and state.

The blow fell upon the Jews in the early seventh century when, in the year 613, King Sisebut commanded that they all be baptized by force. As a result there began a tragic century of crypto-Jewish life, of underground Judaism, of "Marrano" Judaism (though the term did not yet exist), with strenuous but ultimately unsuccessful efforts by the Crown and the Church to uproot it.

This was the first Jewish experience of mass conversion in the Iberian Peninsula, an experience which, as we shall see, was to be repeated three times: in the twelfth century in Muslim Spain; at the end of the fourteenth century in Christian Spain; and at the end of the fifteenth century in Portugal. True, in Visigothic Spain there was as yet no Inquisition. The rulers used the coercive means available to them in those days—severe punishments, the selling of Judaizers into slavery, separation of children from their parents to be brought up among Christian families. Yet, for all its erosion, in the end Judaism in Visigothic Spain proved too tenacious to be obliterated.

II

Salvation came suddenly, and from without.

In the year 711 a Muslim commander, Tariq, came to Spain with an army from North Africa across the strait whose famous rock has borne his name ever since: "Jebel at-Tariq"—"The Mountain of Tariq" which we call "Gibraltar." Like a whirlwind the Muslim conquest overran the tottering Visigothic kingdom. Most of the Peninsula came under Muslim rule while the Christians were pushed to the remote mountainous regions in the far North. In this way the Visigothic yoke over the Jews was broken, and they were finally able to remove the Christian mask and to live again openly as Jews.

It is hard to trace precise lines from Visigothic Jewry to what was soon to become "Spanish Jewry." We don't know, for instance, how many Jews survived after a century of persecution. But that is not the crucial issue. Following the Muslim conquest, Spain began to receive large and successive waves of Jewish immigrants from North Africa and from the East. From a spiritual and intellectual perspective, Spanish Jewry became a kind of colony of Babylonia, the world center of Talmudic authority and learning, of the Exilarchs and the Geonim, and it remained so until the middle of the 10th century. During this period Talmudic Judaism sank deep roots into Spanish soil and, what was to be of equal moment, the Arabic culture of Muslim Spain itself impressed its stamp indelibly upon Spanish Jewry for all ages to come.

I have neither the desire nor the time to enter this evening into the details of Hispano-Jewish culture, whose main outlines are familiar to many of you anyway. I should stress that most spheres of Jewish creativity in Spain—*Halakhah* (jurisprudence), Hebrew poetry, philosophy, biblical exegesis, grammar, etc.—all had their beginnings in Babylonia and North Africa, but Spanish Jewry brought these to new peaks of accomplishment, and gave them a character and a style of their own. To these achievements, three important factors contributed:

First—The inspiration of Hispano-Arabic culture, which reached its highest development beginning in the tenth century in the Ummayad Caliphate of Cordoba. This culture, splendid, cosmopolitan, and to a large extent secular, attracted Jewish intellectuals like a lodestone, and aroused in them a powerful desire for participation.

Second—The surprise is that out of this climate there emerged, no mere imitation, but an original Jewish creation. Here, no doubt, a prime factor was the religious rivalry that always hovered above and behind the commonly shared secular culture. Jews wrote philosophical works in Arabic, but in order to clarify and buttress the Jewish faith; they wrote books on philology in Arabic, but in order to analyze the structure and grammar of the Hebrew language. As for poetry, of which the Arabs were justifiably proud, it was not only the inspiring Muse that was at work. There was another very potent impulse—the need to demonstrate that the language of the Hebrew Bible was no less suitable to poetry than the language of the Quran, and the challenge to try and surpass it.

The third factor had to do with the coming of age of Spanish Jewry and its independence from the intellectual and religious tutelage of Babylonian development that took place in the tenth century and coincided with the breaking away of the Spanish Caliphate from the Caliph of Baghdad. With this began the so-called "Golden Age" of Jewish culture in Muslim Spain.

The Golden Age produced not only glittering creations in all branches of literature and of science. Simultaneously there was born a sociocultural ideal of the "accomplished Jew" as that Jewish society conceived of him. Before the inner eye of the Spanish Jewish aristocracy there stands the image of a Jew who combines within himself, and in perfect harmony, elements that other Jewries and other ages have sometimes regarded as contradictory or in tension: A punctilious Jewish observance fused with worldly ways and graces; Torah and Greek wisdom; intense devotion to Jewish tradition, and a genuine openness to the surrounding non-Jewish culture. The image of a rabbi-poet-philosopher-courtier-diplomat all blended together. It is not important that in reality perhaps only a man like Shmuel Ha-Nagid, the scholar-poet who rose to become Vizier of eleventh-century Granada, could combine most of these qualities in his own person. Every society has a different ideal of perfection which, even when incapable of total realization, serves as a standard by which both society and the individual measure themselves. Thus it is sometimes astonishing to see the posthumous influence of certain paradigmatic historical figures as types to be emulated by subsequent generations. Hasdai Ibn Shaprut in the tenth century is not only the first of the long line of Jewish statesmen in Spain that will continue unbroken for five hundred years until the Expulsion. His image also serves as a kind of archetype for all the great court Jews who will rise after him, and into whose hands Spanish Jewry will entrust its destinies.

Still, the "Golden Age" of culture was not so golden in other respects. The picture of an absolute tolerance and mutual understanding in Muslim Spain is a myth we have inherited from nineteenth century Jewish historiography. Having already mentioned Shmuel Ha-Nagid, let us not forget that a decade after his death, in 1066, the Muslim population of Granada rose and perpetrated a pogrom against the Jews which all but wiped out the Jewish community. More than an intrinsic tolerance on the part of Muslim society in Spain, we have a recognition of the usefulness of the Jews, and a certain laxity which was willing to ignore some of the more rigorous demands of Muslim law in the treatment of minorities.

Even this changed in the last decades of the eleventh century. Wars broke out with the Christian kingdoms, who had begun to press southward. The Muslims had to seek outside help, and in 1090 there came the army of the Almoravides, sectarian Muslims from North Africa. In the wake of these wars one can already discern the beginnings of significant Jewish settlement in the now expanding Christian territories. The final, abrupt end to the Jewish communities of Muslim Spain came some fifty years later, with the invasion of the Almohades. They too were a Muslim sect from North Africa, where they had established an empire, and they were possessed of a religious zeal that would not be tempered by merely practical or cultural considerations. The Almohades destroyed the Jewish communities of southern Spain. The Jews fled, most of them to the Spanish Christian kingdoms. Those who were left behind and were caught by the Almohades were forced to convert to Islam. It was the second instance of forced conversion and crypto-Judaism on Spanish sod, but this time Jews became Muslim "Marranos." That period of the Almohade invasions marks the transition of Spanish Jewish life from the Muslim to the Christian orbit.

Only one Jew, at least of those who recorded their thoughts, had sensed what was coming, and that was the great poet and thinker Judah Halevi: "Ha-yesh lanu be-mizraḥ 'o be-ma'arav mekom tikvah nehi 'alav betuḥim?" (Have we either in the East or in the West a place of hope in which we can trust?)

"The East" in this line is Muslim Spain; "the West"—Christian Spain. Halevi, before the cataclysm, had come to despair of Spain altogether, and had left for Palestine. But Halevi was not representative of the spirit of the generation of transition. The dominant feeling of the Jews who crossed the Christian frontier in flight from the Almohades can be seen in the words of Abraham Ibn Daud in his *Sefer Ha-Qabbalah*, written around 1160. There he paints, in vivid strokes, the sufferings of the refugees streaming to the border of Christian Castile, but he continues with praises to God. Telling of the Almohade invasion, he writes:

> However, He who prepares the remedy before afflictions exalted be His name, anticipated the calamity by putting it into the heart of King Alfonso, the *Emperador*, to appoint our master and rabbi Judah the Nasi Ibn Ezra over Calatrava [a fortress near the border] and to place all the royal provisions in his charge. . . . Now when this great Nasi Rabbi Judah was appointed over Calatrava, the city of refuge for the exiles, he supervised the passage of the refugees, released those bound in chains, and let the oppressed go free. . . . At his home and at his table where the refugees found rest, he fed the hungry . . . and clothed the naked. Then, providing animals for all the feeble, he had them brought as far as Toledo in great dignity. This he was able to do because of the awe and respect he commanded among the Christians. . . . When all the nation had finished passing over the border by means of his help, the King sent for him and appointed him lord over his household and ruler over his possessions.

We have here a particularly interesting testimony on the fundamental attitude of the generation that passed from Muslim into Christian Spain. "The Lord prepared the remedy before the affliction." There is a secure refuge in Castile and the other Spanish Christian kingdoms. The king, who is called a "righteous king," receives the refugees willingly. Moreover, within Castile there are already to be found Jewish courtiers of the type of Judah Ibn Ezra, who serves the king faithfully and helps his own people. The image is familiar. This Ibn Ezra continues the aristocratic tradition of his forefathers in Granada. It is thus possible to begin afresh. Or perhaps it would be more accurate to say: It is possible to begin the old—anew.

The history of the Jews in Christian Spain unfolds against a fundamental attempt to reconstruct there the culture and the way of life that the Jews had developed in preceding centuries in the Muslim South.

On the face of it, the attempt succeeded. Despite the pessimism of Judah Halevi as to the viability of Jewish existence in Spain, the Jews more than held their own in Christian Spain for almost three hundred and fifty years after Halevi's death. That fact will not seem insignificant to anyone acquainted with the life-span of other Jewries in medieval Europe.

From several points of view it must even have seemed that the cycle was repeating itself and that the transplant onto Christian soil had really taken hold. The same courtly society and culture were revived. Jews create in all the familiar categories. In Christian Spain, even after the passage of time had made most Jews forget the Arabic vernacular, the traces of Arabic culture remained as strong as ever.

And yet—something *had* changed, something that deserves an extended discussion, but I will only indicate the central datum.

From the end of the eleventh century Spain as a whole reached a decisive turning-point which, in effect, created a new ambiance, different from anything that had come before. This turning-point was the *Reconquista* ("reconquest"), a term that covers the long drawn out process, proceeding through fits and spurts over many centuries, in which Spanish Christendom set itself to realize its dream of recapturing the entire peninsula from Islam.

The *Reconquista* was not only to decide the ultimate historical fate of all Spain; it also had enormous repercussions for Spanish culture as a whole. This war of reconquest, which will not be finally completed until 1492, was literally a Crusade. But at the very time that other European nations who went forth to wage the Crusades against Islam had to wander overseas to the Near East and Palestine, the Spaniards carried on their Crusade in their own house, within Spain itself. Spain is therefore a microcosm of the tremendous worldwide confrontation between Christendom and Islam in the Middle Ages. If we want to discover the special quality of medieval Spanish Jewry, we will get nowhere unless we take into account the special character of Spain itself. This is the only land in which, for eight centuries, three religions and three cultures lived in close proximity, three large groups of Jews, Muslims and Christians, whose web of relationships was exceedingly complex, a tangle of understanding and fanaticism, of respect and denigration, of mutual influence and of unrelenting war.

What was the position of Jewry within this constellation?

Anyone who approaches the history of the Jews of Muslim Spain and of Christian Spain as two distinct episodes will grasp only a half-truth, and perhaps even less of the reality that was Spain. What will be missing is a sense of the dynamic interplay of forces that constituted that reality, in which the Synagogue was caught between the Church and the Mosque and contended with both. If, at first glance, the question of who will rule Spain politically and militarily seemed to concern the Christians and Muslims alone, the very nature of their struggle, a combination of Christian Crusade and Muslim Jihad, created an atmosphere that Jews breathed as well.

Again, without entering into the details of these subtle and important processes, it is worth recognizing that the particular tonalities of Spanish Jewry derived, not merely from the influences it absorbed separately from Muslim or Christian culture (both were also influenced by Jewish culture), but rather out of constant reaction to the intrinsic challenge of both combined.

No medieval religious polemic, for example, created so rich and varied a literature as that of Spain. Nowhere else is there a parallel to that enormous tension of Spanish Jews who, on the one hand, acquired more political and economic power than any other medieval Jewry, and precisely for that reason they chafed all the more under restrictive legislation that prevented them from playing the game of power to its end. Similarly, we begin to understand that even the proverbial pride and arrogance of Spanish Jewry was not only the result of its real achievements, but a response to the triumphalist onslaughts of Christendom and Islam, who never tired of declaring that their political-military successes were proof that God has rejected the Jews and chosen them instead. In the face of this hubris of Edom and Ishmael, Spanish Jewry, *Galut Yerushalayim 'asher bi-Sefarad*, "The exile of Jerusalem that is in Spain," loudly proclaimed its moral superiority, its antiquity on Spanish soil, its distinguished lineage, and above all, its absolute conviction of the truth of its religion and the certainty of its messianic hopes.

In retrospect we can also see that the very existence of Spanish Jewry depended, in the long run, upon the *Reconquista*. So long as the two sides were in genuine confrontation, there was a place for the Jews. But after the first great stages of the *Reconquista* were completed, a different attitude was in the making. In the fourteenth century there is a general erosion in the legal and social position of the Jews of Spain, and the century ends in catastrophe. In 1391 a wave of massacres swept throughout Spain and into the Balearic Islands. Entire communities were destroyed irrevocably, thousands were killed, tens of thousands were forced to convert to Christianity. All through the fifteenth century Spanish Jewry is split in two, into two populations, one of professing Jews, the other of converts and Marranos. This last century of Spanish Jewry in its own land has much of the tragedy of the final century of Visigothic rule. In the end, as you know, in 1492, the last Muslim stronghold (Granada) was taken by the Christian armies, and with this the *Reconquista* was completed. Ferdinand and Isabella ruled over the whole of Spain. It was more than coincidence that within a few months the Jews were expelled.

IV

But have we not learned that the "remedy" is prepared before the "affliction"?

The Sephardic diaspora did not begin, as is commonly supposed, with the Expulsion of 1492. It began at least a hundred years before, with the massacres of 1391. Through the entire fifteenth century Jews continued to leave Spain and settle around the Mediterranean basin. At the time of the Expulsion there were already nucleal Sephardic communities in North Africa, Egypt, Turkey, the Balkans, even a handful in Palestine, and when the exiles of 1492 arrived, they could be received and helped.

This and more. In the century between the massacres of 1391 and the Spanish Expulsion a new Muslim power arose in the world, the empire of the Ottoman Turks, and from the mid-fifteenth century, when the Turks conquered Byzantine Constantinople, Christian Europe began to tremble for fear of the Ottoman peril. The rise of the Ottomans had vast significance for Jewish history, and in order to appreciate it, we must glance momentarily at the situation in Europe following the Spanish Expulsion.

At the beginning of the sixteenth century almost all of Western Europe, and not only Spain, was closed to Jews. The expulsion from Spain was part of the final stage of a chain of expulsions, begun two hundred years earlier, as a result of which most of Europe was emptied of Jews. Had I lived in the year 1500, and had I wanted to come to Europe as an openly professing Jew, I would have found that most countries were closed to me. At the end of the thirteenth century the Jews had been expelled from England; in the fourteenth century—from France; in the fifteenth—from most of the large cities of Germany; in 1492—from Spain. The process did not even end there.

When the Jews were expelled from Spain, Portugal was still open (at any rate—for a price). Many of the Spanish refugees entered Portugal, which was just across the border. But only five years later, in 1497, King Manuel decreed a total forced conversion, the likes of which had not been seen in the Iberian Peninsula since the days of the Visigoths. At one stroke all Jews living in Portugal, including the Spanish refugees, were baptised, so that even without an expulsion, open Judaism came to an end or was forced underground.

Expulsions continued from other places: Provence, various parts of Germany and Austria, Southern Italy. The Scandinavian countries had never had a Jewish settlement. Sicily and Sardinia were under Spanish rule, and the Jews were forced to leave. Spain also ruled the Low Countries through most of the sixteenth century, and no Jewish residence was allowed.

And so—to the East.

For the third time, Sephardic Jewry is transplanted from one sphere to another. It returns now from the sphere of Christian rule to that of Islam—to North Africa, and to the Ottoman Empire which extends its conquests through the Balkans and, twenty-five years after the Spanish expulsion, conquers Egypt and Palestine. In the sixteenth-century Ottoman Empire, Sephardic Jewry enters its second Golden Age.

I should like to stress that life under the Turks was not all roses, even in the glorious days of the sixteenth-century sultans. But everything, of course, remains relative. Compared to Christian Europe which had barred its doors, the Ottoman Empire seemed like salvation itself, just as once Christian Spain had been a haven for the refugees from the Muslim South. Recall, now, the words of Abraham Ibn Daud in the twelfth century, and listen to Elijah Capsali on the island of Crete, in the sixteenth: "Behold, our brothers the sons of Esau [i.e., the Christians] have expelled us, and devoured and destroyed us . . . first Spain and then Portugal. Had it not been for the Lord of Hosts who left us a remnant . . . and let us find favor with Sultan Bayazid of Turkey, who received the Jews into his Empire graciously, we would have been destroyed like Sodom or Gomorrah. . . ."

Spanish Jewry now seemed scattered to the winds, yet—though dispersed, they were not disintegrated. One of the most interesting phenomena in Jewish history of the last four centuries is the manner in which Sephardic Jewry retained its Hispanic character after leaving Spain and in every place it settled. Spanish Jews kept their Castilian language (Ladino), and the popular ballads they had brought with them from Spain, down to our own time. Not only did they not "assimilate" in their new lands of residence, but during the sixteenth century the process often went in reverse. The Sephardim inundated local Jewries, and the latter assimilated to them and became — "Sephardic."

Certainly some significant changes did take place as a result of new conditions. Within Spain before the expulsion, the Jewish community of any city coincided with the total Jewish population of that city, and all were ruled by a single communal administration. In the cities of the Sephardic diaspora such an organization was impossible. Not only were there communities in each city that had existed before the Sephardim arrived, but they themselves organized according to their areas of origin in Spain and Portugal, and even according to their cities of origin for example — the "Holy Community of Castile," of Aragon, of Catalonia, but also the "Holy Community of Barcelona," of Lisbon, of Evora. It was a situation without precedent that carried a potential danger of anarchy. Nevertheless, as time went by, structures were found that enabled the various congregations within each city to resolve differences, and to act together in matters affecting the welfare of the city as a whole.

Another important change took place in the economic sphere. We have no evidence that the trade of the Jews of Spain before the Expulsion was of anything beyond relatively petty and local dimensions. Not so, however, in the Sephardic diaspora, where Spanish and Portuguese Jews developed an international commerce of the first rank that their forefathers had not dreamed of. From the sixteenth to the eighteenth centuries the Sephardic diaspora was a global commercial factor of great significance, and this derived from the nature of the Sephardic dispersion itself. The Sephardic merchants and financiers had special international connections, not only with Jews in other countries, but an entire network of relations with other Sephardim that included also Marranos in Christian countries. Often these were family connections. Within a given family there could be members living as Jews in Greece and Turkey, Morocco and Italy, and others who were still "New Christians" in Spain and Portugal, or in the Spanish and Portuguese colonies in the New World or in India. Such close ties cut across all the religious and geopolitical barriers that divided the Christian and the Muslim world, or Protestant from Catholic countries. Here, perhaps, was the secret of Sephardic commercial success, which deserves a lecture in itself. For the moment let me only mention that the first theoretical treatise on the workings of a stock-exchange was written in Spanish in the seventeenth century by a Sephardic Jew of Amsterdam,

Joseph Penso de la Vega, and was entitled, appropriately—*Confusion de confusiones* ("Confusion of Confusions"). Those of you who are interested will find that an abridged English translation was published some years ago by the Harvard Business School. But I would now turn instead to one last dimension of Sephardic history I have in mind—the Marranos.

V

From the beginning of the sixteenth century, another diaspora may be said to have been added to the Sephardic dispersion, related to it in origins, and yet—different: The Marrano diaspora.

For some three hundred years, down to the end of the eighteenth century, many Marranos succeeded in fleeing from the Iberian Peninsula. Thousands came to established Sephardic communities, returned to the open practice of Judaism, and were absorbed into those communities. Some found the adjustment difficult, and out of the ensuing ideological and intellectual ferment emerged those currents which formed the background of a Spinoza. But there were many other Marranos who, for various reasons, continued the double life of crypto-Jews even after leaving Spain and Portugal, and who formed a dispersion all their own. These Marranos were to perform an historic task for the Jewish people at large. They were, in effect, the pioneers of Jewish colonization and resettlement in modern times.

We've seen that around the year 1500 almost all of Western Europe as well the far-flung Spanish and Portuguese empires were closed to Jews. That is—residence was forbidden to *professing* Jews, but not to Marranos who, outwardly at least, passed as Christians. And so, to all those places from which Jews had been expelled in prior centuries, and to places where Jews had never yet set foot, the Marranos began to come and settle—nominally as Christians. The rule is: the arrival of Marranos paves the way for the later arrival of openly professing Jews, for as the Christian mask was gradually dropped, Jewish residence became a fait accompli. The Marrano settlements beyond the Iberian Peninsula were thus to become the nuclei of some of the most important Jewries of the modern era. This is true of England, Holland, Denmark, the cities of northern Germany, France (except for Alsace, which was Ashkenazic), and, in a different way, of North and South America as well.

In this way the Sephardic diaspora, together with the Marrano diaspora, developed by the mid-seventeenth century into a truly global dispersion. In the middle of the seventeenth century it is already possible to speak of Eastern Sephardic Jewry, which includes all the countries of North Africa and the Ottoman Empire, and Western Sephardic Jewry, which already embraces not only most of Western and Central Europe, but also parts of South America, the islands of the Caribbean, and even New York (which is still New Amsterdam), to which a group of Sephardic refugees arrived from Brazil in 1654.

There are palpable differences between East and West. The Eastern Sephardim live under Muslim rule, and their vernacular is (besides the Judeo-Arabic of North Africa)—Ladino. The Western Sephardim live everywhere under Christian rule, and their vernaculars are Castilian and Portuguese. Nevertheless, there are fundamental unities within the global dispersion. Jewish literatures are created in all three vernaculars, while Hebrew creativity remains fundamental to all, in both East and West. The various Sephardic segments are linked, not only by family and commercial ties, but by an irreducible Sephardic identity. The young communities in the New World receive instruction in religious matters from Amsterdam and London. The Society for Dowering Orphan Brides established by the Sephardim in Venice sends dowries for orphan girls to Salonika and Adrianople. From the island of Curaçao funds arrive for the Sephardic community of Jerusalem. Such examples could be multiplied at will.

VI

I can only indicate the developments since then. In the eighteenth century the outward fortunes of the Western Sephardim rise (for example, after the French Revolution they become citizens of France), while the legal status and security of masses of oriental Sephardim decline, until, by the mid-nineteenth century there is a wide disparity between them. But in that same period there takes place a serious demographic decline among the Western Sephardim whose causes we still do not understand completely. The fact is that already in London and New York at the end of the eighteenth century the number of Ashkenazim far exceeds the Sephardim. Many Western Sephardic Jews move toward total assimilation. In the nineteenth and twentieth centuries, Sephardic Jewry is, in effect, that of the Middle East. And this Jewry, living often under corrupt and venal regimes, retains an immense vitality in literature as in life. Research into the modern history of the oriental Sephardim has only begun to flower in our time. It is a history that is yet to be written.

And so, as you see, we have traveled wide and far since our initial encounter with poor little Annia Salomonula, who died so young and so long ago. You are entitled to ask—What does all this amount to?

I have tried, throughout this excursion, to present essentially one central thesis, though its implications exceed what I have been able to encompass here. *The specificity of Sephardic Jewry is not to be sought in this or that area of cultural activity.* Other Jewries have also produced important poetry, philosophy, biblical commentaries, scientific works, and have achieved great things. I have put forth only one concept, because I believe it is basic to all else—that Sephardic Jewry has had a *history* unique unto itself, and its uniqueness lies in the fact that this Jewry alone has had such extensive and profound experiences of life in both Muslim and Christian lands. It received from two cultures, and contributed to both; it contended with two religions, and out of the totality of these relationships and experiences emerged that fusion of East and West which, without our needing to define it prematurely, strikes us immediately as— "Sephardic."

To summarize:

The history of Sephardic Jewry is the history of four great transmigrations:
In the eighth century: from Christian Visigothic Spain to Muslim Spain.
In the twelfth century: from Muslim to Christian Spain.
At the end of the fifteenth century, with the Expulsion: from Christian Spain to the lands of Islam.
By the mid-seventeenth century: a worldwide dispersion, divided between Muslim and Christian countries.

Throughout these metamorphoses, Sephardic Jewry reveals its continuities, and an astonishing capacity for creative adjustment to new conditions. Now, in our lifetime, Sephardic Jewry has entered yet another, unprecedented, perhaps ultimate phase. Since 1948 most of the Eastern Sephardic diaspora has been ingathered in Israel. Others have been scattered from Seattle, Washington, to Buenos Aires, to Marseilles, and many places along the way.

The future? If philosophers are not yet kings, how should mere historians lay claim to prophecy? Our task here at Harvard is of a more sober order, yet it is not, I believe, without its meaning and purpose. To paraphrase the well-known parable—though we may no longer be able to light the fire, we can tell the story of how it was done, and that may create its own radiance. Indeed, the more careful study, teaching, research, the better the story will eventually be told. In this way the Sephardic past can be fed into the present, as part of a many-chambered storehouse from which all, Sephardim and Ashkenazim, Jew and gentile, the community of scholars and the community at large, can draw and be enriched.

It is Mr. Edmond Safra's vision and generosity that have made this more possible than ever before, and we are grateful. Safra professors will come and go; the Safra Chair in Jewish History and Sephardic Civilization, established at a great and venerable university, will endure. To Mr. Safra, then, I address the Ladino maxim, with its characteristic mixture of Hebrew and Castilian: "El *kavod* es a quien lo da, no a quien lo toma. . . ." (Honor belongs to him who gives it; not to him who takes it.)

8 : THE RE-EDUCATION OF MARRANOS IN THE SEVENTEENTH CENTURY

Originally delivered as the Rabbi Louis Feinberg Memorial Lecture in Judaic Studies at the University of Cincinnati, March 26, 1980.

This piece originated as the Rabbi Louis Feinberg Memorial Lecture in Judaic Studies, hosted by the Judaic Studies Program at the University of Cincinnati. Yerushalmi delivered the lecture in 1980, the year in which he moved from Harvard to Columbia to take up the chair named for his teacher Salo W. Baron.

Up to this time, the bulk of Yerushalmi's scholarly output, including both of his books, had been concerned with the Marranos.[1] Many thousands of Jews converted to Christianity on the Iberian Peninsula in the century after the anti-Jewish riots of 1391. In 1492, the Jews were expelled from Spain; all who remained were required to convert to Christianity. Five years later, the tens of thousands of Jews who had fled the expulsion to Portugal were forced to convert en masse in that country. Marranos were those among the converts or *conversos* who continued to maintain a Jewish identity in secret. It was they whom the Inquisition specifically targeted for their "judaizing" heresy. As a result, the lives of the Marranos or crypto-Jews were particularly tenuous. In the sixteenth and seventeenth centuries, many crypto-Jews left the Iberian Peninsula for Muslim or Protestant countries, particularly the Maghreb, the Levant, and the Netherlands, where they could once again adopt an open Jewish identity. By this period, all of them were at least fourth-generation Catholics and had been raised in places where Jewish education, books, and practice were strictly outlawed. The "re-education" of the Marranos, as reflected in the mechanisms they used to acclimatize themselves to the Jewish communities that they joined, was the subject of Yerushalmi's lecture.

Yerushalmi identified two kinds of activities by which Marranos committed themselves to their new Jewish lives. The first were "emotional, symbolic." Marranos replaced their Christian names with Jewish ones, and some submitted themselves to a penitential flogging. Males underwent circumcision and married couples were remarried in a Jewish ceremony.

The other kind of activity was a more intellectual endeavor. After the returning Marranos had openly recommitted to Judaism through the rituals mentioned above, they had to acquire knowledge of the Jewish tradition necessary to take

---

1. Some prefer the term "crypto-Jew," because of the pejorative origin of the term "Marrano" in the Old Spanish word for "pig."

part in the Jewish community. A slew of books were published in Spanish and Portuguese during the sixteenth and seventeenth centuries to help them do so. Yerushalmi surveyed this new Jewish literature, which included Bibles, Hebrew grammars, histories, and other works. In particular, he described various halakhic manuals and the way they changed over time, initially being published in Ladino in Hebrew characters but before long being published in ordinary Castilian in Latin characters.

The tone and methodology of this article were typical of Yerushalmi's wider oeuvre. He covered vast ground by relying on evocative pieces of evidence to illustrate his careful generalizations. He used ostensibly arcane bibliographic details to shed light on shifts in attitude. He drew on a wide variety of historical sources, including rabbinical responsa, royal charters, and Inquisition records. He also evinced a special sensitivity to the inner experience of his subjects, as, for instance, in his reference to "the psycho-symbolic significance of names," which hints at his later interest in Freud.

It should also be noted that Yerushalmi made brief references in this article to the ongoing historiographical debate regarding the Marranos in Inquisitorial Iberia. Some historians, notably Benzion Netanyahu (mentioned in the introduction to chapter 5), claimed that the vast majority of the Spanish *conversos* led fully Christian lives and that the extent of crypto-Judaism described in the records of the Inquisition was a fabrication motivated by racial hatred.[2] Others, such as Yitzhak Baer, claimed that the many Marranos identified firmly as Jews.[3] Yerushalmi offered a somewhat more complex version of Baer's approach, acknowledging the "metamorphosis" required for a Marrano to join the Jewish community. Here Yerushalmi took issue with the claims of Netanyahu by asserting that the Inquisition records constitute, on the whole, reliable historical evidence. In particular, he pointed out that these records provided Marranos in Iberia with the opportunity to learn about traditional Judaism by making public reference to Jewish practices and sources. Accordingly, "[w]e should disabuse ourselves," he insisted, "of the common notion that the Marranos in Spain and Portugal knew nothing of post-biblical Judaism." Ironically enough, the Inquisition, sincere in its conviction

2. Benzion Netanyahu, *The Marranos of Spain from the Late 14th to the Early 16th Century, according to Contemporary Hebrew Sources* (Ithaca, NY, and London: Cornell University Press, 1999). The book was first published in 1966. It was followed some thirty years later by a more exhaustive version of the same thesis, *The Origins of the Inquisition in Fifteenth-Century Spain* (New York: Random House, 1995).

3. Yitzhak Baer, *A History of the Jews in Christian Spain*, 2 vols. (Philadelphia: Jewish Publication Society of America, 1983). Yerushalmi's review of this book is in chapter 3.

to root out heresy, provided some of the key material, Yerushalmi argued, for the "judaizing" practices of Marranos.

In one of the rare autobiographical accounts to come to us from a former Marrano, the poet João (Moshe) Pinto Delgado, who returned to Judaism in France, writes poignantly of his parents in Portugal as having planted in his soul "the trees of the Most Holy Law whose fruits were late in coming" (*los árboles de la Santíssima Ley, de que tardaron los frutos*).[1] That metaphor could well have served as the title of this lecture on the means by which those thousands of Marranos who still fled from the Iberian Peninsula in the seventeenth century managed to make the transition from a truncated clandestine Judaism to full and open Judaism, and who were thus absorbed into Jewish communities the world over.

At the very outset we must be astonished at the phenomenon itself. We are dealing in this period with Marranos of the fourth, fifth, even sixth generation, born and raised as Christians in Spain and Portugal where, since the end of the fifteenth century, open Jewish life had ceased to exist. These were men and women whose grandparents had already known neither synagogue nor house of study, yet they continued to flee abroad in order to bring their Jewish faith to full flower, and to rejoin the living body of the Jewish people throughout the vast Sephardic diaspora.

To be sure, some fled—and failed. The tragic case of Uriel d'Acosta is the best and most famous example of this. But most succeeded. Da Costa and some others who came into collision with the Judaism that awaited them achieved notoriety precisely because they were not typical. Most of the Marranos who fled took their places quietly within established Jewries. Some went on to become communal leaders, scholars and rabbis. The galaxy of former Marranos who contributed to every sphere of seventeenth-century Jewish life far exceeded the number of heretics among them, and I shall not weary you with their names. In any case, for our present purposes we are as concerned with the anonymous as well as the illustrious.

How was this metamorphosis achieved? How did a person who had reached maturity in Catholic Spain or Portugal acquire those Jewish traditions, skills and attitudes that would enable him to feel at home in the Jewish community and become an active participant in both its religious and mundane life?

The answer depends, in part, on how one views the problem. In general, two assumptions obscure our view of what actually took place:

> That between the Iberian Catholic ambiance and that of such
> contemporary Jewish communities as Amsterdam or Venice there
> lay an almost unbridgeable chasm.
> That before leaving the Iberian Peninsula Marranos had access
> only to the Bible, that they were totally ignorant of post-Biblical
> Judaism and that all they encountered once they arrived in a
> Jewish community was a complete novelty for them.

I shall have occasion to indicate that both assumptions are exaggerated and that the real problems lay elsewhere. For the moment we would best plunge in directly and begin to look closely at the Marrano emigrants themselves.

I

The transition of the Marrano from what I. S. Révah has called a "potential Judaism"[2] to active Judaism began before his arrival in a Jewish community. It began with the very decision to flee, with the flight itself, despite the dangers involved. In a responsum written in 1655 Rabbi Jacob Sasportas speaks of "those Marranos whose entire effort is to come to a Jewish community, and who have risked their lives and endangered themselves, and the uncircumcised detected them . . . and they gave up their lives for the sanctification of the Name." And yet, others continue to flee, "for they believe that there is yet hope for them, and they seek the nearness of God . . . and they reckon their lives as nothing in accepting the yoke of the kingdom of Heaven lovingly. . . ."[3]

In short, the flight was itself already an act of intense Jewish commitment, not to be undertaken easily or capriciously. And this was true not only of those who fled voluntarily, but even of those who were menaced by the Inquisition and who fled to escape arrest. Once abroad even the latter were now at liberty to live securely as Christians and, to be sure, some did precisely that. If many still chose to enter a Jewish community that choice too was an act of Jewish volition. Both types, then, came to the Jewish community with a prior existential investment and, as one may well imagine, with great expectations.

The primary aspect to ponder is that once the Marrano arrived in a Jewish community his "re-education" or, if you will, his "re-judaizing" began on a non-cognitive plane. Indeed, it began on a deep, emotional, symbolic—one would almost say sacramental—level, which preceded any intellectualizing, and which was all the more powerful for that very reason. Before any systematic study the returning Marrano performed a series of acts and rituals, rites of passage in the fullest sense, which could not fail to impress on him that in reclaiming his spiritual patrimony he was indeed beginning a new life. Some practices were specifically geared to Marranos. Others stemmed from the natural consequences of what Jewish law demands of any Jew. Even the latter, however, often had a different meaning for the Marrano than for other Jews.

For the adult male the act of prime significance was, of course, his circumcision, generally performed as soon as was feasible. We can only begin to imagine the impact of such an experience. Gentile proselytes to Judaism have obviously known it, but I am not aware that they have ever written about it. Some former Marranos did. Here, for example, is Isaac Cardoso who, at age forty-five, abandoned his career as court-physician in Madrid to become a Jew in Venice: "For it is not like some light wound in the leg or an easy bruise on the arm, but rather something hard and difficult which no one would undertake unless he were moved by great awareness and zeal to embrace the Law of the Lord. This is also the reason why it is done at the tender age of eight days, when the pain is not so great as later, and the imagination is still weak. But all this increases with maturity, when a man becomes apprehensive and fears things before they happen. . . ."[4]

Little wonder that some were reluctant to submit to circumcision. With these persuasion was necessary and, when that failed, various forms of coercion. In the Sephardic community of London, for example, one of the earliest ordinances of the seventeenth century barred any uncircumcised male, as well as his family, from burial in the communal cemetery.[5] In some Italian communities the returning Marrano was allowed to perform various ritual commandments even before his circumcision, while others disagreed and denied him the right of putting on phylacteries, or raising the Torah in the synagogue, arguing on psychological grounds "that they will delay in entering into the covenant of our father Abraham, since they see that although they are uncircumcised nothing is withheld from them and they can use all holy objects as Jews."[6]

Yet the evidence indicates that most did undergo circumcision as soon as possible. Indeed, it is not surprising that perhaps nowhere in Jewish literature do we find so great an emphasis on the rite, or such glowing praise of it, as in the writings of former Marranos. In Cardoso's terminology it is a "mysterious sacrifice" (*sacrificio misterioso*). It, and not the Crucifixion as the Christians claim, made full restitution for Original Sin. "Without this seal of circumcision the Jew cannot be saved" (*sin este firmamento de berit no se puede salvar el judío*).[7] The seventeenth-century Venetian rabbi Samuel Aboab was upset that some former Marranos seemed to believe that their sins began to count only from the moment they are circumcised, and that therefore they did not sufficiently regret their past deeds.[8] But Aboab saw only the negative side of this belief, and so missed the point. It was really a measure of the centrality of circumcision in the eyes of those very Marranos that they regarded it as the crucial event separating their Jewish from their Marrano lives, the mark of a truly new beginning.

What I have tried to sketch thus far is not merely a speculative reconstruction. In an inquisitorial trial still preserved in the archives in Madrid there is a uniquely graphic description of the absorption of a Marrano into a Jewish community. The case is that of Cristóbal Méndez, alias Abraham Franco de Silveira, arrested in Madrid in 1661.[9] He had fled originally in 1643 to Venice, where he fully embraced Judaism, and had lived as a Jew for years both there and in Amsterdam. In 1649 he had returned to Spain in order to bring his sister and stepmother out of the country. Now he had returned once more, probably on a similar mission, but was caught. His description of his reception into the Venetian Jewish community, revealed in the course of an inquisitorial interrogation, is of concern to us here.

Upon his arrival in Venice in April of 1643 Méndez was taken to the house of an uncle, Abraham Suárez. Twenty years old at the time, Méndez had some natural hesitations about undergoing circumcision, but was persuaded to agree to it by the uncle and by a rabbi, Moses of Toledo, himself a former Marrano. The latter gave him a Spanish bible (*la Biblia en romance*), and in particular discussed with him Psalm 19:18 ("The law of the Lord is perfect"). The circumcision took place a month later, the mohel being Solomon Foro, an elderly Jewish merchant who, we are told, considered it a special merit for himself to perform the ritual. The circumcision was accomplished according to all the requirements of Jewish law, including *periah*. In retrospect Méndez recalled that he had barely heard the benedictions recited on the occasion because of the great pain he felt (*con el gran dolor que sentía*). As soon as he was circumcised the uncle gave him a prayer-shawl (*tallit*) and phylacteries (*tefillin*). He also gave him a Spanish translation of the prayer book which he perused during the twenty days it took him to recuperate from the operation. Once recovered he came to the Sephardic synagogue, the Scuola Spagnola, in the Venetian ghetto. He put on his *tallit* and *tefillin* and was called to ascend to the open ark, where he recited the traditional blessing of deliverance (*birkat ha-gomel*) in Hebrew, repeating it word for word after the cantor. His formal transition to Judaism was accomplished.

II

There were other elements as well.

Anyone who appreciates the psycho-symbolic significance of names, and especially of a change of names, will readily understand the importance of the fairly universal custom whereby the returning Marrano exchanged his Iberian Christian name for a Jewish one.[10] Usually this took place at circumcision or, in the case of women, at their ritual immersion. Some Marrano families even succeeded to transmit the original Jewish surname from the fifteenth century down through the generations, and where this name was known it would now be adopted openly.[11] Similarly, while still in the Iberian Peninsula some Marrano parents would give their children a secret Hebrew first name with the admonition that this should be used by them if they ever managed to depart.[12] More surprising is the fact that the genealogical traditions of Marrano families were generally respected and accepted as accurate. Thus, if a man claimed that he was descended from *kohanim* or *levi'im* he was given the priestly or levitical prerogatives in the synagogue without further inquiry. A case preserved in the rabbinic responsum concerns a Marrano who came to Salonika and did not know his Jewish family name, so he picked one at random. After a while he received a letter from an old woman in Safed, Palestine, who said she knew he was from a priestly family. On the basis of this testimony he now named himself Cohen, and was allowed to deliver the priestly benediction in the synagogue and to be called up first at the reading of the Torah. "And thus it is the custom with regard to all Marranos (*'anusim*) who declare themselves to be *kohanim*, and they are called thus upon their own word, and there is no suspicion whatever."[13]

Given the guilt that some Marranos felt for the life they had led as Christians, it is no surprise that penitential rites also existed, including flogging, though here the practice varied widely. Some rabbis saw fit to impose them; in most cases Marranos sought and undertook them voluntarily.[14] Most widespread was the custom of observing a private fast, a practice that obtained even within the Iberian Peninsula. The inquisitorial documents reveal instances in which an active Judaizer would persuade another New Christian to join him and urge that he begin to become an "observer of the Law of Moses" (*observante de la ley de Moysen*) by first undertaking a fast.[15]

Finally, after arriving in a Jewish community Marrano couples who had married in Spain or Portugal were now re-married in a Jewish ceremony. In Livorno, and probably elsewhere as well, it was the custom to place any children who had been born in the Peninsula under the bridal canopy (*ḥuppah*) together with their parents. This practice was apparently at the request of the parents themselves, who believed that in this way they were legitimizing their children. In a rabbinic responsum we read: "And at that time they declare their children to be *legítimos*, for it seems to them that if they will not do so (the children) are *bastardos*. . . ."[16]

All such experiences, I repeat, were undergone by the Marrano shortly after coming to a Jewish community, before any formal "education" had taken place. He was now already a member of the community. It need hardly be added that from the beginning he attended the services in the synagogue, usually with a Spanish translation of the prayerbook in his hands, while presumably a neighboring worshipper pointed out which prayer was being recited in Hebrew at the moment. But it is a truism that Judaism also requires substantive knowledge of its adherents. What kind of Jew the former Marrano would turn out to be, the measure of his adjustment and contribution to the community, would be affected to a considerable degree by the knowledge he acquired. The awareness of the new "Law of Moses" which he brought out of the Iberian Peninsula had now to be expanded into a knowledge of Judaism as lived and practiced by his fellow Jews. Where they had grown into that knowledge and had absorbed it organically, he had to acquire it rapidly and artificially. Where they had learned it as children, he must now learn it as an adult. It was not an easy task.

III

Yet it was also not as impossible as it might seem at first glance.

To begin with, the Marrano refugee often arrived with more knowledge than modern scholars have credited to him. We should disabuse ourselves of the common notion that the Marranos in Spain and Portugal knew nothing of post-biblical Judaism. The mass of them must have known at the very least that a post-biblical Jewish tradition existed, if only because every Iberian polemic against them and virtually every sermon at the public autos-da-fé heaped invective upon the Talmud and the rabbis. Many knew more than that. The intellectuals gleaned a mass of Jewish information from the works of Christian scholars. Businessmen brought back information on Jewish life from their trips abroad. The Iberian Peninsula in the seventeenth century was not hermetically sealed to Jewish information, nor even to occasional visits by professing Jews. I have dealt with these aspects elsewhere and need not repeat the data here.[17]

The problem was not that they knew nothing of Judaism, but that what they knew was often a pastiche of fragments inherited from parents, gleaned haphazardly from books, disorganized, with significant gaps, sometimes distorted. There was an obvious need for systematic instruction. In Venice Samuel Aboab called for a special brotherhood (ḥebrah) that would devote itself to this task.[18] I do not know whether it was actually established. But even if it was, the returning Marrano remained essentially an autodidact and, like all autodidacts, he needed books to read.

I cannot possibly give a complete description of this literature within the confines of a lecture,[19] but I will attempt to outline some of its more important characteristics. Some of the works produced for the benefit of former Marranos were obviously geared toward the rapid acquisition of what might be termed "basic Judaism." The rest was intended for deeper study and a more intensive awareness. Let us examine each in its turn.

Certain works were staples and probably to be found in most homes. Of these the Bible was the cornerstone. The first Jewish translation into Spanish appeared in Ferrara, Italy, in 1553, and this served as the basic text for all subsequent editions.[20] The Jewish liturgy was also available in Spanish, and here again Ferrara could claim a "first" (1552: *Libro de oraciones de todo el anno* [*sic*] *traducydo del Hebrayco de verbo a verbo*).[21] Throughout the seventeenth and eighteenth centuries many other Spanish prayerbooks were printed, in various formats, especially in Amsterdam. In addition, a very popular work was the Spanish translation of the Aramaic paraphrase (*Targum*) to the Song of Songs (*Paraphrasis Caldayca en los Cantares de Selomoh en lengua española*), which was often printed together with the Spanish version of the "Chapters of the Fathers" (*Pirke Abot*), the ethical tractate of the Mishnah.[22]

It is interesting to note that the Bible and the liturgy were always printed in Spanish, never in Portuguese, even though from the end of the sixteenth century most of the Marranos were of Portuguese rather than of Spanish extraction.[23] It is not that Portuguese was never heard in the synagogue, for sermons were sometimes delivered in that language. But where prayer was not in Hebrew, it was in Spanish, which was considered equally acceptable. In a responsum of Samuel Aboab, who had been asked by a group of "vernacular-speaking Jews" (*Yehudim lo'aziim*), apparently former Marranos, whether they may pray entirely in the vernacular (*lo'azit*), the answer given is that it is perfectly acceptable. The reference is undoubtedly to prayer in Spanish, and only one exception is specified. The priestly blessing (*birkat kohanim*) must be recited in Hebrew, for the biblical verse (Numbers 6:23) specifies: "*Thus* shall ye bless. . . ."[24]

In any case, Bible, liturgy, the *Targum* and *Pirke Abot*, were not in themselves sufficient to inculcate and sustain a Jewish way of life. There was still the all-important area of halakhah, of Jewish law and its observance. Halakhic works were therefore produced in Ladino, in Spanish and in Portuguese. These assumed two forms: practical halakhic manuals which summarized the laws a Jew must observe, and books of precepts arranged according to the 613 commandments, both positive and negative. The latter genre, a venerable one in Hebrew, was on the borderline between law and philosophy, because such works also included discussions for the reasons for the commandments (*ta'amey ha-mizvot*). The first such work to appear in Spanish was printed in Venice in 1627 and reprinted in Amsterdam in 1649. Its author was Rabbi Isaac Athias, and it bore the sonorous title: *Thesoro de preceptos, adonde se encierran las joyas de los seis cientos y treze preceptos que encomendó el Señor a su pueblo Israel; con su declaración, razón y dinim, conforme a la verdadera tradición, recibida de Mosé y enseñada por nuestros sabios de gloriosa memoria* ("A Treasury of Precepts, in which are enclosed the jewels of the 613 commandments which the Lord commanded to His people Israel, with their declaration, reason and the laws deriving from them, conforming to the true tradition received from Moses and taught by our sages of glorious memory").[25]

The most urgent need was served by the halakhic manuals, for these were concerned with daily praxis. Yet throughout the sixteenth century there had been a notable reticence to print them in the vernacular. This despite the fact that the very first work printed in Ladino of which I am aware was of a practical halakhic character, a little book giving instructions for the ritual slaughtering of animals entitled *Dinim de seḥitah y bedikah* (1510).[26]

Nothing further of a halakhic character appeared for almost the next six decades. But in 1568, only some three years after the first publication of Joseph Karo's great code of Jewish law, the *Shulḥan Arukh*, a Ladino abridgment, printed in rabbinic Hebrew characters without vowels, appeared in Salonika.[27]

In 1602 a new edition was published in Venice by Rabbi Isaac Gershon, entitled: *Sefer shulḥan ha-panim; Livro llamado en Ladino Meza de el Alma, porke es konpuesto de todos los dinim nesesarios para el hombre, tiresladado del livro del Gaon kebod morenu ha-rab Yosef Karo, zikhro le-ḥayye ha-'olam ha-ba*[28] ("The Book of the Table of the Shew-Bread; a book called in Ladino The Table of the Soul, because it is composed of all the laws necessary for a man, translated from the book of the eminent scholar our honored master Rabbi Joseph Karo, may his memory endure for the life of the world to come"). Despite the precedent of the Salonika edition this one carried an apologetic preface by the editor which is of considerable interest. This preface appeared in Hebrew, which indicates that it was intended, not for former Marranos, but for Isaac Gershon's fellow rabbis. He apologizes generally for printing such a work in the vernacular, and appeals to the example of Maimonides, who wrote in Arabic. Still, he warns sternly against any attempt to transcribe the book into Latin characters. He tells of someone who, several years before, had sent *dinim* printed in the vernacular and in Latin characters to Flanders, an act that had angered him greatly. But he himself recognizes that the English are reading the Talmud in Latin, and he alleges that all that rolls off the Italian presses is sent to Paris and Salamanca—codes, commentaries and Kabbalah. "If so," he writes, "now that these are being studied by the gentiles, it will surely not occur to anyone that we should not also translate them into a language that the members of our own people will understand."

He then discusses his method, claiming that he only included those laws that are really in need of being known, as well as the customs observed in Italy. Because he aimed at brevity many matters were deliberately excluded from the book, because of any of the following reasons:

a) If their prohibition is universally known and recognized, so that no further statement was deemed necessary.
b) Matters concerning which we know that they (i.e. former Marranos) do not proceed first without asking a rabbi.
c) Things that are done in the synagogue, and that can therefore be seen directly and emulated.
d) "A few things against which the idolaters respond. These are

omitted so that, God forbid, the Marranos should not come to ridicule them."[29]

e) Where there is a dispute, and Karo adopted the stringent position, that is not recorded, so that Marranos will not say—"How is it that it is forbidden, and yet everyone does it?"

The introduction to the book itself, addressed directly to the returning Marrano, is in Ladino. He wrote the book, Gershon states, *palavra por palavra en breve y en Ladino de letra entera kon puntos, para ke todos se puedan aprovezhar de el, afilu el ke no conose mas ke las letras y los puntos* ("word for word, in brief, and in a Ladino of full [i.e. square Hebrew] letters with vowel-points, so that all can make use of it, even he who knows no more than the letters and the vowels").

He admonishes his potential audience to read a chapter and practice it right away. *Y no basta leerlo, sino de usar para ponerlo luego en obra* ("and it is not enough to read it, but it is to be used in order to put it immediately into action").

One should study the book every day, or at least on the Sabbath—*ke no ay kosa ke les estorbe* ("when there is nothing to hinder you").

The husband should teach his wife—*lo ke toca para su muzher, tanto en los dinim de la nidah, y de la ḥalah y candela de Shabbat, como en los dinim de kashrut* ("that which concerns his wife, whether in the laws of menstrual purity, the Sabbath bread and candle, or in the dietary laws").

The daughter should be taught to read (apparently the wife was considered either too old or too busy to learn).

And the end result of all this will be: *Y no havra zhudeo ke sea 'am ha-'areẓ* ("and there will be no Jew who will be an ignoramus").

There is no question but that this was the way many former Marranos learned the rudiments of Jewish law. The book apparently proved so useful that only seven years later yet another edition appeared.[30] This time, despite Isaac Gershon's injunction, it was transcribed by Moses Altaras into Latin characters, *por ver que ay muchos que no saben leer otra letra que la presente* ("seeing that there are many who do not know how to read any other letter than the present one"). Thus, from 1568 to 1609 we have a pedagogic progression of three editions in which the abridgment of Karo's *Shulḥan Arukh* was printed first in Ladino with unvocalized rabbinic characters, then in Ladino with vocalized square Hebrew characters and finally in ordinary Castilian with Latin characters.

IV

Thereafter we encounter no more hesitations. Indeed, the seventeenth century proved to be the heyday for such translations, and for Ibero-Jewish vernacular literature generally. To appreciate some of what was achieved, let us glance at what a seventeenth-century library for Iberian vernaculars could have contained:

1. For Bible—in addition to the text—paraphrases in prose and poetry and commentaries synthesizing the views of medieval Jewish exegetes.[31]

2. At least five Hebrew grammars in Spanish or Portuguese.[32]

3. No less than ten Spanish or Ladino "books of precepts" and halakhic manuals, beside those I have mentioned, of which one is in Portuguese by Manasseh ben Israel (*Thesouro dos preceptos*, Amsterdam, 1645).

4. Of classical and medieval rabbinic literature—two editions of the Mishnah in Spanish (Venice, 1606, and Amsterdam, 1663); Isaac Aboab's *Menorat Ha-Ma'or* (Spanish: *Almenara de la luz*, Livorno, 1656); and individual sections of Maimonides' *Mishneh Torah*, including the particularly relevant laws of repentance (*Tratado de la tesubah o contrición*, Amsterdam, 1613).

5. In the realm of Jewish history and messianism: Samuel Usque's *Consolaçam as tribulaçoens de Israel* ("Consolation for the Tribulations of Israel"), Ferrara, 1553; Amsterdam, late 16th or early 17th century. Manasseh ben Israel's *Esperança de Israel* ("The Hope of Israel"), Amsterdam, 1650. Josephus Flavius' "Against Apion," translated into Spanish as *Respuesta de Josepho contra Apion Alexandrino*, Amsterdam, 1687. Solomon ibn Verga's *Shebet Yehudah* ("The Scepter of Judah"), translated into Spanish as *La vara de Juda*, Amsterdam, 1640.

6. Ethics, mysticism, philosophy: Elijah de Vidas' *Reshit ḥokhmah*, abridged and translated as *Tratado del temor divino* ("Treatise on the fear of God"), Amsterdam, 1633. Selections from Isaiah Hurwitz's *Sheney luḥot ha-berit* in Portuguese, Amsterdam, 1666. Judah Halevi's *Kuzari*, translated into Spanish by Jacob Abendana, Amsterdam, 1663. Bahya ibn Pakuda's *Ḥobot ha-lebabot* ("The Duties of the Heart"), in Ladino, Constantinople, 1569; in Spanish, Amsterdam, 1610; in Portuguese, Amsterdam 1670.[33]

These are only some of the highlights. Even more impressive than the fact of translation is the manner in which both translators and original writers conveyed not only the content but the textures of Jewish sources. Even when the language was not Ladino, but Castilian or Portuguese, the forms of Hebrew names were retained, in prayerbooks God was addressed as *Adonay*, and everywhere key words like *miẓvah*, *din*, *minyan*, etc., tend to appear as such, without being translated at all.[34]

Conversely, Iberian idioms and forms often facilitated the comprehension and absorption of Jewish materials. The works that were published for the use of former Marranos took full cognizance of their background and mentality, and attempted to express Jewish concepts and values in ways that would be congenial to them. A striking example of such adaptation is the *Fundamento sólido* ("The Solid Foundation") by Yehuda Leon Pérez.[35] It is written in the form of a catechism, with questions and answers on the foundations of the Jewish faith *para los niños y para los ignorantes* ("for children and for the ignorant"). Thus it is a perfect instance of the appropriation of a Catholic form, familiar to anyone who had been raised in Spain or Portugal, but now filled entirely with Jewish content.

V

In sum, we have seen that there were numerous bridges to help the former Marrano effect his transition to normative Judaism. If, nevertheless, some came into conflict with the community, it was due to any number of factors that had little or nothing to do with mere lack of knowledge. For ignorance there were always available remedies, so long as there was a desire to learn. The success of the transition largely depended, not upon the Jewish knowledge brought out of the Iberian Peninsula by those who fled, but upon their mental attitudes. The Marrano while still in Spain or Portugal had perforce to be his own "rabbi" in Jewish matters, and some, having rejected the authority of the Church, now found it equally difficult to accept the authority of the Synagogue. Others, in their repudiation of Christianity, had recoiled into a relativism that made it difficult for them to accept the absolute claims of any revealed religion, Judaism included. It is among such factors that we should seek the roots of subsequent maladjustment. For the Marrano skeptic and heretics, however, there was yet another large literature in the Iberian vernaculars—that of polemic and apologetics. But that is easily a subject for a separate lecture. I have not been concerned here with those Marrano emigrants who failed to adjust to Jewish life, only with those who succeeded.

Today the books that helped them bring to fruition that which had been planted in their souls in Spain and Portugal lie unread on the dusty shelves of great libraries. By the end of the eighteenth century their task had been achieved.

But perhaps we can try to imagine, by an act of historical empathy, the feelings of a father in Amsterdam several centuries ago, who, having himself grown up a crypto-Jew in the Iberian Peninsula, now held the *Fundamento sólido* before him and asked his son:

—*Quien eres tú, mi hijo?*
(Who are you, my son?)

And the son replied:

—*Yo soy Hebreo, y a Adonay Dios de los cielos y la tierra sólo adoro.*
(I am a Jew, and I worship only the Lord God of the heavens and the earth.)

—*Dime: qual es la principal razón de seres judío?*
(Tell me: what is the principal reason that you are a Jew?)

—*Soy judío por la gracia de Dios, y por ser de la descendencia de los Santos Padres amados de Dios, haviendo escogido a sus descendientes para en ellos establecer su pueblo. "Ve-taḥat ki 'ahab 'et 'abotekha"—por aver amado a tus padres. Y el Real Psalmista dize: "Ki Ya'akob baḥar lo Yah, Yisrael li-segulato"—que a Yacob escogió para si Yah, Israel por su tesoro. . . .*

(I am a Jew by the grace of God, and by being the progeny of the holy patriarchs beloved of God, having chosen their descendants in order to establish His people through them. *And because He loved your fathers* [Deut. 4:37]. And the royal Psalmist says: *For God chose Jacob unto Himself, and Israel for His treasure* [Psalm 135:4].)

NOTES
1. I. S. Révah, "Autobiographie d'un Marrane: édition partielle d'un manuscript de João (Moseh) Pinto Delgado," *Revue des études juives*, CXIX (1961), 93.

2. I. S. Révah, "Les Marranes," *Revue des études juives*, CVIII (1959-60), 55.

3. Jacob Sasportas *'Ohel Ya'akob* (Amsterdam, 1737). no. 3.

4. Isaac Cardoso, *Las excelencias de los Hebreos* (Amsterdam, 1679), p. 48, paraphrasing Maimonides, *Guide for the Perplexed*, III, xlix.

5. *El libro de los acuerdos*, ed. L. D. Barnett (Oxford, 1931), p. 23.

6. See the responsa of Rafael Meldola, *Mayim rabbim* (Amsterdam, 1737), II, nos. 51–53.

7. See Y. H. Yerushalmi, *From Spanish Court to Italian Ghetto* (New York–London, 1971), p. 380.

8. Samuel Aboab, *Sefer ha-zikhronot* (n.p., n.d.; ca. 1650), fol. 75. For details see Yerushalmi, *From Spanish Court*, p. 200.

9. Madrid: Archivo Histórico Nacional, Inquisición de Toledo, Judaizantes, Leg. 165, no. 12 (562), fols. 61r–62v. I plan to publish a full study of this case in the near future.

10. Sometimes both the Christian and the Jewish names continued to be used, depending on the circumstances. Merchants and travelers, for example, often found it safer. On occasion it may have been commercially advantageous. In the *Livornina*, the charter of privileges granted in 1593 by Ferdinand, Grand Duke of Tuscany, in his successful effort to attract Jews (among them former Marranos) to settle and trade in his new free port of Livorno, the sixth clause states: "We grant you the right to traffic and trade in all of the cities, territories, fairs, markets, villages, and other places of our states, and to set sail for the Levant, the West, Barbary, Alexandria and elsewhere, *under your own names or under a Christian name. . . .*" (My thanks to Prof. Bernard Dov Cooperman of Harvard for making his translation of the document available to me.)

11. For an example of this in the case of the Aboab family, see *From Spanish Court*, p. 56, n. 17.

12. Joseph Ibn Leb, *She'elot u-teshubot* (Amsterdam, 1762), III, no. 87.

13. See S. Assaf, "Anusey Sefarad u-Portugal be-sifrut ha-teshubot," in his *Be-'oholey Ya'akob: Perakim mi-ḥayyey ha-tarbut shel ha-Yehudim bi-yemey ha-beinayim* (Jerusalem, 1943), p. 163.

14. The question of the need for an ordained rabbinic tribunal to impose biblical stripes upon former Marranos was cited as a major issue in the controversy over the revival of ordination that erupted in Palestine in 1538 between Jacob Berab of Safed and Levi ben Habib of Jerusalem. See Assaf, op. cit., p. 179.

15. See *From Spanish Court*, p. 181.

16. Assaf, op. cit., p. 157.

17. See *From Spanish Court*, pp. 276–99, my study of "Professing Jews in Post-Expulsion Spain and Portugal," *Salo W. Baron Jubilee Volume* (New York, 1974), II, 1023–1058, and my Hebrew lecture on "Conversos returning to Judaism in the seventeenth century: Their Jewish Knowledge and Psychological Readiness," *Proceedings of the Fifth World Congress of Jewish Studies* (1969), vol. II (Jerusalem, 1972), Hebrew section, pp. 201–209.

18. See the excerpts from Aboab's *Sefer ha-zikhronot* in *From Spanish Court*, p. 199.

19. A comprehensive and analytic bibliography of Jewish works in Spanish, Portuguese and Ladino, is still a desideratum. For the time being Kayserling's pioneering attempt of 1890 is still indispensible. See: Meyer Kayserling, *Biblioteca Española-Portugueza-Judaica and other studies in Ibero-Jewish bibliography by the author and by J. S. da Silva Rosa*, selected with a prolegomenon by Y. H. Yerushalmi (New York, 1971). Abbreviated henceforth as BEPJ, with the pagination of the 1890 edition in brackets [i.e., parentheses, eds.].

20. For such editions consult BEPJ, pp. 50–53 (28–31). Cf. T. H. Darlow and H. F. Moule, *Historical Catalogue of the Printed Editions of Holy Scripture in the Library of the British and Foreign Bible Society* (London, 1903; reprinted New York, 1963), vol. II, pt. 3, s.v. "Spanish," passim.

21. A list of printed prayerbooks in Spanish, quite incomplete, is given by Kayserling in BEPJ, pp. 81–86 (59–64), s.v. "Liturgie."

22. BEPJ, pp. 93 f. (71 f.), s.v. "Misnajoth."

23. A sixteenth-century manuscript of Jewish prayers in Portuguese, possibly unique, is in the collection of Alfonso Cassuto in Lisbon. The Portuguese version of the piyyut *'Et sha'arey raẓon* from this manuscript has been studied by H. P. Salomon, "The Last Trial in Portuguese," *Studi sull'ebraismo italiano in memoria di Cecil Roth* (Rome, 1974), pp. 161–183.

24. Samuel Aboab, *Debar Shemuel* (Venice, 1702), no. 321.

25. BEPJ, pp. 36 f. (14 f.), s.v. "Athias (Atias), Yshac."

26. BEPJ, p. 57 (35).

27. BEPJ, pp. 56 (34) and 89 (67).

28. There is as yet no satisfactory scheme for transliterating Ladino. Here, as in the Ladino citations to follow, my transliteration of the Hebrew characters is generally based (except where it would prove misleading) on the system employed by Henry V. Besso in his bibliography of *Ladino Books in the Library of Congress* (Washington, D.C., 1963).

29. Gershon does not explicate this pedagogically intriguing but cryptic statement. "Idolaters" was a standard epithet for Catholics among Marranos. It would be interesting to know precisely which customs (obviously of a non-obligatory nature) were glossed over in order to avoid "ridicule."

30. BEPJ, p. 33 (11). Cf. M. B. Amzalak, *A tradução espanhola do livro de Joseph Caro . . . feita por Mosé Altaras sob a denominação de 'Libro de mantenimiento de la alma'* (Lisbon, 1927).

31. For examples of these genres see Kayserling's introduction to BEPJ, pp. xiv f.

32. Ibid., p. xv.

33. BEPJ, p. 37 (15), s.v. "Bachya"; p. 106 (84), s.v. "Pardo."

34. One small and random example will suffice. In Manasseh ben Israel's *Thesouro dos preceptos* we read: "E assi aquelle que está em terra donde ay Esnoga, e não entra *has ve salom* nella, se chama mão vezinho" ("and so he who is in a place where there is a synagogue and does not enter it, *God forbid*, is called a bad neighbor"). The phrase "God forbid" has been retained in Hebrew in the midst of the Portuguese sentence.

35. *Fundamento solido; baza y thypo de la Sacro Sancta y divina Ley, siendo doctrina legal y moral para instruir, enseñar, plantar, y raigar sus fundamentos, imprimiendolos en los coraçones del pueblo escogido de Dios, a fin de que mamen la leche de la doctrina de nuestros Sanctos Padres* (Amsterdam, 1729).

9 : ASSIMILATION AND RACIAL ANTI-SEMITISM
THE IBERIAN AND THE GERMAN MODELS

Leo Baeck Memorial Lecture, New York, 1982.

Named for the German rabbi and scholar, the Leo Baeck Institute, based in New York, is an organization devoted to the study of German-speaking Jewry. This article originated as the Leo Baeck Memorial Lecture that Yerushalmi delivered in 1982. In it, Yerushalmi drew a series of intriguing historical parallels between the experience of people of Jewish ancestry in medieval Spain and in modern Germany. Whereas chapter 8—"The Re-education of Marranos in the Seventeenth Century"—focused on the experience of the descendants of converts as they returned to Judaism, this lecture dealt with the experience of those converts who attempted to integrate fully into Christian society and religion.

Throughout the lecture, Yerushalmi acknowledged the somewhat unorthodox endeavor of comparing historical periods that are as different as "apples and pears." He maintained, however, that just as apples and pears are both fruits, so the experiences of those who converted away from Judaism in medieval Spain and in modern Germany bear "phenomenological affinities" worth exploring. In particular, he was interested in the way in which each society, or elements within each, ascribed racial characteristics to groups of former Jews, asserting that they possessed biological qualities as Jews that lingered for generations after their abandonment of Judaism.

Given that the address was the Leo Baeck Memorial Lecture, and thus his audience was more familiar with modern Germany than with medieval Spain, Yerushalmi devoted the bulk of his remarks to a discussion of the latter. Around half of Iberian Jews converted to Christianity, mostly under extreme duress, during the course of the fifteenth century. When many of the *conversos* took advantage of the social mobility that came with their new religious identities, "the traditional mistrust of the Jew as outsider now gave way to an even more alarming fear of the Converso as insider." A backlash took place, which began with a series of popular riots from the middle of the fifteenth century. It spread to formal regulations that banned "New Christians" from many roles of authority and other socially significant positions. Because the people against whom these regulations were aimed were formally Christian by faith, they had to be differentiated by their ancestry. "Not religion but blood was their determining factor." Thus, the regulations were known as *estatutos de limpieza de sangre* (statutes of purity of blood). Initially resisted in some quarters, they were eventually embraced by the crown and the papacy in the mid-sixteenth century and, in some places, remained in force well into the modern period. The racial underpinnings of the attitude to "New Christians" embodied in these statutes (and in other sources that Yerushalmi discussed) came "perilously close" to the modern notion of race that anchored Nazism.

Yerushalmi used this comparison to interrogate a common historiographical distinction between medieval antisemitism, motivated by theology, and modern antisemitism, motivated by new sciences such as biology. In fact, one of the proponents of this distinction, the Israeli historian Uriel Tal, had delivered a lecture on that very topic at the Leo Baeck Memorial Lecture eleven years previously, entitled "Religious and Anti-Religious Roots of Modern Anti-Semitism." Yerushalmi's analysis indicated, however, that "the assumption of a total absence of racism in pre-modern anti-Semitism may yet have been too glib and facile." Racial antisemitism did not mark a complete break with premodern attitudes to Jews, and "secularism did not create modern racial anti-Semitism." Rather, racial antisemitism, based on the perceived "essential immutability" of Jewish biological characteristics, arose out of circumstances in which Jewish assimilation was possible or mandated, including in premodern times. This recognition led Yerushalmi to identify "an imminent dialectic in the process of Jewish assimilation into societies constrained by new circumstances to accept them, but conditioned by deeply ingrained attitudes to reject them."

Yerushalmi ended the lecture with a brief introduction to a related area of inquiry. He noted that in both medieval Spain and modern Germany, people of Jewish descent who had left their faith were often overrepresented in cultural fields that exhibited a "special creativity." He suggested that this was to be explained by the fact that assimilated Jews suffered "the anxiety of hovering between acceptance and rejection, integration and marginality" and "found release for their inner tensions and anxieties along paths that were somehow off the beaten track." Yerushalmi did not have the opportunity to expand on these comments in his lecture, but they contain the seeds of his later work on Sigmund Freud. Freud, after all, was the classic modern assimilated Jew situated on the border of acceptance and rejection, and he occupied Yerushalmi's scholarly attention for much of the 1980s.

The title of this lecture may have already forewarned you that I am about to make a foray into comparative history, in this instance—between certain tragic aspects of Jewish fate in pre-modern Spain and Portugal on the one hand, and in modern Germany on the other. I am quite aware that this can be a perilous venture since, initially at least, it may seem to violate the sacred injunction not to compare "apples and pears." That timid and intimidating cliché, however, has always puzzled me, for of course apples and pears can most certainly be compared. Despite their differences they are, after all, both edible fruits that grow on trees and have cores and seeds within, and it is precisely the combination of difference and similarity that makes the comparison viable and possibly even instructive. At any rate, this pomological digression is only meant to ease us gently toward our theme. Should I require a closer warrant to bring Spanish perspectives to a lecture sponsored by an institute devoted to the study of German Jewry, I shall simply invoke the authority of Heinrich Heine who, albeit instinctively and poetically, already sensed certain more than vague affinities. One well-known poem is worth recalling. In the mordantly ironic *Donna Clara*, that bigoted beauty is in the process of being seduced by a Spanish knight she has just met, and she swears she loves him by the Savior "whom the God-damned Jews once wickedly and maliciously murdered." When he asks her if she has not sworn falsely she replies:

Falsch ist nicht in mir, Geliebter,	There is nothing false in me, beloved,
Wie in meiner Brust kein Tropfen	Just as in my breast there's
Blut ist von dem Blut der Mohren	Not the slightest drop of blood
Und des schmutzgen Judenvolkes.	of Moors and the filthy Jewish people.

And when, just before they part, she begs him finally to reveal his name to her, the knight replies with this exquisite coup de grâce:

Ich Sennora, Eur Geliebter	I, Senora, your beloved,
Bin der Sohn des vielbelobten	Am the son of the much-praised,
Grossen, schriftgelehrten Rabbi	Great and learned Rabbi,
Israel von Saragossa.	Israel of Saragossa.

I need hardly remind this audience that the knight in the poem is but a mask for Heine himself, a German-Jewish convert in an age of conversions and other attempts at radical Jewish assimilation. The knight, be it noted, is not to be understood as a secret Jew, even though he is obviously aware of who his Jewish father was. The same is true of Heine's other Spanish knight, the so-called "Don Isaac Abravanel" in *The Rabbi of Bacherach* ("I myself came from the House of Israel; my grandfather was a Jew, perhaps my father even . . ."), whose vestigial Judaism amounts to a fondness for Jewish carp and other Sabbath delicacies ("I love your cooking much better than your faith"). What is interesting is the fact that Heine should sense in what had happened in Spain long ago a viable paradigm for his own existential situation and for that of others like him. Clearly, it is no longer Judaism that is at issue here, but the consequences of Jewish descent for those who are really no longer Jews and do not regard themselves as such. The humor and irony are a thin surface under which lurk darkness and pathos. And in the words given to Donna Clara (*kein Tropfen Blut*) there is even a passing but specific allusion to that Spanish preoccupation with "purity of blood" of which I shall yet have much to say.

To raise all the legitimate methodological questions and qualifications that my theme requires would, I fear, leave no room for the theme itself. Suffice it for me to state that in juxtaposing two obviously different historical settings I do not intend the analogies and parallels that may emerge to be considered as equations. Nor am I suggesting any historical continuity between the two. I merely propose that there are some phenomenological affinities between—the terms are anachronistic but unavoidable—assimilation and anti-Semitism in the Iberian Peninsula of the fifteenth to the eighteenth centuries, and in Germany of the nineteenth and twentieth; that such affinities are too striking to be ignored; and that the earlier phenomena can, in some ways, illumine the latter. But here I am already running ahead of myself. We have first to define the problem.[1]

I

It is generally recognized today that anti-Semitism is not a monolith, that its historical manifestations differ from one period to another, that its varieties require special adjectives ("religious," "secular," "social," "political," "racial," are some of the most common), and that even these can figure in various combinations and permutations. Viewed chronologically, there is at least a working agreement on an overall tripartite periodization of anti-Semitism: "Ancient-Pagan"; "Medieval-Christian"; and, finally, "Modern-Secular." It is natural, of course, that the roots of modern anti-Semitism should continue to generate the most intense debate, with widely diverging opinions as to its elements of novelty or continuity, and the relative importance of each. Such complex discussions need not be surveyed here. Of moment for us is the fact that, whatever their disagreements on other matters, there seems to be a virtual consensus among scholars that racial anti-Semitism is a peculiarly modern and secular, rather than medieval, phenomenon. Indeed, even those who insist most emphatically upon the Christian "teaching of contempt," not only as the decisive preparation for modern anti-Semitism, but as an ongoing and powerful stream within it, seem to accept the axiom that racial anti-Semitism per se is a uniquely modern development not to be found in medieval Christendom. Such a scheme seems at first glance to be entirely plausible. Even the concept of "race" as we know it did not exist in the Middle Ages, or so we are told. True, the more vulgar forms of medieval anti-Semitism did express themselves more than occasionally in sheer physical terms—the notion of a distinct Jewish odor (*foetor Judaicus*; a slur that is even older than Christianity),[2] or the so-called "Curse of the Twelve Tribes" which posited that, in perpetual punishment for the Crucifixion, the Jewish descendants of each of the tribes of ancient Israel are born with physical defects so loathsome that I shall relegate them to a footnote when the lecture is printed rather than enumerate them here.[3] But even these and similar manifestations do not really constitute racial thinking, for the same sources inform us that immediately after a Jew accepts baptism any such physical defect miraculously disappears. Here, surely, is the litmus test for non-racial thinking. Once baptized, a Jew is on a par with all other Christians. In other words, within the medieval frame of reference conversion is the portal to total assimilation into Christian society, if not for the actual convert, then at least for his descendants.[4]

And yet we seem to find disquieting exceptions to this reassuring norm. In the year 613 the king of the Visigoths ordered the forced conversion of all the Jews living at the time in a Spain that was not yet "Spanish" but from then until the Muslim conquest of 711 neither the converts nor their progeny disappeared as a distinct entity. On the contrary, to the very end of the Visigothic state, kings and church councils continued to enact special laws aimed at the descendants of the original converts, in a mounting crescendo of hysteria against "Jews baptized and unbaptized."[5] In 1130, in the midst of a deep split within the papal curia, the majority elected Cardinal Petrus Pierleone as Pope Anacletus II, while the minority elected an anti-pope, Innocent II. In the controversy that erupted across Europe during the next decade there were a number of large issues involved, but it is significant that the enemies of Anacletus laid repeated stress on his Jewish origins (he was the great-grandson of a Roman Jewish convert in the first half of the eleventh century). No less a figure than St. Bernard of Clairvaux regarded the descendant of a Jew on the papal throne as an affront to Christ. One writer depicted Anacletus physically as "dark and pale, more like a Jew or an Arab than a Christian"; with a deformed body and "the bad odor of his ancestor who was a wicked money-lender."[6] Again, in 1290 the Jews of Southern Italy were converted by force. Nevertheless, for the next two centuries the descendants of these Jews were still known as such and were referred to generically in official documents as *Neofiti* (neophytes) or *Mercanti* (merchants).[7]

All this would seem to indicate that not all of medieval anti-Judaism was merely theological or religious. Beyond that, however, the examples I have given are of limited value. We still know all too little about the realities of the converts' lives in Visigothic Spain; much of what occurred in Southern Italy after 1290 remains obscure; and the papacy, after all, may be considered too special a case to yield broad conclusions.

II

Such ambiguities recede when we turn to Spain and Portugal in the late Middle Ages. There Jewish conversion to Christianity took place on a scale unprecedented in earlier periods and unequaled in the rest of Europe, and it is from there that we possess a vast array of documentary and literary sources that bring the question of pre-modern Jewish assimilation and racial anti-Semitism into the sharpest focus.[8]

The mass conversions in the Iberian Peninsula occurred in four main stages. In 1391 anti-Jewish pogroms spread throughout Spain and into the Balearic Islands, in the course of which thousands of Jews accepted baptism rather than be slaughtered. Only two decades later, in 1413–14, the last great public disputation of the Middle Ages between Jews and Christians was held at Tortosa in Aragon. Barely recovered from the havoc and demoralization of the pogroms, to many Spanish Jews it now seemed as though Judaism had been defeated decisively. A new wave of conversions ensued, with thousands more rushing voluntarily to the baptismal fonts. Throughout the fifteenth century Spanish Jewry was bifurcated, with Jews and converts (*conversos*) coexisting side by side. Finally, in 1492 Ferdinand and Isabella gave the remaining Jews the ultimate alternative of conversion or expulsion. Many remained constant and chose the hard road of exile. Others, however, could not or would not leave Spain, and once again the convert ranks were swelled. The epilogue took place in Portugal. In 1497 the Portuguese king, Manuel, decreed the forced conversion of all Jews in the country, including those Jewish refugees who had crossed the border from Spain five years before.

We shall probably never know how many Spanish Jews were converted to Christianity between 1391 and 1492. There are indications that fifty percent may be a conservative estimate, and we must remember that we are speaking of what had been the largest Jewry in medieval Europe. Whatever one's conjecture in absolute figures, it is clear that within a relatively short span of time a large mass of Jews had entered, through conversion, into Spanish Christian society. To be sure, there were many who remained Jews at heart and lived the dual life of Marranos, secret Jews in one way or another. Many others, however, whether out of initial conviction or opportunism, became sincere Catholics, or at least rejected Judaism completely in favor of a functional adherence to the new faith. Modern Jewish scholarship has been preoccupied with the subsequent history of the crypto-Jews and has left it largely to Hispanists to explore that of the genuine converts. Our theme requires that we be concerned primarily with the latter.

In theory, nothing should have prevented the total absorption of the true converts, or at least their descendants, into Spanish society, and, in fact, during the first half-century following the conversions of 1391 the process of integration seemed well under way. Spanish Jews had traditionally performed a host of important economic and managerial functions as financial administrators, tax-farmers, and advisors to the royal courts of Castile and Aragon. Conversos continued and expanded these roles. But now, with the removal of the former religious bars to their further advancement, the Conversos expanded into new areas in which they displayed an extraordinary "upward mobility."[9] Some became large-scale entrepreneurs, others entered the universities and the learned professions, of which hitherto only medicine had been open to Jews. In various cities and towns Conversos gained control of the municipal councils.[10] Many flocked to important careers within the Church. We have only to cite the famous case of Pablo de Santa Maria, the former Rabbi Solomon Halevi, who converted voluntarily in 1390 and subsequently became Bishop of Burgos. His son, Alonso de Cartagena, who was baptized with him as a child, succeeded him in that high office and represented Spain at the Council of Basel in 1434.[11] The powerful monastic order of the Jeronymites was filled with converts,[12] as were some of the most important Cathedral chapters. Daughters of wealthy Conversos married with apparent ease into noble families, rejuvenating tired blood-lines and replenishing empty coffers. Some Conversos were themselves occasionally granted patents of nobility.[13] There seemed to be no further obstacle to the assimilation of those who, like Heine's knight, retained at most certain culinary predilections ("they never lost their Jewish tastes in eating," the chronicler Andres Bernaldez observed sarcastically).[14]

Yet even as the converts and their children were energetically, and even aggressively, fulfilling new ambitions, in certain sectors of the old Hispano-Christian society a profound anti-Converso resentment was gathering force, and by the mid-fifteenth century it erupted into the open. This "backlash" first arose among the urban masses, who began to perceive the entire Converso class as rich and powerful usurpers of positions and privileges to which they themselves aspired, parvenus well on their way to dominating, not only the organs of municipal government, but perhaps the country as a whole. It did not matter that a good many Conversos were actually quite poor, or engaged in humble occupations; the swift ascent of so many others in so many fields was what caught the eye. This, it was felt, could only be explained on the assumption that, although baptized, the Conversos had retained the proverbially "Jewish" traits of cunning, sharpness, and a boundless lust for money and power defying all moral scruples.

III

Thus a mounting tension within Spanish society rapidly approached a point of genuine paradox. Throughout the Middle Ages the whole of Christian Europe had perceived its Jewish problem essentially in one dimension—as one of conversion.[15] The Jews were a group apart because they stubbornly refused to accept the regnant Christian truth. Should the Jews be converted, they would disappear as a distinct entity, and the problem, by definition, would cease to be. Of all countries, Spain had now come closest to making this pan-European dream a reality. Ironically, only then did a growing number of Spaniards begin to feel, with a sense of shock, that far from having resolved the problem, the mass conversions of Jews had only exacerbated it. So long as the Jews had remained within their ancestral religion they could also be contained within well-defined limits through restrictive laws. Now, overnight as it were, the entire corpus of anti-Jewish legislation was no longer applicable to the huge Converso group. Technically and legally Christians, they could do as they pleased, and for many Spaniards that was intolerable. A critical juncture had been reached. The traditional mistrust of the Jew as outsider now gave way to an even more alarming fear of the Converso as insider.

Two texts, one from the mid-fifteenth century, the other from the mid-sixteenth, vividly conjure up the specter of subversion from within. The first is an anonymous satire against the Conversos (here called *Marranos*—a generic epithet that at first simply meant "pigs"), in the form of a royal privilege allegedly granted by King Juan II of Castile to a Christian nobleman also named Juan, descended from "pure Old Christians" (*cristianos viejos lindos*). At Juan's own request, the king grants him formal permission to live the life of a "Marrano," and to employ all their "subtleties, evils, deceits and flatteries" to his advantage. Like them, he is now permitted to acquire through duplicity such lucrative royal appointments as mayor (*alcalde*), magistrate, and public notary, enjoying the municipal rents; to enter the priesthood so that, listening to the confessions of Old Christians he can discover their secret derelictions and denounce them to the courts; to become an apothecary, physician, or surgeon, in order to kill Old Christians, marry their wives, and acquire their property and offices while besmirching their pure lineage; to bring to church, instead of breviaries, the account-books listing the rents and taxes farmed out to him, and to read these during the service while pretending to recite penitential psalms.[16] The second text—the so-called "Correspondence of the Jews of Spain and those of Constantinople"—reflects a similar mentality, but in addition it evokes the notion of an international Jewish conspiracy that almost anticipates the modern "Protocols of the Elders of Zion." Responding to a plea for advice from the alleged leader of the Spanish Jews, who are threatened by the king with conversion or destruction, the putative chief of the Jews of Constantinople responds that they should certainly become Christians and then wreak their revenge from within.[17]

Anti-Converso feeling first erupted into violence in riots that began in Toledo on January 27, 1449.[18] It was an uprising of the urban mass sparked by the sudden imposition of a huge tax on the city for the defense of Castile against a recent invasion by the Aragonese. The tax had been levied by the royal constable Don Alvaro de Luna, but the people suspected that its chief instigator was a Toledan Converso, Alonso Coca. The real roots of the outburst were obviously deeper. Further riots were to take place in Toledo in 1467, in Córdoba and other Andalusian cities in 1474, and, on a very large scale, in Lisbon in 1506.[19]

Still, occasional violence and pillage obviously did not strike at the heart of the problem. How, really, could the advance of the Conversos be checked, now that the old safeguards against Jews had been rendered irrelevant? The very proliferation of terms and epithets applied in the fifteenth century to the converts and their offspring bears witness to the ambiguity of the situation and the elusiveness of the adversary—*converso*, *confeso*, *marrano*, *tornadizo* [turncoat], *cristiano nuevo* [New Christian] or perhaps, indeed, *alboraique* (after the steed of Muhammad, which was neither horse nor mule).[20] What was required was a new legal definition within which to curb the Conversos, and it was out of this need that the Spanish doctrine of *limpieza de sangre*—"purity of blood"—emerged and crystalized.

IV

Laws that came to be known as "Statutes of purity of blood" (*estatutos de limpieza de sangre*) were an attempt, faltering at first but ultimately successful, to bar Conversos from public offices, privileges and honors, now that the old laws that had been enacted against professing Jews were no longer applicable.[21] These new statutes therefore mark the ironic retaliation of Iberian society against the intrusion of the Jew by means of a conversion toward which that same society had labored so long and so assiduously.

If new barriers were to be raised, however, they could no longer be based upon a difference in religion which, formally at least, no longer existed. The only foundation remaining to justify special discriminatory legislation against the Converso and his descendants was necessarily a genetic one. Not religion but blood was to be the determining factor. Certainly there were secret Judaizers among the Conversos, and in order to discover and prosecute these heretics the Inquisition would be established in 1478. With a singular lack of foresight many Conversos seem even to have welcomed the idea of an Inquisition in the hope that, if the Judaizers could be weeded out, their own Catholic orthodoxy would no longer be impugned. It is therefore doubly significant that the statutes of purity of blood never made such distinctions. They were aimed, not at crypto-Jews, but at the entire Converso class. Anyone of known Jewish (or Moorish) ancestry, regardless of his personal Christian piety, would be subject to them automatically and perpetually.[22] Purity of blood came to overshadow purity of faith.

Despite its alarm over the Converso threat, Spain did not easily accept the statutes of *limpieza* in the initial phases. When the first statute, the *Sentencia-Estatuto* excluding all persons of Jewish extraction from municipal offices in Toledo, was adopted some four months after the riots on June 5, 1449, the subsequent outcry caused it to fall into temporary abeyance.[23] It was opposed by King Juan II of Castile, by Pope Nicolas V, and by prominent clergy and statesmen. For a religion that had come into the world proclaiming its indifference to the distinction between Jew and Greek—*non est distinctio Judaei et Graeci*—the theological objections were obvious.[24] Moreover, some authorities sensed immediately the potential dangers of such laws for a land in which Christian, Jewish, and Moorish blood had mingled for ages.[25] But although the controversy over *limpieza de sangre* was to continue for centuries in the Iberian Peninsula, the progress of the statutes was inexorable. The century after 1449 saw a gradual but definite spread of such statutes adopted sporadically by various corporate bodies and institutions.[26]

The most serious impetus came in 1547, when a new statute, instigated by the archbishop Juan Martinez Siliceo, excluded all descendants of Jews from positions in the Cathedral Chapter of Toledo. Again, as had happened a century before, there was considerable opposition. But this statute was destined to endure, and, because of the primacy of Toledo in Spanish Christendom, to serve as a model and sanction for later ones. In 1555 it was ratified by Pope Paul IV and a year later it was upheld by King Philip II, thus setting the final seal of papal and royal approval upon a practice that, while already rooted in many places, was now officially legitimized.[27] It is noteworthy that this occurred at a time when the last active vestiges of Spanish crypto-Judaism seemed to be disappearing, and the Catholic loyalties of most New Christians cannot have been in doubt. Yet from this point on *limpieza de sangre* rapidly became a requirement for entry into almost any important honor or office in Spain. As the network of statutes widened, it was hard to find a significant area of Spanish public life which did not require of the candidate elaborate "proofs of purity" (*pruebas de limpieza*), meticulously documented genealogies and testimonies of witnesses certifying him to be free of any trace of Jewish blood. From Spain the system passed over to Portugal. When Portuguese New Christians began to flow into Spain after 1580, they found the statutes rampant everywhere. By the seventeenth century the corporations with requirements of *limpieza* included the military orders; judicial tribunals, among them the Inquisition itself; cathedrals and chapters; the various monastic and religious orders; the powerful aristocratic colleges (*colegios mayores*) at the universities; certain entire provinces and towns which forbade New Christians to reside or marry in their midst; almost all public and municipal offices; brotherhoods and confraternities.

The statutes of purity of blood, and the mentality they represented, perpetuated the distinction between "New" and "Old" Christians for centuries. That the original converts of the fifteenth century should have been considered literally as *cristianos nuevos*—"New Christians"—was perhaps appropriate and logical; that their known descendants in the seventeenth and eighteenth centuries should still have had to bear that label might seem absurd, were its consequences not so far-reaching and dismal.[28] Though some were able to hide their ancestry, falsify documents, or buy their certifications of purity through outright bribery, most could not. Often a Spaniard or a Portuguese who was totally unaware of his Jewish origins would apply for an official post, only to discover in the course of the mandatory genealogical investigations that there were indeed some Jews on remote branches or even twigs of the family tree. As a result he suddenly found himself not only ineligible for the position but, in a real sense, declassed. For "New Christian" was both a legal category and a social stigma, in a society whose preoccupation with purity of blood and lineage had become a fixation.

Limpieza was to have profound repercussions upon Spanish and Portuguese history and culture, and was to shape important aspects of literature and the peculiarly Iberian sense of "honor." However, we cannot concern ourselves here with the general aspects of the problem. The question for us is whether or not, within the developments I have sketched, we have an example of racial anti-Semitism.

Stressing the social and religious origins of these phenomena, misled, perhaps, by the theological rhetoric and rationales with which apologists for the statutes invariably embellished their arguments, or simply caught up in the conventional dogma that racial concepts are solely a product of the nineteenth century, some modern scholars have denied the racial character of *limpieza* altogether.[29] Yet although we will certainly not find the distilled pseudo-scientific racial jargon of modern times in the Iberian Peninsula, the very fact that the consequences of Jewish ancestry, however remote, were considered by so many to be indelible, perpetual, and *unalterable*, is already sufficient to indicate the racist mentality at work. Indeed, it is worth noting that the Spanish word *raza* (race) was defined in the great Castilian dictionary of Sebastián de Covarrubias in 1611 by the following inverted but illuminating comparison: "*Raza*—the caste of pure-bred horses which are branded with an iron so that they may be recognized as such. *Raza* in [human] lineages is understood in a bad sense, such as having within oneself some of the lineage of Moors or Jews (*tener alguna raza de moros o judíos*)."[30] Other interesting terms and phrases crop up repeatedly in Spanish and Portuguese texts. Descendants of Jews are *maculados* ("tainted") because they have a "stain" (*mácula*) in their blood. They are "impure" (*impuros*). By the end of the sixteenth century it is customary, when candidates seek honors or offices, to search for *limpieza de sangre de tiempo inmemorial* ("purity of blood from time immemorial") and even an adverse rumor is enough to disqualify one.[31] In 1623 the Portuguese Vicente da Costa Mattos cries out: *Pouco sangue Iudeo he bastante a destruyr o mundo*—"A little Jewish blood is enough to destroy the world!"[32]—this, one hundred and twenty-six years after the original conversion of Portuguese Jewry.

Are these only rhetorical flourishes, is "blood" merely a loose metaphor intended to dramatize a suspicion that New Christians actually teach their children to Judaize in secret, or are they meant genetically and biologically? In a defense of the statutes of purity of blood published in 1637, Juan Escobar del Corro declares categorically that the foetus acquires the moral qualities of its parents *at the moment of conception*; therefore, if one member of a family sins, that proves that there is impure blood in the veins of all.[33] Other texts speak even more eloquently and explicitly. In his *Centinela contra judíos* ("Sentinel against the Jews") Fray Francisco de Torrejoncillo offers a definition of "Jews" in 1673 that must bring a slight chill to a reader of our own generation: "To be enemies of Christians, of Christ, and of his Divine Law, it is not necessary to be of a Jewish father and mother. One alone suffices. It does not matter if the father is not [Jewish]; it is enough if the mother is. And even if she is not entirely so, half is enough; and even if not that much, a quarter is sufficient, or even an eighth. And the Holy Inquisition has discovered in our times that up to a distance of twenty-one degrees [of consanguinity] they have been known to judaize. . . ."[34] But Fray Francisco has another point to underscore which renders the biological element even more transparent:

> In the palaces of the kings, and of many princes, the wet-nurses who
> are chosen to suckle their sons must be Old Christians [*cristianas
> viejas*] for it is not proper that the sons of princes should be suckled
> by Jewish vileness, because *that milk, being of infected persons* [*per-
> sonas infectas*] can only engender perverse inclinations. . . . In the city
> of Valladolid, about thirty years ago, they burned alive as a Judaizer
> Don Lope de Vera, a native of the town of San Clemente in La Man-

cha, who was verified to be of illustrious blood, but it was found that the nurse who had suckled him was of infected blood [*era de sangre infecta*; i.e. the nurse had been a New Christian].[35]

Should this not be sufficient, we may turn to the biography of the emperor Charles V by Fray Prudencio de Sandoval, who, in 1604, actually compares Jewishness to Negritude:

> I do not censure the Christian compassion which embraces all, for then I would be in mortal error, and I know that in the Divine presence there is no distinction between Gentile and Jew, because One alone is the Lord of all. Yet who can deny that in the descendants of the Jews there persists and endures the evil inclination of their ancient ingratitude and lack of understanding, just as in the Negroes [there persists] the inseparable quality of their blackness [*negrura*]? For if the latter should unite themselves a thousand times with white women, the children are born with the dark color of the father. Similarly, it is not enough for the Jew to be three parts aristocrat [*hidalgo*] or Old Christian, for one family-line alone [*sola una raza*] defiles and corrupts him. . . .[36]

If, admittedly, we have not quite arrived at the modern concept of race, I submit that we have come perilously close.

V

Germans did not learn about "purity of blood" from the Iberian precedent. *Limpieza de sangre* in Spain and Portugal, and racial anti-Semitism in modern Germany, were independent and indigenous developments, the latter oblivious of the former. For that very reason the similarities are all the more significant.

But let us proceed cautiously. It will not do simply to draw up a list in two parallel columns, one Hispano-Portuguese, the other German, and to record: Toledo riots of 1449 — "Hep-Hep" riots of 1819; exclusion of students from the *colegios mayores* — and from the nineteenth-century German student organizations (*Burschenschaften*);[37] the sixteenth-century *Libro verde de Aragón* or the *Tizón de la nobleza de España*, both of which listed the names of Spanish nobles with Jewish blood in their veins — and the *Semi-Gotha*, which did the same for the German nobility in 1912;[38] Torrejoncillo's fractional definition of Jews — and the Nuremberg Laws of 1935. Such tantalizing lists could easily be expanded, and some specific parallels would certainly be striking enough to merit a fuller exploration. In the end, however, they remain matters of detail that point to deeper structures and larger patterns.

We shall be hindered from perceiving these only if we become entangled in the obvious but, for our present purposes, not really decisive, differences between pre-modern conversion and modern assimilation and emancipation (the apples-and-pears syndrome again). In order to focus on the essential, I should stress once more that, prior to modern times, the only possible road to the removal of all Jewish legal disabilities and to total assimilation into the dominant non-Jewish society, was through religious conversion. From this perspective the conversion of masses of Spanish and Portuguese Jews between 1391 and 1497 may be regarded on one level as an emancipation through baptism. This seemingly paradoxical formulation should not shock you, for it is meant in a very specific sense and is not an endorsement of apostasy. Functionally, the Iberian conversions and modern emancipation both entailed the elimination of prior legal restrictions against the Jews and the prospect, initially at least, of their integration under new conditions into the life of the majority. Thus, at the very core, we are confronted with two parallel problems—the absorption of "New Christians" and "New Germans" into their respective host societies.

Despite the manifold differences between those societies, they share a common pattern with regard to the entry of the Jews into their midst: a period (in Germany several periods) of sufficient acceptance to facilitate a growing assimilation and a significant influx into important areas of economic and civic life; a rising resentment against that very intrusion, in the course of which there surfaces an open and volatile racial hatred; racial discrimination, at first without the official sanction of the state, but ultimately institutionalized in law.

The critical element is, of course, the emergence in both instances of a racial conception of the Jews. But our comparison will still remain little more than historical play unless we are prepared to press its implications. The Iberian experience should not be regarded merely as an exotic adumbration of the later development. It should shift our angle of vision and pose some new questions.

VI

Virtually all scholarly discussions of the rise of racial anti-Semitism in Germany begin within the context of the rise of organized political anti-

Semitism in the 1870's and especially in the 1880's.[39] The treatment is often more descriptive than analytic, concentrating repeatedly on such obvious apostles of anti-Jewish racism as Wilhelm Marr or Eugen Dühring. Attempts to probe the question of origins tend to invoke essentially external influences, whether individual (Gobineau, Renan), or cultural — the general racial currents in contemporary anthropology, biology and even linguistics, which, once absorbed, were applied to the Jews. More penetrating inquiry has made a significant distinction between "Christian" and "anti-Christian" anti-Semitism in late nineteenth-century Germany, with racial anti-Semitism placed squarely within the latter.[40] Most concur that racial anti-Semitism is a consequence of secularization, not in the sense of a secularized metamorphosis of an earlier religious anti-Semitism (that is granted, if at all, for certain other aspects), but as a secular rupture with the past. Whatever the point of departure, the racial component is widely regarded as quintessentially modern, a radical break with the medieval Christian conception of the Jews, its very antithesis.[41]

Precisely here, it seems to me, lies the value of the Iberian juxtaposition. Patently, none of the factors I have just enumerated had been operative in Spain and Portugal. In those profoundly Christian societies an avowed "anti-Christian anti-Semitism" was inconceivable, and, had a Marr or a Dühring arisen, he would have been burned at the stake. Secularism in the modern sense made no inroads until late in the eighteenth century, and even then it was limited to small circles of Francophiles. The nineteenth-century sciences and pseudo-sciences had not been born. Yet, even in the absence of all this, an anti-Semitism with distinctly racial overtones had developed throughout the Iberian Peninsula.

That this should have been so must surely suffice to shake at least some of the conventional wisdom concerning the development of racial anti-Semitism in modern Germany as well. It suggests, in the first place, that however important any of the aforementioned factors may have been, they may not have been decisive. Often lacking in the scholarly literature is a differentiation between causes and catalysts, and, above all, a sense of the dynamics in the process through which modern racial anti-Semitism evolved. By expanding our horizon from modern Germany to pre-modern Spain and Portugal we begin to detect an imminent dialectic in the process of Jewish assimilation into societies constrained by new circumstances to accept them, but conditioned by deeply ingrained attitudes to reject them. When, as happened in both cases, assimilation had become a sufficient reality (Catholic orthodoxy in the Iberian Peninsula;

acculturation and the erosion of Jewish religious identity in Germany) the old religious definition of Jewry became a palpable anachronism and yielded increasingly to a racial one.

Still, the very fact that such a transition could be made in both instances is not so easily explained. Whatever the felt necessity, what made such allegedly radical shifts in mentality possible for so many? Did believing Christians, as we have been led to suppose, somehow first become less Christian? Were racial anti-Semites in Germany necessarily anti-Christian? Or should we not perhaps begin to ask whether the shift was so radical after all? The Iberian case already indicates that the distinction between "Christian" and "anti-Christian," valid and fruitful for an understanding of two specific anti-Semitic trends during the Second Reich, may be too sharp and absolute to embrace the full historical reality of racial anti-Semitism. To ask whether the latter is a Christian or anti-Christian phenomenon, as though these were polar alternatives, may miss the historical point through a semantic evasion. It all depends upon what we mean by "Christian." If we have in mind the official teaching of the Church, the conclusion is obvious. But surely even the entire corpus of Christian dogma and theology does not express the full range of behavior, thought, and feeling of believing Christians, nor can it reveal the latitude of interpretation to which it is itself potentially susceptible. The statutes of "purity of blood" were opposed by some Spanish and Portuguese churchmen on the grounds that they were, in effect, anti-Christian, but they were supported by many others who felt no contradiction whatever. Indeed, the statutes were even ratified by several sixteenth-century popes.[42] In nineteenth-century Germany such racial anti-Semites as Otto Glagau, Franz Perrot, and Rudolph Meyer, were by no means anti-Christian, to say nothing of those pretty bourgeois, urban workers and peasants, who listened as avidly to racial demagogues as to their Christian pastors, and who, unlike the intellectuals, were not liable to lose much sleep over problems of consistency.

"Christian" and "anti-Christian" must finally lead us back to the related question of "medieval" and "modern." The Iberian example is sufficient to indicate that the notion that racial anti-Semitism represents, in and of itself, a total break with all past forms of anti-Jewish hatred, must be tempered, at the very least. Yet it will not suffice merely to concede that Spain and Portugal were the exceptions and to let it go at that, as though out of the whole of medieval Christendom only the Spaniards and Portuguese were somehow prone toward racialism.

In a passing footnote to his magisterial study of Bismarck's Jewish banker, Gerson Bleichröder, Fritz Stern makes this important and challenging observation: "Historians have always fastened on organized anti-Semitism; a comparative study of latent, informal anti-Semitism in different European countries would be a difficult but immensely rewarding venture."[43] The same could be said for what I shall provisionally call latent *racial* anti-Semitism in pre-modern European Christendom. Obviously if this existed it did not label itself as such, for these terms are themselves entirely modern. But this does not mean that a fresh reexamination of medieval conceptions of the Jews would be a search for something entirely vague and amorphous. At the core, any hostile conception of the Jews which implies that their negative characteristics are permanent must already be considered as essentially, or at least potentially, "racial."

In this sense the assumption of a total absence of racism in premodern anti-Semitism may yet prove to have been too glib and facile. On the one hand it has rested on the uncritical assumption of an intrinsic incompatibility between Christianity and racial conceptions; on the other, it has been based upon the wrong kinds of evidence.

The fact that, throughout the Middle Ages, individual Jewish converts were welcomed and absorbed into Christian society does not yet tell us how Jews as a whole were regarded in certain quarters. Yes, the individual Jew lost his odor and his other debilities at the baptismal font, but what of the entire unwashed Jewish people that remained? Granted, again, that the Church firmly held to an ultimate conversion of the whole of Jewry at the end-time of the Second Coming, when everything, including the Jews, would radically change. However, except in moments of apocalyptic enthusiasm, the end of time was a very long way off. When the seventeenth-century English poet Andrew Marvell was trying to entice his coy mistress to bed and needed a metaphor for the infinity of time which he, being mortal, lacked for his enterprise, he wrote: "Had we but World enough and time . . . you should if you please refuse, till the Conversion of the Jews."

The real question, then, is how the Jewish people was regarded collectively, not within the official theology of a remote end of time, but within the long historical time stretching from the present "till the conversion of the Jews." Here centuries of Christian teaching had harped incessantly upon such enduring Jewish qualities as stubbornness, stiff-neckedness, obduracy, rigidity. The Jews were depicted, not only as unyielding, but as unchanged since the primal sins of their ancestors. Their physical attributes became stereotyped in art, folklore, and the popular imagination. The whole of Christian Europe had been conditioned in this way, and this cannot but have contributed profoundly to mold a mental conception of the Jews which Christian dogma did not reflect—one of their essential *immutability*. The eschatological conversion and metamorphosis of the Jews could be accepted safely as an article of faith which did not impinge on present reality, indeed so long as it did not become a reality. The fascination of what occurred in Spain and Portugal is that, there alone, what was expected elsewhere only at the end of time was realized to a large degree in the here-and-now. The rest of Europe could afford to postpone thinking of how they might receive a converted Jewry in the end of days. Only the Spaniards and the Portuguese were put to the immediate test, and they did not pass it. The racial potential that was already implicit everywhere, was actualized here for the first time.[44]

Even when, toward the end of the eighteenth century, new currents of European thought and modes of political organization were preparing the way for modern Jewish emancipation, the long predisposition on the part of many Christians to regard the degenerate traits of the Jews as innate made itself felt immediately. The many debates over Jewish emancipation in France and then in Germany, like the earlier controversies over the statutes of purity of blood in Spain and Portugal, all revolved around a pivotal issue—whether or not the Jews are capable of a genuine and radical transformation. Those who opposed the enfranchisement of the French and German Jews, like those who had opposed the abolition of legal distinctions between "New" and "Old" Christians in the Iberian Peninsula, were convinced that no real change would result, for none was possible, and therein too lay embedded a fundamentally racial conception.[45]

In sum, a re-examination of racial anti-Semitism cannot be confined to late nineteenth-century Germany, nor even to Germany alone, but should include a renewed and meticulous scrutiny of the Christian Middle Ages as well. Whether we style this an investigation of latent anti-Jewish racialism, or protoracialism, or simply the prehistory of racial anti-Semitism, is not of immediate concern.

Far from glossing over the vital differences between medieval and modern, such an undertaking can only help to refine our perception of what is truly new in the latter. If I have myself stressed the affinities between the Iberian and the German models, I trust that the reasons are manifest by now. But I am just as acutely conscious of how much they diverge, and I also know the difference between latent and explicit, potential and actual. Organized political anti-Semitism could not arise in Spain and Portugal, which did not know of politics in the nineteenth-century sense. The racialism behind the statutes of purity of blood was an obsession that had theoretical underpinnings, but it never had the all-embracing claims typical of modern ideologies. The Inquisition, for all its excesses, was not the Gestapo; Spanish and Portuguese anti-Semites were not Nazis. There is no genocide here. The most virulent theoreticians of *limpieza* never called for the physical extermination of the New Christians, only, at the most extreme, for their expulsion—an essentially medieval solution—and the state did not comply even with that.[46] *Limpieza de sangre* in the Iberian Peninsula reveals to us a society straining, as it were, to define itself racially, and the limits to which a pre-modern racial anti-Semitism could attain. We can see it, in retrospect, as though oscillating perpetually within the same fixed arc, capable of making men miserable, incapable of moving beyond certain bounds. That this was due to the gravitational pull of a traditional Christianity to whose basic presuppositions an entire society was still, after all, committed, is not to be doubted. But, by the same token, this does not mean that the impact of modern secularization should be regarded as causal. Secularism did not create modern racial anti-Semitism. It did help to erode the restraints which Christianity, with its inherent ambivalence toward Judaism, had once been able to impose upon its own anti-Jewish animosities.[47] I need not spell out the catastrophic results.

VII

Through all our peregrinations this evening I am acutely aware that I have omitted one major comparative dimension between the Iberian and German experiences—the extraordinary contributions of "New Christians" and "New Germans" to their respective host cultures. The time for a detailed discussion is obviously gone, yet I should be remiss were I not to conclude, in a brief epilogue, with at least some indication of what is involved.

The strikingly disproportionate share of Jews in certain areas of modern German culture continues, justifiably, to draw attention, and is often described as unprecedented. There was a precedent, however, and we find it once more in the Iberian Peninsula. The congruence is not accidental. It points again to parallel forces at work in both places.

For some time, now, a new and burgeoning frontier has opened in Hispanic scholarship. With a mounting body of evidence Hispanists continue to unveil the crucial role of Conversos in Spanish civilization, and a galaxy of illustrious Spaniards in various fields of creative endeavor who were, in fact, descended from Jews.[48] This is not the place for a catalogue. Suffice it to say that it now includes such varied figures as Fernando de Rojas, author of the immortal *Celestina*, one of the truly seminal works in Spanish and European literature; Juan Luis Vives, a thinker of international eminence; the great mystic and poet Fray Luis de León; Diego Laínez, second general of the Jesuit order, chosen personally by Loyola as his successor; no less a figure than Santa Teresa of Ávila; and, possibly, even Cervantes himself.[49] More important, perhaps, is the growing realization that certain vital aspects of Spanish spirituality and literature, from sixteenth-century mystical and Erasmian currents to the pastoral novel, cannot be fully and properly understood without taking account of their New Christian background. I should stress, parenthetically, that here again we are not dealing with "secret Jews," but with descendants of Jews who were thoroughly Christian, yet whose creativity was somehow deviant or innovative.[50]

What has been achieved in Hispanic studies should be of more than passing interest to the student of Jewish assimilation and creativity in modern Germany. The latter faces a central problem that crops up repeatedly: Did the fact of Jewish origin really affect the careers and accomplishments of those who regarded themselves, not as Jews but as Germans, and if so, how? The difficulty in the case of modern Germany is that we usually know *to begin with* those who were born Jewish or were of Jewish descent. Thus, when we contemplate their work, we must always wonder if we are not making an artificial equation by discovering allegedly Jewish traits where none may exist. By contrast, one of the more remarkable aspects of the Spanish case is the fact that by the twentieth century the Jewish origin of so many figures had long been forgotten, indeed, had already been concealed during their own lifetimes. It was often through a highly sensitive and close reading of literary texts that some modern scholars found traits and nuances that made them suspect the writer to have been a Converso. Surprisingly, in a number of instances the documentary genealogical evidence was discovered independently or subsequently.[51]

There is, of course, nothing essentially mysterious about the phenomenon itself. The special creativity of so many Spanish New Christians, as of assimilated German Jews, is not to be attributed to some vague genetic endowment, but is to be explained primarily on sociological and psychological grounds.[52] What we find in Spain was part of a wide spectrum of New Christian responses to life in a society where to be of Jewish ancestry was to carry a blemish which, even if known only to oneself, might at any time be revealed to all. In the shadow of the Inquisition and the statutes of purity of blood some Conversos turned more zealously Catholic than many Old Christians.[53] Others recoiled into crypto-Judaism and fled abroad to lead fully Jewish lives. But many sensitive spirits, believing Christians and loyal Spaniards, found release for their inner tensions and anxieties along paths that were somehow off the beaten track. The student of modern German Jewry who turns to the history of Spanish New Christians will find characteristics that are familiar to him, and may feel almost an inverted sense of déjà-vu. The ambiguity and insecurity of the assimilated Jew, the anxiety of hovering between acceptance and rejection, integration and marginality, *jüdischer Selbsthass*—all are present there, albeit expressed in the vocabulary and under the conditions of another age and culture.[54] Indeed, he will even find Converso poets and writers whose self-deprecating ironic humor marks them as curiously kindred spirits to Heinrich Heine.[55]

However elusive the quest for the actual impact of the Jewish element, whether in Spanish civilization or in Wilhelminian and Weimar culture, it remains a striking fact that the larger society regarded certain qualities as distinctively Jewish, and this had repercussions of its own. Though Spain expelled all professing Jews in 1492, the Conversos remained, and the continuity of what Spanish Old Christians perceived as Jewish remained unbroken. Business and trade were "Jewish" occupations, and medicine a "Jewish" profession. Intellectuality as such was identified as Jewish, hence also suspect and dangerous.[56] Even more ominously, as time went by, certain *types* of thought were labeled "Jewish" and therefore excluded. It is here, above all, that Spanish racialism may have exacted one of its heaviest tolls from a great and talented nation. I leave you with two quotations widely separated in space and time, and I have chosen them deliberately from an unusual context—the physical sciences. The first is by Johannes Stark, one of the high priests of that "Aryan" physics which attacked not only Einstein and relativity, but contemporary theoretical physics generally, as Jewish and un-German, and revised the history of science accordingly. In 1937 Stark wrote: "It can be no accident that the great discoveries belonged almost exclusively to the Germanic race (Galileo, Newton, Faraday, Rutherford, Lenard). They are all in accord in that they direct their attention upon the reality of Nature. . . . Opposed to this spiritual attitude stands the Jewish-dogmatic one. . . ."[57] The other is from eighteenth-century Spain, where only Aristotelian physics was legitimate, and many Spaniards actually believed Aristotle himself to have been an "Old Christian." In 1758 Xavier de Munibe, Count of Peñaflorida, mocked the rampant obscurantism of his contemporaries, and summarized the prevailing Spanish attitude as follows: "Why does anyone have to pay attention to any heretical dogs, atheists, and Jews like Newton, who was a terrible arch-heretic . . . [like] Galileo de Galileis, whose very name implies that he must have been an arch-Jew or proto-Hebrew, and others whose names cause people to shudder?"[58] My epilogue has been only that. Like the lecture itself, it hardly begins to do justice to so large and complex a theme. If it has at all aroused your curiosity, perhaps you may one day allow me another occasion on which to try your indulgence.

NOTES

Every public lecturer, I suppose, tries to imagine his audience long before he actually stands before it, and, in anticipation, shapes his materials accordingly. In preparing this lecture I had in mind a hypothetical audience which, assembled by the Leo Baeck Institute, would presumably be far more knowledgeable about the history of modern German Jewry than of the New Christians of Spain and Portugal. The seemingly disproportionate space allotted to details of the Iberian aspects of the problem is merely a reflection of this concern, and, as the reader should discover, not of the primary thrust of the lecture itself. The same is true of the notes that follow and the bibliographical references they contain. [Y.H.Y.]

1. An initial attempt at a comparison between Spanish and German anti Semitism was made more than four decades ago by Cecil Roth in his brief sketch of "Marranos and Racial Anti-Semitism: A Study in Parallels," *Jewish Social Studies*, II (1940), pp. 239–48. Writing at a time when Hitler's Germany was at the height of its power, Roth was preoccupied with immediate parallels to the anti-Jewish racial policies of the Nazis, and made no effort at a broader and more sophisticated conceptualization of the problem. Moreover, he did not yet have access to the wealth of information on the role of Conversos and of "purity of blood" in Iberian society that has since come to light. Roth's essay did stimulate some polemical discussion as to whether Spanish anti-Semitism should be regarded as "racial" to begin with (see infra, n. 29), but its comparative dimension has hitherto not been systematically explored. In this respect, I find it curious that

Léon Poliakov has compared the Iberian phenomenon, not to German racial anti-Semitism, but to the Boer racism of South Africa as delineated by Hannah Arendt. See his *Histoire de l'antisémitisme*, II: *De Mahomet aux marranes* (Paris, 1961), p. 281.

2. Joshua Trachtenberg, *The Devil and the Jews* (New Haven, 1943; reprint Philadelphia, 1961), pp. 47 ff.

3. The following examples should suffice: Descendants of the tribe of Simeon annually develop bloody wounds on their hands and feet; Asher: their right hands are shorter than their left; Naphtali: they have four large teeth, like pigs, and pigs' ears; Levi: they cannot spit forward, and so the spittle runs down their beards; "Joseph": after age thirty-three the women have live worms in their mouths when they sleep. (Trachtenberg, op. cit., pp. 51 f.). For variations, as well as the belief that Jewish males are subject to a menstrual flux, cf. Y. H. Yerushalmi, *From Spanish Court to Italian Ghetto* (New York–London, 1971; 2nd ed., Seattle-London, 1981), pp. 126–33.

4. See Peter Browe, "Die Kirchenrechtliche Stellung der getauften Juden und ihrer Nachkommen," *Archiv für katholisches Kirchenrecht*, CXXI (1941), 3–22, 165–91. "In keiner mittelalterlichen Regel treffen wir eine Bestimmung, die konvertierte Juden ausschloss; höchstens liess man, im Anschluss an den Kanon von Nicaea, die neu Getauften eine Zeit lang warten, um ihrer Bewährung sicher zu sein" (ibid., p. 6).

5. On the Visigothic persecution see Salo W. Baron, *A Social and Religious History of the Jews* (hereafter: *SRH*), 2nd revised ed. (New York, 1952 et seq.), III, pp. 36–46.

6. Aryeh Grabois, "From 'Theological' to 'Racial' Antisemitism: The Controversy over the 'Jewish' Pope in the Twelfth Century" (in Hebrew), *Zion* XLVII (1982), 1–16.

7. Vito Vitale, "Un particolare ignorato di storia pugliese: neofiti e mercanti," in: *Studi di storia napoletana in onore di Michelangelo Schipa* (Naples, 1926), pp. 233–46.

8. After surveying the favorable reception of Jewish converts outside the Iberian Peninsula, Browe writes (op. cit., p. 9): "Anders als im übrigen Europa lagen die Dinge in Spanien. . . ." In fact, the bulk of Browe's article is devoted to anti-Converso discrimination in Spain, but he draws no conclusions from his data.

9. There is abundant illustrative material on this in most of the standard histories. See, inter alia, José Amador de los Ríos, *Historia social, política y religiosa de los judíos de España y Portugal* (one vol. reprint, Madrid, 1960), Pt. III, chs. 1–2, pp. 557–614; Cecil Roth, *A History of the Marranos* (Philadelphia, 1947), pp. 20 ff.;

Yitzhak Baer, *A History of the Jews in Christian Spain* (Philadelphia, 1961), II, pp. 274 f., 315–22; Julio Caro Baroja, *Los judíos en la España moderna y contemporánea* (Madrid, 1962), 1–11, passim.

10. Francisco Márquez Villanueva, "Conversos y cargos concejiles en el siglo XV," *Revista de archivos, bibliotecas y museos*, LXIII (1957), 503–40.

11. For the Santa Maria family see Baer, *Jews in Christian Spain*, II, pp. 139–51; Luciano Serrano, *Los conversos D. Pablo de Santa María y D. Alfonso de Cartagena* (Madrid, 1942); Francisco Cantera Burgos, *Alvar García de Santa María: Historia de la Judería de Burgos y de sus conversos más egregios* (Madrid, 1952). Writing about Solomon Halevi, Américo Castro observes: "From him stem all the theologians, jurists, and historians named Santa María, whose works fill fifteenth-century letters with distinction" (*The Structure of Spanish History* [Princeton, 1954], p. 537).

12. On the large number of Conversos, including active Judaizers, absorbed into the Order of St. Jerome during the fifteenth century, see Albert Sicroff, "Clandestine Judaism in the Hieronymite Monastery of Nuestra Señora de Guadalupe; *Studies in Honor of M. J. Bernardete* (New York, 1965), pp. 89–125; Haim Beinart, "The Judaizing Movement in the Order of San Jeronimo in Castile," *Scripta Hierosolymitana*, VII (1961), 167–92.

13. For an example, see Francisca Vendrell, "Concesión de nobleza a un converso," *Sefarad*, VIII (1948), 397–401 (on the grant in 1416 of a patent of nobility to a Converso, Gil Ruiz Naiari, by Ferdinand I of Aragón).

14. Andrés Bernáldez, *Historia de los Reyes Catolicos Don Fernando y Doña Isabel* (Seville, 1870), I, ch. 43, pp. 124 f. Among the Jewish foods, Bernáldez mentions *adefina*. The same term appears also in a fifteenth century anti-Converso satire (see infra, n. 16) published by H. Pflaum, who defines it as "un ragoût aux choux et aux épices qu'on prépare le vendredi et qu'on garde sous la braise pour le samedi" (*Revue des études juives* [hereafter: *REJ*], LXXXVI, 146, n. 6). Bernáldez, in other words, refers to a lingering Converso fondness for *tscholnt*, the very *Schalet* that Heine whimsically immortalized in his "Prinzessin Sabbath," and of which he has Borne say "that the renegades who deserted to the new covenant need only smell a Schalet in order to feel a certain homesickness for the synagogue." See *Ludwig Börne: eine Denkschrift*, in Heinrich Heine, *Werke und Briefe*, ed. H. Kaufmann, VI (Berlin, 1962), p. 110.

15. The most thorough account of the Christian effort to convert the Jews in the Middle Ages will be found in Peter Browe, *Die Judenmission im Mittelalter und die Päpste* (Rome, 1942).

16. Heinz Pflaum, "Une ancienne satire espagnole contre les Marranes," *REJ*, LXXXVI (1928), 131–50.

17. Isidore Loeb, "La correspondance des juifs d'Espagne avec ceux de Constantinople;" *REJ*, VI (1887), 262–76.

18. Baer, *Jews in Christian Spain*, II, pp. 279 ff. Cf. Nicholas G. Round, "La rebelión toledana de 1449," *Archivum*, XVI (1966), 385–446; E. Benito Ruano, "Del problema judío al problema converso," *Simposio Toledo Judaico* (Madrid, 1973), II, 13 ff.

19. On the latter see Y. H. Yerushalmi, *The Lisbon Massacre of 1506 and the Royal Image in the "Shebet Yehudah"* (Cincinnati, 1976), pp. 1–34.

20. Hence the title of the anonymous anti-Converso *Libra del Alborayque* (1488), summarized and excerpted by Isidore Loeb, "Polémistes chrétiens et juifs en France et en Espagne," *REJ*, XVIII (1889), 238–42, and by Fidel Fita, "La Inquisición de Torquemada," *Boletín de La Real Academia de La Historia*, XXI (1893), 379–82.

21. The outstanding history of the statutes is Albert A. Sicroff's *Les controverses des statuts de "pureté de sang" en Espagne du XVe au XVIIe siècle* (Paris, 1960). Cf. also Caro Baroja, *Los judíos*, II, 267–380. Américo Castro's hypothesis (*Structure of Spanish History*, pp. 524 ff.) that the Spanish preoccupation with *limpieza de sangre* originated in reaction to an allegedly similar concern with purity of blood among the Jews themselves, has been rejected with good reason, though on different grounds, by both Sicroff (*Les controverses*, p. 88, n. 98) and Antonio Domínguez Ortiz (*Los Judeoconversos de España y América* (Madrid, 1978), pp. 78 f.

22. Although, technically, descendants of both Jews and Moors were stigmatized by the statutes, in effect these were aimed primarily at persons of Jewish origin. See Sicroff, *Les controverses*, p. 26.

23. The text of the *Sentencia-Estatuto* is available in Fritz [Yitzhak] Baer, *Die Juden im Christlichen Spanien*, II: *Kastilien/Inquisitionsakten* (Berlin, 1936), no. 302, pp. 315–19, and in Eloy Benito Ruano, *Toledo en el siglo XV* (Madrid, 1961), pp. 191–96. On the genesis of the statute and the opposition to it see Sicroff, *Les controverses*, pp. 32–62. Cf. also E. Benito Ruano, "La Sentencia-Estatuto de Pero Sarmiento contra los conversos toledanos," *Revista de La Universidad de Madrid*, VI (1957), 277–306.

24. See I Corinthians, 12:13; Galatians, 3:27–28; Ephesians, 1–6; Colossians, 3:11. Such scriptural passages provided some of the proof-texts for the learned and passionate defense of the unity of Christendom by Alonso de Cartagena, written in 1449, a fundamental work whose arguments would be repeated by almost all later opponents of the statutes of purity of blood. See D. Alonso de Cartegena, *Defensorium Unitatis Christianae*, ed. Manuel Alonso (Madrid, 1943). The bull of Nicolas V condemning the *Sentencia-Estatuto* is reproduced as Appendix XV, pp. 367 ff.

25. This was emphasized in a memorandum attacking the Toledan statute that was drawn up almost immediately at the behest of Lope de Barrientos, bishop of Cuenca, by Fernan Díaz de Toledo, himself a Converso. Referring to the Visigothic conversions he claimed that no Spaniard could now be certain that he was not of Jewish descent, and gave detailed examples of the admixture of Jewish blood among the nobility and even the royal family. The text is printed in Alonso de Cartagena, *Defensorium*, Appendix II, pp. 343–56.

26. Around 1482 the guild of stone-masons (*pedreros*) of Toledo forbade their members to teach the art to Conversos, and the province of Guipúzcoa excluded them from residence or intermarriage with Old Christians (see Henry Charles Lea, *A History of the Inquisition of Spain*, II, New York, 1906, p. 285). The further progress of the statutes of purity of blood may be seen in their adaptation by the following: The Order of St. Jerome, 1486, rendered definitive in 1495; the colleges of San Bartolomé (Salamanca) and Santa Cruz (Valladolid), 1488, and San Ildelfonso, 1519; the Dominican monastery at Ávila, 1496, other Dominican establishments from 1531; the Franciscans, from 1525; the cathedral chapter of Seville, 1515, and of Córdoba, 1530. The Inquisition itself did not have a statute of *limpieza* until the mid-sixteenth century, and the Jesuits only in 1593. For details see Sicroff, *Les controverses*, ch. II, pp. 63–94.

27. Sicroff, op. cit., ch. III, pp. 95–139. It should be emphasized that in the century between 1449 and 1557 the statutes had neither emanated from the Crown nor were they necessarily approved by it. The impulses throughout this period came from below.

28. The basic premise behind the term "New Christian" is stated succinctly by Juan Escobar del Carro, inquisitor of Llerena, in 1633: "Appelatur etiam Christianus novus non tam quia de novo ad fidem Christi sit conversus, sed quia ab his descendit" (*Tractatus bipartitus de puritate et nobilitate probanda*, cited by Caro Baroja, *Los judíos*, II, p. 305).

29. Guido Kisch categorically denied any racial element in pre-modern anti-Semitism and sharply criticized Lea (*Inquisition of Spain*, I, 126) and Roth (supra, n. 1) for allegedly "reading modern racist conceptions into medieval sources." See his "Nationalism and Race in Medieval Law," *Seminar: An Annual Extraordinary Number of 'The Jurist,'* I (1943), 71. While granting that medieval man did not have a conscious concept of race in its modern form, Salo Baron found Kisch's position to be too extreme. See Baron, *Modern Nationalism and Religion* (New York, 1947), p. 276, n. 26, and his own reference to "manifestations of racialism in the treatment of Iberian conversos," ibid., p. 15. Kisch, in turn, held fast to his views and rejected even Baron's relatively cautious approach (See Kisch, *The Jews of Medieval Germany*, Chicago, 1949, pp. 314–16 and 531, n. 60). For Baron's more recent

formulation see *SRH*, XIII, pp. 84 ff., in which the section on *limpieza* is explicitly entitled: "Growing Racialism."

Similar divisions of opinion will be found among Hispanists. Even so distinguished and perceptive a student of the Conversos as Francisco Márquez Villanueva has maintained that "the problem of the New Christians was by no means a racial one; it was social and in the second line religious" ("The Converso Problem: An Assessment," in *Collected Studies in Honor of Américo Castro's 80th Year* [hereafter: *Castro Festschrift*], Oxford, 1965, p. 324). "The converso," he continues, "did not carry in any moment an indelible biological stigma. Normally he could only be recognized as such through genealogical investigation or through the police action of the Inquisition . . ."—which simply means that the stigma of Jewish descent, unlike black or yellow skin, was not externally visible, an observation that is irrelevant both to the racial character of *limpieza* and to the indelibility of the Jewish stigma once it was discovered. Contrast Domínguez Ortiz who, although recognizing the religious and social dimensions of the differentiation between Old and New Christians, concedes that already at an early stage it acquired racial nuances (*Los Judeoconversos*, p. 77).

30. Sebastián de Covarrubias y Orozco, *Tesoro de la lengua castellana* (Madrid, 1611), fol. 605r.

31. Sicroff, *Les controverses*, p. 182.

32. Vicente da Costa Mattos, *Breve discurso contra a heretica perfidia do iudaismo* (Lisbon, 1623), fol. 31v.

33. *Tractatus bipartitus de puritate et nobilitate probanda* (Lyon, 1637), fols. 71r–74r. See Sicroff, *Les controverses*, pp. 224 f.

34. Francisco de Torrejoncillo, *Centinela contra judíos, puesta en la torre de la Iglesia de Dios* (ed. Pamplona, 1691), p. 62.

35. Ibid., p. 214. The martyrdom of Don Lope de Vera was a cause célèbre in the seventeenth-century, precisely because he was not only a noble, but entirely of Old Christian stock. See Yerushalmi, *From Spanish Court*, p. 450.

36. Fray Prudencio de Sandoval, *Historia de la vida y hechos del emperador Carlos V* (*Biblioteca de autores españoles* [hereafter: *B.A.E.*], vol. LXXXII, Madrid, 1956, p. 319). Note the blithe coexistence in this passage of traditional Christian dogma on the equality of all men in Christ, and an acutely racist conception of the Spanish New Christians.

37. On the *colegios mayores* see Yerushalmi, op. cit., p. 87, and the bibliography cited there; on the German student organizations see Oskar F. Scheuer, *Burschenschaft und Judenfrage: Der Rassenantisemitismus in der deutschen Studentenschaft* (Berlin, 1927).

38. For the *Libro verde* (actually a number of such works had circulated widely

under this title until their official suppression in 1623) and the *Tizón de la nobleza* (Blight of the Nobility), see the discussion and bibliography in Baron, *SRH*, XIII, pp. 99, 359, n. 43. The actual title of the "Semi-Gotha" was *Weimarer historisch-genealogisches Taschenbuch des gesamten Adel jehudäischen Ursprunge* (Weimar, 1912; 2nd ed., Munich, 1913). It should be noted parenthetically that a similar work on the Provencal nobility entitled *Critique du Nobiliare de Provence* was composed at the end of the seventeenth century by Barcilon de Mauvins, a lawyer of Aix. See Armand Lunel, *Juifs du Languedoc, de la Provence, et des états français de pape* (Paris, 1975), ch. IV, "Une noblesse de souche hebraïque," especially pp. 63 ff.

39. It would be superfluous to list here all the well-known works on German anti-Semitism, or modern anti-Semitism generally, in which this is the case. A notable exception is Eleanore Sterling's *Er ist wie Du: Aus der Frühgeschichte des Antisemitismus in Deutschland (1815–1850)* (Munich, 1956; 2nd ed. retitled *Judenhass: Die Anfänge des politischen Antisemitismus in Deutschland (1815–1850)*, Frankfurt a. M., 1969), pointing to anti-Jewish racial attitudes in Germany before the mid-nineteenth century (see *Judenhass*, pp. 67, 86 f., and especially 125–29). P.G.J. Pulzer, *The Rise of Political Anti-Semitism in Germany and Austria* (New York, 1964), begins his discussion of "Racialism" (ch. 6, p. 49) with the laconic statement that "racial anti-Semitism had appeared in 1848 and even earlier," and then proceeds directly to a discussion of Wilhelm Marr. One of the many merits of Jacob Katz's recent *From Prejudice to Destruction: Anti-Semitism, 1700–1933* (Cambridge, Mass., 1980) is his demonstration of the continuity and transmission of many anti-Semitic ideas from early modern times to the eve of the Nazi era. Yet even he does not refer directly to anti-Jewish racial thinking in Germany until the appearance of J. Nordmann's *Die Juden und der deutsche Staat* of 1861 (see Katz, pp. 213 f.).

In this respect the testimony of Moses Hess in *Rome and Jerusalem* is pertinent. Although the book appeared in 1862, Hess' characterization of German racial anti-Semitism does not present itself as a discovery of something newly arisen, nor as a reaction to individual anti-Semitic thinkers, but as a summary of broad and long standing observations and experiences from which he generalizes: "Keine Reform des jüdischen Kultus ist dem gebildeten deutschen Juden radikal genug. Selbst die Taufe erlöst ihn nicht von dem Alpdruck des deutschen Judenhasses. *Die Deutschen hassen weniger die Religion der Juden als ihre Rasse, weniger ihren eigentümlichen Glauben als ihre eigentümlichen Nasen* [my italics]. Weder Reform noch Taufe, weder Bildung noch Emanzipation erschliesst den deutschen Juden vollständig die Pforten des sozialen Lebens. . . . Die judischen Nasen werden nicht reformiert, und das schwarze, krause jüdische Haar wird durch keine Taufe in blondes, durch keinen Kamm in schlichtes verwandelt . . ."

(*Rom und Jerusalem, die letzte Nationalitätsfrage*, Leipzig, 1862, Vierter Brief, p. 14; d. also pp. 34, 204). As Hess indicates in a short *Nachschrift* placed at the beginning of the book, he did not even become aware of Nordmann's anonymously published pamphlet until his own book was already in printer's proofs and it was too late to deal with it.

It is neither by accident nor oversight that the origins and development of the racial component in modern German anti-Semitism do not figure among the major issues in scholarship analyzed by Ismar Schorsch in his lucid and penetrating survey of "German Antisemitism in the Light of Post-War Historiography," *Leo Baeck Institute Yearbook*, XIX (1974), 257–71. Nor has the situation changed within the last decade. The question has simply been foreclosed prematurely, or else absorbed and obscured in the general concentration on political and other organized forms of anti-Semitism in Germany.

40. See especially Uriel Tal's important study of *Christians and Jews in Germany: Religion, Politics and Ideology in the Second Reich, 1870- 1914*, tr. from the Hebrew by N. J. Jacobs (Ithaca, 1975), ch. V, "Christian and Anti-Christian Anti-Semitism," pp. 223–78, and the further bibliography, ibid., p. 227, n. 5. Cf. also his "Religious and Anti-Religious Roots of Modern Anti-Semitism" (Leo Baeck Memorial Lecture no. 14, New York, 1971).

41. Characteristically, in the collaborative *Judenfeindschaft: Darstellung und Analysen*, ed. Karl Thieme (Frankfurt a. M. and Hamburg, 1963), there is a separate two-part essay by the editor on "Die religiös motivierte Judenfeindschaft," and another by Karl Saller on "Die biologisch motivierte Judenfeindschaft," which opens (p. 180) with the declaration that "Der 'biologische' Aspekt der Judenfrage ist ein Errungenschaft der Neuzeit. Er löste den konfessionellen Aspekt ab in der Mass, in dem die Konfessionen an öffentlicher Bedeutung zu verlieren begannen."

42. On the arguments employed to reconcile the statutes with Catholic theology see Sicroff, *Les controverses*, pp. 170–81. Among the popes, Alexander VI (himself a Spaniard) ratified the statute of the Jeronymites in 1495; the statute of the Colegio de San Ildenfonso was ratified by Clement VII in 1525; those of the cathedrals of Córdoba and Toledo by Paul IV in 1555. Cf. also supra, n. 36.

43. Fritz Stern, *Gold and Iron: Bismarck, Bleichröder, and the Building of the German Empire* (New York, 1977), p. 497.

44. One need hardly speculate as to what would have occurred had German Jewry followed Theodor Mommsen's friendly but naive advice that they accept (an admittedly diluted) Christianity and thus remove the presumed final barrier to their total assimilation. See Mommsen, "Auch ein Wort über unser Juden-

thum" (1880), reprinted in *Der Berliner Antisemitismusstreit*, ed. Walter Boehlich (2nd ed., Frankfurt a. M., 1965), pp. 225 f.

45. From this perspective, a careful review even of fairly well-known works can be enlightening. To take but two examples: When we find that in 1791 the German anti-Semite Karl Grattenauer published a work entitled *Über die physische und moralische Verfassung der heutigen Juden*, and stated that the baptism of Jews is as effective as "trying to wash a blackamoor white," we should be fully alert to the assumptions and implications of both the title and the comparison. The same is true of Fichte's observation only two years later that "the only way to give them citizenship would be to cut off their heads on the same night in order to replace them with those containing no Jewish ideas." The brutal image has caught the attention of many, but it is the implicit conception of the Jews as unalterable that is of primary importance. I dare say that even a fresh re-reading of the Abbé Grégoire's pro-Jewish *Essai sur la régénération physique, morale et politique des juifs* (Metz, 1789) could be instructive if approached from a somewhat different angle than usual. An inverse reading, so to speak, would focus, not on the "physical regeneration" of the title, but on the current physical *degeneration* the phrase implies. Indeed, we find a rather appalling catalogue of Jewish biological defects enumerated in the book, doubly revealing because they crop up so prominently within a passionate advocacy of Jewish emancipation. Grégoire, to be sure, was able to transcend (though not quite abandon) these particular prejudices and argue for the Jewish cause, trusting that ultimately the physical debilities of the Jews, along with their morals, could be positively transformed. Be that as it may, his championship of the Jews was idiosyncratic, while his biological prejudices were surely symptomatic of the views of masses of Frenchmen who shared neither his philo-Semitism nor his liberal optimism concerning a possible change in the Jews themselves.

46. By contrast, the Moriscos (Christians of Moorish descent) were expelled from Spain in 1609. Admittedly, their expulsion was facilitated by the fact that they lived together more compactly, were more easily recognizable, and were, on the whole, less important as a group than the New Christians of Jewish origin.

47. My own view of the nature and importance of this historical Christian ambivalence, with its delicate balances and tensions between a simultaneous desire for the degradation and the preservation of the Jews, is expressed in my "Response to Rosemary Reuther," in *Auschwitz: Beginning of a New Era?*, ed. Eva Fleischner (New York, 1977), pp. 97–107.

48. The re-evaluation of the Conversos may be said to have begun with the investigation of Manuel Serrano y Sanz of "The Aragonese Friends and Protec-

tors of Columbus" in his *Orígines de la dominación española en América* (Madrid, 1918). Another landmark was the publication in 1937 of Marcel Bataillon's *Érasme et l'Espagne*. However, the major impetus came with the appearance of Américo Castro's *España en su historia* in 1948 (Eng. tr.: *The Structure of Spanish History*, Princeton, 1954; revised ed. entitled *La realidad histórica de España*, Mexico, 1962). The central thesis of this seminal book, and others that followed, is that the history of Spain cannot be understood without taking full account of the interaction of Christians, Moors, and Jews in the Middle Ages, and of "Old" and "New" Christians from the fifteenth century onward. I cannot pause here to consider the controversy that continues to surround Castro's work, nor the occasional flaws in his own understanding of Jewish history and religion. The fact remains that in the renaissance of scholarship on the Conversos, Castro's fructifying influence has been decisive, not only upon his disciples, but as a stimulant to others. For an overview of what had been achieved in the field up to 1965 see Antonio Domínguez Ortiz, "Historical Research on Spanish conversos in the last 15 years," *Castro Festschrift*, 63–82. For more recent bibliography see Robert Singerman, *The Jews in Spain and Portugal: A Bibliography* (New York–London, 1975), and the rich bibliographical notes to Baron, *SRH*, especially vols. XIII, ch. lvi, XV, chs. lxv–lxvi.

49. Américo Castro was convinced that Cervantes was of Converso origin. (See in particular his *Cervantes y los casticismos españoles*, Madrid, 1975, pp. 73, 264). Definite genealogical documentation for this is lacking, though there is some indirect evidence that cannot lightly be dismissed. Cf. the judicious summary of the problem by William Byron, *Cervantes: A Biography* (Garden City, N.Y., 1978) p. 24. Whatever his actual lineage it is clear by now that Cervantes was acutely aware of the tensions between Old and New Christians and of the obsession with *limpieza* in Spanish society, and that this consciousness is reflected significantly in his works.

50. Bataillon, *Érasme et l'Espagne* (Paris, 1937); 2nd rev. ed., *Erasmo y España* (Mexico–Buenos Aires, 1950). Cf. Eugenio Asensio, "El Erasmismo y las corrientes espirituales afines: Conversos, franciscanos, italianizantes," *Revista de filología española*, XXXVI (1952), 31–99. Concerning Converso influence on reformist and spiritual tendencies in the Spanish religious sentiment of the sixteenth century Domínguez Ortiz observes: "Here one can be much more positive . . . for how could a converso be a common Christian, a Christian of routine?" (*Castro Festschrift*, p. 79). Cf. Francisco Marquez (ibid., pp. 328 f.): "Whoever takes the trouble today to read with some understanding the writings of Santa Teresa, Fray Luis de León, Fray Diego de Estella, the Blessed Juan of Ávila, and so many others [of converso origin], will find there the same detestation of the ecclesiastical organization of the time, of imperialist policy, of violent conversions, of Caesarism, of

limpieza de sangre and of the Inquisition. . . . All of them were feeling a painful longing for a society without caste, for a state without violence, and for a spiritual church, free from the structure of social power."

51. Among the more impressive examples: The Jewish origin of Santa Teresa of Ávila was documented through the discovery of a lawsuit filed at the beginning of the sixteenth century by members of her family, the Sánchez de Cepedas, claiming exemption from local taxes because they were *hidalgos*. In the course of the investigation it was revealed that their father (Teresa's grandfather Juan Sánchez) had been penanced by the Inquisition of Toledo in 1485 for relapsing, by his own admission, into his former Judaism. Nevertheless, whether through bribery or benevolence, the court of appeals allowed his sons to retain their presumed *hidalguía*, and the derelictions of Juan Sánchez were hushed up. See Narciso Alonso Cortés, "Pleitos de los Cepedas," *Boletín de la Real Academia de la Historia*, XXV (1946), 86–110, and cf. H. Serís, "Nueva genealogía de Santa Teresa," *Nueva Revista de Filología Hispánica*, X (1956), 365–84. Perhaps even more dramatic are the facts which have emerged concerning Juan Luis Vives, whose Jewish origin was already suspected by Castro in 1948 (*España en su historia*, pp. 682–85). The inquisitorial records have since revealed that he was of Jewish extraction on all four sides, that until the age of ten he attended a clandestine "synagogue," that his father was burned alive as a Judaizer and the bones of his mother were exhumed and burned as well, and that his entire family was destroyed by the Inquisition. See M. de la Pinta Llorente and José M. Palacio, *Procesos inquisitoriales contra la familia judía de Juan Luis Vives* (Madrid, 1964). Though Vives' own Catholicism remained firm (he even wrote a theological polemic against Judaism), he understandably left Spain and never returned.

52. In other words, the mere fact that one's forebears were Talmudists does not, of itself, bequeath a "Talmudic mind," and while intelligence may be, in part, biologically inherited, its Jewish characteristics, if such exist, are not. Nor is the special creativity to which I allude to be identified as "Jewish" in content, or in the sense that it is necessarily nurtured by anything in Jewish religious or cultural tradition. I need hardly add that I do not propose to include Santa Teresa, or any of the other major Converso figures, in some pantheon of illustrious Jews, or in the often inflated roster of "Jewish contributions to civilization." It is not the fact of Jewish descent that is of moment for our purposes, but the inner and outer tensions it generates, and the manner in which these are expressed or resolved. Here, obviously, the conscious awareness of being of Jewish origin is decisive. (For one exemplary approach to the treatment of the problem in its modern context see Isaiah Berlin's "Benjamin Disraeli, Karl Marx, and the Search for Identity," reprinted in his *Against the Current: Essays in the History of Ideas*, New York, 1980,

pp. 252–86). That the Conversos I have mentioned were indeed aware of their Jewish ancestry has been established by direct and indirect evidence. Concerning Fernando de Rojas, Vives, etc., there is no doubt whatever. As for Santa Teresa, in a fascinating passage in his *Espiritu de la beata Ana de San Bartolomé*, Teresa's close friend Padre Jerónimo Gracián relates ingenuously that when he asked Ana about her family history she responded readily; but when he told Teresa of Ávila that he had verified the nobility of both her family lines, the Ahumadas and the Cepedas, "she became very annoyed with me for dealing with this, saying that it sufficed her to be a daughter of the Church; and that it would grieve her more to have committed a venal sin than if she were a descendant of the vilest and lowest villains and *confesos*" (cited by Américo Castro, *De la edad conflictiva*, 4th ed., Madrid, 1974, pp. 200 f.). Cf. also Castro, *Structure*, p. 565 (on Mateo Alemán, author of the famous picaresque novel *Guzmán de Alfarache*, who suppressed his mother's surname when asked for his parentage in a public document, "because in Seville the name Enero smelled Jewish a hundred leagues away").

53. Just as many assimilated Jews in Wilhelminian and Weimar Germany became stolid German bourgeois. This point, though quite correct in itself, has been overstressed by Peter Gay in his generally salutary effort to balance exaggerated claims that the avant-garde in modern German culture was predominantly a Jewish phenomenon. See, e.g., his "Encounter with Modernism," as well as "The Berlin-Jewish Spirit" (Leo Baeck Memorial Lecture XV, 1972), reprinted in his *Freud, Jews and Other Germans* (Oxford, 1979). The fact that many German Jews were cultural conservatives or, conversely, that many German avant-garde artists were not Jews, helps to refine the problem, but does not cause it to disappear. Gay himself is careful to concede that "whatever hyperbole the skeptical historian detects and discounts, the Jewish share in German Modernism remains noteworthy" (ibid., p. 131). It is this, precisely, that still invites further investigation, and I suggest that the manner in which Castro and his followers have approached similar questions of the Converso factor in Spanish culture may well prove relevant and instructive.

54. These qualities are abundantly evident throughout the scholarly literature on the Conversos. The English reader will find a powerful portrayal and documentation of most of them in Stephen Gilman, *The Spain of Fernando de Rojas* (Princeton, 1972). As for *Selbsthass*, it will suffice to cite an anonymous Franciscan who writes in 1581 that one would have to be blind not to see that there is no *confeso* in Spain "who would not prefer being descended from paganism rather than Judaism, and almost all of them would give up half their lives to have that pedigree ... for they abhor the lineage they have received from their parents" (Sicroff, *Les controverses*, p. 150).

55. See e.g., Caro Baroja, *Los judíos*, I, 282–92, "El converso que se burla de su propria condición."

56. Vivid examples of this, from all ranks of Spanish society, in Castro, *Structure*, pp. 472, 635–39 ("Thought as a Great Danger"); idem, *The Spaniards* (Berkeley, 1971), pp. 550–53, 576; idem, *De la edad conflictiva*, pp. 162 ff.

57. Léon Poliakov and Josef Wulf (eds.), *Das Dritte Reich und seine Denker: Dokumente* (Berlin-Grunewald, 1959), p. 298. On Stark and Aryan physics see Alan D. Beyerchen, *Scientists under Hitler: Politics and the Physics Community in the Third Reich* (New Haven, 1977), especially chs. 6–8.

58. Xavier de Munibe, *Los aldeanos críticos* (Évora, 1758), reprinted, but erroneously ascribed to Padre José Francisco Isla, in *B.A.E.*, vol. XV (Madrid, 1850), p. 375; cited by Castro, *The Spaniards*, p. 577 (the date 1786 given there is incorrect).

10 : SPINOZA ON THE SURVIVAL OF THE JEWS

English translation of a lecture in Hebrew, the Israeli Academy of Arts and Sciences, Jerusalem, Israel, May 3, 1977.

This selection was initially delivered as a lecture in Hebrew at the Israeli Academy of Arts and Sciences in Jerusalem in May 1977, when Yerushalmi was spending a sabbatical year in Israel. It reveals his ongoing interest in themes central to his first book, *From Spanish Court to Italian Ghetto*, namely, the Iberian Jewish experience and the condition of the crypto-Jew, or Marrano. At the same time, the lecture evinces Yerushalmi's concern for large questions about Jewish history, including the history of historiography, the nature of the secularization process, and the explanation for the Jews' surprising survival over millennia.

At the center of this set of overlapping inquiries stands the renowned philosopher from Amsterdam Baruch (Benedictus) Spinoza (1632–1677). The fulcrum of the lecture is Yerushalmi's new reading, against the grain, of Spinoza's views about the survival of the Jews expressed in the *Theologico-Political Treatise*. Yerushalmi drew on his textured historical knowledge of the Iberian context from which Spinoza drew and the Dutch context in which Spinoza dwelled, to tie together various facets of Spinoza's life and strands of Spinoza scholarship into a masterful synthesis.

He began the talk by identifying various stages of research into Spinoza. The shift toward a more a more historically sensitive approach to Spinoza, one that focused on his crypto-Jewish origins, began with the German scholar Carl Gehardt in the 1920s and was later taken up by the French scholar I. S. Révah. The historical approach gained considerable momentum in Yerushalmi's time, with the discovery of new documentary sources on the Amsterdam Jewish community, as well as on the history of New Christians in Spain, Portugal, and beyond. Notwithstanding this trend, Yerushalmi observed a lingering tendency among scholars to regard Spinoza in rather one-dimensional terms, as a pure "philosophical intelligence" who "sits alone in his room, grinds lenses, and ponders his ideas with a serenity of spirit so absolute that his thoughts have no origin beyond the pure spirit itself." By contrast, Yerushalmi proposed a more multidimensional historical approach that explored the way in which Spinoza's past figured in his thought.

He went about this task through the prism of an age-old question: What explains the survival of the Jews? In contrast to the competing (and, at times, overlapping) theological explanations of Jews and Christians, Yerushalmi pointed to Spinoza as the progenitor of a new, secular response to the question. It is, somewhat counterintuitively, the hatred of the Gentiles that explains the survival of the Jews. Spinoza stated this quite openly in the third chapter of the *Theologico-Political Treatise*. What intrigued Yerushalmi the scholar of Iberian Jewish history even more was what Spinoza asserted following this statement: namely, that while the forced conversion of Jews in Spain paved the path to their assimilation, the same was not true in Portugal. Rather, in Portugal, *conversos* always lived apart from their old Christian neighbors. In fact, however, the path of converted Jews to "all honorable offices" in Spain was no more open than it was in Portugal. Why then did Spinoza get it wrong, given that he had access to sources that would prove the opposite of his statement?

Yerushalmi set out to solve the mystery of this historical inaccuracy, leading the reader on a captivating tour of the labyrinthine byways of seventeenth-century Portuguese and European history, noting possible motives and personalities that might have influenced Spinoza's misreading. He argued that the pervasive view in Portuguese circles that tolerance might encourage the New Christians to assimilate was flipped on its head by Spinoza, who maintained that it was the very absence of tolerance—namely, Gentile hatred—that had the ironic effect of preserving the Jews. In exploring this inversion, Yerushalmi revealed his considerable talents as historical sleuth and close textual reader. More generally, he shed important new light on Baruch Spinoza as the discoverer of an unlikely key to Jewish survival: antisemitism.

I

I should explain at the very outset that I did not choose this topic as a philosopher or a historian of philosophy. In fact I did not begin with Spinoza. I arrived at my theme through a longstanding preoccupation with the history of Sephardic (Hispano-Portuguese) Jewry and with the history of Jewish historiography, and these two concerns merged and led me to Spinoza. Let me add that, in fact, it was not the philosopher called Benedictus who will concern us here but rather the Sephardic Jew Baruch Spinoza, who started on his path as a member of the Portuguese Jewish community in 17th-century Amsterdam, and even after he was excommunicated by that community, there remained in Benedictus not a little of Baruch.

I will admit also that I first approached the subject with some hesitation. The scholarly literature dealing with Spinoza is so vast and wide-ranging as to seem to leave almost no room for innovation. Nevertheless, anyone who carefully examines the Spinoza bibliography will find some interesting characteristics. It turns out, for example, that in terms of sheer quantity it is his *Ethics* that has attracted most of the toil and effort, while less has been written on the *Theological-Political Treatise* (*Tractatus Theologico-Politicus*). In research on the *Tractatus* itself, pride of place has been given to Spinoza's views on the separation of religion and state and his pioneer contribution to Bible criticism. But details of other topics still await exposition. In terms of the study of Spinoza, scholars have examined his sources in medieval Jewish philosophy and biblical exegesis, and of course they have dealt extensively with the notorious excommunication, concerning which the flames of polemic have not subsided to this day. Similarly much has been written on the question of the "Jewish character" of Spinoza's teaching generally, some affirming it, others denying it, each according to their definitions and preconceptions of the nature of Judaism itself. But in the writings of Spinoza there are passages that speak explicitly of Judaism and of the Jews, passages that have been neglected or subjected to arbitrary and tendentious commentaries.

Spinoza research has passed through various cycles. Some scholars did not want to see in Spinoza's teachings simply a chapter, albeit an important one, in the history of ideas, but sought to understand them within the immediate historical reality and environment in which Spinoza grew up and created, and so they searched for "influences" in various places. Some pointed to certain streams in contemporary Dutch Christianity, especially the Collegiants or the Mennonites.[1] Others argued that one should look for the important influences, in the years in which he matured and his thought developed, precisely in the midst of Amsterdam Sephardic Jewry itself. This approach was essentially correct, but for a long time these scholars did not find the tools and the material necessary to validate it. Research in the history of Sephardic Jewry had not yet attained the level at which it was able to present the details required for an understanding of the actual background of Spinoza. Because of this deficiency one episode alone was emphasized—the famous and tragic drama of the Marrano heretic Uriel Da Costa, who was twice excommunicated and then committed suicide. In all the discussions that surrounded the question of the influence of the Jewish environment on Spinoza, Da Costa stood at the center, and this conception, for all its distortion, became common.[2]

A major change in Spinoza studies occurred with the appearance in the 1920's of the important publications of Carl Gebhardt. And not only because he issued model editions of Spinoza's works and gathered much important material on the Da Costa affair,[3] but particularly because he emphasized the fact that not only Da Costa but also other Marranos who fled to Amsterdam held skeptical and dangerous opinions within the community. The study by Gebhardt of the physician Juan de Prado,[4] who was also a former Marrano and who is worthy of being regarded as the real teacher of Spinoza in matters of disbelief, opened new doors to an understanding of the rationalist-heterodox circles to which the youthful Spinoza had access. Gebhardt's studies were extended and broadened later, particularly in the work of I. S. Révah.[5] These studies and others contained much more than the disclosure of hitherto unknown documents; they bore a new approach to the study of Spinoza.

Since then there has been a renaissance of research into the history of the Marranos after the expulsion from Spain. Manuscripts have been discovered and documents have been published from the archives of the Inquisition which shed new light on the thought of the Marranos in the 17th century. We are now better informed than ever before about the Portuguese Jewish community of Amsterdam and about other Sephardic centers.[6] Although much still remains buried in libraries and archives, we have before us even now rich material sufficient to contribute to a concrete historical understanding of Spinoza's background, if we only desire and know how to use it. Simultaneously there has been intensive and ongoing research on the character and fate of the New Christians, descendants of the original Jewish converts who remained in the Iberian Peninsula, their place and influence in the history and literature of Spain and Portugal, the hatred directed against them, and other reactions of the Old Christian community toward them.[7] This too, as I hope to show, is of the highest relevance to the subject of Spinoza.

But there is another obstacle to our understanding of Spinoza, and since this discussion is to place us within the borders of Spain itself, I will invoke the words of one of the great Spanish writers and thinkers of modern times, Miguel de Unamuno. In his well-known book *The Tragic Sense of Life* (*Del sentimiento trágico de la vida*), Don Miguel sought, among other things, to recall to his readers a simple truth which many tend to ignore, and that is—that even a philosopher is an "*hombre de carne y hueso*"—a man of flesh and bone—a man fully alive and destined for death, who rejoices and suffers, despairs and exults; not merely a disembodied intellect, but possessed of a variety of emotions that even influence his thinking.[8] In Spinoza, however, the man of flesh and bone is especially hard to expose, and for a reason. It is doubtful if in all the history of philosophy you will find another image of a philosopher that so conceals the man within—in any case, as that image has been accepted and sanctified through the course of generations. Socrates, at least, had his *daemon* and a wife, Xanthippe, to disturb occasionally his intellectual tranquility. Not so Spinoza. The Spinoza hagiography created from its inception a seductive myth of a philosophical intelligence immune to the influence of any alien thought, and thus is he viewed by his admirers and even by his critics to this very day: He sits alone in his room, grinds lenses, and ponders his ideas with a serenity of spirit so absolute that his thoughts have no origin beyond the pure subject itself.[9] Possibly there is some truth in this, but the skeptic in me whispers that it cannot be the whole truth. I do not make this point in order to disparage Spinoza's philosophical achievement. I shall try only to illumine one passage in his writings, a passage that itself has a special place in the development of modern conceptions of Jewish history. And perhaps, along the way, it will be possible for us to glimpse, if only for an instant, the man behind the philosopher.

II

What, after all, has preserved the Jewish people in dispersion these thousands of years? I would propose that rather than "the Jewish faith," or "the messianic idea," or the power of Jewish law (*halakhah*), or "the authority of the autonomous Jewish community," most will respond: The hatred of the Gentiles for the Jews is what preserved both the identity of the Jewish people and its religion. According to this view, the Jewish people preserved itself for lack of an alternative, because the hatred that surrounded it did not allow it any other possibility; one might say, it was not possible for it to disappear. Doesn't every schoolboy know that precisely in the Middle Ages, in the days of oppression and persecution, Judaism flourished, while under liberal regimes in modern times, assimilation became rampant? Ernst Bloch once wrote that anti-Semitism is an international society for the preservation of Judaism,[10] and this is but a playful formulation of a serious view widespread, indeed prevalent, in our time.

In the past, however, this view was not common at all; in fact it was unknown, whether among Jews or Christians. The two groups agreed, as it were, that the preservation of the Jewish people is to be viewed first and foremost as a result of Divine providence in history, except that the Jews saw here a kind of positive Providence, in the sense of "I have betrothed thee to Me forever," while the Christians saw it as a kind of negative Providence, an eternal punishment for the death of their savior, an expiation that must continue until his second coming at the End of Days, when finally the Jews too will recognize him as the Messiah.

It is not my intention to claim that earlier generations did not recognize the power of gentile hatred to affect Judaism and the Jewish people. From the medieval Church arose occasional voices of popes and others who contended that oppression and persecution reinforce the obstinacy of the Jews. In his treatise "That Jesus Christ was Born a Jew" (*Dass Jesu Christus ein eborener Jude sei*) Martin Luther wrote that in light of the foolishly harsh treatment by the Catholics of the Jews, he is not surprised that in the past the Jews did not change their faith and become Christians. The ancient rabbis too did not disregard the potential effects of the hatred of the nations on Israel. We read: "Rabbi Abba bar Kahana said, 'The removal of the ring [which Ahasueros gave to Haman as a sign that he can proceed to destroy the Jews] is greater than the forty-eight prophets and seven prophetesses who prophesied to Israel, because all of them could not make the Jews repent, while the removal of the ring (in other words, the threat of persecution) made them repent'" (Megillah 14a). But all these and similar voices saw in the hatred of the nations only a secondary cause, because regardless of its importance, it does not contradict or displace the primary and superior cause, which is Divine Providence. The hatred of the nations may profoundly affect the *behavior* of Jews in various times and circumstances but it is not an explanation for the *survival* of Israel through the ages. For this concept—the hatred that preserved the Jewish people from disappearing through assimilation—there is a beginning and therefore a history of its own. This notion that sees in anti-Semitism and not in Providence the primary cause of the survival of the Jews could emerge only after the belief was abandoned that it was God who preserved them. The entire contention depends on the severing of Jewish history from Divine Providence or, in other words, on the secularization of Jewish history in the most literal and radical sense—its transformation from sacred to profane.

As is well known, already in the 18th century the view which placed Divine Providence as the central factor in the history of the Jewish people was under open attack. Rejecting the providential conception as expressed in Bossuet's *Discours sur l'histoire universelle*, Voltaire proclaimed blandly: "We shall speak of the Jews as if we were speaking of Scythians or Greeks."[11] Yet it was not Voltaire who was the first to perceive Jewish history in purely secular terms. The first to do so was also the first to relate the survival of Israel among the nations to the hatred of the nations, and he is that very Sephardic Jew who was Baruch before he became Benedictus.

III

The passage central to our theme is found in the third chapter of the *Tractatus* which appeared in print anonymously in the year 1670. The passage appears in the course of an argument that denies the eternal election of the Jewish people by God. After Spinoza rejects the concept that God has chosen the Jews and declares that, if indeed they were chosen, this was only for the sake of limited political rule in the time of the Bible, he continues with these words:

> At the present time, therefore, there is absolutely nothing which the Jews can arrogate to themselves beyond other people.
>
> As to their continuance so long after dispersion and the loss of empire, there is nothing marvelous in it, for they so separated themselves from every other nation as to draw down upon themselves universal hate, not only by their outward rites, rites conflicting with those of other nations, but also by the sign of circumcision which they most scrupulously observe.
>
> That they have been preserved in great measure by Gentile hatred, experience demonstrates. When the king of Spain formerly compelled the Jews to embrace the State religion or to go into exile, a large number of Jews accepted Catholicism. Now, as these renegades were admitted to all the native privileges of Spaniards, and deemed worthy of filling all honourable offices, it came to pass that they straightway became so intermingled with the Spaniards as to leave of themselves no relic or remembrance. But exactly the opposite happened to those whom the king of Portugal compelled to become Christians, for they always, though converted, lived apart, inasmuch as they were considered unworthy of any civic honours.[12]

Even a cursory reading of these lines suffices to recognize that Spinoza is here denying the concept of Providence for both Jews and Christians. While he does not rely on the theological assumptions of Christianity, he accepts the essence of the classical Christian argument that the election of the Jewish people by God has lapsed and come to an end. However, from this he does not reach the Christian conclusion which maintains that instead of the Jews, a "New Israel" was chosen. And this is not a mere coincidence. It fits well the place of Spinoza in the history of the Jewish people, as it was defined by the eminent historian Yitzhak (Fritz) Baer when he wrote, "He was the first Jew to depart from his faith and his people without a religious conversion."[13]

Before we delve into the heart of the matter, let us comment on one detail in the passage, whose source is quite apparent. The idea that the Jews originally "so separated themselves from every other nation as to draw down upon themselves universal hate," is drawn directly from Tacitus, something that should not surprise us, since the *Tractatus* is permeated with influences from that Roman historian.[14]

The great innovation appears in one sentence: "That they have been preserved in great measure by Gentile hatred," and this is really something new. True, it is possible to gather various passages from Jewish literature before Spinoza which at first sight seem to contain similar thoughts, such as the statement of Rabbi Yohanan (*Menahot*): "Why is Israel compared to an olive? To teach you that just as an olive does not produce its oil except through pounding, so Israel does not repent except through suffering." But the similarity to Spinoza is only apparent. Such homilies, which recur in every generation, have an entirely different purpose and meaning (and the same applies to the words of Rabbi Abba, which I quoted earlier). They do not deal with the very survival of the Jewish people, but with its conduct and behavior, and their entire function is only to arouse Jews to repentance. Other apparent parallels will also be revealed as illusory if we but take into account the context in which they were expressed. Close to the generation of Spinoza the rationalist Simhah (Simone) Luzzatto in his essay on the Jews of Venice—*Discorso circa il stato de gl'Hebrei di Venetia* (1638)—writes as follows:

> Even though servitude and dispersion are among the very greatest blows that are capable of befalling a nation and people, sufficient to render them degraded and despised, and to make them a byword among the nations—they nevertheless serve as a very effective therapy for the survival of the nation and its preservation, because the servitude and the dispersion remove envy and suspicion from the hearts of the rulers, and pride and arrogance from the heart of the dispersed people, and make them humble and accepting of authority.[15]

This passage is but a marginal note to the consistent view of Luzzatto, according to which it is better for the Jews, from a practical standpoint, to bow their heads and not become excessively conspicuous in the eyes of the Gentiles. Let us not be misled by the language of the passage; there is no attempt here to relate the basic survival of the nation to its despised status in the diaspora. The proof is in the sentence preceding this passage, where Luzzatto writes explicitly: "There is no doubt that it would have been beyond the power [of the Jewish people] to endure by themselves before the devouring teeth of time and to escape the severe blows over so long a period—about 1600 years—had it not been the desire of God, blessed be He, who has watched over them for the sake of purposes that are known to Him." Surely the most interesting contrast to Spinoza's words is found in the commentary of Isaac Abravanel, the scholar and last great Jewish statesman at the time of the Expulsion from Spain, on Ezekiel 20:33. In the words of the verse, "As I live, says the Lord God, I will reign over you with a strong hand, with arm outstretched and with wrath outpoured," Abravanel sees a "tremendous" prophecy of what occurred in his time. Here he deals with the question of Divine providence specifically in connection with the New Christians of Spain. He points out that among the converted Jews and their offspring, there are those who "because of the woes of the decrees and the persecutions, and because of the swords of the enemies, left the [Jewish] religion and intended to resemble the nations of the earth, and they thought that in so doing Divine Providence would be removed from them." Indeed, more than a century and a half before Spinoza, Abravanel forecasts that the Christians will not allow the converts and their descendants to assimilate even if they would want to, and that "against the will" of the converts, the Christians would continue to relate to them as Jews. But this hatred on the part of the Gentiles is only the rod of God's anger. In Abravanel's eyes the entire phenomenon is a manifestation of a never-ceasing Divine providence, which does not permit *even those Jews who changed their faith* to escape the destiny of the entire people. These are his words:

> Regarding the apostates and the Marranos who left the religious community, God said, "With wrath outpoured shall I reign over you." This signifies that even though they and their descendants after them try to be like thorough Gentiles, that will not be, because the nations of the earth will always call them Jews, will label them Israelites against their will, will consider them Jews, will accuse them of

secretly Judaizing, and will burn them in the flames for it. All this is included in God's saying "With wrath outpoured shall I reign over you," because even though they wish to exhibit themselves as Gentiles, despite themselves they will be regarded as Jews, because the Lord God of Hosts will rule over them against their will.[16]

The examples I have cited suffice to show that these and similar instances derive from a different *Weltanschauung* from Spinoza's. So far as I can see, Spinoza was the first to advance the contention that it was not Providence but hatred that preserved the Jewish people. It is appropriate, therefore, to inquire if this contention, notwithstanding its originality, is simply the result of his own thought or whether it may have roots elsewhere.

At first blush we might think that it was a direct and organic consequence of the totality of his thought as he expounded it in the *Tractatus*. For if Spinoza's principal objective was to sever the state from religion and to liberate philosophy from theology, he was first compelled to sever all of history from both Revelation and Divine Providence. But in the Europe of the 17th century, and even later, the history of the Jewish people still stood at the center of almost every *non-Jewish* historical conception, and from this stemmed the internal necessity of the *Tractatus* to establish a new view of Jewish history. For this reason it would not suffice for Spinoza to deny biblical prophecy alone—a thesis to which he devoted the first two chapters of his work. As a stumbling block to his argument stood the survival of the Jewish people in exile and dispersion, that unique historical "miracle" at which not only the Jews were astonished. As a matter of fact, ancient and well established Christian tradition, beginning with the Church Fathers and continuing to Spinoza's time, saw in the continued survival of the Jewish people a clear result of Divine Providence (albeit for the purpose of Divine Punishment) and indeed a miraculous sign and proof of Divine Providence itself.[17] One might say, therefore, that because of these considerations, Spinoza was compelled not only to limit the election of the Jewish people to political sovereignty in the biblical period, but also to postulate a natural explanation for Jewish survival from that point until his own time.

But the search for a natural cause does not necessarily lead to Spinoza's conclusion. For even from a secular view of Jewish history it is possible to draw and propose a large number of other rational explanations for the survival of the Jews. If so, the question remains: Why did Spinoza particularly choose this explanation, which makes Jewish survival dependent on the hatred of the nations?

I venture to say that between the lines of the passage under discussion, as in other places in the book, one can sense Spinoza's resentment and even contempt for his former brethren who had excommunicated him. But even though such feelings may be perfectly understandable, we are still obliged to examine his words and their implications as he presented them. When Spinoza declared that it was hatred that preserved the Jews, he did not state this in a vacuum, and there is no reason to assume that he did not know what he was attacking and whom he was wounding. The thought itself that the survival of Israel is not in the hands of its God does not yet constitute the wound. The real blow is that Spinoza places the source of Jewish survival into the hands of the enemies of the Jews. This attack obviously touches the Jewish people as a whole, but its immediate target must be sought, I propose, in that group of Sephardic Jews that was especially close to him, in the community in which he grew up and knew so intimately. Most of its members were refugees from conversion and the Inquisition, fiercely proud to have succeeded in preserving their Judaism in the Iberian Peninsula *despite* the hatred of the Gentiles, not because of it. In order to appreciate the full sting in Spinoza's words, it will suffice to compare them with those written on the same subject by Isaac Cardoso, a Marrano who left Spain in the middle of the 17th century and returned to Judaism in Italy. In his Spanish book *The Excellencies of the Jews* (*Las excelencias de los Hebreos*), which was published in Amsterdam only nine years after the appearance of the *Tractatus*, we can find a genuine expression of the emotions of that entire generation of Sephardic Jewry:

> The election of Israel to be the people of God, this sacred betrothal, was neither temporary nor conditional but eternal and absolute. . . . God is not like earthly rulers who at one time choose a favorite or minister and at another time repudiate him. . . . In this very abasement and general degradation of the Jews, the Lord has performed miracles with them, and more continuously than in ancient times. What greater marvel than to see a lamb among seventy wolves, as the people of Israel is among the seventy nations of the world, who like carnivorous wolves or rapacious lions desire to tear them to pieces and swallow them alive, but God, like a true shepherd, does not allow it?[18]

I have quoted these words — and it is possible to cite many similar ones from the literature of the Sephardic diaspora of the time — in order to emphasize that Spinoza was not simply firing in the air, but was shooting at a target visible to all. Still, when we come to analyze Spinoza's idea, we should not rely on the subjective factor alone, but also seek other sources for it. It is quite conceivable, for example, that Spinoza knew the commentary of Abravanel on Ezekiel 20 and appropriated it selectively for his own purposes. But there is an even better direction in which to search. Facing Spinoza there stood something else, closer and more dramatic, and it is embedded in that very passage in the *Tractatus* with which we are dealing. I refer to the historical example on which Spinoza relies, and it is appropriate that we now turn to it again and analyze it closely.

IV

Let us refresh our memories by recalling Spinoza's actual words:

That they have been preserved in great measure by Gentile hatred, experience demonstrates. When the king of Spain formerly compelled the Jews to embrace the State religion or to go into exile, a large number of Jews accepted Catholicism. Now, as these renegades were admitted to all the native privileges of Spaniards, and deemed worthy of filling all honourable offices, it came to pass that they straightway became so intermingled with the Spaniards as to leave of themselves no relic or remembrance. But exactly the opposite happened to those whom the king of Portugal compelled to become Christians, for they always, though converted, lived apart, inasmuch as they were considered unworthy of any civic honours.

That Spinoza chose to support his thesis that hatred has preserved the Jews with a historical example from the Iberian Peninsula should not surprise us, in light of his personal background. However, there is here a rather blatant incongruity between Spinoza's general thesis and the historical evidence that accompanies it. In order to prove that the hatred of the nations is what preserves the Jews, he does not turn to the history of the Jews in its usual sense, but to the history of the Marranos, that is to say — not to the history of normative Jews but to that of Jews who had already changed their faith and become Christians, and he does not even pause to consider that the lives of converts may reveal a different dynamic, unique to them.

Nevertheless, one detail in Spinoza's historical example can be accepted as plausible. Although the subject still requires examination, there is certainly a basis for his assertion that most of the Marranos of Spain assimilated in the course of the 16th century, while the converts of Portugal continued to live clandestine Jewish lives for generations, indeed down to our own time. Toward the end of the 15th century the Spaniards were of the opinion that the problem of a secret Judaizing heresy in their country had already been solved. If, in the 17th century, the problem arose anew and more acutely, this was mainly the result of the mass migration of Portuguese Marranos into Spain itself.[19] Thus far, then, Spinoza seems to be on firm ground. But I propose that all the rest of the passage is an instructive example of Spinoza's tendentious use of historical facts for his special purposes.

The impression Spinoza tried to create is transparent enough. In Spain, he argues, the Jewish converts and their descendants were received into all levels of Spanish society and therefore they assimilated completely. By contrast, in Portugal they met with opposition, and as a result of this opposition they did not assimilate. This is proof that it is the hatred of the Gentiles that preserves the Jews.

What could be simpler than that? But this is not how matters developed in the Iberian context. There was no significant difference between Spain and Portugal, either in relation to the admission of the New Christians to "honourable offices" and important posts, nor in the hostility that surrounded them. The two countries merely operated on a different time schedule.

If Spinoza wanted to prove that the admission of the New Christians to "honourable offices" was an important cause contributing to their assimilation, then he did not present the facts correctly. It can be demonstrated that at least during the forty or fifty years after the compulsory conversion of all of Portuguese Jewry in 1497, the New Christians in Portugal *were* in fact admitted to high office, a parallel to what occurred with the converts in Spain in the initial periods of their conversion.[20] If so, then according to Spinoza's own theory, the Portuguese converts too should have assimilated. Conversely, if indeed it was hatred that maintained the converts in their secret Judaism in the Iberian Peninsula, there was no reason to expect different consequences in Spain, on the one hand, and in Portugal, on the other. On the contrary, the converts of Spain too would necessarily have kept their Jewish character and would not have assimilated. For in everything that concerned hatred toward them, identical factors were at work in both countries alike:

First, the Inquisition (which Spinoza does not even mention in his remarks on the hatred of the Gentiles) was established in Spain in 1478 and in Portugal in 1536. The Inquisition in Spain was the prototype of the institution that was later created in Portugal in its likeness and image.

Second, the intense hatred toward the Marranos and the New Christians in general was widespread virtually from the start, in Spain no less than in Portugal. Moreover, even on this score, it is clear that it was in Spain that we first find those phenomena that served as precedents for what occurred in Portugal. The riots against the New Christians in Toledo in 1449 already prefigured the massacre of the New Christians in Lisbon in 1506. We must pause to wonder: Is it conceivable that Spinoza, who grew up in an important refuge for the Marranos of Spain and habitually read Spanish literature, really did not know that Spain too, and not only Portugal, was permeated with hatred of Judaism and of the Marranos?[21]

Third, and above all: the bar to "honourable offices," which is the single detail Spinoza expressly mentions and which he regards as a central point. Even if he did not employ the technical legal designation for this type of discrimination, there can be no doubt that he had in mind the racist legislation in the Iberian Peninsula known by the name of *estatutos de limpieza de sangre*—the laws of purity of blood. These laws were well known to him, just as he knew of the general situation in the Peninsula, as did most of the Amsterdam Jews, not only from books, but from the reports of Marranos who continued to stream into the Dutch capital. It is therefore odd that Spinoza writes about the laws of purity of blood as though they were only a Portuguese phenomenon, without even hinting that their birth and development occurred specifically in *Spain*, and that the Portuguese copied them from the Spaniards.[22]

The laws of purity of blood reflected in essence the reaction of Spanish Christian society to the massive penetration of a huge number of Jews into its midst as a result of conversion. The self-same society that had previously labored to convert the Jews to Christianity subsequently saw in the converts an alien and suspect growth, doubtful Christians and doubtful Jews, and from then on it tried to restrict their influence. Suddenly, as it were, Spaniards discovered that all the anti-Jewish legislation that had crystallized over centuries had now lost its force overnight. From the standpoint of the existing legislation the converts and their descendants were legally Christians and entitled to all the rights previously withheld from them. New discriminatory laws against them could only be created on a new foundation, not on the religious difference on which the traditional legislation had been based, but on a new distinction—on a racial difference, on "purity of blood" (*limpieza de sangre*). From this new, revolutionary standpoint, it was not faith that determined the scope of one's rights but family origin, and the appellation "New Christian" (*cristiano nuevo*) became an official term that would adhere forever even to the descendants of the converts, down to the early nineteenth century. In other words, the degree of personal Catholic orthodoxy of any New Christian determined and changed nothing. Anyone known to be of Jewish origin was disqualified from participating in certain areas of state and society. The first attempt to impose a law of this type had already been made in the middle of the 15th century in Toledo, and its aim was to prevent New Christians from holding office in the local cathedral. This effort failed, not only through the opposition of the New Christians but of Christian theologians who saw in a distinction of this sort a negation of the fundamentals of Christianity. The authorities too sensed, perhaps instinctively, that in this approach lay an explosive potential for a land in which the blood of Christians, Muslims and Jews had long mingled.

At the beginning of the 16th century the pressure to restrict the New Christians prevailed. The efforts to enact the laws of purity of blood in Spain were renewed, and this time they were crowned with success. By the middle of the century the laws of purity of blood spread to almost every locality in Spain. Theoretically they affected the entire population. Any Spaniard who desired, for example, to serve in a municipal or governmental office, or who wished to be accepted to one of the aristocratic colleges (*colegios mayores*) at the universities, or who was a candidate for one of the most privileged chivalric military orders, was required first to receive a certificate from the Inquisition—and this was given him only after a thorough investigation of his family tree—declaring that he was *limpio* ("pure"); that is—that there is no trace of Jewish or Moorish blood in him. The laws of purity of blood turned into an inseparable component of Spanish historical experience and had a profound impact on the Spanish way of life and culture. The same doctrine of purity of blood, which was definitively a Spanish creation, was thereafter adopted in Portugal.

In this phenomenon of the laws of purity of blood, which is essentially the historical proof that Spinoza places before the reader, or more precisely in the controversy that surrounded these laws, one can find, as I shall now attempt to show, the key to the understanding of Spinoza's dictum that hatred preserves the Jews.

V

The situation engendered by the enactment of the laws of purity of blood aroused a stormy debate, both in Spain and Portugal, that continued until the end of the 18th century. The laws of purity of blood not only haunted the descendants of the Jews, but at times turned into a nightmare for many Spaniards and Portuguese. No one could be sure that the dark shadow would not fall on him, either because of some family flaw which the investigators of the Inquisition were liable to reveal, or as a result of denunciation by enemies, or from zealots who were prepared to defame even the faultless. A fundamental theoretical dispute on the subject erupted both from a theological perspective and with regard to the efficacy of such laws in solving "the Jewish problem" in the Iberian Peninsula.

The New Christians in Spain and Portugal of the 16th and 17th centuries had both enemies and defenders, the latter of course not defending the Judaism of the New Christians but, on the contrary, the sincerity of their Christianity. The defenders contended that if there were still suspicion that the New Christians had not yet reached perfection in their Christian faith, this was due not to a lack of willingness but to the obstacles that society placed before them. This aspect of the controversy bears directly on our subject. Among the arguments advanced by the defenders of the New Christians against the system of purity of blood was the recurrent claim that, in one form or another, it was precisely the discriminatory laws that *caused* the preservation of Judaism among the New Christians. If only the New Christians were allowed to live like other people, they would assimilate and be absorbed among the Old Christians until all differences between them would disappear. Instead the laws of purity of blood strengthen them in their Judaism, either because they do not allow them to forget their Jewish origins or because they teach them that no amount of good will or loyalty to Christianity could change their standing in society to the slightest degree. In despair they revert to their evil ways and fall again onto the bosom of Judaism.[23]

From all the arguments advanced in this controversy let us select one of the more interesting. One of the eminent personages in the history of Portugal and a central figure in the 17th century was the Jesuit father António Vieira. Vieira served both in Portugal and in Brazil, was close to the royal court, and was a great preacher and fervent messianist. Toward the end of his life he was even harassed by the Inquisition.[24] He was also the most important supporter of the New Christians in Portugal, on both religious and patriotic reasons. Vieira was convinced that the division between "New" and "Old" Christians had brought and was bringing economic catastrophe to the country; time after time he pleaded with the Crown to change the methods of the Inquisition and to repeal the laws of purity of blood, which to his mind were the root of the evil.[25] In 1646, when Spinoza was twelve, Vieira proposed to King John IV of Portugal a three-point plan, of which the second stated: "It should be recognized that every 'Man of the Nation' [*Homem da Nação*, one of the stereotypical synonyms in Portugal for a New Christian] should be eligible for every office, honor or appointment;" that is to say, that the laws of purity of blood be abolished. Vieira explains: "This is the greatest war which it is possible to wage against Judaism to destroy it and finish it"[26] (*Esta é a maior guerra que se pode fazer ao Judaismo Para o extinguir e acabar*). The underlying theory was simple: What preserves the Judaism of the Marranos of Portugal is the discrimination and hostility that they suffer.

Whether these words of Vieira reached Spinoza—something that is entirely possible—or whether they did not, the views of Vieira were known among the Hispano-Portuguese Jewish diaspora. Vieira himself came to Holland twice in 1646–1647. He visited the synagogue in The Hague and even had conversations with Rabbi Manasseh ben Israel and other Jews.[27] His desire to abolish the laws of purity of blood was certainly known to various circles of Jews and New Christians, for he proposed, among other things, to work for the abolition of these laws in exchange for financial assistance they would give for the purpose of establishing a commercial company for trade with Brazil. One can assume that those he talked to knew the nature of the arguments he advanced in his appeal to the King of Portugal.[28] But the primary importance of Vieira's words is that they reflect a state of mind that others shared in the 17th century. The dispute over purity of blood in Spain and Portugal was notorious and had reverberations throughout Europe.[29] The content and wording of the passage in Spinoza testify eloquently that its source lies in this context. This is the actual background of his thesis, indeed, the source of the historical example that he cites as proof. But in the *Tractatus* Spinoza chose to pass in complete silence over the *Spanish* legislation on purity of blood, for otherwise his proof would lose its force. And, for his own reasons, he broadened the explanation according to which discrimination preserves the crypto-Judaism of the Marranos to the global pronouncement that the hatred of the nations is what preserves the entire Jewish people.

Spinoza knew other interesting things that he preferred not to mention in his book. In his collected correspondence there is a letter addressed to Albert Burgh. Burgh was at first a Protestant and a disciple of Spinoza in Holland, but after he traveled to Italy he converted to Catholicism. In September 1675 Burgh wrote a letter from Florence, arrogant and aggressive in tone, announcing that he had undertaken no less a task than to persuade Spinoza that he too should convert to the Catholic faith. Of course Spinoza completely rejected Burgh's proposals, but there is something of special interest in his reaction to one of Burgh's arguments. When speaking in praise of the Catholic Church, and noting a mark of its truth, Burgh mentioned the long record of Catholic martyrdom. On these grounds, Spinoza replied, the Christians have no reason to boast in comparison to the Jews:

> But the matter in which they [i.e., the Jews] glory and take special pride is the large number of martyrs which has no parallel in any other nation, and daily the number increases of those who accept torture in a very steadfast and wonderful way, in order to sanctify their faith. And this is not a lie. I myself knew, among others, of a man named Judah, who in the midst of the flames, when he was already thought dead, began to sing the hymn which opens with the words "Into Thy hands do I entrust my spirit" and, while singing, he expired.[30]

We know very well who this Judah was who is mentioned in the passage. He was Judah the Believer (in Spanish "Juda Creente"), among the most renowned victims of the Inquisition in the 17th century, who earned fame and glory throughout the Sephardic diaspora. It is likely that Spinoza knew about him by reading Manasseh ben Israel's *The Hope of Israel* (*Esperança de Israel*), which was dedicated to the communal leaders of Amsterdam, among whom is inscribed the name of Spinoza's father. The particularly striking detail in the episode of "Judah the Believer"—and it is important for our subject—is that the man called *Juda Creente* was not born a Jew, and did not even come from a family of New Christians. His true name was Don Lope de Vera y Alarcón. He was a Castilian nobleman of the purest Old Christian ancestry, who studied Hebrew at Salamanca, became convinced that the religion of Moses was the true faith, and was imprisoned as a Judaizer by the Spanish Inquisition. Even in prison he refused to return to Christianity, and by his free choice he died a martyr's death, burned at the stake in the auto-da-fé of Valladolid in 1644.[31]

The question arises: How is the phenomenon of Don Lope de Vera, to which Spinoza refers, consistent with his thesis that it is the hatred of the nations that preserves Judaism? Obviously, although Spinoza wrote both passages, there is no linkage here, but rather two different contexts. In the *Tractatus* Spinoza wants to dispel the idea that the preservation of the Jewish people is the result of Divine Providence, and he therefore renders a judgment that denies to this people any active role in determining its destiny. Five years later, however, when he is refuting the Catholic arguments of Burgh, Spinoza informs us of the story of a Christian whom he knew to be a voluntary convert to Judaism, of singing amidst the flames, and of the martyrdom of the Jews. In his letter to Burgh there is no trace or echo of the thesis concerning the hatred of the nations. On the contrary, in his response to the Catholic who tried to advance as further proof the antiquity and firm foundation of the Church, Spinoza writes about the Jews:

> Their pedigree they trace back to Adam. In that arrogance itself they take pride that their church stands, and to this very day maintains its growth, its permanence and stability, despite the bitter hatred of the Gentile idolaters and the Christians. They principally claim credit for themselves by reason of their antiquity. They unanimously proclaim and announce that they received the religious tradition from the hands of God Himself and they alone observe the words of God, written and unwritten. And indeed no one can deny that all the dissenters separated from them, while they themselves are preserved and endure for thousands of years with no compulsion whatsoever from any government and with only the force of this superstitious faith.[32]

In the *Tractatus* the Jewish people did not earn even this limited appreciation—namely, that it is preserved by virtue of its faith, albeit a superstitious one. Apart from the causal factor of the hatred of the nations, Spinoza mentions in the *Tractatus* only the distinguishing and preserving force of circumcision; this is presented without connection to faith, but rather as a physical and outward mark alone, like the pigtails of the Chinese.

There is no reason whatever to assume that Spinoza changed this earlier position, or that any evolution had taken place in his opinions from the time that he wrote the *Tractatus*. After all, even the letter to Burgh exhibits a derogatory attitude toward the Jews and their religion. The two quotations I have cited do not point to a new sympathy, but only teach us about the weapons Spinoza took in hand to beat off his adversary. Herein lies their importance for our subject. If, in the *Tractatus* we heard nothing of "Judah the Believer," and if in the letter to Burgh there is no mention of the assimilation of the Marranos of Spain, there can be only one conclusion, and that is that Spinoza remained after all a man of flesh and blood, and that he had personal considerations beyond pure theorizing. Like many others, both before and after him, Spinoza used historical examples or disregarded them when it suited him, with full awareness and in accordance with various and changing objectives.

VII

Spinoza's thesis on the preservation of the Jewish people bore implications for the future, and I shall conclude by briefly pointing to one of them.

I see in the third chapter of the *Theologico-Political Treatise* an important station on the road to the secularization of Jewish history and to the historicization of Judaism,[33] two tendencies that would gain momentum in the 18th century in various influential non-Jewish circles.

In the passage on the survival of the Jews there lay a paradoxical potential. The idea that it is the hatred of the nations that preserves the Jews can be turned into an argument in favor of tolerance toward them as human beings. For if in fact the hatred of the nations preserves the Jews in their Judaism, it follows that benevolence will lead to their assimilation amongst the nations.[34] And in fact this was one of the fundamental assumptions of the partisans of the Jews in the debate on the emancipation of the Jews of France at the end of the 18th century, and later in other countries. By this I do not mean to say that the key personages who participated in the debate drew their arguments directly from the *Tractatus*. At the threshold of the French Revolution there was no longer any need for this. The essence of Spinoza's teachings had already become the common property of the liberal intelligentsia in France, and the same is true of the philosopher's views on the survival of the Jewish people. On the other hand, we know that in the second half of the 18th century, many in France read the writings of Spinoza, and it is natural, therefore, that directly or indirectly, and along with other influences, something of Spinoza would be absorbed.[35]

In retrospect it is clear that in the era of Emancipation it was precisely the champions of Jewish equality who advocated their assimilation. The crucial point is that neither their enemies nor their friends wanted the Jews as they were. The great debate turned, at the end of the day, on the prospects and capacity of the Jews to change, to assimilate, in short— to cease to be Jews. Of course there is no comparison between the rhetoric of the French Revolution and that of Spain and Portugal in the 16th and 17th centuries. In revolutionary France it was no longer fashionable to demand religious conversion, and instead there was much talk of national assimilation. Nevertheless, from a phenomenological standpoint, striking parallels can be seen between the debate over emancipation in France and the controversy over purity of blood in the Iberian Peninsula. The opponents of Jewish emancipation in France were absolutely convinced that even the granting of equal rights to the Jews would obliterate neither their Jewish characteristics nor their national-religious identity, and that it was impossible for them to merge successfully with the rest of the population. By contrast, the proponents of emancipation contended that if only discrimination and restrictions were ended and the difference in their legal standing abolished, the Jews would become, after a while, "human beings" like all others. Here we have the final transformation of the Spinozist idea. The survival of the Jewish people is conceived not in metaphysical terms but as a product of history alone; this history was made neither by God nor by the Jews, but by the nations of the world, and therefore the nations have the ability to change it completely and radically.

Where have we arrived?

I have tried to show how a view that was widespread in Spain and Portugal—namely, that tolerance would bring about the total assimilation of the New Christians, whose Judaism was solely the result of discrimination—was molded by Spinoza into a more general thesis according to which the hatred of the nations was the cause for the survival of the Jews. This thesis was destined to evolve into arguments in favor of equal rights for the Jews in the era of Emancipation. Our journey has led us from the Iberian Peninsula to Holland, and from there to France. And with that, the circle is closed.

[Editors' note: The text included here is an English translation of the Hebrew lecture that Yerushalmi delivered in Jerusalem in 1977. It lacks Yerushalmi's usual stylistic felicity, deviates from the Hebrew at various points, and thus, in all likelihood, is not of Yerushalmi's hand. The editors have slightly altered the translation to assure greater fluency. The original Hebrew lecture was subsequently published as "Divre Shpinoza 'al kiyum ha-'am ha-Yehudi" in *Divre ha-akademiyah ha-yisre'elit le-mada'im* 6:10 (1982/83), 171–213. A French version of the lecture, "Propos de Spinoza sur la survivance du peuple juif," was published in 1998 in a collection of Yerushalmi's papers on Sephardic themes, *Sefardica: Essais sur l'histoire des juifs, des marranes et des nouveaux-chrétiens d'origine hispano-portugaise* (Paris: Chandeigne, 1998). A year later, a German version of the lecture was published as *Spinoza und das Überleben des jüdischen Volkes* (Munich: Lehrstuhl für Jüdische Geschichte und Kultur, Institut für Neuere Geschichte, Ludwig-Maximilians-Universität, 1999). The English translation of the lecture, a copy of which we received from Yerushalmi's French translator Eric Vigne, did not have the footnotes that were included in the published Hebrew version of the lecture. A handwritten copy of the notes, however, was found in the Columbia University Rare Book and Manuscript Library, Yerushalmi Papers Box 7/5, Folder 12. The handwriting of the notes does not belong to Yerushalmi. And similar to the lecture, the notes lack his literary flair and are likely a translation from Hebrew made by someone other than Yerushalmi. Accordingly, we have relied heavily on the Hebrew original in producing the notes here. We have *not* included here the article's appendix, which discusses and lists Spanish books and books about Spain in Spinoza's library.]

The origin of this paper lies in an address that I delivered before the Israeli National Academy of Sciences on 3 May 1977, and for technical reasons its publication has been delayed till now. While I have here broadened the discussion in a number of places and have added footnotes and an appendix, I did not think it proper to change the style of presentation in the body of the text, and I preferred to commit my remarks to print in the manner in which they were delivered before the assembled group.

1. What is mainly discussed are the influences that were likely to distance the youthful Spinoza from traditional Judaism. On the Dutch sects, see, for example, K. Meinsma, *Spinoza en zijn kring*, The Hague, 1898 (German translation: *Spinoza und sein Kreis*, Berlin, 1909); C. Hylkema, *Reformateurs — Geschiedkundige studien over de godsdienstige bewegingen uit de nadagen onzer gouden eeuw*, I–II, Haarlem, 1900–1902; J. Severijn, *Spinoza en de gereformeerde theologie zijner dagen*, Utrecht,

1919. For an opposing view, see Madeleine Frances, *Spinoza dans le pays néerlandais de la seconde moitié du XVIIe siècle*, Paris, 1937.

2. This is how the subject was presented even at the beginning of our century. In the first edition of the outstanding biography of Freudenthal (J. Freudenthal, *Das Leben Spinozas*, Stuttgart, 1904), the fourth chapter deals with Spinoza's alienation from Judaism. When dealing with the Jewish context, only the skepticism of the YaShaR (Joseph Solomon Delmedigo) of Candia and the excommunication of Uriel da Costa are mentioned.

3. C. Gebhardt, *Die Schriften des Uriel da Costa (Bibliotheca Spinozana*, II, Amsterdam-Heidelberg-London, 1922).

4. C. Gebhardt, "Dr. Juan de Prado," *Chronicon Spinozanum*, III (1922), pp. 269–291.

5. See: I. S. Révah, *Spinoza et le Dr. Juan de Prado*, Paris–La Haye, 1959, as well as his articles: "Aux origines de la rupture spinozienne—Nouveaux documents sur l'incroyance dans la communauté judéo-portugaise d'Amsterdam à l'époque de l'excommunication de Spinoza," *Revue des études juives* [= *REJ*], III [CXXIII] (1964), pp. 358–431; "Aux origines de la rupture spinozienne—Nouvel examen des origines, du déroulement et des conséquences de l'affaire Spinoza-Prado-Ribera," *Annuaire du Collège de France*, LXX (1970–1973), pp. 562–568; LXXI (1971–1972), pp. 574–589; LXXII (1972–1973), pp. 641–653. For additional information on de Prado see Y. Kaplan, "Nueva información sobre la estancia de Juan de Prado en Amberes," *Sefarad*, XXXV (1975), pp. 159–163.

6. Among the monographs and articles that have recently appeared on Sephardic Jewry in Amsterdam alone, and on its religious and intellectual currents in the 17th century, we may cite as examples: Y. Kaplan, "R. Shaul Morteira ve-ḥiburo 'Ta'anot ve-hasagot neged ha-dat ha-notsrit,'" in *Meḥkarim 'al toldot yahadut Holand*, v. 1, Jerusalem, 1975, pp. 23–29; K. R. Scholberg, *La poesía religiosa de Miguel de Barrios*, Madrid [undated]; Wilhelmina C. Pieterse, *Daniel Levi de Barrios als geschiedschrijver van de Portugees-Israelietische Gemeente te Amsterdam in zijn "Triumpho del Govierno Popular*," Amsterdam, 1968; A. Altmann, "Eternality of Punishment—A Theological Controversy within the Amsterdam Rabbinate in the Thirties of the Seventeenth Century," *Proceedings of the American Academy for Jewish Research*, XL (1972), pp. 1–88. (In the debate described in this article, Isaac Aboab da Fonseca and Saul Levi Morteira took part.) On the background of Uriel da Costa, as well as a discussion of the later writings of I. S. Révah, see G. Nahon, "Les Sephardim, les Marranes, les Inquisitions péninsulaires et leurs archives dans les travaux récents de I.-S. Révah," *REJ*, XII [CXXXII] (1973), pp. 5–48.

7. For a useful bibliography see J. Caro-Baroja, *Los Judíos en la España mo-*

derna y contemporánea, III, Madrid, 1961. Although this book suffers from serious errors and distortions, it contains important information on the New Christians in Spain from the time of the expulsion, even though the author did not always grasp its significance.

8. See M. de Unamuno, *Del sentimiento trágico de la vida*, chap. 1, in: *Ensayos*, II, Madrid, 1966, pp. 729 ff.

9. "His story has passed into a legend: his life is held up as that of a saint" (L. Roth, *Spinoza*, London, 1929, p. 15). Examples of this can be found in the collection containing words of praise of Spinoza by various authors: *Chronicon Spinozanum*, I, The Hague, 1921, pp. vii–xviii; E. Altkirch, *Maledictus und Benedictus—Spinoza im Urteil des Volkes und des Geistigen bis auf Constantin Brunner*, Leipzig, 1924. Graetz harshly criticized Spinoza's thinking to the point that he even regarded it as a justification for the Inquisition: "Die Scheiterhaufen der Inquisition gegen die Marranen waren nach diesem System doppelt gerechtfertigt." At the same time, he maintained that it was Spinoza's personality that prevented the danger from spreading to the Jews: "Allein Spinoza hatte eine Charactereigenschaft, welche dem Judentum damals zu statten kam. Er liebte zu sehr Frieden und Ruhe, als dass er mit seinen kritischen Grundsätzen hatte Propoganda machen wollen. 'Friedfertig und ruhig zu sein,' das war für ihn das Ideal des Lebens. . . . Bis an sein Lebensende führte er ein ideal-philosophisches Leben" (H. Graetz, *Geschichte der Juden*, X, Leipzig, 1900, pp. 178–179).

10. Cited by S. Baron in his article, "World Dimensions in Jewish History," *History and Jewish Historians*, Philadelphia, 1964, p. 38.

11. In his *Discours dur l'histoire universelle*, Bossuet placed Jewish history at the center of human history, and then explained the general course of history as the result of divine will and providence. For Voltaire's views, see *Dictionnaire philosophique* (1764), s.v. *Histoire*. On the two, see K. Löwith, *Meaning in History*, Chicago, 1949, chaps. V, VII.

12. Baruch Spinoza, *Ma'amar teologi-politi* (translated from the Latin by Ch. Wirszubski, Jerusalem, 1962, pp. 42–43). In the original: "Quare hodie Judaei nihil prorsus habent, quod sibi supra omnes Nationes tribuere possint. Quod autem tot annos dispersi absque imperio perstiterint, id minime mirum, postquam se ab omnibus nationibus ita separaverunt, ut omnium odium in se converterint, idque non tantum ritibus externis, ritibus caeterarum nationum contrariis, sed etiam signo circumcisionis, quod religiosissime servant. Quod autem Nationum odium eos admodum conservet, id jam experientia docuit. Cum Rex Hispaniae olim Judaeos coëgit Regni Religionem admittere, vel in exiliym ire, perplurimi Judaei pontificiorum Religionem admiserunt; sed quia iis, qui religionem admiserunt, omnia Hispanorum naturalium privilegia concessa sunt, iique

omnibus honoribus digni, existimati sunt, statim ita se Hispanis immiscuerunt, ut pauco post tempore nullae eorum reliquiae manserint, neque ulla memoria. At plane contra iis contigit, quos Rex Lusitanorum religionem sui imperii admittere coëgit, qui semper, quamvis ad religionem conversi, ab omnibus separati vixerunt, nimirum quia eos omnibus honoribus indignos declaravit" (B. Spinoza, *Tractatus Theologico-Politicus*, ed. C. Gebhardt [*Opera*, III], Heidelberg, 1924, pp. 56–57].

It is strange that scholars of Spinoza, even those who were especially interested in his Jewish side, almost ignored this important passage. Thus, for example, Joel, in his book on the sources of the *Theologico-Political Treatise*, mentions only Spinoza's views on the customs of the Jews, not on the hatred of the Gentiles: "Ebenso erklärt Spinoza die Erhaltung der Juden durch die Natur ihrer Riten, statt richtiger zu sagen, die Erhaltung der Riten folge aus der Natur der Juden' (M. Joel, *Spinoza's Theologisch-Politischer Traktat auf seine Quellen geprüft*, Breslau 1870, p.49).

By contrast, H. Cohen quotes the passage in the course of his sharp attack on Spinoza without commenting on it. See H. Cohen, "Spinoza über Staat und Religion, Judentum und Christentum," *Jüdische Schriften*, III, Berlin, 1924, pp. 332–333. Nor is the passage mentioned at all in Freudenthal's book (J. Freudenthal, *Spinoza Leben und Lehre*, ed. C. Gebhardt, Heidelberg, 1927), nor even by Strauss (L. Strauss, *Die Religionskritik Spinozas*, Berlin, 1930). Wolfson's important book (H. A. Wolfson, *The Philosophy of Spinoza*, v. I, II, Cambridge [Mass.], 1954) is devoted entirely to "The Ethics." Although Wolfson comments on our passage, for some reason, he passes silently over its negative tone: "Speaking of his own people, Spinoza says that the Jews have maintained their historical continuity as a people because they have preserved the continuity of certain institutions, and he refers to the fact that a number of Jews in Spain who have broken away from their past have disappeared as Jews even though they were not physically exterminated." (Ibid, v. II, p. 250).

Even in the works of J. Klatzkin (*Barukh Shpinoza*, Leipzig, 1923), N. Sokolov, *Shpinoza u-vene doro*, Paris, 1929) and E. Shmueli, *Masoret u-mahpekhah*, New York, 1942), Spinoza's view of Gentile hatred did not merit special attention. It seems to me that Yitzhak Baer was the only one to grasp the historical significance of this passage (see below, n. 34). Generally speaking, it is not the passage under discussion but its continuation that raises, as it were, the possibility of the reestablishment of a Jewish state, that has attracted the attention and enthusiasm of students. It is not within our purview to discuss here the details of what was included in *Sefer ha-tsiyonut* of B. Dinur. I will only note that, to my mind, there is no affirmative content whatsoever in Spinoza's reflections on this subject.

The various efforts to present him as one of the precursors of Zionism are an especially interesting chapter of the Spinozist myth, that exerted an influence, for the most part, without any connection at all to Spinoza's own intention.

13. Y. F. Baer, *Galut* (Engl. trans.), New York, 1947, p. 105. Already in the 17th century Spinoza is portrayed in an anti-Dutch treatise in these words: "C'est un homme qui est né juif, qui n'a point abjuré la religion des juifs ny embrassé la religion chrétienne: aussi il est très méchant juif et n'est pas meilleur chrestien" (*La religion des Hollandais*, Paris, 1673, p. 90).

14. See Ch. Wirszubski, "Spinoza's Debt to Tacitus," *Scripta Hierosolymitana*, II, Jerusalem 1955, pp. 176–186.

15. Simhah Luzzatto, *Ma'amar al Yehude Venetsyah*, trans. D. Lats (Jerusalem, 1950), p. 151.

16. Abravanel, *Perush nevi'im aharonim*, Ezekiel 20:33. In the continuation of these remarks he again emphasizes: "'And with wrath outpoured' is directed at those who transgressed against their faith, and in this lies the explanation for the fact that a Jew, despite having sinned, remains a Jew, and even if the Jews worshipped foreign idols, they did not depart from God's providence and guidance."

17. This idea had already been expressed by Augustine: "Et nunc quod per omnes fere terras gentesque dispersi sunt, illius unius veri Dei providentia est . . ." (*De Civitate Dei*, IV, 34). And in the 17th century, Pascal, a contemporary of Spinoza, offered this impression of the Jewish people: "Ce peuple n'est pas seulement considérable par son antiquité; mais il est encore singulier en sa durée, qui a toujours continué depuis son origine jusqu'à maintenant. Car, au lieu que les peuples de Grèce et d'Italie, de Lacédémone, d'Athènes, de Rome, et les autres qui sont venus si longtemps après soient péris il y a si longtemps, ceux-ci subsistent toujours, et malgré les entreprises de tant de puissants rois qui ont cent fois essayé de les faire périr, comme leurs historiens le témoignent, et comme il est aisé de le juger par l'ordre naturel des choses, pendant un si long espace d'années, ils ont toujours été conservés néanmoins (et cette conservation a été prédite); et, s'étendant depuis les premiers temps jusqu'aux derniers, leur histoire enferme dans sa durée celle de toutes nos histoires." (Pascal, *Pensées* [*Oeuvres complètes*, ed. J. Chevalier], Paris, 1954, No. 408, p. 1196.)

18. Isaac Cardoso, *Las excelencias de los Hebreos*, Amsterdam, 1679, pp. 5, 13 f.

19. On these developments, see Y. H. Yerushalmi, *From Spanish Court to Italian Ghetto*, New York–London, 1971, pp. 3–11.

20. As is well known, after the mass conversion in Portugal, King Manuel on May 30, 1497, issued a proclamation in which he promised that, for twenty years, no law would be passed that would discriminate against the New Christians. This

assurance was renewed in 1507, 1509, and 1512, and then by João III in 1522 and 1524. See A. Herculano, *Da origem e estabelecimento da Inquisição em Portugal*, I, Lisbon, 1854, pp. 129, 161, 179. It is possible to gather information on New Christians who occupied high office from various sources; a few examples will suffice. The tax farmer João Rodriguz Mascarenhas, who was killed in the Lisbon massacre of 1506 is noted by Solomon Ibn Verga in his *Shevet Yehudah*, ed. Y. Baer and A. Schochat (Jerusalem, 1946/47), p. 126. The non-Hebrew sources concerning him are discussed in my article, "The Lisbon Massacre of 1506 and the Royal Image in the 'Shebet Yehudah,'" *Hebrew Union College Annual*, Supplement No. 1, Cincinnati, 1976, pp. 11–12. (Concerning another tax farmer, who is mentioned in a document from 1509, named Ammrique Fernandez Abarbanell, see ibid, n. 33.) Duarte de Paz, among the leaders of the New Christians in the time of João III, held an important government post before his departure from Portugal to Rome, and was a knight in the order of nobles, Ordem de Christo (Herculano, p. 266). The testimony of Samuel Usque is particularly important; Usque states that the New Christians in the first generation after the conversion "sank into the temptations of power" and "felt themselves secure in their imitation of the Christians, although they never converted in the depths of their souls." See S. Usque, *Consolaçam as tribulaçoens de Israel*, ed. J. Mendes dos Remédios (Coimbra, 1906–1908), III, chapter 30. Immanuel Aboab, for his part, mentions no statutory discrimination against the New Christians in the time of King Manuel. See Immanuel Aboab, *Nomologia o discursos legales* (Amsterdam, 1629), p. 292. In fact, discrimination of this sort is not mentioned in any source, and it is simply an invention of Spinoza in order to explain the preservation of Judaism among the Marranos of Portugal. See also n. 22 below.

21. On the hatred toward Spanish Marranos in the 16th century, see Y. Baer, *Toldot ha-yehudim bi-Sefarad ha-notsrit* (Tel Aviv, 1965), chapter 6. For a survey, albeit incomplete, of the anti-Semitic books written in Spain after the Expulsion see Caro-Baroja (supra, n. 7), v. II, chapter VI: "El Arsenal Antijudio." Edward Glazer has studied Spanish anti-Semitism as it was reflected in *belles-lettres* and the theatre; see especially E. Glazer, "Referencias antisemitas en la literatura peninsular de la Edad de Oro," *Nueva Revista de Filología Hispánica*, VIII (1954), pp. 39–62. In Spinoza's time there was no recognizable difference between expressions of anti-Semitism in Spain and in Portugal (see my book, supra, n. 19, passim, and the literature referred to there). Concerning Spinoza and Spanish literature and on the anti-Semitic elements in the books he kept in his library, see the Appendix, below. [Editors' note: The appendix, "Spain and Spanish in Spinoza's Library," is a catalog and analysis of all the books in Spanish and about

Spain in Spinoza's library, and their possible influence on his thought. It remains valuable to students of Spinoza, but it has not been republished here due to its specialized nature.]

22. The Spanish purity of blood laws have been the subject of important studies, most significantly A. Sicroff, *Les controverses des statuts de 'pureté de sang' en Espagne du XVe au XVIIe siècle*, Paris, 1960; A. Dominguez Ortiz, *La clase social de los conversos en Castilla en la edad moderna*, Madrid, 1955. While purity of blood laws were in force in Spain in the 16th century, they did not yet have official standing in Portugal. The big push came after 1580, when Philip II annexed Portugal to his kingdom, and the country was subjected to Spanish hegemony and influence for the next sixty years. See A. J. Saraiva, *Inquisição e Cristãos-Novos* (Porto, 1969), pp. 165–174, chapter VII: "A limpeza de sangue."

23. At the end of the 16th century, the Dominican monk Fray Augustin Salucio wrote an article on the need for fundamental reform of the purity of blood laws: *Discurso acerca de la justicia y buen gobierno de España en las estatutos de limpieza de sangre, y si conviene o no alguna limitación en ellos*. One of his important contentions was that no matter how much the New Christians tried to forget that they were of Jewish stock and hide their origin from their children, the purity of blood laws exposed the "blemish" of their origins to everyone. It was at that moment that the risk arose that they would be tempted to choose the faith of their fathers. Here are his words: "Pues no es cosa de lástima, que haya muchos que para asegurar á sus hijos deseen grandemente que no sepan de la infidelidad de sus abuelos, y que el rigor de los estatutos los oblique (mal que les pese) á descubrirlos, lo que forzosamente en gente flaca les ha de ser tentación y tropiezo? Clara es, que viendo que la deshonra de aquella secta no la pueden echar de si, corren peligro de buscar consuelo en creer, que quizá era la major ley la de sus antepasados" (Sicroff [supra, n. 22], p. 201).

In 1637 Jerónimo de la Cruz's book appeared which sought to uphold the principle of purity of blood: *Defensa de los estatutos y noblezas españolas*. The author completely rejects the views of Salucio, but nevertheless acknowledges that many people of Jewish descent, upon seeing that they are denied positions of honor in Spain, "pass over to the synagogues of Holland and Salonika" (cited in Sicroff, p. 249). Similar views were held even by an anonymous inquisitor, who put them in writing in the days of Philip IV (ibid., 176–177, 213). It is interesting that, without specifically mentioning the laws of purity of blood, David Abenatar Melo, a former Marrano, wrote in his preface to the Spanish paraphrase of The Book of Psalms, that the Inquisition was a "school" in which the Marranos learned to recognize God, and in which "their lost blood was renewed." That is, it was through the Inquisition that they came to recognize their Jewish origins. See David Abenatar Melo, *Los CL Psalmos de David in* [*sic*] *lengua española, en varias rimas* (Franquaforte [Amsterdam] 5386 [1626]), fol. 2. Similar to the status of New Christians of Jewish origin was the status of the Moriscos, Christians of Muslim origin, before their expulsion from Spain in 1609–1614. Claims about the adverse effect of the laws of purity of blood were also directed at them. Thus, for example, Pedro Fernández de Navarrete argued that if only the marks of shame (that is, the laws of purity of blood) were lifted from the Moriscos before the expulsion, then they might have become true Catholics, perhaps through the "Gates of Honor": "con todo esto me persuade á que si antes que estos hubieron llegado á la desesperación . . . se hubiera buscado forma de admitirlos á alguna parte de honores, sin tenerlos en la nota y señal de la infamia, fuera posible que por la puerta del honor hubieran entrado al templo de la virtud y al gremio; obediencia de la Iglesia católica" (Pedro Fernández de Navarrete, *Conservación de monarquias*, Madrid, 1626, Discurso VII).

24. On the life and works of Vieira, see J. Lúcio d'Azevedo, *História de António Vieira*, I–II, Lisbon, 1931. On the Inquisition's case against him see ibid., II, pp. 5–88 and the appendices. See also António Vieira, *Defesa perante o tribunal do Santo Ofício*, I–II, ed. H. Cidade (Bahia, 1957).

25. His main works on the New Christians, purity of blood and the Inquisition were gathered in António Vieira, *Obras escolhidas*, ed. A. Sergio & H. Cidade, IV [*Obras varias*, II: *Os Judeus e a Inquisição*] (Lisbon, 1951).

26. Vieira (supra, n. 25), IV, p. 50. This idea appears in his work in various formulations. The legal differentiation between New and Old Christians damaged both the collective and the individual, and the elimination of this distinction was the most effective way to bring about the automatic disappearance of Judaism in Portugal: "por ser esta distinção causa de grandes danos, assim públicos como particulares, e a indistinção o meio mais efficaz de se extinguir o Judaismo" (ibid., p. 44). In another work of 1674, which some attribute to Vieira, the argument is advanced that if the laws of purity of blood would be repealed in Portugal, Judaism would be eliminated there within twenty years: "e se isto se extinguir em Portugal, em vinte anos se extinguirá o Judaismo" (ibid., p. 124).

27. On Vieira's visit to France and Holland, see d'Azevedo (supra, n. 24), I, chaps. 3–6, pp. 92–148. On his meeting with Manasseh ben Israel, see ibid., pp. 140–141. And recently, A. J. Saraiva, "Antonio Vieira, Menasseh ben Israel, et le Cinquième Empire," *Studia Rosenthaliana*, VI (1972), pp. 25–56.

28. On the interesting episode of Vieira's plans for a trading company in Brazil, for which he gained the cooperation of Portuguese Jesuits, New Christians, and Jews of Portuguese origin in France and Holland, see especially I. S. Révah, "Les Jésuites portugais contre l'Inquisition—La campagne pour la fondation de

la Compagnie Générale du Commerce du Brésil (1649)," *Revista do Livro*, III–IV (1956), pp. 29, 53.

29. Already in the middle of the 15th century, a book appeared in France opposing the purity of blood law of Toledo, which was the prototype of laws subsequently enacted elsewhere. The author, Henri Mauroy, was a Franciscan monk and professor of Bible at the Sorbonne. On his book see Dominguez Ortiz (supra, n. 22), p. 43 ff.; Sicroff (supra, n. 22), p. 158 ff. Other books dealing with the protracted dispute were published in Spanish Flanders, such as the well-known book of Diego de Simancas in defense of the laws, which was published in Antwerp in 1575. However, it was not only books that disseminated information about what was occurring in the Iberian peninsula. The doctrine of purity of blood was widely known throughout Europe and became an object of derision. Spaniards and Portuguese often complained that when they traveled abroad, they were a laughing stock and called "Jews." See the anonymous work, "Noticias reconditas do modo de proceder da Inquisição com os seus presos" (Vieira [supra, n. 25], IV, p. 182): "vulgarmente entre as mais: nações da Europa se equivoca portugues com judeu." As late as the beginning of the 19th century, the English poet Lord Byron recalls with much humor the Spanish fanaticism reflected in purity of blood laws in his renowned poem "Don Juan." Concerning the Spanish origin of the hero he writes,

> His father's name was José—*Don*, of course,
> A true Hidalgo, free from every stain
> Of Moor or Hebrew blood, he traced his source
> Through the most Gothic gentlemen of Spain. . . .

And on Doña Julia:

> The darkness of her oriental eye
> Accorded with her Moorish origin;
> (Her blood was not all Spanish, by the by;
> In Spain, you know, this is a sort of sin).

(*Don Juan*, Canto I, ix, lxvi, in: *The Poetical Works of Lord Byron* [New York–London 1946], pp. 638, 643).

30. Baruch Spinoza, *Igrot*, trans. E. Shmueli (Jerusalem, 1963), p. 272. The Latin original is in Gebhardt's edition of Spinoza, *Epistolae*, Opera, IV (Heidelberg, 1924), pp. 321–322. The sentence, "ipse enim inter alios quendam Judam, quem fidum appellant, novi" is translated by Shmueli as "I myself knew, among others, a man named Yehuda." I thought it proper to alter this translation to "I myself knew, among others, *of* a man," since, as will be clarified presently, it is

impossible that Spinoza was personally acquainted with Don Lope de Vera. Cf. J. Weill, "Spinoza et le Judaïsme," *REJ*, XLIX (1904), p. 167.

31. The story of Don Lope de Vera is cited in several other sources: Isaac Cardoso, *Las excelencias de los Hebreos*, p. 363; Daniel Levi (Miguel) de Barrios, *Triumpho del govierno popular*, Amsterdam, 5443, pp. 43 f. An elegy in Spanish on de Vera by Antonio Enríquez Gómez is found in manuscript at the Bodleian Library (Neubauer Catalogue 2481.5). Another version of the elegy was published by Cecil Roth, except that he mistakenly attributed it to the martyr himself. See: C. Roth, "Le chant du cygne de Don Lope de Vera," *REJ*, XCVII (1934), pp. 105–111. The incident of Don Lope de Vera left a strong impression in Spain itself, where there was astonishment that a "pure" Spanish nobleman was prepared to convert and die for his faith. The anti-Semitic Franciscan monk Francisco de Torrejoncillo, who described the incident, tried to explain the puzzling episode with the claim that Don Lope had once had a wet-nurse of Jewish origin. See his *Centinela contra judios* (Pamplona, 1691), p. 214. The first edition of this work appeared in Spinoza's lifetime.

32. *Igrot* (supra, n. 30), p. 272; and in the Latin original: "Stirpem deinde suam ad Adamum usque proferunt. Eorum Ecclesiam in hunc usque diem propagatam, immotam, & solidam invito hostili Ethnicorum, & Christianorum odio permanere, pari arrogantiâ jactant. Antiquitate omnium maximè defenduntur. Traditiones ab ipso Deo acceptas, seque solos Verbum Dei scriptum, & non scriptum servare, uno ore clamant. Omnes haereses ex iis exiisse, ipsos autem constantes aliquot annorum millia absque ullo imperio cogente, sed solo superstitionis efficaciâ mansisse, negare nemo potest" (*Epistolae* [supra, n. 30] p. 321).

33. Although Spinoza wrote almost exclusively in the *Theologico-Political Treatise* of the ancient "Hebrews" and the religion of the Bible, there is no doubt that his views were interpreted as applying to Jews and Judaism more generally. This is suggested by the French translation of the *Treatise*, which appeared in 1678: *Traitté des ceremonies superstitieuses des juifs tant anciens que modernes.*

34. On this point, only Yitzhak Baer correctly explained, in my view, the significance of Spinoza's words: "If it is true that the Jews are held together only by hate, as Spinoza claims, then there is a simple consequence to be drawn from his concept of history; a conclusion he never expresses directly, to be sure, but which he approaches in his consideration of the situation in the Iberian peninsula. In Spain, where the Jews (New Christians) are admitted to all offices, they have assimilated, but not in Portugal. The Inquisition is to be blamed for the flare-up of religious-national feeling among the Jews, and not the Jewish fidelity for the Inquisition. This interpretation is historically untenable, and it entails a bitter

insult to the Amsterdam Jews, who celebrated the memory of their martyrs in Portugal with fanatical pride. But from this argument there follows the practical doctrine that it is wiser not to persecute the Jews, so that they may of themselves be submerged in the gentiles . . ." (Baer [supra, n. 13], p. 104).

35. On the influence of Spinoza in France see P. Vernière, *Spinoza et la pensée française avant la Révolution* (Paris, 1954), and especially vol. 2, which deals with the eighteenth century. Cf. A. Hertzberg, *The French Enlightenment and the Jews* (New York, 1968), chapter 3. On Spinoza's approach to Judaism, the two authors mention only his views on the ancient Hebrews (Vernière interprets them favorably), but do not discuss his notion that the survival of the Jewish nation was the result of Gentile hatred. The various iterations of this idea among thinkers up to the French Revolution still require examination; I hope to return to this subject elsewhere.

11 : SERVANTS OF KINGS AND NOT SERVANTS OF SERVANTS SOME ASPECTS OF THE POLITICAL HISTORY OF THE JEWS

Original English text delivered as the Tenenbaum Family Lecture in Judaic Studies, Emory University, Atlanta, Georgia, February 8, 2005.

This piece was originally delivered as a lecture in German in Munich in 1993 and reprised in the original English in 2005 as the Tenenbaum Lecture at Emory University. The title of the talk, taken from the fifteenth-century Spanish scholar Isaac Arama, announces Yerushalmi's major theme: the *longue durée* of the "royal alliance" of the Jews, their vertical relationship with state power, extending from the Babylonian Exile in the sixth century BCE to the twentieth century. In a sweeping display of historical learning, Yerushalmi traced two intersecting currents: first, the striking and counterintuitive tradition of royal—and, for that matter, papal—protection of Jews, in stark contrast to the more local medieval practice of *de non tolerandis Judaeis*; and second, the deeply ingrained perception of Jews that monarchic rulers, regardless of their religious differences or biases, consistently acted on behalf of their well-being. The unmistakable termination of this tradition and of the accompanying perception of kingly benevolence came with Nazism. "In the entire historical experience of the Jews," Yerushalmi asserted, "there was nothing to prepare them intellectually or psychologically for what befell them between 1940 and 1945."

Rather than judge the resulting shock as a moral blemish (as did Hannah Arendt, whom he treats with a mixture of respect and criticism), Yerushalmi evinced considerable powers of empathy in explaining how Jews invested so much faith over the centuries in Gentile kings. That account was not a story of political passivity, but of a sophisticated and skillful Jewish politics, indeed, part of what he imagined to be "a history of Jewish diplomacy." In this regard, and for much of this essay, one sees the clear influence of Yerushalmi's mentor at Columbia, Salo Baron. It was Baron who first insisted that the status of Jews under medieval kingdoms as *servi camerae* be translated not as serfs, but as servants of the court—and indeed, as protected and even privileged servants at that. And it was Baron whose classic 1928 essay "Ghetto and Emancipation" sought to restore to Jews in premodern times, especially as a collective, a degree of agency and normalcy often undone by "lachrymose" renderings of their past.

For his own part, Yerushalmi followed an organizational pattern made familiar by his book *Zakhor*: the lecture is divided into four main, chronologically sequenced parts (with the addition of a brief fifth concluding section). The first section features the well-known instance of popular violence against Jews in Alexandria in 38 CE as a way of demonstrating the efficacy of the Jewish entreaty to the emperor Caligula in Rome to reaffirm Jewish autonomy. The second section focuses on the Middle Ages, with Yerushalmi combining his discussion of the formal legal instruments of the royal alliance (e.g., charters and privileges) with a review of important works of medieval Jewish political theory that acknowledged and validated the alliance. This section culminates with a discussion of one of Yerushalmi's most enduring and favorite subjects, Solomon Ibn Verga, whose *Shevet Yehudah* offers up, he declared, the most "articulate exposition of the royal alliance" in all of medieval Hebrew literature. The third section makes its way to the Age of Emancipation, noting how the new path toward citizenship for Jews in the eighteenth and nineteenth centuries upheld the alliance but with one important difference: in lieu of the medieval king came the modern state. The fourth section deals with the twentieth century, thereby affording Yerushalmi the opportunity to engage with Hannah Arendt. He observed the keen historical insight into the royal alliance that she had evinced in *The Origins of Totalitarianism*, whose sage observations he found lacking in her *Eichmann in Jerusalem*. Looking back on the long history of Jewish political engagement, he read the evidence very differently from Arendt. Whereas she saw the behavior of the *Judenräte* (Jewish councils) as continuous with a tradition of ingrained and self-defeating passivity, he emphasized that "the phenomenon of a state purposely seeking the destruction of the Jews [was] unprecedented and therefore unanticipated." Contra Arendt, Yerushalmi pointed to the skill of Jewish communal leaders in conducting relations with royal or state power over the millennia—until the moment that the rules of the game changed so suddenly and inexplicably, with such ferociously tragic consequences. Marked by neither triumphalism nor stern judgment, this essay balances erudition and empathy in applying, in moving fashion, the lessons of the distant past to our own times.

In 1986, while examining the splendid collection of Hebrew manuscripts at the Academy of Sciences in Budapest, I was introduced to a Hungarian scholar who turned out to be a Tibetologist. Duly impressed, even awed, I said: "You really know Tibetan? How astonishing!" Whereupon he smiled and replied with a wink: "Of course. But I am really an expert on two Tibetan dialects. There is only one other such specialist outside of Tibet, and therefore only he can criticize my work!"

In pondering a topic for this occasion, I confess that I thought more than once of that happy Tibetologist and was tempted to take refuge in some remote corner of Jewish history in which I would be almost as immune to criticism as he. But a more imperative inner voice persuaded me that this is an occasion neither for exoticism nor for mere antiquarianism. I have therefore decided to risk, within the narrow space of one lecture, a very large topic that I consider essential to an understanding of certain vital aspects of Jewish history. My theme revolves around what I shall provisionally call the "royal alliance," its concrete realities, its theoretical underpinnings, its mythological inflations, and its consequences for Jewish destinies.

I

Jews seem to have discovered early in their experience of exile that their ultimate safety and welfare could be entrusted neither to the erratic benevolence of their gentile neighbors nor to the caprice of local authorities. It was natural, therefore, that they should strive to come within the uniform jurisdiction of the highest governmental power available. Not only the physical survival of a people in dispersion, but Jewish communal and judicial autonomy, crucial to the practice of the Jewish religion and the vital substructure of Jewish civilization, all depended on as much stability and continuity in the rule of law as was possible, and on the establishment of a mutuality of interest with those ruling powers most capable of providing it. Jews, in other words, sought direct vertical alliances, even if at times this meant alienating lesser jurisdictions and seemed to be forged at the expense of horizontal alliances with other segments or classes of the general population.

This phenomenon did not escape the sharp eye of Hannah Arendt. In the second chapter of the *Origins of Totalitarianism* she wrote, à propos the entry of the Jews into modern times:

> [T]he Jews had no political tradition or experience. What little knowledge or traditional practice they brought to politics had its source first in the Roman Empire, when they had been protected, so to speak, by the Roman soldier, and later, in the Middle Ages, when they sought and received protection against the population and the local rulers from remote monarchical and Church authorities. From these experiences they had somehow drawn the conclusion that authority, and especially high authority, was favorable to them and that lower officials, and especially the common people, were dangerous.[1]

Since her book is exclusively concerned with the modern period Arendt's statement is properly succinct and, at its core, it is unimpeachable. Only two points require modification. That the Jews had "no political tradition or experience" is, as I hope to indicate, simply not true. And in the remark that from their historical experience they had "somehow" drawn the conclusion she mentions, the intrusive adverb seems to imply that such a conclusion was almost haphazard, that other conclusions were possible. But we do not know this. On the contrary, the available evidence would seem to indicate that, within its various historical contexts, the Jewish gravitation toward vertical alliances was, if not inevitable, at least thoroughly realistic.

To begin to realize what is involved let us plunge abruptly in medias res to first century Alexandria with its large and flourishing Jewish community, possessing long established and extensive privileges which, nonetheless, had to be guarded vigilantly. With which group in the city could a horizontal alliance be forged? Though culturally assimilated, Alexandrian Jewry was separated from the pagan Greek population by the irreducible otherness of Jewish monotheism, a tension often aggravated by economic rivalry. The indigenous, non-hellenized Egyptians had no power to lift even themselves from their degraded and oppressed condition. Foreign ethnic colonies in the city had no special reason to make common cause with the Jews. Under the circumstances one can hardly be surprised that the Alexandrian Jews should look to Rome as the ultimate guarantor of their rights.

One example will suffice.[2]

In the year 38 CE, after the Greek mob failed, against fierce Jewish resistance, to force images of the emperor into the Alexandrian synagogues, a pogrom ensued. Though the local Roman prefect, Flaccus, may not have instigated it, he certainly did nothing to stop it. And so the eminent Jewish philosopher Philo and a group of communal leaders made their way to Rome to denounce Flaccus to the Emperor and ask for a confirmation of the rights granted by his predecessors. Regrettably, the current emperor was Gaius Caligula, and the Jewish delegation did not have an easy time of it. In the end, after many tribulations, Caligula granted at least the minimal Jewish demands.[3]

The entire episode reveals both idiosyncratic and exemplary elements. Idiosyncratic—not only because Caligula happened to be insane, but because at this time, although vassal to Rome, Judea still had an aura of quasi-independence, and because the Roman Jewish diaspora, vast in number, was perceived as powerful and capable of armed revolt. Indeed, within the next hundred years three major Jewish revolts against Rome would erupt, two of them in Judea and one, under Trajan, in the diaspora itself.[4] All this and much else would, of course, change in time. Yet one can also discern a basic configuration which, for all its subsequent variations, will remain strikingly constant.

The Jewish community of Alexandria, like those elsewhere both before and after, was not a mere conglomeration of Jews but a highly organized corporate entity.[5] It enjoyed a sweeping degree of collective self-rule that would be inconceivable in any modern state. The community regulated all its internal affairs, not merely "religious" in the narrow modern sense, but embracing the whole of life—civil litigation between Jews adjudicated in Jewish courts according to Jewish law, communal discipline, taxation, regulation of markets, social welfare. To supervise and implement the network of these and other activities, there existed a well-defined body of leaders, ranging from the head of the community through a governing council and a host of judicial and administrative officials. These men both ruled the community and represented it in all dealings with the government. In times of stress or danger, it was from their ranks, or those specially appointed by them, that emissaries or lobbyists were sent to negotiate or plead with the powers that be.

Rome invented neither the Jewish communal structure nor the relationship. Each was inherited from the past, the one by the Jews, the other by the Romans. The essential characteristics of the diaspora Jewish community can already be detected in the Babylonian exile following the destruction of the First Temple in 586 BCE and display their continuity and ongoing evolution through the Persian and Hellenistic periods. In accepting the right of Jews to the free exercise of their religion, by exempting them from participation in those aspects of the civic and imperial cult that they considered idolatrous, in recognizing the wide self-governing powers of the Jewish community, imperial Rome was following a policy long established by Persian, Macedonian, Ptolemaic and Seleucid rulers. For all the changes that would take place, its fundamental contours would remain constant long after the demise of Rome, in fact, as we shall see, up to the French Revolution.

One may well wonder why the highest authority not only tolerated the Jews and their alien faith, but allowed them such a wide latitude of autonomous privileges. Obviously it was not out of mere generosity. Among the many factors involved, certainly the most important was the overriding perception that on the whole the Jews were a useful element. Above all, they were an important source of revenue, paying for their privileges in the form of special taxes. Their internal self-government was convenient, for it relieved the ruler of many administrative and other burdens. They were potentially the most loyal element in the population since, especially after their loss of an independent state they were the most exposed and vulnerable, the most dependent on the ruler, those with the most to lose by betraying him. In short, the royal alliance was based on a reciprocity of interest.

On their side, Jewish perceptions of their relation to their non-Jewish rulers were based not only on their actual historical experience, but on their own inner religious traditions, beginning with Scripture itself which, studied and interpreted from one generation to the next, became an equally potent historical force in shaping Jewish mentalities.

The need to come to terms with the reality of exile is already present in the famous letter sent by the prophet Jeremiah (ch. 29) to the first exiles carried off to Babylon a decade before the destruction of the First Temple, arguing against the other prophets and soothsayers who were blithely forecasting an imminent return:

> Thus says the Lord of Hosts . . . unto all the captivity whom I have caused to be carried away captive from Jerusalem to Babylon: Build houses and dwell in them, plant gardens and eat the fruit of them; take wives and beget sons and daughters . . . and multiply there and be not diminished. And seek the peace of the city to which I have caused you to be carried away captive, and pray unto the Lord for it; for in the peace thereof shall you have peace. . . . Let not the prophets that are in the midst of you, and your diviners, beguile you, for they prophesy falsely in my name. I have not sent them.

Here we have the root of the long tradition of the Jewish prayer for the government, still recited in synagogues around the world. But the passage also hints at one of the tensions that would run through most of subsequent Jewish history. The same Jeremiah who counseled his brethren to accept their exile as divine punishment, and to accommodate themselves to it, believed just as fervently in their restoration. Indeed, he was convinced that the messianic redemption would occur after seventy years. In this, of course, he was misled. Exile became a permanent feature of Jewish life, the diaspora continued and expanded even after the partial return under Cyrus and the later creation of a second independent

Jewish commonwealth by the Hasmoneans. The dialectics of exile and redemption are a leitmotiv of Jewish history which I have explored elsewhere.[6] Suffice it to say that the three revolts against Rome to which I alluded were all, at their core, messianic in nature. All ended for the Jews in bloody defeat. Following these catastrophes the dominant attitude of the responsible lay and rabbinic leadership of the people, perceptible even earlier, was to place the Redemption in the hands of God alone, at His will and in His own time. A genuine faith in the ultimate messianic redemption was universally shared; any form of messianic activism, any attempt to "hasten the End" by human means, was discouraged. Jews lived simultaneously, as it were, on an eschatological and a historical plane. On the one, they were fully persuaded that they were in exile and prayed daily to return to the ancestral homeland for which they yearned. On the other, except in times of active persecution, they were genuinely attached to the lands of their dispersion and employed thoroughly realistic means to live there in peace.

A statement by Rabbi Hanina, a first-century Palestinian sage, begins with an echo of Jeremiah and concludes with words that could have been written by Thomas Hobbes: "Pray for the welfare of the government—for were it not for the fear of it, men would swallow each other alive."[7] There is certainly no love here for imperial Rome, destroyer of the Temple, only a thoroughly pragmatic attitude that must have been shared by many. Jews indeed benefited from the Pax Romana. Rome declared Judaism a legitimate religion, a *religio licita* recognized by the state. In the year 212–213, under the emperor Caracalla, virtually all the Jews of the empire received citizenship and were henceforth *cives romani*.[8]

Nor were Jewish scholars and leaders oblivious to the fact that despite their recognized and jealously guarded judicial autonomy they were still obliged to obey the laws of their rulers, at least insofar as these did not directly involve a violation of the essentials of Jewish faith. Sometime in the early third century the Babylonian scholar Mar Samuel enunciated his famous dictum *dina de-malkhuta dina*, "the law of the kingdom is law,"[9] meaning that Jewish law recognized the authority of state legislation affecting all its inhabitants. Happily, perhaps, he formulated it as a general principle, leaving its wide practical implications to be elaborated in detail by future generations.

The rise of Christianity, and especially its adoption in the fourth century as the state religion of Rome, could not but have profound effects on Jewry.[10] Between Judaism and paganism there had been no organic links. Christianity, like Islam later on, was a daughter religion of Judaism that claimed to have replaced it in the favor of God. No anti-Jewish accusations voiced by pagans could compare to the charge that the Jews had crucified the Son of God, or that they had rejected the prophet who brought His final revelation. Moreover, whereas earlier the Jews had to face one power, now they would face two—the state and the Church.

That God's repudiation of the Jews must somehow be visibly reflected, not only by the fact of their exile but by their actual condition in exile, must have seemed axiomatic. Between the fourth and sixth centuries the Christian Roman empire forbade Jews to proselytize, to own Christian slaves or to convert even pagan ones, to build new synagogues without special permission. They were barred from most municipal and governmental offices. Their Roman citizenship was, in effect, revoked.

In light of these and other measures it is all the more astonishing that the basic tradition of toleration was carried over from pagan Roman legislation and remained intact. Judaism, for Jews, was still a *religio licita*, both in the eyes of the state and of the Church. Synagogues, though occasionally destroyed by fanatical Christian mobs, were to be protected. Though sporadic attempts were made to restrict Jewish communal autonomy, in practice it remained virtually undiminished in scope.[11]

It could easily have been otherwise. Had Judaism been declared a heresy, nothing could have prevented either the forced conversion or the total and deliberate physical destruction of the Jews. That both church and state adopted a policy of degradation and preservation was the result of a combination of factors too complex to detain us now.[12] But the essential policy of toleration, whatever its attendant ambiguities, was absorbed, after the demise of Rome, into the Middle Ages.

II

It is in the Middle Ages that we can observe the full dynamics of the royal alliance through a documentation so abundant that all I can offer you here are only highlights and chapter-headings. I shall confine my observations to Christian Europe.[13]

Without minimizing the importance of early European legal codes incorporating laws concerning the Jews,[14] for our purposes the charters granted to Jews across the centuries are even more revealing, as these were the result of direct negotiation. Jews, of course, had settled in most parts of Roman Europe before the barbarian invasions, but the first surviving charters actually granted to Jews emanate from the Carolingian period. These are three charters issued by Louis the Pious, most probably modeled on earlier ones issued by Charlemagne himself which have been lost.[15] All three are granted to individuals, who are named, and it is they who must have taken the initiative in soliciting them for themselves and their associates. Whatever the differences in some details and phrasing, these charters all guarantee the Jews concerned protection of their lives, property, freedom to trade and, significantly, freedom of religion (*liceat eis secundum illorum legem vivere*—"they have been allowed to live . . . according to their law"). It is made abundantly clear that in all this they are directly under the protection of the Emperor, circumventing all other authorities. In one of the charters granted to Abraham of Saragossa, we hear that he has placed himself in the emperor's hands and taken an oath (*in manibus nostris se commendavit, et eum sub sermone, tuitionis nostre recepimus ac retenemus*), the language and ceremonial of a direct feudal relationship. The Jews are the emperor's men. Lest there be any doubt about this, it is stipulated that should a Jew be killed, the murderer must pay the huge sum of ten pounds of gold—*decem libras auri*—roughly twice what would be paid for the killing of a Christian knight, the money going directly to the imperial treasury.

The subsequent history of Jewish charters is not one of a change in essence but in details, according to changing circumstances, and above all in their scope—from individuals to cities and finally to entire countries or empires.

Thus in 1084 (we are in the period of the building and expansion of cities) the archbishop Rüdiger of Speyer who, along with the emperor Henry IV was also its temporal lord, invited Jews, as a particularly desirable urban element, to come and settle in Speyer by giving them a charter with extensive privileges.[16] The preamble to the charter is worth quoting: "In the name of the Holy and undivided Trinity. When I wished to make a city out of the town of Speyer, I, Rüdiger, surnamed Huozmann . . . thought that the glory of our places would be augmented a thousand-fold if I were to bring Jews (*putavi milies amplificare honorem loci nostri si et Iudeos colligerem*)." In 1090, at the request of the Jewish leaders of the Speyer community, Henry IV renewed and extended the charter and issued a similar one for Worms.[17] The Worms charter was renewed in 1157 by Frederick I Barbarossa, who also issued another for Regensburg in 1182.[18] Implicit in these twelfth century charters was the notion that the privileges mentioned were not merely local. This became explicit in the thirteenth century when, in 1236, the Emperor Frederick II issued a charter for all of German Jewry.[19] Notwithstanding the imperial claim over all the Jews, in 1244 Frederick II, Duke of Austria, issued a charter of his own for the Jews of his lands.[20]

The Austrian charter provided the model for those that now traveled eastward, along with the migrations of the Jews: 1251—Hungary (Bela IV);[21] 1254—Bohemia (Premysl Ottakar II).[22] In 1264, in a Poland trying to reconstruct itself from the devastations of the Tatar invasions, Boleslas the Pious of Kalisz, Duke of Great Poland, issued a charter to the Jews encouraging them to come from the West, just as Germans were attracted to settle and live in Poland under Magdeburg law. Indeed, for the next few centuries Jews and Germans were, in effect, the bulk of the middle class in the Polish cities. In 1334 Casimir the Great reconfirmed the charter of Boleslas for a now reunited Poland. He would reissue and extend it three times in the 1360s, in 1364 at the request of the elders of the Poznan community (*seniores judei civitatis Posnaniensis*). A similar charter was granted to the Jews in 1388 by the Grand Duke Witold of Lithuania. The definitive version of the Polish charter would be reached under Casimir IV in 1453. Thereafter it would be reconfirmed by almost every king of Poland, down to the very last, Stanislaw August Poniatowski.[23]

We shall not undertake even such a bare survey of Jewish charters in England, France or the Spanish kingdoms (though we shall turn back to Spain for other purposes). Suffice it to say that all charters, as well as actual legislation concerning the Jews, show the same pattern—along with varying restrictions, the commitment of the central authorities to the maintenance and protection of the basic rights of Jewish life, property, and permission to practice their religion. But what of the church, especially the papacy?

Though motivated by both temporal and particular theological considerations, we find here the same commitment to basic protection of the Jews. The famous *Edict in Favor of the Jews* (*Constitutio pro Judeis*), first issued by Calixtus II in the early twelfth century and, in its definitive form by Innocent III in 1199, is representative of papal policy through the ages.[24] Innocent, who was to vigorously pursue the effort at the degradation and restriction of the Jews (it was he who would preside over the Fourth Lateran Council in 1215 which, among other decrees, imposed the Jewish badge), opens with what is only an apparent paradox: "Although the Jewish perfidy is in every way worthy of condemnation, nevertheless, because through them the truth of our own faith is proved, they are not to be severely oppressed by the faithful." It goes on, in a sentence lifted almost verbatim from Gregory the Great at the end of the sixth century: "Therefore, just as license ought not to be granted the Jews to presume to do in their synagogues more than the law permits them, just so they ought not to suffer curtailment in those privileges which have been conceded them." The rest of the text specifies that they shall not be baptized by violence or force, they are not to be wounded, killed or robbed, their festivals are not to be disturbed, their cemeteries are not to be desecrated.

Neither for the Jews nor for the popes was this empty rhetoric. In times of stress or danger Jews looked ultimately not only to kings but to popes as their protectors, and they could at least count on a response. The same Innocent, so implacably hostile to Judaism and contemptuous of Jews, wrote in 1215 to the archbishops and bishops of France: "It is commanded them to forbid all Christians, especially crusaders, to hurt the Jews or their families."[25] Innocent's successor Gregory IX, the first pope to order the confiscation of the Talmud, responded to continuing crusader attacks upon Jews in 1236 with the powerful bull *Lachrymabilem Judeorum* addressed to Louis IX of France: "We have received a tearful and pitiful complaint from the Jews who live in the Kingdom of France. . . . Since, however, it is for kings to render judgment and to do justice . . . we ask your Royal Excellency and we warn you and urge you in the name of the Lord to use the power with which God entrusted you to correct and to punish those who in their rashness dare commit these crimes so unspeakably and terribly offensive to God in whose image the victims were created."[26]

Who negotiated charters, who dealt with kings and nobles when traditionally recognized Jewish rights were infringed, who brought the "tears" of the French Jews before the pope, if not the recognized leadership of the Jewish communities and their delegates and emissaries? All this and more is part of an as-yet-unwritten comprehensive history of Jewish diplomacy which, when it is written, should finally explode the myth of Jewish passivity in the face of history. Ideally these diplomats might be "court Jews," with influence both among their own people and among their rulers. Here we must think far beyond our stereotyped image based on the Central European *Hofjuden* of the seventeenth and eighteenth centuries. In medieval Spain Jewish courtiers constituted an entire class. From the caliphate of Cordoba in the tenth century until 1492 Jews served their Muslim and Christian rulers wholeheartedly, not merely as tax farmers and financiers, but as advisers, diplomats, translators, and physicians.[27] In a vital sense the archetype of the Jewish courtier in the diaspora is already to be found in the Hebrew Bible itself and was hence long part of Jewish collective memory and consciousness. The archetypal court Jew is the biblical Joseph, who saves Egypt from famine and is thus able to help his brethren as well, or Mordecai in the Book of Esther who saves both the life of the King Ahasueros and, as a result, the lives of the Jews of Persia.

From beginning to end in medieval Europe, the royal alliance was predicated on the assumption that the Jews belonged to the king. In England, they were "the king's Jews"; in the Kingdom of France, *juifs du roi*. In the thirteenth century what had always been a latent assumption became manifest in official terminology. Already in the renewal of the Worms charter in 1157 Frederick Barbarossa had asserted exclusive imperial authority over the Jews "since they belong to our treasury" (*ad cameram nostram attineant*). It remained for the Emperor Frederick II to refer to the Jews, for the first time, as *servi camerae nostre*—"serfs of our treasury." This famous phrase, over which much scholarly ink has been spilled, has misled many. That it did not mean that Jews were literally in the status of serfs should be clear to anyone with a knowledge of the realities of medieval Jewish life. No Jews were ever bound to the land, none were enslaved; in principle, all had freedom of movement. The group to which their way of life most closely corresponded was that of the burghers. Frederick himself showed his benevolence to the Jews on more than one occasion. My late master, Salo Wittmayer Baron, advanced a very persuasive argument that the real background to Frederick's use of the term was the general conflict between the empire and the papacy, here manifesting itself in the issue of which of the two has authority over the Jews.[28] For us at the moment, the more interesting question is how Jews themselves perceived their status, which brings us into the realm of medieval Jewish political theory.

Perhaps the most pertinent comment on what this *servitus judaeorum* really meant to the Jews was voiced in the fifteenth century by Isaac Arama, who wrote that it was part of Divine Providence that the Jews in their dispersion should not be handed over as slaves to ordinary masters, but "that they should remain in the hands of the kings of the earth and that they should be servants of kings and not servants of servants" (*'avadim la-melakhim ve-lo 'avadim la-'avadim*).[29] Earlier, Bahya ben Asher of Saragossa had explained: "He who is a vassal of one of the king's nobles is not of such high station as though he were vassal of the king, for the vassal of the king is feared even by the nobles and ministers, out of fear of the king himself."[30] In short, far from seeing their servitude to the king as a humiliation, these and others regard it as a mark of high status and something to be fostered.

In a *responsum* of the great thirteenth-century Rabbi Solomon Ibn Adret of Barcelona, we find one of the clearest definitions of the relation between Jewish law and royal law and, by extension, between the Jews and royal authority.[31]

Here a primary theoretical distinction is drawn between a Jewish king of a sovereign Jewish state in the Land of Israel, and the gentile rulers under whom Jews actually lived. Mar Samuel's *dina de-malkhuta dina*— "the law of the kingdom [or rather the king] is law"—can apply only to a gentile king. For the hypothetical Jewish king is not regarded as a creator of law, only as the enforcer of the law that was given by God. Similarly, in theory a Jewish king does not own the Land of Israel, since it is the common inheritance of the entire Jewish people. By contrast, gentile kings have acquired dominion over their Jews through conquest. Moreover, the land itself is the gentile king's property. The Jews are allowed to live on his land subject to his will. Should he so desire he can expel them. Jews are therefore bound to obey the king's decrees, with the significant condition that these must not exceed the bounds of law, that is, they must not violate long established Jewish rights.

Ibn Adret was also aware, however, that in the Spanish kingdoms not only the king's law was operative, but a bewildering multitude of often conflicting customary laws and privileges (*fueros*) of nobles, municipalities, regions. In this legal labyrinth Jews realized that the greater the number of jurisdictions over them, the greater their obligations and their taxes, as well as the risk of unfair treatment by local authorities. It was therefore important to stress their obedience to royal legislation as opposed to those of others. "*Dina de-malkhuta dina*"—"the law of the king is law"—Ibn Adret emphasized; "*dina de-'ummata lav dina hu*"—"the law of the nation [meaning that which is not the king's law] is not law for us." One can perhaps ask for no more succinct expression of the Jewish perception of the Royal Alliance.

I need hardly tell you that here as elsewhere the royal alliance was an ideal model. The realities to be faced were often more complicated. In the Spanish kingdoms Jews were occasionally handed over with their revenues by the king to the great military orders or to nobles to whom he was indebted or whose support he required. In France they were often under the jurisdiction of the barons, though by the thirteenth century royal centralization had reasserted most of the king's prerogatives. In Poland, however, from the sixteenth century on the nobility became more powerful than the king and often gained direct control over Jews. Sometimes royal or papal protection, however sincere, was ineffective or came too late.[32]

Sometimes, indeed, the royal alliance came apart altogether. In two instances—Sisebut in Visigothic Spain in 613, and Manuel of Portugal in 1497—kings actually decreed the forced mass conversion of all the Jews in their lands.[33] Beginning in 1290 in England, entire Jewries were expelled from one country after another in a chain that would culminate in the Spanish expulsion of 1492 and beyond. Significantly, none of these phenomena was able to fundamentally alter the dynamics or the Jewish understanding of the royal alliance itself.

Nowhere in medieval Europe was the Jewish alliance with the crown more reciprocal, of longer duration, or operative on more levels than in Spain. Nowhere else did conditions favor the rise of so large and powerful a class of Jewish courtiers, servants of the king and rulers of the community. And nowhere in medieval Hebrew literature will one find a more articulate exposition of the royal alliance than in the *Shevet Yehudah* (*The Scepter of Judah*) of Solomon Ibn Verga, himself an exile from Spain. In this work, through a combination of historical chronicle and fictional dialogue, Ibn Verga tries to understand all the catastrophes of Jewish history, including the expulsion, by going beyond the traditional categories of divine punishment and invoking, for the first time, "*ha-sibbah ha-tiv'it*"—"natural cause." In this sense, the *Shevet Yehudah* is a precocious first attempt at a sociopolitical analysis of the Jewish condition in exile.[34]

In Ibn Verga's eyes kings, and royal officials generally, are always ardent protectors of the Jews against the attacks of the rabble. When the Jews are not saved it is not for lack of royal will, but because of the obstinacy and power of the *vulgus*. To be sure, this was often enough the case in medieval Europe, and some of the examples cited can be independently documented. In others, Ibn Verga freely invents or elaborates in order to score his point.

That the Jews belong to the king, and that this creates a bond of common interest between them, is a recurrent major theme. Thus, when Gonzalo Martínez de Oviedo counsels Alfonso XI to expel the Jews, the Archbishop of Toledo vehemently opposes the plan: "So the archbishop said to Gonzalo: 'Have they indeed made you an advisor to the king? You have counseled shame upon your house! For truly the Jews are a treasury for the king, a good treasury, but you seek to destroy them, and you urge the king to do what his father did not do. You are not an enemy of the Jews, but of the king!'"[35]

Of course, ultimately even Ibn Verga cannot completely ignore the fact that sometimes kings have proceeded against the Jews on their own initiative. These are seen, however, as rare departures from the norm, and they are few in number. Convinced that kings are fundamentally committed to the rule of law and the preservation of their Jews, Ibn Verga is always prepared to give them the benefit of the doubt. Where kings appear sometimes to violate the pattern, he will extend himself to find some mitigating factor to explain such aberrations. "For in general," he writes, "the kings of Spain and France, the nobles, the men of knowledge, and all the distinguished men of the land used to love the Jews, and hatred obtained only among the masses, who were jealous of the Jews."[36] Incidentally, Ibn Verga does not shrink from occasionally criticizing the Spanish Jews themselves for aggravating popular hatred by their own arrogant behavior, but the hatred remains out of all proportion to this. In a crucial passage, the Jews are threatened with an unspecified expulsion unless they convert:

> The documents were written and sealed at the king's command. When the Jews heard, they went to one of the king's ministers, for he loved them greatly, as in Spain they were beloved by the kings, the nobles, and all their wise men and savants, and were much honored by them. The expulsions emanated only because of some of the lower classes who claimed that because of the Jews and their arrival in the kingdom their own food became expensive and that the Jews also encroached upon their trades. The expulsions also derived from the priests, for in a display of piety, and in order to show the people that they seek to honor and exalt the religion of Jesus the Nazarene, they would daily preach bitter things against the Jews. But by the other Christian classes they were honored as though they were living in their own land, and they were much loved by them, as is known to the elders of Spain.[37]

The thrust of such passages is evident. Throughout the *Shevet Yehudah* Ibn Verga shows himself well aware that Jews everywhere face a constellation of different forces. On the one hand, kings (along with the aristocracy) and the papacy (along with the higher clergy); on the other, the masses and the lower clergy. The former are generally well disposed toward the Jews, the latter usually hostile. The kings and the masses are especially in tension over the Jews. Though ever ready to protect the Jews, kings are often prevented from doing so by their own subjects.

Ibn Verga never budges from this position. Not once do we hear that the Expulsion of 1492 was due to a fundamental change in attitude on the part of the Crown. The change occurred in the growth of religious fanaticism and popular hostility, both welling up to such a pitch that they could no longer be resisted. There is neither word nor hint that the royal alliance itself had reached an impasse, that for various reasons the Spanish Crown now felt it no longer needed the Jews and would gain from their banishment.[38]

If, in the *Shevet Yehudah*, the royal alliance sometimes reaches almost mythical proportions, Ibn Verga was far from alone in clinging to its essential features. Certainly Jews knew of good and evil kings and, among themselves, of good and corrupt leaders. But they never lost faith in kingship per se, nor in the absolute need for organized Jewish leadership. It is a significant historical fact that after 1492, in the refugee communities of the Ottoman Empire, the pre-Expulsion Sephardic leadership was not repudiated and the Turkish sultans were now exalted as saviors.[39]

What did Jews distill from their medieval experience and incorporate into their mentality? That in a relative world vertical alliances were generally the more favorable for them; that such alliances were predicated on the usefulness of the Jews to their rulers; that if, at any time, the ruler should no longer regard them as such, diplomacy, lobbying, even outright bribery, could sometimes avert a harsh decree; that if all else collapsed and failed, the worst measures of which the medieval state was capable were forced baptism (historically exceptional) or expulsion. These were terrible enough. But there was no slaughter here. No medieval king ever decreed it, no pope ever sanctioned it. Where it occurred it did not emanate from above. No more eloquent testimony is needed than Isaac Arama's commentary to chapter three of the Book of Esther where Haman, enemy of the Jews, persuades King Ahasueros to decree that they be destroyed and letters are sent "to destroy, to slay, to annihilate, all Jews both young and old, little children and women." On which, against the plain meaning of the biblical text, Arama writes: "his saying 'let it be decreed that they be destroyed' does not mean 'to destroy, to slay, to annihilate,' for this is something that human nature could not tolerate. But it means that they should be expelled or enslaved."[40] That a king should deliberately seek the physical annihilation of the Jews was inconceivable.

I shall devote the shortest space to the modern period since it is generally the most familiar and because, with regard to our specific theme, Hannah Arendt has caught some of the major ramifications in her *Origins of Totalitarianism*.

That the often abrupt transition of European Jewries to modernity not only brought unprecedented opportunities but involved often traumatic ruptures and profound transformations must be evident to all: the end of Jewish communal autonomy and the inevitable constriction of the force of Jewish law to the private and purely religious ritual spheres; an ever-widening assimilation into the surrounding cultures; new crises in individual and collective Jewish identity and new ideologies intended to cope with them; the emergence of a full-blown racial anti-Semitism. The catalogue could easily be extended. What is of moment for us is the fact that for all these and other changes the modern period also betrays certain underlying continuities, one of the most significant being the persistence of the royal alliance, albeit in a metamorphosed form. No longer was it an alliance with the person of the king, but an equally compelling vertical alliance with the modern state.

It is no coincidence that the first truly modern nation-state, which came into being with the French Revolution, was also the first to give the Jews, in 1790–1791, a legal equality that would have been unimaginable in the earlier corporate state that was now swept away. The intrinsic link between the nascent nation-state and Jewish emancipation was not lost on the Jews. Remove the legal disabilities of the Jew, grant him the rights of citizenship, Mirabeau had argued two years before the Revolution, and "*son pays deviendra sa patrie.*" In the actual debate in the Assemblée Nationale, Clermont-Tonnerre went farther because he understood the implications better. The Jews must become citizens, he declared, and if they do not wish it, let them be banished from France, for there cannot be "a nation within a nation."[41] Emancipation meant that in exchange for individual rights the Jews must relinquish their former corporate and communal rights. Personal allegiance to the ruler must give way to patriotism.

The vanguard of French Jewry was more than willing. Jews not only embraced the new French state with fervor; they were eager to do all in their power to prove themselves worthy of the gift that had been bestowed. In 1791 Berr-Isaac Berr wrote, in a letter to his fellow Jews in Alsace and Lorraine: "We are now, thanks to the Supreme Being, and to the Sovereignty of the Nation, not only Men and Citizens; we are Frenchmen!"[42] (The latter phrase was, regrettably, premature.) "Let us examine with attention what remains to be done on our part . . . and how we may be able to show, in some measure, our gratitude for all the favors heaped upon us." Citizenship and equality were a gift from above, a lesson that was soon learned elsewhere, especially when the Napoleonic armies brought the first experience of emancipation to Jews in Italy, Holland, parts of Germany and Poland. Napoleon's defeat and the Congress of Vienna put a temporary halt to that. Heinrich Heine understood it all quite well. Having tasted emancipation à la française he was now barred as a Jew from a civic or academic career. Once baptized, he would write sardonically: "My becoming a Christian is the fault of those Saxons who suddenly changed saddles at Leipzig, or of Napoleon, who really did not have to go to Russia, or of his teacher of geography at Brienne, who did not tell him that Moscow winters are very cold."[43]

Most Jews, of course, were not prepared to give up their religion, though some were ready to divest it of its national elements. They wanted equality of rights without totally surrendering their Jewish identities, for they regarded the two as thoroughly compatible. "Germany is our Zion," cried an early-nineteenth-century rabbi, "and Düsseldorf our Jerusalem!" Nor did organized Jewish communities disappear, though their character changed radically. Even if the old unity of an all-embracing Jewish law was progressively shattered, there was no city or country that did not have some form of recognized Jewish leadership. Through the variegated spectrum of forms, there remained the ingrained conviction that Jewish affairs could not be left passively to chance or whim, but required stable and responsible guidance.

Beyond France, the struggle for Jewish emancipation extended through most of the nineteenth century. (In Russia, it was not achieved until 1917; in the Habsburg and Russian successor states, not until Versailles.) Without even attempting to trace this intricate development, the salient point remains. Jews instinctively recognized that the attainment of civic and political equality depended not only on the emergence of nation-states but of unified states, for only a centralized state could grant and sustain these rights. The unifications of Germany and of Italy, each almost immediately followed by full Jewish emancipation, are the most vivid examples.

Jews, by and large, supported German unification, just as in the fifteenth century they had supported the union of Aragon and Castile under

Ferdinand and Isabella. They played a prominent role in the Italian Risorgimento. If some of them also participated actively in the Revolutions of 1848 or later in Russian revolutionary movements, it was not out of an intrinsic repudiation of the state, but out of a felt need to change its current character, not merely as Jews, but as patriots. Even Zionism was not so much a rejection of the state as of the state of living in exile. Even so, the vast majority of European Jews were not radicals in either sense, but waited and worked patiently to convince the regimes under which they lived of their loyalty and utility. Through all vicissitudes the vertical alliance remained a dominant element in Jewish consciousness, as well it might.

For we can ask again, of modern as of earlier times, with what group of any significance could a horizontal alliance have been forged? Where legal emancipation had been achieved, Jews soon discovered that social equality by no means followed. The growing tide of nineteenth-century anti-Semitism only widened the gap. We are not speaking here of individuals but of groups. On what group in Western or Central European society could the Jews look upon as natural allies should their rights be threatened? Anti-Semitism was endemic even among the intellectuals and in the universities. The bourgeoisie resented the intrusion of the Jews in their midst. The workers were preoccupied with their own problems and tended to identify the Jews with wealth and exploitation. Socialism East and West, as well as Communism, could welcome Jews into its ranks, but not qua Jews. Neither had any concern for the special plight of Jews, to say nothing of the strand of anti-Judaism inherited from Marx himself.[44] In Russia in the early 1870s, idealistic young Jewish university students identified themselves with the Russian populist movements of "going to the people" and later with the *Narodnaia Volia* ("the people's will"), and went to live and work among the peasants. When the leaders of the Narodvoltsy began to condone anti-Jewish pogroms, most Jews withdrew in disillusion.[45] The year of the First Zionist Congress, 1897, also witnessed the creation of a separate Russian Jewish socialist organization—the Bund—which, within a few years, attracted masses of followers. As it began increasingly to assert its Jewish character and even to demand recognition of certain Jewish national rights, Lenin opposed it as unnecessary and in contradiction to the universalist goals of socialism, while the Bund leaders tried to explain that Jewish workers suffered doubly—as workers and as Jews.[46]

The failure of modern Jewry to establish horizontal alliances, and hence its excessive reliance and faith in the state, was due on the one hand to inherited attitudes and, I am convinced, not so much to a lack of desire or effort on their part as to the reluctance of other groups to enter such an alliance. Hannah Arendt argued that Jews miscalculated the changed relationship between state and society in modern times and, as a result, never really understood the nature of modern anti-Semitism. Perhaps. But whatever the explanation, the essential fact remains, and Arendt stated it with singular clarity: "For more than a hundred years, antisemitism had slowly and gradually made its way into almost all social strata in almost all European countries until it emerged suddenly as the one issue upon which an almost unified opinion could be achieved. The law according to which this process developed was simple: each class of society which came into conflict with the state as such became anti-semitic because the only social group which seemed to represent the state were the Jews."[47]

The two outstanding examples she gives are, as you know, the Third French Republic at the time of the Dreyfus Affair, and Weimar Germany. Neither instance, I think, requires commentary.

IV

We are nearing the end of our journey. At the outset I indicated that my subject would not be merely antiquarian, and now I must redeem that pledge. The most important conclusion that emerges from even this cursory survey of what I have called "the royal alliance" is that in the entire historical experience of the Jews there was nothing to prepare them intellectually or psychologically for what befell them between 1940 and 1945. Rulers might be capable of oppressing the Jews in various ways, but destruction was never dictated from above. We have seen this vividly for antiquity and the Middle Ages. The same, until Nazism came to power, was true of modern times. Even the worst of modern governments, as Jews perceived them, did not initiate physical attacks against the Jews, let alone plan their systematic extermination. Russian tsars might keep the Jews in that geographical ghetto known as the Pale of Settlement and vex them in a hundred ways. But the pogroms of 1881 and even that of Kishinev in 1903 were not the work of the government. (Can we still conceive that Kishinev, where a total of forty-nine Jews were killed and some five hundred wounded, sparked protests throughout the Western world?) Romania, which had grudgingly guaranteed full citizenship to its Jews as one condition of its independence, did its best, once the Treaty of Berlin was signed in 1878, to sabotage it. The Polish government, especially in the 1930s, actively fostered what was almost an economic war against the Jews. But in all these and other instances there was no hint of genocide. Outside Germany, even fascism was not intrinsically linked to anti-Jewish violence. Franco's Spain saved some fifty thousand Jews during World War II.[48] In Mussolini's Italy not a few Jews were members of the party, patriots to the last. The farthest Mussolini would go were the racial discriminatory laws of 1938. The ultimate annihilation of a fifth of Italian Jewry was not his work.

Nothing, I repeat, in the Jewish experience in dealing with ruling powers could have prepared European Jewry for the fate that awaited it. Not only the inherited perception that in the last resort governments were their protectors, but that even hostile governments could be open to negotiation, could be appealed to for their self-interest. And what of proven patriotism? In 1932 the Reichsbund Jüdischer Frontsoldaten published a *Gedenkbuch* listing the names and statistics of some 12,000 German-Jewish soldiers and officers killed while fighting for Germany in the First World War. It included a letter from Hindenburg dated October 3, accepting the book for his eighty-fifth birthday, "*mit kameradschaftlichem Gruss.*"[49] In 1935, in a pathetic gesture, the same organization published an anthology of deeply moving *Kriegsbriefe gefallener Deutscher Juden* with a lithograph by Max Liebermann of a grieving woman, and an opening caption—"*Wir starben für Deutschland!*" Pathetic, in the naive hope that the New Order could be swayed in any way by such memories. In the years immediately after 1933 the worst that German Jews expected was that they would be driven out of Germany, and some sought parallels to the expulsion from Spain.[50] When the Nuremberg Laws were adopted they were perceived, naturally though mistakenly, as a kind of return to the Middle Ages, involving much suffering, but still endurable. In November 1940, when the Warsaw Ghetto was completed and sealed off, we are told that initially many Jews almost felt a sense of relief that their hitherto uncertain situation seemed now to be stabilized and defined. After all, ghettos were nothing new; Jews had survived them.[51] Jews would and did work for German industries, so they were useful after all, and so long as they were useful who could imagine that they would be utterly destroyed? And when the deportations began, what reason not to believe that the camps were labor camps? The first eyewitness reports of what was really happening at Treblinka were not believed. Only when the Ghetto itself began to resemble a death camp, only after less than 40,000 out of 430,000 Jews remained, and it was certain that the Nazis aimed at total destruction, did the revolt erupt.

I must add that not only was the phenomenon of a state purposely seeking the destruction of the Jews unprecedented and therefore unanticipated, but the fact that this should emanate from Germany made it all the more so. I shall not offend your intelligence by informing you of what you already know, the passionate identification of so many modern German Jews with all that was great and noble in German tradition. What you may not be aware of is the image of Germany in the eyes of the East European Jewish intelligentsia prior to the cataclysm. For them too Germany was Bildung, Kultur and Wissenschaft. Young Polish and Lithuanian Jews flocked to German universities to receive their doctorates. Along with Hebrew, German was until 1939 the international language of modern Jewish scholarship.[52] For those East European Jews who did not read German, there were translations into Hebrew and Yiddish, now all but forgotten, of the best of German literature and thought. Even a bibliography of such translations would come to most, Jews and Germans alike, as a revelation. Would it surprise you to know that Goethe already appeared in Hebrew in Warsaw in 1857, Nietzsche's *Zarathustra* in 1912, Schiller's *Gesammelte Schriften* in Yiddish in 1929? In 1930 Thomas Mann's *Der Zauberberg* was published in a four-volume Yiddish translation (*Der Tzoiberbarg*) in Vilna. The translator was none other than Isaac Bashevis Singer.

I close by returning to Hannah Arendt, this time to her *Eichmann in Jerusalem* where, in a curious way, she seems to have forgotten the insights she had attained in *The Origins of Totalitarianism*. I do so not in order to debate with her about the "banality of evil," the kind of bon mot that first seduces with its paradoxical novelty, and then rapidly becomes itself a banal and unreflective cliché of common discourse. But let us leave an analysis of the "banality of evil" for another occasion. The passage in the Eichmann book that is of direct concern to us is almost as famous and has been equally influential: "Wherever Jews lived, there were recognized Jewish leaders, and this leadership, almost without exception, cooperated in one way or another, for one reason or another, with the Nazis. The whole truth was that if the Jewish people had really been unorganized and leaderless, there would have been chaos and plenty of misery but the total number of victims would hardly have been between four and a half and six million people."[53]

The reference, of course, is to the *Judenräte* which the Nazis set up throughout occupied Europe and which, indeed, cooperated "in one way or another." I am not here to defend the Jewish Councils, for that is essentially irrelevant. I believe that I have always been secure enough to study and teach Jewish history without glossing over the imperfections of the Jews. (Why, indeed must they be perfect? The Hebrew Bible did not think them so.) Mordecai Chaim Rumkowski, head of the *Judenrat* in the Lodz Ghetto, seems to display the pathology of a megalomaniac. Most of the Jewish police in the ghettos were infamous for their brutality. There is no reason to ignore any of this. What is disturbing in Arendt's wholesale condemnation of the Jewish Councils is her uncharacteristic refusal to confront complexity, nuance, context, and the historical background which she herself had elucidated in her earlier work. The result is a series of generalizations which have contributed—though this was surely not her conscious intention—to the increasingly fashionable blurring of the distinction between victims and murderers.

That in the absence of an organized leadership the number of victims would have been diminished is pure and gratuitous speculation, an example of what historians wryly call "history as the story of what should have happened." We need not dwell upon it. Rumkowski strutted about the Lodz Ghetto like a king. But the head of the Council in Warsaw, Adam Czerniakow, committed suicide on the second day of the massive deportation of July 1942. Arendt mentions this in passing, but pays little attention in her rush to indict all the Jewish councils en bloc. To realize the full complexity of the Jewish Councils and the enormous variability in the character of their leaders and members, one must turn to Isaiah Trunk's magisterial, sober, and meticulously documented *Judenrat*.[54]

Perhaps Hannah Arendt did not know all that Trunk knew; his book appeared some nine years after hers. What is surprising is that she should not have realized that an "unorganized and leaderless" Jewish people was a contradiction in terms, an impossibility both because of what Jews had inherited from their history and within the context of the historical moment. What is astonishing is that she could not bring to bear in her discussion of the *Judenräte* her own prior understanding of the age-old relation of the Jews to the state. Granted the worst that can be said about individual leaders or members of the councils, there can be little question that when most were told to serve they acquiesced not because it was their duty to the Nazis but to their fellow Jews.[55] In this, they were simply following the millennial archetype of Jewish leadership in its dealings with power. The men who went daily to negotiate with the SS or the Gestapo were, in essence, no different in their conception of their role than Philo on his mission to Gaius Caligula.

Even when the *Judenräte* in the Nazi ghettos became aware that the Jews they were delivering for deportation were going to their deaths, there remained a lingering legacy from the past that one could still somehow maneuver to at least limit the losses, to postpone by delivering quotas rather than risk the total and immediate slaughter of all. We can reflect today and say that they were wrong, that they miscalculated, that the ghetto revolts should have taken place earlier. But we say these things only with hindsight, for we know in retrospect that it was all of no avail, that Caligula had not prepared the Jews for Hitler, that between the medieval *seniores Judei* and the Nazi term *Älteste der Juden* there lies not a translation, but an abyss. At the time, however, in situations of such extremity that we can hardly imagine them, every day gained, every choice left, however ruthless, seemed a gamble worth taking.

Could the horror be repeated? In 1945 I thought it impossible. By now I have lost that absolute certainty. If it happened again, would Jews react as they did before? I do not really know, though I should think not. I know only that the destruction of European Jewry half a century ago has now itself become part of Jewish historical experience and collective memory and that something decisive has changed as a result. The royal alliance, in the sense of the dependence of diaspora Jews on the states in which they reside, may remain a fact of life, but I think it has finally been demythologized. Jews now know something that they never knew before. They know that even the highest powers of the state can deliberately decide to destroy them. In the minds of the mass of contemporary Jews everywhere, there is only one state upon which they can utterly rely—the Jewish state, for all its imperfections. The nightmare that haunts the Jewish imagination is not merely the recollection of what happened, but the possibility, however remote, that the Jewish state might itself be destroyed.

Jews know other things as well. They know that during the Second World War the allied governments, who were fighting a common enemy, virtually abandoned the Jews in Nazi Europe to their fate; that the extent of the active and willing complicity of the Vichy regime in the deportation of French Jews is only now being revealed; that in contrast to his medieval predecessors, the Pope, whatever his reasons, was silent.

I put it to you that all this is not a merely internal Jewish affair. We have all lost whatever remained of our innocence, and by this I mean not only

Jews but the entire world. For all their terrors, the Middle Ages, at least on the highest levels of power, still knew limits that could not be trespassed. We have learned that there are no longer any restraints. Out of the ashes of the death camps there grew a grotesque new Tree of Knowledge, and we have all tasted its bitter fruit, and we know what our forebears knew not—that once this is possible, anything is possible. The global atrocities since World War II, and indeed those being committed at this very moment, have only confirmed it.

Do not misunderstand me. I harbor no nostalgia for the Middle Ages. One is, after all, always born at the wrong time. But if we cannot choose the time in which we are fated to live, it does not follow that we must accept its depravities as inevitable. In the current desperate struggle for human decency and justice all peoples have a stake.

NOTES

[Editors' note: This lecture was initially delivered in Germany on the occasion of Yerushalmi's acceptance of a prize from the Siemens Stiftung and published as *"Diener von Königen und nicht Diener von Dienern": einige Aspekte der politischen Geschichte der Juden* (Munich: Carl-Friedrich-von-Siemens-Stiftung, 1995). It was also published subsequently in French as "'Serviteurs des rois et non serviteurs des serviteurs': Sur quelques aspects de l'histoire politique des Juifs," *Raisons politiques* 7 (2002), 19–52.]

1. Hannah Arendt, *Origins of Totalitarianism*, 2nd ed. (New York: Meridian Books, 1958), 23.

2. Philo (*Legatio ad Gaium*, xxxvi: 280) states characteristically that the Jews always had been *philokaisares* and, despite his antipathy to Caligula, calls the emperor a "savior" and "benefactor." Since the Roman annexation of Egypt in 30 BCE, one of the major sources of anti-Jewish hostility among the Alexandrian "Greeks," now themselves a subject population, was their perception of Jewish loyalty to Rome and of the alleged favoritism of the Roman emperors toward the Jews. How easily the intense anti-Roman feeling of Hellenized Egyptian nationalists could express itself also in anti-Semitism is exemplified in the so-called "Acts of the Pagan Martyrs," commemorating the deaths of Alexandrian patriots in the struggle against Rome. See Baron, *A Social and Religious History of the Jews*, 2nd revised ed. (New York: Columbia University Press, 1952–1983) (hereafter: *SRH*), 1:190. The extant texts of the "Acts" are assembled in Herbert A. Musurillo, ed. and trans., *The Acts of the Pagan Martyrs: Acta Alexandrinorum* (Oxford: Clarendon Press, 1954).

3. The events leading to the pogrom as well as the Jewish embassy to Rome

are described by Philo, *In Flaccum* and *Legatio ad Gaium*. See also Arnalda Momigliano, "Aspetti dell antisemitismo in due opere de Filone," in *La rassegna mensile de Israel* 5 (1930): 275–86; Erwin R. Goodenough, *The Politics of Philo Judaeus: Practice and Theory* (New Haven: Yale University Press, 1938), chs. 1–3; E. Mary Smallwood, *The Jews under Roman Rule, from Pompey to Diocletian: A Study in Political Relations* (Leiden: Brill, 1981), ch. 10.

4. The two great revolts of Palestinian Jewry, in 66 CE and again in 132 CE, are too well known to require bibliographic comment here. Regarding the revolt under Trajan by the Jews of Egypt, Cyrenaica, and Cyprus, see Baron, *SRH*, 2:94–97; Smallwood, *Jews under Roman Rule*, ch. 15; Marina Pucci, *La rivolta ebraica al tempo di Traiano* (Pisa: Giardini, 1981).

5. The political status, corporate autonomy, and communal structures of the Jews of Alexandria are discussed by Baron, *The Jewish Community: Its History and Structure to the American Revolution* (Philadelphia: Jewish Publication Society of America, 1942) (see the index in vol. 3, s.v. "Alexandria") and more recently in considerable detail by Arieh Kasher, *The Jews in Hellenistic and Roman Egypt* (Tübingen: J.C.B. Mohr, 1985), esp. chs. 4, 7–9. Cf. also Victor (Avigdor) Tcherikover, *Hellenistic Civilization and the Jews* (Philadelphia: Jewish Publication Society of America, 1961), 269–377, passim; Erwin R. Goodenough, *The Jurisprudence of the Jewish Courts in Egypt: Legal Administration by the Jews under the Early Roman Empire as Described by Philo Judaeus* (New Haven: Yale University Press, 1929).

6. Yerushalmi, "Exile and Expulsion in Jewish History," in *Crisis and Creativity in the Sephardic World, 1391–1648*, ed. Benjamin R. Gampel (New York: Columbia University Press, 1997), 3–22; German translation in idem, *Ein Feld in Anatot: Versuche über jüdische Geschichte* (Berlin: K. Wagenbach, 1993), 21–38.

7. *Mishnah Avot*, 3:2.

8. The Jewish acquisition of citizenship was due to the famous "Constitutio Antoniana de civitate," which gave this status to almost all free men in the empire. See Baron, *SRH*, 2:109, 374 n. 25, and the literature cited there. Cf. Elias Bickerman, *Das Edikt des Kaisers Caracalla in P. Giss 40* (Berlin, 1926).

9. Babylonian Talmud, *Gittin*, 10b.

10. For the impact on the Jews of the Christian triumph, see James Parkes, *The Conflict of the Church and the Synagogue* (London: Soncino Press, 1934), esp. chs. 5–7; Marcel Simon, *Verus Israel; Études sur les relations entre chrétiens et juifs dans l'Empire Romain (135–425)* (Paris: E. de Boccard, 1948), ch. 4; the laws collected and analyzed by Amnon Linder, *The Jews in Imperial Roman Legislation* (Detroit: Wayne State University Press; Jerusalem: Israel Academy of Sciences and Humanities, 1987), and his remarks, ibid., 67–78. Jean Juster's classic *Les*

juifs dans l'Empire Romain: Leur condition juridique, économique et sociale, 2 vols. (Paris: Paul Geuthner, 1914) remains fundamental for all aspects.

11. See the conclusions of Smallwood, *Jews under Roman Rule*, ch. 21.

12. See Yerushalmi, "Response to Rosemary Ruether," in *Auschwitz; Beginning of a New Era?*, ed. Eva Fleischner (New York: Ktav Pub. Co., 1977), 97–108. The book arose out of an international symposium on the Holocaust held at the Cathedral of St. John the Divine in New York in 1974. The French translation is "Persecution et préservation: Une réponse juive à Rosemary Ruether," in *Les Temps Modernes* 47 (1991): 112–25.

13. The attitudes toward the ruling power among Jews in Islamic countries do not seem to have differed significantly from those of their European brethren. See Shelomo Dov Goitein, "The Muslim Government as Seen by Its Non-Muslim Subjects," *Journal of the Pakistan Historical Society* 12 (1964): 1–13; Baron, "Some Medieval Jewish Attitudes to the Muslim State," in his *Ancient and Medieval Jewish History* (New Brunswick: Rutgers University Press, 1972), 77–94.

14. The main provisions concerning the Jews in the early European codes such as the *Lex Romana Visigothorum (Breviarium Alarici)* were adopted from the Roman Theodosian Code. See Baron, *SRH*, 3:35.

15. Full texts of the three charters can be found in Karl Zeumer, ed., *Formulae Merovingi et Carolini aevi* Monumenta Germaniae Historica, Legum sectio V (Hannover, 1886), nos. 30, 31, 52; abridged with comments by Julius Aronius, *Regesten zur Geschichte der Juden im frankischen und deutschen Reiche bis zum Jahre 1273* (Berlin: L. Simion, 1902), nos. 81–83.

16. Text in Alfred Hilgard, ed., *Urkunden zur Geschichte der Stadt Speyer* (Strassbourg: K. J. Trübner, 1885), no. 11.

17. Ibid., no. 12.

18. Worms, 1157: Ludwig Weiland, ed., *Constitutiones et Acta Publica Imperatorum et Regum* Monumenta Germaniae Historica, Legum sectio IV, vol. I (Hannover, 1893), no. 163; Regensburg, 1182: Aronius, *Regesten*, no. 314a.

19. Aronius, *Regesten*, no. 496.

20. Ibid., no. 547.

21. *Monumenta Hungariae Judaica*, vol. 1 (1092–1539), ed. Armin Friss et al. (Budapest: Wodianer F. és Fia bizománya, 1903), no. 22.

22. Gottlieb Bondy and Franz Dworsk, *Zur Geschichte der Juden in Böhmen, Mähren und Schlesien von 906 bis 1620* (Prague: G. Bondy, 1906), vol. 1, no. 24.

23. The charter of Boleslas has not survived but can be reconstructed from its confirmations by Casimir the Great. For the texts of these charters and the subsequent Polish renewals mentioned here, see Phillip Bloch, *Die General Privi-*

legien der polnischen Judenschaft (Poznan: J. Jolowicz, 1892); Jacob Goldberg, *Jewish Privileges in the Polish Commonwealth: Charters of Rights Granted to Jewish Communities in Poland-Lithuania in the Seventeenth-Eighteenth Centuries* (Jerusalem: Israel Academy of Sciences and Humanities, 1985).

24. Latin text with English translation in Solomon Grayzel, *The Church and the Jews in the XIIIth Century* (Philadelphia: The Dropsie College for Hebrew and Cognate Learning, 1933; rev. ed., New York: Hermon Press, 1966), no. 5.

25. Ibid., no. 32.

26. Ibid., no. 88.

27. This is not to say that even in Spain there were not individual Jewish courtiers who put their own quest for power above the interests of the community. However, the fundamental ideology out of which this class arose, and which continued to sustain it, runs through the whole of Hispano-Jewish history. See Gerson D. Cohen's perceptive analysis of the Jewish courtier ideal in Islamic Spain in his edition of *The Book of Tradition (Sefer Ha-Qabbalah) of Abraham Ibn Daud* (Philadelphia: Jewish Publication Society of America, 1967), 263–89; Eliyahu Ashtor, *The Jews of Moslem Spain* (Philadelphia: Jewish Publication Society of America, 1973–1984), vol. 1, ch. 5; vol. 2, ch. 2; vol. 3, ch. 3; and passim; Yitzhak Baer, *A History of the Jews in Christian Spain* (Philadelphia: Jewish Publication Society of America, 1966) (consult the index to vol. 2, s.v. "Court officials, Jewish"); Haim Beinart, "Demutah shel ha-hatzranut ha-Yehudit bi-Sefarad ha-Notzrit" ("The Image of Jewish Courtiership in Christian Spain"), in *Kevutzot 'ilit u-shekhavot manhigot* (Elites and Leading Groups: Tenth Convention of the Historical Society of Israel) (Jerusalem: The Historical Society of Israel, 1966), 55–71.

28. S. W. Baron, "Plenitude of Apostolic Powers and Medieval Jewish Serfdom," in his *Ancient and Medieval Jewish History*, 284–307; "Medieval Nationalism and Jewish Serfdom," ibid., 308–22; *SRH*, 9:135–92 ("Serf of the Chamber").

29. Isaac ben Moses Arama, *'Akedat Yitzhak* (Venice, 1565), fol. 318v.

30. Bahya ben Asher, *Perush 'al ha-Torah*, ed. Chaim Dov Chavel (Jerusalem: Mosad ha-Rav Kook, 1968), 3:423 (ad Deut. 28:10).

31. Solomon ben Abraham Adret, *Sefer Toldot Adam* (Livorno, 1657), no. 134, and *Sefer she'elot u-teshuvot*, vol. 6 (Warsaw, 1868 [1908]), no. 149.

32. For Spain, see Abraham A. Neuman, *The Jews in Spain* (Philadelphia: Jewish Publication Society of America, 1944), 1:16–18. Examples from France are given by Baron, *SRH*, 4:58 f., 10:56–59. The jurisdiction of the Polish magnates over the Jews in the estates, towns, and villages owned by them was a natural consequence of the enormous growth of the power of the nobility from the sixteenth century onward. See Baron, *SRH*, 16:120–39 and, more recently, the excellent study by M. J. Rosman, *The Lord's Jews: Magnate-Jewish Relations in the*

Polish-Lithuanian Commonwealth during the Eighteenth Century (Cambridge, MA: Harvard University Press, 1990). It is important to note that the reciprocal relationship of Jews and magnates paralleled that of Jews and the king and, under Polish conditions, was often more beneficial for them. As Rosman observes: "In 1539, the Polish king relinquished to the noblemen full jurisdiction over the Jews resident in their lands, so that for all practical purposes a Jewish resident of a privately owned town viewed his lord or lady as his king" (39). Moreover, from the sixteenth century on, many Jews tended voluntarily to move into magnate-owned territories. "The tolerance and economic opportunity offered by the magnates encouraged the majority of Jews to become inhabitants of magnate holdings, mainly as town dwellers" (41).

33. The forced conversion in Visigothic Spain is succinctly analyzed by Baron, *SRH*, 3:36–39. The story of the forced baptism in Portugal often has been told. See, for example, Alexandre Herculano, *Historia da origem e estabelecimento da Inquisição em Portugal* (Lisbon, 1854–1859), 1:118–30; Meyer Kayserling, *Geschichte der Juden in Portugal* (Leipzig: O. Leiner, 1867), 129–39; Maria José Pimenta Ferro Tavares, *Os Judeus em Portugal no século XV* (Lisbon: Universidade Nova de Lisboa, 1982), 483–500.

34. The standard edition is *Sefer Shevet Yehudah*, ed. Azriel Shochat, intro. Yitzhak Baer (Jerusalem: Mosad Bialik, 1946). A complete German translation, together with the Hebrew text, is available in M. Wiener, *Das Buch Schevet Jehuda* (Hannover, 1856; rpt., 1924).

35. *Shevet Yehudah*, ch. 10, 54; *Schevet Jehuda*, 63.

36. *Shevet Yehudah*, ch. 24, 70; *Schevet Jehuda*, 91.

37. *Shevet Yehudah*, ch. 44, 117 f.; *Schevet Jehuda*, 177.

38. For a more detailed analysis of Ibn Verga's views on the "royal alliance," see my monograph *The Lisbon Massacre of 1506 and the Royal Image in the Shebet Yehudah* (Cincinnati: Hebrew Union College-Jewish Institute of Religion, 1976). French version in *Sefardica: Essais sur l'histoire des juifs, des marranes, et des nouveaux-chrétiens d'origine hispano-portugaise* (Paris: Chandeigne, 1998), 34–173.

39. Regarding the continuity of the courtier ideal and of Sephardic leadership after the Spanish expulsion, see Haim Hillel Ben-Sasson, "Dor goley Sefarad ʾal ʾatzmo" ("The Generation of the Spanish Exiles on Its Fate"), *Zion* 26 (1961): esp. 28–34. The idealization of the Ottoman Turkish sultans finds its most extravagant expression in the chronicle of Elijah Capsali of Crete, *Seder Eliyahu Zuta*, ed. Aryeh Shmuelevitz, Shlomo Simonsohn, and Meir Benayahu, 3 vols. (Jerusalem: Ben-Zvi Institute and the Hebrew University, 1976–1983). Employing biblical messianic language, Capsali perceives the sultans in the image of Cyrus the Great, who returned the Jews to their land from their Babylonian captivity.

40. Quoted by Barry Walfish, *Esther in Medieval Garb: Jewish Interpretation of the Book of Esther in the Middle Ages* (Albany: State University of New York Press, 1993), 187.

41. Gabriel de Riquetti Mirabeau, *Sur Moses Mendelssohn, sur la réforme politique des juifs* (Paris, 1787); rpt. in Robert Badinter, *Libres et égaux: l'émancipation des Juifs sous la Révolution française* (Paris: Fayard, 1989), 1:67; opinion de M. Le Comte Stanislas de Clermont-Tonnerre, député de Paris, le 23 Décembre 1789, ibid., 7:13.

42. Berr-Isaac Berr, *Lettre d'un citoyen, membre de la ci-devant communauté des Juifs de Lorraine, à ses confrères, à l'occasion du droit de citoyen actif, rendu aux Juifs par le décret du 28 septembre 1791* (Nancy, 1791); *La Révolution*, 8:3 f., 6.

43. Heinrich Heine, "Aphorismen und Fragmente," in *Werke und Briefe*, ed. Hans Kaufmann (Berlin: Aufbau-Verlag, 1962), 8:396.

44. Regarding all these aspects, see Edmund Silberner, *Sozialisten zur Judenfrage: Ein Beitrag zur Geschichte des Sozialismus vom Anfang des 19. Jahrhunderts bis 1914* (Berlin: Colloquium Verlag, 1962); idem, *Kommunisten zur Judenfrage: Zur Geschichte von Theorie und Praxis des Kommunismus* (Opladen: Westdeutscher Verlag, 1983). Cf. also Julius Carlebach, *Karl Marx and the Radical Critique of Judaism* (London: Routledge and Kegan Paul, 1978).

45. Baron, *The Russian Jew under Tsars and Soviets* (New York: Macmillan, 1964), 165–67; Jonathan Frankel, *Prophecy and Politics: Socialism, Nationalism, and the Russian Jews, 1862–1917* (Cambridge and New York: Cambridge University Press, 1981), 98 ff. and passim.

46. Henry J. Tobias, *The Jewish Bund in Russia from Its Origins to 1905* (Stanford: Stanford University Press, 1972), esp. chapters 15–16, 19; Zvi Y. Gitelman, *Jewish Nationality and Soviet Politics* (Princeton: Princeton University Press, 1972). For Lenin's views, see V. I. Lenin, "The Bund's Position in the Party," in *Collected Works* (Moscow: Foreign Language Pub. House, 1964), 7:92–103; idem, "Critical Remarks on the National Question," ibid., 20:17–51.

47. Arendt, *Origins of Totalitarianism*, 25 (my italics).

48. Either by providing temporary passage through Spain or by protecting those Sephardic Jews whose families, by a law of 1924, had been registered as "Spanish nationals" without actually having lived in Spain. For the complex story, not without its darker aspects, see Haim Avni, *Spain, the Jews, and Franco* (Philadelphia: Jewish Publication Society of America, 1982). Cf. also Caesar C. Aronsfeld, *The Ghosts of 1492: Jewish Aspects of the Struggle for Religious Freedom in Spain, 1848–1976*, Jewish Social Studies Monographs No. 1 (New York: Columbia University Press, 1979), 47–55.

49. *Die Jüdischen Gefallenen des Deutschen Heeres, der Deutschen Marine und*

der Deutschen Schutztruppen, 1914–1918 (Berlin: Verlag Derschild, 1932). Hindenburg's letter appears following the title page.

50. In this respect, it was no mere coincidence that the *Almanach des Schocken
Verlags auf das Jahr 5697* (1936–1937), published in Berlin, included the essay "Die
Vertreibung der Juden aus Spanien" by Yitzhak (Fritz) Baer, who had been teaching at Hebrew University in Jerusalem since 1930. Similarly, Valeriu Marcu's book
with the same title, was published in Amsterdam in 1934 by the well-known publisher of "Exil-Literatur," Querido Verlag. There were also works of fiction—for example, Hermann Sinsheimer's *Maria Nunnez: Eine Jüdische Überlieferung* (Berlin:
Philo Verlag, 1934). This historical novel, set in the sixteenth century, traces the
flight of a Marrano girl from Lisbon to London and finally to Amsterdam, where
she could practice Judaism openly and freely. At the very end of the book, we read:
"Von dem ferneren Leben der Maria Nunnez erfahren wir nichts mehr. Aber Gott,
der Herr, der in sie einzog wie ein Sturmwind, das sie jung war, wird sie zu einem
gesegneten Alter und zu einem seligen Ende gefordert haben. *Worum auch wir ihn
für uns und die Unsrigen bitten. Amen*" (my italics).

51. On November 9, 1940, the eminent Polish-Jewish historian Emmanuel
Ringelblum wrote in Warsaw: "There's been the growth of a strong sense of his-
torical consciousness recently. We tie in fact after fact from our daily experience
with the events of history. We are returning to the Middle Ages." See Emmanuel
Ringelblum, *Notes from the Warsaw Ghetto*, ed. and tr. Jacob Sloan (New York:
Schocken Books, 1958), 82. See also Sloan's remarks, ibid., 97.

52. The most prestigious and longest-lived journal of modern Jewish scholarship in the world was the *Monatsschrift für Geschichte und Wissenschaft des Judentums*, founded in 1851. The eighty-third and last volume (1939), edited by Leo
Baeck, was confiscated and destroyed by the Nazis. This volume, a tragic yet
heroic monument to German-Jewish scholarship, was reproduced in 1963 by the
Leo Baeck Institute from one of the very few surviving copies.

53. Hannah Arendt, *Eichmann in Jerusalem: A Report on the Banality of Evil*
(New York: Viking Press, 1963), 111.

54. Isaiah Trunk, *Judenrat: The Jewish Councils in Eastern Europe under Nazi
Occupation* (New York: Macmillan, 1972). Czerniakow was by no means the only
member of a ghetto council to take his life rather than hand Jews over for deportation. Moreover, in 1942 there were two attempts—one successful—at collective
suicide of entire ghetto councils (in Bereza Kartuska and Pruzana; in the latter
the people, except one, were revived). Trunk observes: "Characteristically this attempt at collective suicide was resented by the ghetto community. People maintained that the intelligentsia should not have let the community down, yielding
to desperation rather than serving as an example to prevent the community from

a spiritual breakdown at such a crucial time" (446). For the excruciating moral dilemmas facing the councils, and their varied responses, see especially ch. 7: "The Strategy and the Tactics of the Councils toward the German Authorities."

55. A striking case in point is Leo Baeck, whom Arendt (*Eichmann*, 105) castigates for serving as honorary president of the Ältestenrat in the Theresienstadt concentration camp and for not telling his fellow inmates that when they left the camp, they would be gassed at Auschwitz. His conduct can be debated endlessly and fruitlessly; however, Arendt does not mention the central fact, which was common knowledge, that Baeck easily could have left Nazi Germany but refused numerous offers from abroad to serve as rabbi or professor, declaring that he chose to remain so long as there was still a *minyan* (prayer quorum) of Jews left in Germany. He was deported to Theresienstadt in 1943.

12 : ISRAEL, THE UNEXPECTED STATE

MESSIANISM, SECTARIANISM, AND
THE ZIONIST REVOLUTION

Address delivered on receiving the 2005 Leopold Lucas Prize at the University of Tübingen. Published in a parallel German and English edition as *Israel der unerwartete Staat: Messianismus, Sektierertum und die zionistische Revolution* (Tübingen: Mohr Siebeck, 2006).

The following text was based on a lecture delivered by Yerushalmi on the occasion of receiving the Lucas Prize at the University of Tübingen. The prize, named for Dr. Leopold Lucas, a German rabbi and scholar who died in Theresienstadt in 1943, is awarded annually to those who have "rendered outstanding services to the dissemination of the concept of tolerance." The lecture was delivered in 2005, amidst growing international criticism of Israel and calls for an academic boycott. Although Yerushalmi retained his typical scholarly objectivity, he acknowledged that his "concern with Israel," as with all of Jewish history, was "profoundly personal and existential."

The speech explored the relationship between Zionism and messianism. Whereas Yerushalmi frequently addressed the latter subject in his research and teaching, he discussed the former much less often. Zionism, he claimed, is at once a continuation of and a radical departure from traditional Jewish messianism. Certainly, Zionism "channeled Jewish messianic energies" and was built upon the ancient desire for a return to a Jewish state. However, the State of Israel bears little resemblance to the irenic Davidic kingdom imagined by centuries of believers who intoned the ideal of a "return to Zion" in their daily prayers. For Jews, Israel is an "in-between state," in which they are clearly no longer in exile but are also not fully redeemed. This confusion, this "messianic syndrome," Yerushalmi suggested, lay at the root of the dangerous tensions within Jewish society in Israel.

Christianity and Islam also lack categories into which to fit the State of Israel. Both religions understood Jewish exile as confirmation of their supersession of Judaism. Christianity in particular conceived of the return of the Jews to the Holy Land principally in the context of the Second Coming. These theologies continue to inform modern attitudes, Yerushalmi noted: "Such legacies do not simply disappear, even in the so-called secular modern world, but continue to exert a powerful if subliminal influence." Jews and Gentiles unconsciously desire Israel to be the perfect messianic state. Gazing through his wide historical lens, Yerushalmi asserted that unbalanced criticism of Israel, what he considered to be the widespread tendency to hold it to higher standards than any other state, should be viewed against the backdrop of that theological contestation.[1]

Although this is Yerushalmi's only published work that concentrates entirely on Zionism and the State of Israel, the article shares a certain spirit and method with his other areas of scholarship. His inquiry into the relationship between messianism and Zionism mirrored his work on Jewish historiography, Iberian *conversos*, and Freud, all of which dealt with the ways in which ancient structures of belief are both preserved and transformed by the conditions of modernity. Ever the historian, Yerushalmi not only added a rich measure of historical perspective, but also a bit of succor from the past. History, he concluded his speech, teaches us that the future is always open. "No matter how grim the situation may appear at any time," he declared, "it can always change for the better in unforeseen ways." This sentiment is a striking contrast to the dolorous tone in *Zakhor*, in which history is famously cast as "the faith of fallen Jews." "Messianism," he told his audience in 2005, "is not the only possible form of human hope." He would develop this theme in an essay devoted entirely to "the history of hope," which appears in the next chapter.

The thesis I shall present to you today is that Zionism and the State of Israel represent a major and unanticipated rupture in Jewish history, a revolt against Jewish messianism, at least in the form that messianism had assumed. I shall propose further that a full recognition of the tensions between modern Zionism and traditional Jewish messianism is vital to an understanding of the problems inherent in the Jewish State and what it represents, both for Jews and non-Jews. You will readily understand that I am not suggesting that messianism is the sole source of these problems, only that it is a necessary even if insufficient cause that is often overlooked and deserves far greater emphasis. It should be equally obvious that the subject of Jewish messianism is far too vast for a single lecture (at my own university I occasionally devote an entire year's course to it and feel that even this is not adequate). What I can offer you are merely chapter headings.

I confess that I have chosen this topic with some trepidation, conscious of the risks involved. To my dismay, in today's turbulent cultural and political climate it has become increasingly difficult to find a forum,

---

1. See his comments on what he regarded as unfair criticism of Israel rooted in old theological biases in Goldberg, *Transmettre l'histoire*, 214–216.

even in academic and intellectual circles (and sometimes precisely in such circles), where either Zionism or Israel can be discussed calmly and reasonably, and without provoking fiercely agitated reactions, whether pro or contra. If I finally decided to plunge ahead, it is because I think that the singular honor of the Lucas Prize demands that I not hide in some obscure or esoteric corner of Jewish history where I will be safe from criticism, and because the reputation of the University of Tübingen is such that I can expect a fair and open hearing even from those who, in the end, may disagree with me.

I

In a famous essay Gershom Scholem made an important distinction between the "restorative" trend in Jewish messianism, the return to an ideal or idealized past, and the "utopian" strand which envisioned radical changes in humanity and even in nature itself. He also stressed the "price" the Jewish people paid for its messianism by devaluing the present through a "life lived in deferment."[1] We shall yet return to the question of the "price." But first I want to make another, equally basic distinction in the history of Jewish messianism, namely—between messianic belief and messianic activism (especially messianic movements).[2]

The messianic belief was forged by the classical prophets of ancient Israel. Its essential contours are well known and easily summarized. In the "end of days" God will redeem his people and gather them to the land from which they have been exiled because of their sins. Their enemies will be confounded. The Temple will be rebuilt. They will be ruled by a perfectly just messianic king of the House of David. Israel shall dwell in peace in a world at peace, for nations shall not make war anymore. To be sure, this cluster of themes was later subject to myriad and often diverse interpretations and elaborations, but one core remained firm. Whatever else it might be, the messianic redemption must be visible and collective, not merely inner and individual. It is on this, and not on the validity of the Law, that Judaism and Christianity first separated and it was to this that Judaism, whether Talmudic, philosophical or kabbalistic, clung tenaciously in the face of all challenges. This hope, this belief in a visible redemption of the entire Jewish people became the common property of all Jews everywhere and throughout the ages, at least up to modern times.

However, there is also a psychological dimension to messianic belief. It is important to realize that originally "the end of days" was not conceived as pointing to a far distant future (the same was true of the expectation of the early Christians). Though he foresaw the Babylonian conquest and destruction of the First Temple, Jeremiah thought that the Redemption would come in seventy years.[3] Indeed, up to the second century CE it was still possible to believe that the coming of the Messiah is imminent and to act upon this belief. In the final revolt against Rome in 132–135 so towering a rabbinic figure as Rabbi Akiva hailed Bar Kochba as the Messiah.[4]

The Bar Kochba Revolt is, I think, a kind of watershed. Three messianic revolts against Rome had ended in disaster. Thereafter we find a growing tendency to postpone the messianic advent. All messianic activism, even "calculating the End," was discouraged: *Tippaḥ ruḥan shel meḥashvey kitzin—* "Perish all those who calculate the End [for men will say] since the predicted end is here but the Messiah has not come, he will never come."[5] The messianic era will be ushered in by God alone and in his own time, not through human initiative. In an exquisite appropriation from the Song of Songs, one must not attempt "to awaken or arouse love until it wishes."[6] While theoretically the Messiah could arrive at any moment ("for every second of time was the strait gate through which the Messiah could enter," as Walter Benjamin observed)[7] and although, as we shall soon see, messianic activism never ceased, the passive view that Israel must remain faithful and wait became by far the dominant view.

We should note that from the perspective of the responsible rabbinic and lay leadership of the Jewish people this was the only way. Experience had shown, and would show time and again, that active messianic adventurism led either to the vain shedding of Jewish blood or to disillusion in the messianic hope itself. And yet, messianic activism in all its forms continued nonetheless. We shall focus on messianic movements.[8]

II

What is a messianic movement? In the simplest and crudest terms—a Jew arises and proclaims: "The End of Days is *now* and I am he for whom you have waited [or I am his harbinger, his messenger]." If more than ten Jews believe and follow him, you have a messianic movement.

In the last two thousand years there has been almost no age in Jewish history without such a movement. There is a messianic movement in progress right now—among thousands of Lubavitch Hasidim who continue to believe passionately that their leader Rabbi Menahem Schneerson, who died in 1994, is the Messiah, that he will soon be resurrected and return, or that he did not really die but God has temporarily hidden him.

Sometimes Jewish messianic movements have been small, sometimes large, sometimes armed. Most important, they were always the work of a minority of the Jewish people. With the exception of the worldwide movement around Shabbetai Tzvi in the 17th century, the majority remained passive. The responsible leadership of the Jewish people always fought these movements tooth and nail. And therefore, in Jewish history messianic movements were fated to become sectarian, even heretical movements. It is possible that a few of the so-called false messiahs may have been charlatans, as their opponents always insisted, but most of them surely believed in their mission. What is a false messiah? A messiah who fails.

III

Within these perspectives Zionism cannot possibly be regarded as the heir to the Messianic belief. It had to overthrow that belief (in the form that it had crystallized) or perish at birth. Thus, Zionism predicated a return to Zion in the here and now, not at some presumed end of days; redemption, not by God, but by human initiative; not by any miracle of angelic hosts descending from heaven, but by the miracle of manual and agricultural labor by young pioneers of a people that had been forcibly alienated from both for centuries. In short—modern Zionism arose, and the State of Israel was built, on revolutionary secular foundations.[9]

To make this point more vivid and concrete, we have only to consider that the first group of genuine Zionist pioneers who came from Russia to the Land of Israel called themselves *BILU*, an acronym for the Hebrew *Bet Ya'akov lekhu ve-nelkhah*—"House of Israel let us arise and go!" which is a quotation from the Book of Isaiah in the Hebrew Bible.[10] But there the original verse reads: *Bet Ya'akov Lekhu ve-nelkhah be-or Adonay*—"O House of Israel let us arise and go *in the light of the Lord*."

Or let us turn to some famous Zionist Hannukah songs (do not worry, I shall not sing), with just two examples:

Mi yemalel gevurot Yisrael—"Who shall recount the mighty deeds of Israel"—from the Book of Psalms, but there the verse reads—*Mi yemalel gevurot Adonay*—"Who shall recount the mighty deeds *of the Lord*."[11]

Another song for Hannukah (a festival celebrating in Rabbinic tradition not so much the Maccabean victory as the discovery of the cruse of pure oil in the Temple desecrated by Antiochus, which burned miraculously for eight days). The song, which has no biblical phrases, begins—*Anu nos'im lapidim be-lelot afelim*—"We are carrying torches through dark nights" and the refrain is: *Nes lo karah lanu / paḥ shemen lo mat-zanu*—"No miracle occurred for us / We found no cruse of oil."

It could hardly be otherwise. For a new beginning Zionism had to shatter the hypnotic spell of messianic passivity which had gripped Jewry for almost two millennia. And I know that this audience is too sophisticated to think that in stressing the radical breaks that Zionism entailed I am implying in any way that it was therefore illegitimate or somehow "not Jewish."

But in the beginning Zionism was fated to be a "sectarian" movement, opposed from every Jewish quarter: by assimilationists—for obvious reasons; by most of Orthodoxy—as a threat to belief in the Messiah and lack of trust in God; by classical Reform—as a perversion of Israel's mission to spread light among the nations, for which Jews must continue to live among them; by the Jewish Socialist Bund, Zionism's great rival in Eastern Europe, which saw the Jewish problem as part of the class struggle, to be solved where Jews are.[12]

If not with the dominant messianic belief, it would seem that Zionism may have had something in common with the messianic movements of the past, with the crucial difference that those movements still operated within a religious framework. But there is another, more fundamental difference. Unlike all the messianic movements in Jewish history, Zionism did not fail; it succeeded. And along the way, especially with the beginning of Nazi persecution and the Holocaust, it came to command the support of the bulk of world Jewry.

IV

Now let us pause and ask—if Zionism did not flow directly out of the messianic belief, what was its proximate source?

The answer may appear paradoxical, for it was 19th-century assimilation that unwittingly prepared the ground for the rise of Zionism.[13] But how is this possible, when Zionism and assimilation seem a contradiction in terms?

Assimilation had many facets. True, there were those who wanted to completely lose their Jewish identity. The majority wanted to remain Jews, whether religiously or culturally. For most it was a desire for national assimilation and social equality in their host countries, and this was of course tied to legal and political emancipation.

Assimilation was not just a process of erosion, but an enthusiastic ideology. In its inner core, what gave assimilation its passion, its élan, was the age-old desire to put an end to *Galut*—Exile—an end not only to a separate and inferior legal status, but an end to being and feeling alien, the passionate desire to finally be and feel at home. If Jews would be given equal rights and citizenship, they would indeed be "at home." From the first emancipation in revolutionary France, through the 19th century struggle for emancipation in Germany, Italy, the Austro-Hungarian Empire, Russia, Jews were willing, while retaining their religious or cultural identity, to renounce their national identity and to become Frenchmen, Germans, etc. In Germany a Reform rabbi announced from the pulpit: "Germany is our Zion and Düsseldorf our Jerusalem," while his counterpart across the Atlantic put it as "America is our Zion and Charleston our Jerusalem."

In short, assimilation paved the way for Zionism by arousing a fervent craving to put an end to *Galut*, an end to both the reality and existential condition of exile in the present, to be and to feel at home in the here-and-now. Only when it gradually became clear that legal emancipation did not necessarily mean social emancipation, that anti-Semitism could thrive even where the Jews had equal legal rights, indeed that the new racial anti-Semitism arose and flourished precisely in those countries where legal equality had been achieved, did a new vanguard begin to think that the only end to "exile" in all its dimensions was to return to Zion itself.[14] It should therefore come as no surprise that some of the most prominent fathers of Zionism—Moses Hess, Leo Pinsker, Max Nordau, Theodor Herzl himself, began as highly assimilated Jews who found their way back to their people.

V

But let us return to our central theme. To say that Zionism represented a break with Messianism and with Jewish religious tradition is both true and yet oversimplified. Zionism may have been a revolution against messianism, but its rhetoric was often messianic, and that certainly was one source of its appeal. Classical Zionist literature is saturated with biblical quotations and allusions. Strands of the messianic tradition were woven, visibly and invisibly as it were, into Zionism itself, which marshaled and channeled Jewish messianic energies to new ends. Herzl became for many a virtual messianic figure. Even when parts of biblical verses were amputated, as in the examples I cited earlier, they were still uncannily present, just as amputees still somehow feel the presence of the limb that was cut off.

Today we confront a paradox. The state that began as a minority sectarian dream became the vital center of the entire Jewish people. But—in a profound sense neither Israeli Jewry nor diaspora Jewry, nor the world, were prepared to cope with the reality of a Jewish State. Israel just does not seem to fit into any prepared slots. Efforts to integrate the Jewish State into a broader religious framework have convinced only those who desperately seek it. In synagogues around the world the standard prayer for the State of Israel reflects an obvious ambiguity when it refers to Israel as *reshit tzemiḥat ge'ulatenu*—"the beginning of the sprouting of our redemption."[15]

Zionism broke with Jewish messianic tradition; it did not liquidate it. Overtly or unconsciously Jewish messianism is very much alive. As a result, both Israel and the Jewish Diaspora carry a messianic burden on their shoulders, even when they do not use the word. Israel has expected a messianic ingathering, though that has been tempered of late. The Diaspora expects, in many ways, a messianic State. Both apply impossible standards.

Jewish visitors to Israel often express shock that there should be corruption, bureaucratic bungling, ethnic tensions. Be it so. One could wish that it would be otherwise, and certainly there are many Israelis working to solve such problems. But why the shock? When these tourists return to their own countries, do they not find the same? A diaspora Jew who visits his own synagogue at most once or twice a year comes back and tells of his dismay at encountering so many Israelis who are irreligious, even antireligious. What is normal in Paris or New York should not be so in Tel-Aviv.

The point cannot be emphasized often enough. Without even realizing it, many Jews want Israel to be a perfect, messianic state. Instead they are faced with a real, imperfect state, and they do not seem to understand the difference. But you cannot live through a revolution and then pretend to ignore it.

For instance, there are those both within and outside Israel who demand that the Jewish state be governed in all aspects by *halakhah*, by Jewish law. But is there a *halakhah* for this Jewish state? No, because such a state as now exists was never expected in Jewish tradition. Maimonides' great Code of Jewish law—the *Mishneh Torah*—contains ritual, ethical, civil, and criminal laws for two Jewish states: The ancient state and the future messianic state at the end of time. There is nothing in between.

And here is the fundamental novelty of the Zionist revolution—an independent Jewish state, not at the end of days but in the midst of time, in the midst of history. Israel is neither the kingdom of David and Solomon, nor is it the state of the Messiah. It is precisely the in-between state, the unanticipated and unexpected state to which traditional categories cannot be applied. One calamitous result is that the Israeli population has become polarized as never before, and the messianic syndrome lies at the heart of it.

VI

To view it merely as a struggle between "religious" and "secular" is to distort. The situation is far more complex. There are wide and intricate variations and conflicts among the religious, even among the "Orthodox," just as among the secular. There are Orthodox Jews who accept the State, are culturally modern, work within the framework of the State, are scientists and professors at the universities. Their sons, even those educated in Yeshivas, serve in the army. There are religious Kibbutzim. But there are also thousands of Yeshiva students who do not serve at all.

And then there is the phenomenon of those ultra-pious (I refer to the *Neturey Karta* [the "Guardians of the City"] and in general the Satmar Hasidim both in Israel and abroad) who have never recognized the Jewish State at all. For them the State is anathema, not only because it was founded and is governed by heretics, but precisely because it is to them a revolt against God and his Messiah. They told Yassir Arafat, as they told the Jordanians in the 1948 War of Independence, that they would be quite content to live under Arab rule so long as they would be allowed to pursue their way of life. Shocking though this may sound to some, within their world view they are probably the most consistent in clinging to the tradition of messianic waiting. They, at least, know that the State of Israel is not the messianic state.

Conversely, there are many secular Israelis who have a warm empathy for Jewish tradition, who celebrate the traditional holidays albeit in modified forms, and who ask only that the religious political parties not create a theocracy, especially in areas they already control and beyond— marriage and divorce, and the definition of who is a Jew.

Unfortunately, each camp has at the end of its spectrum an extreme fringe capable of savagery and of throwing the country into civil war and chaos. For the religious extremists the category is the holiness of the entire Land of Israel, conceived of in biblical terms.[16] For the secular extremists the category is *Eretz Yisrael ha-shelemah*—"The whole Land of Israel"—which can have no other source, even when unacknowledged, than the Bible. For each, to give up an inch of territory, even for the sake of peace, is a betrayal to be fought, if necessary, by acts of violence against both Arabs and Jews.

Both types of fanatics are driven, at their core, by a messianic conception of what the Land of Israel should be, a conception that is totally ahistorical, that harks back to promises recorded in ancient times, that refuses to realize that Judaism has never been a closed system but betrays both continuity and change throughout history, that the Bible may be sacred but that as Maimonides knew, the gates of interpretation have never been closed to us.[17]

The result is that the same messianism that was such a crucial factor in the survival of the Jews through the ages is now capable of exacting a terrible new price. In some circles the focus of study is on those portions of the Talmud that deal with the details of the ancient Temple and its service, obviously in preparation for the imminent building of the third, messianic, Temple. But what of Al-Aksa and the Mosque of Omar which now stand on the Temple Mount? Presumably the Messiah will take care of that. But periodically, Israeli security forces uncover and arrest groups that actively plot to blow up the mosques. Do they not realize that should they succeed they could provoke a *jihad* against Israel from the entire vast Muslim world? Though I cannot prove it, I feel that they know this very well and perhaps even want to provoke it. Does not one strand in Jewish (and Christian) apocalyptic tradition emphasize that the messianic age will be preceded by terrible global wars, the so-called Wars of Gog and Magog?

In 1995 Prime Minister Yitzhak Rabin was assassinated by a young law-student, Yigal Amir. No, Amir was not insane, only absolutely convinced that he knew God's will and was carrying it out. By a bitter irony, similar threats are now hurled against Ariel Sharon for his plan to withdraw from the Gaza strip and parts of the West Bank.

VII

If Jewry has not yet fully grasped the revolution that occurred in its midst, for the rest of the world the reality of a Jewish State has become even more contentious. Indeed, I know of no other state that is today subject to more vilification than the State of Israel, and this not only from

Arab countries but in the West as well. It is with the West that I am primarily concerned today. I am not speaking of criticism, however harsh. Israel is surely not immune to criticism, indeed some of the fiercest criticism can be heard from Israelis within the state itself. Nor do I automatically equate criticism of Zionism or Israel with anti-Semitism, though occasionally the link is too evident to be ignored. But whereas many countries can be and are criticized for this or that policy or behavior, in the case of Israel we have an additional dimension. I put it to you that of all the many countries in today's world, only Israel's very right to exist as a sovereign state is challenged, and measures against it are called for that have no parallel. One telling case in point from the sphere I know best will suffice—the petition printed in England in the *Guardian* on April 6, 2002, and almost immediately circulated worldwide via the Internet, asking that all ties with Israeli universities and research institutions be severed. Such a grotesque attempt to isolate and ghettoize Israel's thriving academic and intellectual life has never been threatened against even the most endemic dictatorial and genocidal regimes who blatantly and deliberately violate human rights daily.

VIII

The difficulties Israel continues to encounter in securing a normal place among the nations cannot be explained in current political terms alone. If the creation of such a state was unanticipated in Jewish tradition, the same is true for Christian and Muslim tradition. Christianity knows of a future restoration of the Jews to their land, but only at the time of the Second Coming. In Islam such a restoration was never even contemplated. Both had in common a basic toleration of the continued existence of autonomous Jewish communities in their midst, a fact whose importance is evident. Yet both saw in the loss of Jewish sovereignty a sure sign that God had repudiated the Jews in their favor, and sought additional confirmation of this by ensuring their subsequent degradation. Such legacies do not simply disappear even in the so-called secular modern world, but continue to exert a powerful if subliminal influence. Whether in religious or in secular terms, the State of Israel does not seem to fit into any conventional conceptual categories.

But we live in an age of *térribles simplificateurs* and ever-diminishing historical memory. Discussions of Israel in the media begin with the Intifada, or the June War of 1967, or at most the establishment of Israel in

1948. Throughout we find a depressing ignorance of the history of the Jews and Judaism,[18] of Zionism, indeed of the history of the Middle East as a whole. I limit myself to a few examples.

Zionism is today often equated with colonialism. But what European colonial power ever sent Jews to settle in Palestine? My teacher, Salo Baron, once observed that it has been common in history for mother countries to establish colonies; but where do we have another example of colonies establishing a mother country? Yes, in 1917 the British issued the Balfour Declaration, just as they made promises to the Arabs, neither really fulfilled. But what seems to be forgotten is the essential point — that much of the contemporary map of the Middle East is entirely the creation of Great Britain and France when they dismantled the Ottoman Turkish Empire after World War I and, with the blessings of the League of Nations, received mandates over Iraq, Syria, Lebanon and Palestine, the latter divided by the British into two separate entities, west and east of the Jordan River. None of these new countries had historical precedents or national identities and they were not given full independence until World War II and after.[19] Yet their legitimacy is not in question.

If not as colonialism, Zionism is presented as merely another example of 19th-century nationalism (the term is currently in disrepute), a glib judgment that explains little, because it ignores its special, if not unique, characteristics. Zionism began and remained throughout a movement of national liberation. Certainly it was aware of other such 19th-century movements. Moses Hess pointedly entitled his major proto-Zionist work "Rome and Jerusalem" because, with the Risorgimento in mind, he saw the liberation of Italy as signaling the time for the liberation of the Jewish people as well.[20] Yet when we actually compare Zionism with the other European national movements we realize that it began with a reversal of obstacles and assets. Unlike the other peoples the Jews did not possess a common territory nor a common vernacular. On the other hand, Zionism did not have to invent the concept of a Jewish "nation," but merely to revive and reinvigorate it. As for language, while not spoken in the everyday, Hebrew had a continuous and unbroken literary history, both religious and secular, throughout the diaspora and through the ages.

But how can the Jews be considered a nation? Today, outside Israel, it is not easily apparent and many diaspora Jews would deny it outright, or use the softer term "the Jewish people." But from ancient times until the French Revolution Jews were conscious of themselves as a nation, a nation dispersed in exile, and were viewed as such by the non-Jewish world as well. Striking proof of this can be found in the grand debate on Jewish emancipation itself, as it was first voiced in France in the revolutionary National Assembly. Both those in favor of granting citizenship and equal rights to the Jews in the new nation-state that was in the process of being born, as well as those opposed, agreed that the Jews have at least hitherto been a nation. Mere ethnicity was not the issue in this truly defining moment. On December 23, 1789, Count Stanislas de Clermont Tonnere, one of the prime advocates of Jewish citizenship declared: "Everything must be refused to the Jews as a nation. Everything must be given to them as individuals. They must become citizens. It is thought that they do not want to be such. Let them say it and let them be banished. There cannot be a nation within a nation. . . ."[21] To which the Abbé Jean-Siffrein Maury, a conservative opponent of Jewish emancipation responded: "I observe to begin with that the word *Jew* is not the name of a [religious] sect, but of a nation that has its laws which it has always followed and which it still wants to follow. *To call the Jews citizens would be as if one said that, without letters of naturalization and without ceasing to be English and Danes, the English and Danes could become French.*"[22] The seemingly anomalous persistence of a Jewish national self-consciousness for almost two millennia following the loss of its state is a fact that, rather than be dismissed, should elicit astonishment and creatively challenge any conventional definition of what constitutes a nation.[23] But even if the continued national character of the Jews in dispersion be granted, is continuous residence in a land since antiquity a necessary criterion for claiming sovereignty over it? To insist on this would be to ignore the role of migrations and conquests in history, to create a test that even European nations could not pass, let alone those of the Western Hemisphere.

In the Jewish case the essential point lies elsewhere, in the myriad ways through which Jews everywhere until modern times fused their collective memory and collective hope and focused both on what they continued to regard as their true home. This was so even though Jewish life in the Middle Ages was far from being merely a vale of tears and Jews were often very attached to the lands in which they lived.[24] Although Rabbi Judah Loew (the MaHaraL) of Prague noted that the Bohemia of his time was a relatively mild exile, he succinctly defined exile as anything that is not in its proper natural place and how much more so the Jewish people dispersed outside its land.[25] The real question is whether a nation such as this, in a unique instance, had a right to reclaim its ancestral land, especially when they were not coming as conquistadores to destroy the Arab population and, when Zionist settlement began, they felt that they were not displacing another nation. For in the 1880's there was no Palestinian nation and even the term "Palestinian" was not in use.

IX

Since then, however, a Palestinian nation has certainly come into being, and I would be the first to reject any attempt to deny this reality merely on the grounds that it is a relatively recent historical development. Nor is this the place for a recital of the convoluted history of Arab-Jewish relations in Palestine since the 1920's which each side will interpret in its moral favor. Certainly, in retrospect, at crucial junctures both sides made grievous errors — the Arabs by not accepting the United Nations partition plan in 1947, the Israelis by not following Ben Gurion's advice after the Six Day War to return the conquered territories and not become an occupying power, Arafat's refusal to accept Ehud Barak's peace proposals as a basis for negotiations, the policy of building Israeli settlements on the West Bank and in Gaza. Of course there is no guarantee that had these policies not been followed a genuine peace would have been achieved, but at present that has become irrelevant. History is not the story of what should have happened. In the course of events the Palestinians became a nation, and as such they deserve a sovereign state of their own. Two rights, each with a different source have clashed. Must one choose one instead of the other? Is it not possible in principle to be both pro-Palestinian and pro-Israeli?

And so all along. By all means, criticize Israel for its faults, but also acknowledge its remarkable achievements. Try at least to understand the faults, and let your criticism be out of friendship and concern, not predetermined antagonism. After one of Israel's reprisal raids against terrorists in Gaza in which, tragically, there were also civilian Palestinian casualties, one of my acquaintances said to me that Israel is no different from any fascist aggressor. By what criterion, I asked. "We judge Israel," he replied, "not by the standards of the Middle East, but by what we would expect from a Scandinavian country." Yet what do we know of how the Swedes or Danes would react if they were perpetually vulnerable to sworn enemies, not armies but invisible individuals that are difficult to identity as such, if in Stockholm or Copenhagen, as in Jerusalem, Tel Aviv or Haifa, you went to the market in the morning, or with friends to a café in the evening, and knew in the back of your mind that you might not return, that when you put your children on a bus they might be blown up by a suicide bomber? And yet Israelis try to maintain a normal life. The markets and cafés are filled, the buses run. No, I suggested, your standard is not Scandinavian but unconsciously messianic, with no room for Israel's imperfections or effort to comprehend them. What else can explain the double standard constantly applied to Israel? From 1950 to 1988 the West Bank was annexed by Jordan, yet no one in the West condemned the occupation. I mention this not in order to justify the Israeli occupation, only to exemplify the double standard.

One more facet of Christian messianism deserves to be noted. If Israel is neither the messianic state envisioned by Jewish or Christian tradition, ironically, for one current in contemporary Christianity, at least in the United States, it already has an absolute messianic significance no matter what its failings. I refer to the fundamentalist Christian far right, numbering in the millions and growing rapidly, who are totally convinced that the rise of the State of Israel is the most potent proof that the apocalypse and the Second Coming are just round the corner. Since the Christian Right now exerts an unprecedented influence on the present administration and Congress, I am sorry to say that even many American Jews and Israeli rightists regard and welcome them as Israel's staunchest friends. They choose to ignore that this too is part of a messianic legacy, that for these "friends" the Jewish state is an immediate prelude to the eschatological conversion of the Jews. If politics makes strange bedfellows religion sometimes makes unholy alliances.

So what is to be done? I am neither a political scientist nor a diplomat, and have no recipe to solve the problems of the Middle East. Perhaps they are insoluble. I am only personally convinced that the violent extremists on both sides are, at this moment, still a minority, that the majority of Israelis and Palestinians are tired of war and want peace, if it can be achieved with some measure of justice and equity by their leaders. As a mere historian I can really only offer the one thing I have learned from all my studies—that history is always open, never inevitable.

Permit me a personal anecdote.

In the summer of 1967, shortly after the June War, my wife and I came to Jerusalem and entered the Old City for the first time. We made our way toward the Western Wall and as we walked I found myself wondering how I would react. Would I hug the Wall and weep? Nothing of the sort occurred when we arrived. For all its historical and emotional associations which I knew so well, I was impressed by the size of the stones, even left a slip of paper in a crevice on which we had written a simple prayer, as was the venerable Jewish custom, and that was all. From there we climbed onto the Temple Mount and saw the two mosques guarded by Israeli police and paratroopers and then we went to the Church of the Holy Sepulcher and found it similarly guarded. No, I did not gloat. But these two sights jangled all my historical nerves. I stared almost with disbelief and could think only that for centuries Christendom and Islam fought over these very places without even a thought that the Jews might also have a stake in the struggle (except for the massacres of Jews along the way by the Crusaders of the Christian *jihad*). Who would have thought that one day Jews would be standing guard over these Christian and Muslim holy sites? History is always open.

I remember a time when everyone said that no Arab state will ever make peace with Israel, but now there is peace with Egypt and with Jordan, a cold peace to be sure, but better than a hot war. History is always open.

When I was in Israel last November, the Beijing Opera came from China to perform in Tel Aviv. Who, even a few years ago, could have imagined this? I repeat again—history is always open, for better or for worse. Certainly conditions can become even worse. But it also means that no matter how grim the situation may appear at any time, it can always change for the better in unforeseen ways. Messianism is not the only possible form of human hope.

NOTES

As is my custom, in publishing this lecture I have retained the text as it was orally presented, with only minor alterations and the addition of some footnotes. Bibliographical references have also been kept to a minimum. Readers should also be aware, if they are not already, that despite my Hebrew name and fluency in Hebrew I am not an Israeli. Though ultimately focused on current problems my intent here has not been "political" but historical. At the same time I freely admit that my concern with Israel is profoundly personal and existential, as it is with the whole of Jewish history, but I have never thought that such a concern contradicts or prevents a sincere attempt at historical objectivity. My position on this is close to that of the American historian Thomas L. Haskell in his significantly titled book *Objectivity Is Not Neutrality*, Baltimore, 1998.

I take this opportunity to record my thanks to Prof. Dr. Eilert Herms, Dean of the Theological Faculty, for his generous *laudatio* and cordial hospitality, to Prof. Dr. Hermann Lichtenberger who, beyond the call of duty, took the time and trouble to satisfy my every need and whim, to Dr. Frank Lucas, grandson of Rabbi

Leopold Lucas, who represented the family, to the warmly receptive audience, and to my son Ariel, who made a long and difficult journey just to be with me in Tübingen.

1. G. Scholem, "Toward an Understanding of the Messianic Idea in Judaism," in *The Messianic Idea in Judaism and Other Essays on Jewish Spirituality*, New York, 1971, pp. 1–36. German original: "Zum Verständnis der messianischen Idee im Judentum," *Eranos Jahrbuch*, 28 (1959), 193–239.

2. I shall not deal here with Jewish apocalyptic writings. Although they give the appearance of messianic "activism" and on occasion may provide some of the background for the emergence of a particular messianic movement, apocalyptic speculation is essentially, in my opinion, another form of passivity, in which messianic energies are exhausted by the speculative preoccupation itself.

3. Jer. 29:10.

4. Jerusalem Talmud, *Ta'anit*, 4:8 fol. 68d. But his colleague Rabbi Yohanan ben Torta responded: "Akiva, grasses will grow from your cheeks and the son of David will not yet come."

5. *Yalkut Shimoni*, Habbakuk, no. 562.

6. See Babylonian Talmud, *Ketubot*, 111a (based on Cant. 2:7).

7. W. Benjamin, "Theses on the Philosophy of History," in *Illuminations*, ed. Hannah Arendt, tr. Harry Zohn, London. 1968. p. 266. German original: "Über den Begriff der Geschichte." Zohn's translation was made from the text in *Die Neue Rundschau*, 61, 3 (1959). This passage does not appear in the now standard edition of the text by Rolf Tiedemann and Hermann Schweppenhäuser (*Gesammelte Schriften*, I.2) but in the Anmerkungen, ibid., I.3, p. 1252.

8. A comprehensive study of Jewish messianic movements is still a desideratum. For the moment A. Z. Aescoly's collection of texts *Ha-tenu'ot ha-meshihiot be-Yisrael* (The Messianic Movements in Israel), 2nd ed., Jerusalem, 1987, remains basic and deserves to be translated. See also: *Essential Papers on Messianic Movements and Personalities in Jewish History*, ed. Marc Saperstein, New York, 1992; *Toward the Millennium*, ed. Peter Schäfer and Mark Cohen, Leiden-Boston, 1998: all with ample bibliographies. The most important study of a single movement is, of course, G. Scholem's magisterial *Sabbatai Sevi: The Mythical Messiah*, tr. R. J. Zwi Werblowsky, Princeton, 1973. Since then new researches and perspectives on Sabbatianism have appeared. The most important attempts at critical revisions of Scholem are those of Moshe Idel, e.g. in his *Kabbalah: New Perspectives*, New Haven, 1988; idem, *Messianic Mystics*, New Haven, 1998, especially ch. 6; and Yehuda Liebes, *On Sabbatianism and Its Kabbalah: Collected Essays* [in Hebrew], Jerusalem, 1995.

9. I do not mean by this to deny the significance of modern religious Zionism

in the formation of the Jewish state, or its continued political importance since 1948. But the fundamental character of Israeli culture, society, and the state itself, was forged by secular Zionism. The various streams of religious Zionism developed a common readiness to view even secular efforts to reclaim and develop the Land of Israel in messianic terms, as the beginning, though hardly the end of the divine plan for the redemption of the Jewish people. Their major tension with the secular mainstream has been, from the beginning, their rejection of cultural Zionism, for example their desire to control education. In this, largely because all Israeli governments have been coalitions, they have forced compromises and concessions for their own views and institutions.

10. Is. 2:5.

11. Ps. 106:2.

12. On the Bund see Henry Tobias, *The Jewish Bund in Russia from Its Origins to 1905*, Stanford, 1972; Henri Minczeles, *Histoire générale du Bund: un movement révolutionnaire juif*, Paris, 1995; Claudie Weill, *Les cosmopolites: socialisme et judéité en Russie, 1897–1917*, Paris, 2004.

13. In what follows I am essentially indebted to Yehezkel Kaumann's great work *Golah ve-nekhar* (Exile and Alienage), Tel Aviv, 1930, vol. II, ch. 4, pp. 191 ff., 204 ff. and passim.

14. Not all Zionists were at first committed exclusively to Palestine. Given the urgent problems of masses of Jews, especially in Eastern Europe, there were those, including Theodor Herzl, who were willing, albeit reluctantly, to entertain the possibility of a Jewish national settlement elsewhere, if it were feasible. That is why they were prepared to consider seriously the British offer of such a settlement in East Africa (Uganda). The issue came to a head at the Sixth Zionist Congress in 1903 when, largely because of the revolt of the Russian delegates against any "territorialist" solution, it was abandoned. Some of those who still believed in it left the Zionist movement and, after Herzl died, formed the Jewish Territorial Organization (ITO).

15. The prayer was written by the Hebrew novelist and Nobel laureate S. Y. Agnon. The phrase certainly reflects a belief common to all religious Zionists. Its appropriateness has been defended, at least as a reflection of how masses of Jews have interpreted major events leading to and since the establishment of the State in 1948, by the late eminent historian Jacob Katz. See his "Israel and the Messiah" [1982], reprinted in *Essential Papers* (above, n. 8), pp. 475–491. But then, both Agnon and Katz were themselves religious Zionists.

16. For a fine and nuanced historical analysis of the religious right see Aviezer Ravitzky, *Messianism, Zionism, and Jewish Religious Radicalism*, tr. M. Swirsky and J. Chipman, Chicago, 1996.

17. See Maimonides, *The Guide of the Perplexed* (II:25), tr. and ed. Shlomo Pines, Chicago, 1963, vol. 2, p. 327.

18. This is so with regard to one of the key elements in any understanding of Jewish history—the unique fusion and interdependence of Jewish religion and Jewish peoplehood, so much so that even the challenge and stresses of modern times have not been able to separate them completely. The best account and analysis of this phenomenon is to be found in Salo Wittmayer Baron, *A Social and Religious History of the Jews*, 2nd revised edition, vol. 1, New York, 1952, Introduction.

19. Wherever "independence" was technically granted earlier it was illusory, the mandate powers retaining control in all vital matters, such as foreign affairs, finances, and the continued maintenance of military bases. Without going into the intricate history of each of the countries it will suffice to note that despite formal independence granted to Iraq by Britain in 1932, full independence was not really achieved until the overthrow of the monarchy in 1958. Syria and Lebanon, both French mandates, became fully independent in 1946. The division of Palestine was made definitive by the British in 1923 when they gave so-called independence to the territory east of the river Jordan ("Transjordan") under the Emir Abdullah and forbade Jewish settlement there. But again, real independence came to Jordan only in 1946, after which Abdullah proclaimed himself king.

20. Moses Hess, *Rom und Jerusalem: Die letzte Nationalitätsfrage*, Leipzig, 1862.

21. "Il faut tout refuser aux juifs, comme nation, il faut tout leur accorder comme individus; il faut qu'ils soient citoyens. On prétend qu'ils ne veulent pas l'être; qu'ils le disent et qu'on les banisse; il ne peut y avoir une nation dans une nation" (Achile-Edmond Halphen, *Recueil des lois, décrets, ordonnances . . . concernant les Israélites depuis la Révolution de 1789, suivi d'un appendice concernant la discussion dans les assemblées legislatives . . .* , Paris, 1851, p. 185).

22. "J'observe d'abord que le mot juif n'est pas le nom d'une secte, mais d'une nation qui a des lois, qui les a toujours suivies, et qui veut encore les suivre. *Appeler les juifs des citoyens, ce serait comme si l'on disait que, sans lettres de naturalisation et sans cesser d'être Anglais et Danois, les Anglais et les Danois pourraient devenir Français*" (ibid., p. 186). My italics. Though I am fully aware that prior to the French Revolution "nation" did not yet have all the connotations of the modern nation-state, I regard the exchange between Clermont Tonnere and Maury as a defining moment in revealing how the Jews were seen by others prior to emancipation. Here it is clear that neither regards Jewry merely as a religious or ethnic group but, as Maury says explicitly, as a nation somehow comparable to the English and the Danes. Both know that despite some erosion of Jewish communal autonomy in the 17th and 18th centuries, Jewish law which governs Jewish life is

not merely ritual law, but civil and even criminal law as well. It is these juridical spheres that make the Jews a "nation" that cannot be tolerated in the nation-state that is now coming into being and that will be taken away from the Jews by the state when they are granted citizenship.

23. The question continues to be the subject of lively debate among historians. For an excellent and succinct analysis of the various currents see Anthony D. Smith, *The Nation in History: Historiographical Debates about Ethnicity and Nationalism*, Hanover, New Hampshire, 2000.

24. See on this my "Exile and Expulsion in Jewish History" in *Crisis and Creativity in the Sephardic World*, ed. Benjamin Gampel, New York, 1997, pp. 3–22.

25. See Judah Loew ben Bezalel (MaHaRaL), *Netzaḥ Yisrael*, Prague, 1599, ch. 1.

PART V *The Yoke of Memory*

13 : TOWARD A HISTORY OF JEWISH HOPE

Originally published as "Un champ à Anathoth: Vers une histoire de l'espoir juif," *Esprit* 104/105 (1985), 24–38.

This article was originally delivered as a lecture in December 1984 at the Colloque des intellectuels juifs de langue française (made famous by Emanuel Levinas's Talmudic readings) and subsequently published in the French literary journal *Esprit* in 1985. It continues Yerushalmi's work on the relationship between history and memory in *Zakhor* that appeared in 1982, as well as his long-standing interest, familiar to his doctoral students from his regular seminar, in the history of Jewish messianism.

Here Yerushalmi tried to disentangle the phenomenon of messianism, which had attracted so much scholarly attention in Jewish studies, from the broader and more amorphous current of hope, which had received relatively little serious scrutiny. To a great extent, his lecture was a programmatic call for scholarly engagement with the neglected history of Jewish hope. This topic would seem especially appropriate for the intellectual climate in France, where the talk was delivered. For there is in Yerushalmi's address more than a little of the spirit of the *Annales* School tradition, particularly the study of the "histoire des mentalités" made famous by the renowned French historian Lucien Febvre. Yerushalmi quoted a 1941 essay by Febvre in which he called for a new kind of scholarly labor that focused on emotions or frames of mind that had previously escaped the attention of historians: love, death, pity, cruelty, and joy. While noting that Jewish historiography had not yet found its Febvre, Yerushalmi added hope to the list.

Yerushalmi began his essay (the French title translates, "A Field in Anathoth") by quoting a passage from the Book of Jeremiah (chapter 32) in which the prophet was instructed by God in 587 BCE to buy a field on the outskirts of Jerusalem just as that city was to be overrun by the Babylonians. Jeremiah's investment in the future in the face of imminent destruction was the prototypical act of Jewish hope for Yerushalmi, and one that had vexed him since childhood. In seeking to make sense of it, Yerushalmi understood that one "cannot explore the history of Jewish hope without at the same time exploring the history of Jewish despair." And in fact, much of his essay does just that by exploring Jewish despair in a variety of sources, from the Second Book of Baruch to the medieval Hebrew chroniclers of the Crusades to the early modern Iberian Jewish figures Isaac Abravanel, Solomon Ibn Verga, and the Portuguese Samuel Usque. The account is a lachrymose rendering of the way in which Jewish tragedy has been memorialized. It serves as preface and foil to Yerushalmi's attempt in the last third or so of the lecture to lay out the broad contours of what a history of Jewish hope might look like. To begin with, he declared in an *Annales*-like formulation, it must "seriously investigate those facets of collective tradition and group consciousness that, at any given time, made hope possible for those who were potentially disposed to it."

A major obstacle to gaining access to that collective consciousness was messianism, with its recurring disruptions of Jewish history. Yerushalmi aimed to dig beneath the surface to apprehend the more constant *"interim* Jewish hopes" that nurtured and sustained Jews between episodes of messianic rupture. These hopes, he noted, did not follow a universal script among Jews the world over, but rather were situated in discrete local contexts. Of particular interest to him was the hope that attended migration, which was such a common motif in the annals of the Jews. It was not just economic deprivation or discrimination that propelled Jews into an orbit of ceaseless mobility. It was also the hope of finding a new promised land. This is what Yerushalmi called "the geography of hope," a phrase that was borrowed by his friend the French Jewish sociologist Pierre Birnbaum, in *Géographie de l'espoir: L'exil, les Lumières, la désassimilation* (Paris, 2004).

At the end of the day, what most intrigued Yerushalmi was the ability of Jews, a small and oft-persecuted people, "to endure the tension of waiting" for ultimate redemption. He proposed, as he had done in the second chapter of *Zakhor*, a careful examination of liturgy and ritual as sources and salves of daily hope. In these genres, not only was memory preserved, but the mechanisms of adaptation that allowed for continued resilience were honed. Similarly, Jews had for centuries developed the ability to engage in "a midrash of history" that allowed them to dig beneath the surface of events to find inner meaning, or even invisible triumphs, in the wake of what otherwise seemed to be instances of manifest defeat.

Yerushalmi ended his essay with two sobering contemporary reflections. First, he observed with concern the "current crisis of the Jewish state" that resulted from confusing messianic and other forms of Jewish hope. And second, he commented that since the Holocaust, large numbers of Jews have "order[ed] their collective lives . . . largely out of an obsession with the era of destruction and death." A robust history of hope may not cure this obsession. But at a minimum, he concluded melancholically, it can "assuage our loneliness."

I am gratified and honored that you have invited me to participate in this Colloque des Intellectuels Juifs de Langue Française, but I do not want to begin under false pretenses. Although I am certainly a Jew, and though I like to regard myself as an intellectual, I cannot claim to be an "intellectuel de langue française." If I read French fairly well and, on occasion, even try to speak it tolerably, the fact remains that I neither think nor write in French. What I have to say this evening was written in English and translated by Eric Vigne, the translator of *Zakhor*.

"Mémoire et Histoire" is a theme on which, in that book, I have already expressed my thoughts.[1] I am now eager to hear what others have to say. But memory of the past is incomplete without its natural complement— hope for the future. Because I do not regard this forum as an occasion for a safe and cautious "pointillisme," some of you may conclude that I have gone to the other extreme. The topic I have chosen is certainly too large for a single lecture, and perhaps too rash in itself. I approach it with some trepidation. The title, on the other hand, evokes a text that is undoubtedly familiar to you, for it derives from the 32nd chapter of the Book of Jeremiah. The year is 587 BCE. Jerusalem is surrounded by the Babylonians and Jeremiah is in the palace prison for having proclaimed that the city and the Temple will be destroyed and the king and his people exiled from the land. The essential parts of the text will bear repetition:

> And Jeremiah said: The word of the Lord came unto me, saying: Behold, Hanamel the son of Shallum your uncle shall come unto you, saying: Buy for yourself my field that is in Anathoth. . . . And I bought the field that was in Anathoth of Hanamel my uncle's son, and I subscribed the deed and sealed it, and called witnesses, and weighed him the money in the balances. . . . And I delivered the deed of the purchase to Baruch the son of Neriah . . . in the presence of Hanamel . . . and in the presence of the witnesses . . . before all the Jews that sat in the court of the guard. And I charged Baruch before them saying: Thus saith the Lord of Hosts the God of Israel: Take these deeds . . . and put them in an earthen vessel that they may continue many days. For thus saith the Lord of Hosts the God of Israel: Houses and fields and vineyards shall yet be bought in this land.

Our vast distance from the ancient events, our overfamiliarity with the text, and the actual return of the Jewish people to its land in modern times, prevent us from feeling the full original impact of what must have seemed, by any human standards, the most absurd of all real estate transactions. We only catch a glimmer of this when the prophet himself, after meticulously obeying the instructions he recognized as divine, cries out in anguished frustration: "Behold the mounds they are come unto the city to take it; and the city is given into the hand of the Chaldeans that fight against it, because of the sword, and of the famine, and of the pestilence; and what You have spoken is come to pass; and behold, You see it. Yet You have said to me, O Lord God: Buy yourself the field for money, and call witnesses; whereas the city is given into the hand of the Chaldeans!"

The entire chapter has haunted me for years. Indeed, although as a child in school it seemed perfectly clear to me (prophets, as the teacher blithely pointed out, know everything in advance), I confess that as I grow older I find I understand it less and less. Prophets are men before they are prophets and, as Jeremiah knew above all others, the voice of God can be aped in many ways. To buy a field on the very eve of destruction and exile is a quintessential act of hope that is hardly an inevitable response to hopelessness. What do we really understand of such matters?

In a recent book an eminent colleague at Columbia University, the historian Morton Smith, has asked flatly: "Why is it that, although hope is one of the fundamental factors that have shaped history, it has almost never been the subject of direct historical investigation for its own sake?"[2] Ernst Bloch's massive work *Das Prinzip Hoffnung*[3] does not diminish the force of the question. Despite occasionally brilliant flashes, Bloch's seemingly endless rumination is essentially unhistorical and, despite its avowed Marxism, I doubt that it can even satisfy the requirements of a responsible Marxist historian.

Now if the history of hope may be important for the history of mankind, it must surely be pivotal for an understanding of Jewish history. And yet, for all its diverse lines of investigation and its genuine triumphs in recovering unknown aspects of the Jewish past, contemporary Jewish scholarship has betrayed little interest in such matters. The prodigious energy invested in reconstructing the social, economic, and intellectual history of the Jews has not been matched by an equal passion to fathom how Jews have felt, viewed, and endured that history. Thus, although some tentative beginnings have been made, even the history of Jewish historiography remains a major desideratum, while the far more subtle problem of the history of Jewish *perceptions* of history is barely on the horizon. Recently, to be sure, there has been a growing preoccupation with Jewish literary responses to major historical catastrophes,[4] while interest in messianism and messianic movements continues unabated. But though each of these subjects is relevant, they cannot add up to what we require, for the issue extends beyond them. A history of Jewish hope that would reveal something of its phenomenology remains to be written.

I should emphasize that in speaking of Jewish hope I exclude for the moment such manifestations of individual hope as the longing for life after death or the belief in reincarnation. Rather, I have in mind Jewish hope in its collective, historical dimension, hope in the face of historical defeat. And that includes not only particular catastrophes, but the constant existential condition of historical defeat that lasted at least from the destruction of the Temple until 1948. Such a history need be neither sentimental nor tendentious. On the contrary, it can be rigorous and densely documented. No new texts need be discovered. Those we have will suffice, if we learn to read them afresh, closely and between the lines.

Yet the obstacles to the inquiry I envision are not to be taken lightly. They are not limited to the obvious difficulties in treating any aspect of so seemingly elusive a theme. Any projected history of Jewish hope must first cope with two major obstacles that derive from the same source — our fundamentally patronizing attitude, whether explicitly or latent, toward the Jewish past itself.

The first obstacle concerns our conception of the *Jews* of the past. Whether we admit it or not, we regard them as somehow more naive, certainly more pious, at any rate — simpler than we. Believing firmly in God they, as it were, always had ready answers to historical suffering.

The second obstacle concerns our attitude toward the *experiences* of the Jews of the past. Living as we do a generation after the Shoah, we take it as axiomatic that even the most tragic experiences of our forebears were totally incommensurate with our own. They did not know, they could not have known, the terror of history as we do.

Both assumptions lead us astray. They imply that hope came so much more easily in the past that we can afford to dismiss it, or at least to underrate it. And why not? Hope that comes too easily is a hope that cannot impress. This, therefore, is crucial: We cannot explore the history of Jewish hope without at the same time exploring the history of Jewish despair. Only when we become painfully aware of the historical depths of Jewish despair, only when we take it seriously, will we begin to realize that Jewish hope is not an historical "given" to be taken for granted, but an historical problem that we have not yet begun to recognize, let alone comprehend.

The Jewish people has not, as we would like to believe, simply marched through history with its faith firm and intact. Though the people as an entity has survived, countless Jews — we will never know how many — have fallen along the way. They have been lost not only through slaughter and martyrdom, but through defection and conversion; and these not merely (as again we should like to think) for the sake of worldly ambition and profit, but out of a genuine despair in a Jewish future. Yet how are we to begin to approach this? Most of our sources, even those that are direct responses to catastrophe, are already distortions. They rarely reflect the full and immediate shock of the experience. Literary texts, be they chronicles, laments, or accounts that appear in other genres, are already an assimilation of the experience and an interpretation of it. They were written by those who had managed to overcome at least the initial wave of despair, to give the experience a theological rationale or an aesthetic form. Those who utterly succumbed to despair did not write or, if they did, their writings were not preserved.

Still, after taking all this into account, even in the literary texts something of the original force of despair seeps through the cracks and crevices:

> Blessed is he who was not born
> Or he, who having been born, has died.
> But for us who live, woe unto us,
> Because we have seen the afflictions of Zion,
> And what has befallen Jerusalem. . . .

> Ye farmers, sow not again. . . .
> And thou vine, why dost thou further give thy wine . . . ?
> And you, ye bridegrooms, enter not in,
> And let not the brides adorn themselves with garlands. . . .

> For why should they bear in pain only to bury in grief,
> Or why, again, should mankind have sons?

> . . .

> Would that thou hadst ears, O Earth
> And that thou hadst a heart, O dust,
> That ye might go and announce in Sheol
> And say to the dead:
> "Blessed are you more than we who live."

The words are from the Second Book of Baruch,[5] written after the destruction of the Temple by the Romans. An anthology of similar texts throughout the ages can easily be compiled, but I shall not attempt it here. Instead, let me focus momentarily on a specific event, the expulsion from Spain in 1492. The most famous, almost canonical, account is that of Don Isaac Abravanel in the introduction of his *Commentary on the Book of Kings*: "In every place where the word of the king and his decree arrived there was great mourning among the Jews. . . . But each said to the other: 'Let us fortify ourselves for our religion and the Torah of our Lord. . . . We shall not desecrate our covenant nor turn our hearts back, and we shall walk in the name of the Lord our God.' And so without strength three hundred thousand people . . . and I among them, young and old, babes and women, went forth from all the provinces of the king to go wherever the wind took them."

But we know from documentary evidence that it was not so simple. Faced with the choice of baptism or exile, many chose the former. Even among those who left there was subsequent widespread demoralization. In other works Abravanel himself reveals that there were many who felt that "our hope is lost, we are clean cut off," and again—"our bones are dried up, our hope is lost. . . . The Messiah of the God of Jacob is dead, or broken, or captive; his sun, the sun of righteousness and healing will not come. . . ."[6]

Stronger still is the paradoxical tale told by another Spanish exile, Solomon Ibn Verga, as he attempts to describe the horrors encountered by the wanderers:

> In a certain ship the plague broke out and the captain cast them ashore in an uninhabited place. There most of them died of hunger, while a few braced themselves to walk on foot until they should find a settlement.
>
> Now one Jew among them tried to walk together with his wife and two sons, but the wife, who was not accustomed to walking, fainted and died. The man began to carry the children, until he and they also fainted from hunger. When he awoke he found his two sons dead, and in his great distress he got up on his feet and cried out: "Lord of the Universe! Though you are doing much to make me abandon my religion, know for certain that despite the heavenly host I am a Jew and a Jew will I remain, and nothing You have brought or will yet bring upon me will help You!"[7]

To remain a Jew in spite of God may have a sufficiently modern ring to startle us out of some of our neat and familiar categories. "Europe, O Europe, my hell on earth!" does not come from a survivor of 1945, but from a former Portuguese Marrano, Samuel Usque, in 1554. It does not matter that Usque found his "Consolation for the Tribulations of Israel"[8] in a rigid messianism that will not suffice for most of us. I do not seek in any way to minimize the genuine differences between the age of Usque and our own. Yet any attempt at comparative catastrophe is not only distasteful, but beside the point. From where we stand after the Shoah, in terms of numbers, methods, and the motivations of the persecutors, the Iberian catastrophe may seem, objectively, a lesser event. Yet all our texts testify that, *subjectively*, for the generation that experienced within a mere twenty years the expulsion from Spain, Sicily and Sardinia, the total forced conversion in Portugal, the expulsions from Navarre, Provence and the Kingdom of Naples, all links in a terrible chain, the trauma may well have been comparable.

Certainly hope is facilitated by belief in God. Still, to explain hope with a mere shrug of the shoulders by saying "but of course, they believed in God," is merely to postpone the question at one remove and therefore to explain nothing. Is belief in God immutable? *Let din ve-let dayyan*— "There is no law and there is no Judge"—so Elisha ben Abuyya cried out when he saw a child absurdly die while fulfilling a biblical commandment. That cry was recorded in the Talmud because Elisha was a great rabbi who became a great heretic. But can belief in God not be shaken by history as well? Are we really to think that there were not other Jews, anonymous and not famous, who felt the same absurdity in the face of historical calamity, but whose cries, unrecorded, were dissipated in the winds of time? True, the Jews of the past could not conceive of the death of God. But in every age they experienced the silence of God with frightening intensity. With the mere introduction of a single letter into one word in a biblical verse, an ancient midrash[9] inverts the verse from a rapturous praise of the Divine into a terrifying question: *Mi kamokha ba-'elim Adonay*—"Who is like unto Thee among the gods, O Lord!" becomes *Mi kamokha ba-'ILMIM Adonay*—"Who is like unto Thee among the *silent*, O Lord?!" The point of this midrash was not lost. Many centuries later, sometime after the First Crusade, a poem by Isaac bar Shalom begins:

> There is none like Thee among the silent,
> Mute and keeping silent toward those who torment us,
> Our many enemies who have arisen. . . .[10]

In a recently published Hebrew text written shortly after the expulsion from Spain, God speaks, but only as a furious destroyer of the Jewish people. We hear none of the conventional wisdom about sin and punishment, and nothing of consolation. The anonymous author is not merely concerned with the expulsion itself. In his vision God is pursuing even those who escaped, so that not even a vestige will survive. He writes:

> The voice has gone forth from the Lord of Compassion to destroy, to kill, and to annihilate the entire House of Israel. . . .
>
> He desires to destroy us until no remnant is left of us. For this I mourn and wail and roll in the dust, for the evil calamity that has descended from God, to extinguish our last ember, to destroy our last remnant. . . .
>
> Do not rush to console me, for the comforter and restorer of my soul has gone far from me. The Lord has departed from me and become my enemy. . . .[11]

A dead god, or a silent or even hostile god—I leave it to others to ponder which is the more difficult to bear. I merely want to indicate that "belief in God" is an empty phrase unless we know how this god was perceived and experienced.

Whatever else the God of Israel may be in Jewish tradition, He is preeminently the God of History. Precisely because of this, Jewish belief in God, and hence also Jewish hope, were always potentially vulnerable to the assaults of history. Christendom knew this (as did Islam) and used it to good advantage. Historical despair emanated not only from sporadic physical attack, but from a far more constant psychological onslaught. Let us not deceive ourselves into thinking that the anti-Jewish polemic was merely a matter of conflicting biblical exegesis. Beneath the profusion of biblical texts and interpretations by both sides there runs a fateful argument about the nature and evidence of history. *The scepter shall not depart from Judah, nor the ruler's staff from beneath his feet, until Shiloh come.* The crux of the debate was not so much over the enigmatic word "Shiloh," which even most Jewish commentators interpreted as the messiah, but over the departure of the "scepter" from Judah, whether the loss of Jewish sovereignty and the consequent suffering and dispersion of the Jews signified their rejection by God and hence their replacement by a visibly triumphant "New Israel."[12] Like hammer blows this prime argument *adversus Judaeos* repeats itself over and over again: How can you Jews be so blind? Do you not see that once you had kings and prophets, Temple and priestly sacrifices, glory and honor, and now you are perpetually scattered and enslaved among the nations? Once beloved of God, you are now accursed by Him.

Are we to imagine that this argument had no effect? Jewry witnessed world-shaking changes. In succession Rome, Persia and Byzantium, Christendom and Islam, all triumphantly divided the world among themselves while Jewish exile and servitude remained unchanged. Here is Eliezer bar Nathan at the end of the eleventh century:

> Surely You, O Lord, have abandoned us to oblivion
> More than a thousand years in anguish and groaning,
> You have moved our souls from peace to turmoil and screaming,
> And for You are we killed all day like sheep to the slaughter.
>
> Time after time have we waited
> But the course of our end has lengthened and no cure has come.
> In the year "Sing aloud for Jacob" [1096] we awaited redemption,
> We hoped for peace, but no good has come,
> We hoped for the time of healing, and behold—horror. . . .[13]

Or Amitai ben Shefatiah two centuries earlier in Byzantine Southern Italy:

> How, of all nations, have I been lowered to the abyss
> And from the day I was laid waste there is no help nor revival?
> Why are all my neighbors rebuilt from their ruins
> While I, for so many years, weep over two destructions?
>
> Those who know me revile me: "What has happened to you, O poor
>   and wretched ones,
> That once you were regarded as sons, and now like a dirty vessel or
>   like dogs?
> How long will you foolishly await an end to your exile?
> Do you not realize that your hope is vain and frivolous?!"[14]

We shall not pause to dwell on the essential irony that Christianity, which came into the world as the religion of the Crucified One, and was able to survive its birth only because it denied the manifest evidence of history in favor of what it regarded as a deeper reality, did not hesitate afterward to use its own mundane historical triumphs as a weapon against those whom history had defeated. The important thing is that the polemic was not only verbal or occasional. In one way or another the pressure was continuous. There was even an architectural polemic experienced daily in every city in which Jews lived. The *altercatio Ecclesiae contra Synagogam* was not merely an allegory, as in the statues of the two women, one blindfolded and with a broken staff, at Strasbourg and elsewhere; it was a daily visual fact. We no longer sense the psychological reality behind the legislation that a synagogue must not be higher than a church (or a mosque). Most physical vestiges of the Jewish past have been destroyed. But go even today to Toledo, to the so-called "Sinagoga del Transito," undoubtedly one of the largest and most opulent synagogues in medieval Europe; you will surely be impressed. But then look up toward the Cathedral of Toledo, hovering over the city like a huge triumphant eagle, and you will begin not merely to understand intellectually, but to feel viscerally, the full weight of Christian victory.

Am I attributing my own thoughts to the Jews of the past, or perhaps hewing mere stones into metaphors? I can only reply that if I must speculate it is because the subject demands it, but I trust I do not do so arbitrarily. The essential notion of an architectural polemic is more than speculation. The anti-Christian *Nizzaḥon Yashan* contains a dispute, historically fictitious but psychologically revealing, between Rabbi Kalonymous and the Emperor Henry III, on the relative glories of the new cathedral in Speyer and the ancient Temple in Jerusalem.[15] The author of the twelfth-century *Megillat Aḥimaaẓ* found it necessary to insert a similar argument between Rabbi Shefatiah and the Byzantine Emperor Basil I, as to which cost more to build—hence which is the more splendid—Hagia Sophia in Constantinople or the Jerusalem Temple?[16] Of course the answer in both cases is in favor of the Temple. These are, after all, Jewish texts. But the fact remains that the Speyer cathedral and Hagia Sophia stood proudly for all to see, while the Temple, whatever its ancient glories, was no more. It is against such backgrounds that we can perhaps better appreciate the force of the famous poem by Aḥimaaẓ's ancestor Amitai ben Shefatiah, still recited annually in the synagogue toward the end of the Day of Atonement:

> I remember, O Lord, and I moan,
> When I see each city standing upright on its foundation,
> While the City of the Lord is abased to the very bottom of Sheol.
> Yet despite all this we remain loyal to God,
> And our eyes look toward Him. . . .[17]

It is this and all the other "despites" of Jewish history that cannot be taken for granted, and that point us toward the necessity for a history of Jewish hope. At the moment I cannot even sketch such a history in any detail, not only because of limited time, but because I do not yet know it myself. I trust you will not be disappointed if I only offer you some very preliminary observations, a few problems to be addressed, hypotheses to be tested, and even these in a fragmentary way and without ample discussion.

We can rarely, if ever, discover why one individual continued to hope while another succumbed. Moreover, in the Jewish case we face an extreme paucity of autobiographical sources prior to modern times. However, we can seriously investigate those facets of collective tradition and group consciousness that, at any given time, made hope possible for those who were potentially disposed to it.

Though I speak of a history of Jewish hope I do not conceive of hope as a single principle, idea, or article of faith, whose evolution is to be traced. We should rather think of a plurality of hopes, of fluid and shifting configurations of ideas, beliefs, states of mind, emotional affects, with varying elements of continuity and discontinuity, but always rooted concretely in time and place. Thus, neither a disembodied *Ideengeschichte* in the old academic sense, nor a fashionable "psychohistory" with its often irresponsible presumptions and reductions.

As always, what we understand of the past will be largely determined by the questions we address to it. I shall limit myself at present to three such questions that are meant to be exemplary rather than exhaustive.

What is the relation between messianism and hope in Jewish history? Despite the common assumption, I propose that the two are neither synonymous nor coextensive. A history of Jewish hope may well include the history of Jewish messianism as a primary component, but it would also have to include much more. Even in the Bible a multitude of future-oriented hopes precede the emergence of messianism. Conversely, by no means have all subsequent Jewish hopes been eschatological. Yet the fascinations of Jewish messianism have absorbed historians to the total exclusion of other kinds of hope, of what might be called *interim* Jewish hopes for the times before the end of Time.

If certain perennial hopes for an ultimate redemption united world Jewry, there remained significant differences in the way various Jewries perceived their prospects while in exile. Different Jewries had different thresholds of expectation at different times, and these in turn often conditioned their reactions to pressures and events. The proud and even inflated hope of the Hispano-Jewish elites for permanence and glory in medieval Spain[18] were for them a guiding myth that was not paralleled among Ashkenazic Jews in Northern France and Germany. These differences were not due to their innate temperaments. They were the result of different historical experiences, and are therefore susceptible to historical analysis.

Is it only the hope of a global and final restoration that is worthy of a history of hope, and not, let us say, the efforts to restore a devastated community by its survivors? We will scour the records for information about communal organization and social conflict, taxation and governmental relations, charity and education, all worthy subjects to be sure, all history as usual. But we do not sift the same sources for the revealing acts, phrases, even a certain tonality, that might help us understand the spirit in which a community rebuilds its ruins. Was it habit? Lack of alternative? Hope that such a calamity will not recur, and if so—on what was this hope based? We do not know, because we have not asked.

We have a strong interest in the history of Jewish migrations, but none in the geography of hope. Are migrations to be understood solely in terms of oppression or poverty at home and economic opportunity elsewhere? Beyond the political and material realities there are also mythologies that become active historical forces, in which certain places loom at different times as lands of hope. It is hard to recall today that Poland was once such a land of hope, and, after the Union of Lublin, Lithuania. Reread Ibn Daud's account of the transplantation of Jewish life from Muslim to Christian Spain in the twelfth century,[19] or Isaac Zarfati's impassioned call to the Ashkenazic Jews in the fifteenth century to settle in the Ottoman Empire.[20] The myth of the Golden Land and of the New Beginning was born long before Jews came en masse to America.

I shall not dwell on the complex problematics of Jewish messianism itself. Much has been achieved, many desiderata remain. We still know all too little about the social history of Jewish messianism. We have made no use of the phenomenological insights obtained by anthropologists and social psychologists in a vast and growing corpus of millenarian research. There have been few comparative studies. Gershom Scholem was able to provide a magisterial reconstruction of the origins of the messianic eruption around Sabbatai Zevi in terms of an imminent dialectical process that leads from the Spanish expulsion, through Lurianic Kabbalah and its subsequent diffusion.[21] But we have yet to explain why not only Jewish Sabbatians, but radical English Puritans and Portuguese Sebastianists were all expecting their different versions of the messianic advent in 1666. And so we say "it was in the air," an indolent approach that turns history into meteorology, and historians into weather forecasters.

But let us retain our central focus. Are all the many forms of Jewish messianism to be regarded, almost by definition, as manifestations of hope? Certainly they are all related to hope, but perhaps we should begin to make distinctions. There was a core of messianic belief, rooted in classical prophecy, which became part of the common heritage of the entire Jewish people. It was a hope for redemption that was willing to wait, seemingly to infinity, without attempting to storm the gates of heaven, or, in the striking phrase based on the Song of Songs, not "to awaken love" prematurely. By contrast, in every age there were those, few or many, who could not or would not wait, who feverishly computed an imminent End out of obscure hints in the Book of Daniel, or who launched active, sometimes violent, messianic movements. We tend today to sympathize more with the impatient than with the patient. We regard them as precursors of modern Jewish revolt and feel that history has vindicated them. Their charisma and daring attract us. We understand them more readily.

Yet I wonder if such judgments are not distortions, and whether such a reading of history is not anachronistic. We should find it possible to consider dispassionately whether often, behind the flaring up of an intense but evanescent hope, much of apocalyptic thinking and messianic activism was not itself an expression of the most profound despair. Freud, at least, has sensitized us to such inversions. Perhaps it is those who were willing to wait, those we stigmatize as "passive," that we must now try to fathom. The pendulum of scholarship often swings to wide extremes. In nineteenth-century Jewish historiography the messiahs and their prophets appear as villains and their opponents as heroes. By now, in compensation, the roles have virtually been reversed. Paradoxically, we now understand Abraham Abulafia better than Solomon ben Adret; David Reubeni more than Ishmael da Rieti; Sabbatai Zevi, Nathan of Gaza, and their successors, more than Jacob Sasportas or Moses Hagiz. It is not only a question of granting the opponents of messianic activism the imaginative historical empathy that had enabled us to understand those they opposed. What is at stake is nothing less than the larger enigma: How Jews were able to endure the tension of waiting, despite the passage of a time ever longer than had been originally anticipated, despite all the taunts that they waited in vain, while yet clinging firmly to their messianic hope.

I shall pose the two large remaining questions with a brevity they do not deserve.

What was the relation, among Jews, between memory and hope, or, if you will, between their sense of the past and hope for the future? The Jewish people, even so-called ordinary Jews, had access to a vast and unique reservoir of the past. Its channels were certainly not through historical works, nor merely through Bible and Talmud. I have discussed these matters in some detail in *Zakhor* and will not repeat myself here. For the moment it will suffice to point out that the tale of the field in Anathoth, with which we began, was not internalized through biblical study alone. Chapter 32 of Jeremiah is also the *haphtarah*, the fixed supplement to the public Torah reading in the synagogue that comprises Leviticus 25. It is this aspect that is crucial and paradigmatic. A Jew heard this text read aloud annually, at the same time, every year of his life. In similar ways he was heir to an entire constellation of shared memories and beliefs in which past pointed to both present and future because, in some measure, it seemed to anticipate them. Egyptian servitude and exodus, Nebuchadnezzar and Cyrus, Haman and Mordecai, prophecies of doom and of restoration—these are obvious. But also the eternality of the Covenant and of the Law, the promise of the "saving remnant" and hence the eternality of the Jewish people itself. All these and other beliefs vital to the sustenance of Jewish hopes remain abstractions without historical reality so long as we continue to treat them as concepts or dogmas and do not explore how they were internalized in the hearts and minds of Jews, and concretized in daily life. For that historians should have turned long ago to the richest sources of all—liturgy and ritual, those most sensitive mirrors of Jewish consciousness in any time or place. But we have surrendered the one to philologists and literary scholars, and the other to folklorists and scholars of *halakhah*. I dare say that we may yet learn as much about the dynamics of Jewish hope from the prayers recited thrice daily by all Jews, those added by different generations or different communities, the ritual practices that were standard and those deriving from local custom, as we will from reading explicit messianic tracts.

Finally, the relation between history and hope, by which I mean the impact of ongoing historical events, and the ability to endure and overcome them, to see beyond them. Biblical religion endowed the Jews with a view of history that is hard to define. It is neither myth in the pagan sense, for that was abandoned, nor history in the Greek sense, for that remained alien, nor history in our sense, for that was never achieved. I cannot find an adequate term for it, and so, faute de mieux, I shall call it a midrash of history. It is as though history became a text, capable of interpretation through a hermeneutic that flowed naturally and unselfconsciously out of the fundamental premises of Israelite faith. History was imbued with supreme meaning, but that meaning was most often to be sought beneath its manifest surfaces. While Judaism never affirmed an Augustinian dichotomy, so long as the visible text of history was in conflict with its invisible sub-text (and, except for a few intervals of ancient glory this was always the case), Judaism regarded the latter as decisive. From such a perspective the triumphs of empires could be viewed as transient episodes, mundane victories a sign of error rather than truth, the degradation of Jewry a badge of honor, its suffering a mark of its chosenness. Only at one juncture is visible history decisive—the coming of the Messiah and the manifest redemption of Israel and the world, for then the gap between visible and invisible will exist no more. Until that final resolution of history, no event, no catastrophe, can be final, and all that manifest history can prove is that the true messiah has not yet come. This midrash of history was always potentially available as a bulwark against the terror of history. But even if I have understood it correctly, it remains a generalization that cannot satisfy the historian within us. The task remains to see how this midrash functioned in specific historical contexts, and why, powerful as it was, it sometimes did not suffice.

I close with a feeling of malaise. "Jewish hope" is a theme which, as Ortega once said of Cervantes's *Don Quixote*, cannot be taken by direct assault; it must be taken like Jericho. I have tried to circle this theme from several directions, well aware that I have hardly breached the walls. Though I have concentrated deliberately on pre-modern times, such an inquiry, if it is ever pursued, must surely extend into the modern era as well. We will never appreciate the particular passion of the beginnings of modern Jewish assimilation and the struggle for emancipation without examining them as further metamorphoses of Jewish hope, or even, as Yehezkel Kaufmann suggested, as an inverted Jewish messianism.[22] Diametric opposites on so many levels, both nineteenth-century assimilation and Zionism intensely craved an end to Jewish exile, the latter by an actual return to Zion, the former by transforming the lands of exile into Zion. "Germany is our Zion, and Düsseldorf our Jerusalem"; and in South Carolina—"America is our Zion, and Charleston our Jerusalem." Gershom Scholem correctly stressed that Zionism was a revolt against Jewish messianism, but it is doubtful whether Zionism could have succeeded in becoming a mass movement had it not absorbed traditional messianic energies and employed a blatantly messianic rhetoric. The current crisis of the Jewish State is in no small part the result of an inevitable confusion of different kinds of hope that remains to be unravelled.

Is such a history possible, are any of the lines I have tentatively traced viable? I can only bring you back to Lucien Febvre's seminal essay of 1941, "La sensibilité et l'histoire," in which he wrote: "Nous pourrons, je crois, entreprendre une série de travaux qui, tous, nous font défaut; et tant qu'ils nous feront défaut, *il n'y aura pas d'histoire possible*. Nous n'avons pas d'histoire de l'Amour. . . . Nous n'avons pas d'histoire de la Mort. Nous n'avons pas d'histoire de la Pitié, ni non plus de la Cruauté. Nous n'avons pas d'histoire de la Joie. . . ."[23]

Had Febvre been an historian of the Jews he might well have added "nous n'avons pas d'histoire de l'espoir," and perhaps something might have been accomplished. I do not propose an exact parallel. But Jewish historiography has not yet had its Febvre, whether to achieve what he achieved, or to stimulate some and irritate others. And I, alas, am not he.

Why a history of Jewish hope? For purely historical reasons, some of which I have tried to indicate, and for some personal ones I somewhat hesitantly share with you.

I find myself among those who fear that, since the Shoah, large sectors of the Jewish people are ordering their collective lives, and even determining present and future policy, largely out of an obsession with the era of destruction and death. The fact that I understand this development leaves me no less troubled. It is as though we have forgotten the admonition of Joshua ben Hananiah after the Temple was destroyed: "Not to mourn at all is impossible. . . . But to mourn too much is also impossible. . . ."

I am under no illusion whatever that a history of hope will give us any solutions to our own problems. The specific modalities available to our forebears are simply no longer possible for many of us. In fact, I anticipate that, like all good history, this one may well increase our sense of distance from them in many ways. But distance is not emptiness, and a distant past is still a past. Why a history of hope? To assuage our loneliness. To realize that we are not the first to whom despair was not alien, hope a gratuitous gift, and that by the same token we are not necessarily the last. And that, perhaps, may be a small and modest step toward hope itself.

NOTES

1. Y. H. Yerushalmi, *Zakhor: Jewish History and Jewish Memory* (Seattle and London, 1982). German: *Zachor: Erinnere Dich! Jüdische Geschichte und jüdisches Gedächtnis* (Berlin, Wagenbach, 1988).

2. Morton Smith, *Hope and History: An Exploration* (New York, Harper & Row, 1980), pp. 33 f.

3. Ernst Bloch, *Das Prinzip Hoffnung*, 2 vols. (Frankfurt a. M., Suhrkamp, 1959).

4. See, for example, David G. Roskies, *Against the Apocalypse: Responses to Catastrophe in Modern Jewish Culture* (Cambridge, Mass., Harvard University Press, 1984); Alan Mintz, *Hurban: Responses to Catastrophe in Hebrew Literature* (New York, Columbia University Press, 1984).

5. II Baruch, 10:6–7, 9–10, 13–16, 11:6–7.

6. Abravanel, introduction to *Yeshu'ot Meshiho*. See all his introduction to *Ma'ayeney ha-yeshu'ah*. [Editors' note: The Hebrew original is indeed "shemesh" for sun and not "ben" for son.]

7. Solomon (Shelomoh) Ibn Verga, *Sefer Shevet Yehudah*, ed. A. Shochat (Jerusalem, Mosad Bialik, 1947), ch. 52, p. 122.

8. Samuel Usque, *Consolaçam as tribulaçoens de Israel*, ed. J. Mendes dos Remédios (Coimbra, Francisco França Amado, 1906), vol. I, p. lv.

9. *Mekhilta, Beshalah, Massekhta de-Shirata*, ch. 8.

10. A. M Habermann (ed.), *Sefer gezerot Ashkenaz ve-Zarfat* (Jerusalem, Tarshish, 1946), p. 113.

11. Joseph Hacker, "Khronikot hadashot 'al gerush ha-Yehudim mi-Sefarad, sibbotav ve-toza'otav" [New Chronicles on the Expulsion of the Jews from Spain, its Causes and its Consequences], *Sefer Zikkaron le-Yitzhak Baer* (= *Zion*, vol. 44 [1979]), 223–227.

12. For the Jewish and Christian interpretations of Genesis 49:10, see the texts assembled by Adolf Posnanski, *Schiloh: Ein Beitrag zur Geschichte der Messiaslehre* (Leipzig, J. C. Hinrick, 1904).

13. Habermann, op. cit., p. 82.

14. Benjamin Klar (ed.), *Megillat Ahima'az*, 2nd edition (Jerusalem, Tarshish, 1973); appendixes, p. 99.

15. David Berger, *The Jewish Christian Debate in the High Middle Ages: A Critical Edition of the 'Nizzahon Vetus'* (Philadelphia, Jewish Publication Society, 1979), pp. 23 f. of the Hebrew text, p. 68 of the English translation.

16. *Megillat Ahima'az*, ed. cit., p. 18.

17. Idem, appendixes, p. 95.

18. See Y. H. Yerushalmi, *The Lisbon Massacre of 1506 and the Royal Image in the 'Shebet Yehudah'* (Cincinnati, Hebrew Union College, 1976), pp. 35–66.

19. Abraham Ibn Daud, *Sefer ha-qabbalah: The Book of Tradition*, ed. Gerson D. Cohen (Philadelphia, Jewish Publication Society), 1967, Hebrew text pp. 70–72.

20. See the Hebrew text of Zarfati in Heinrich Graetz, *Dibrey yemey Yisrael*, tr. S. P. Rabbinowitz, vol. VI (Warsaw, 1902), pp. 241 f.

21. Gershom Scholem, *Sabbatai Zevi: The Mystical Messiah*, tr. R.J.Z. Werblowsky (Princeton, Princeton University Press, 1973), ch. I.

22. Yehezkel Kaufmann, *Golah ve-nekhar* (Tel-Aviv, Devir), vol. II, pp.

23. "We could, I believe, undertake a series of works, all of which we ar
ing; and as long as we are lacking them, *no history will be possible.* We hav
history of Love. . . . We have no history of Death. We have no history of Pity, n
of Cruelty. We have no history of Joy. . . ." Lucien Febvre, "La sensibilité et l'histoire," *Annales d'histoire sociale*, III (1941), p. 18; reprinted in *Combats pour l'histoire*, Paris, Armand Colin, 1953, p. 236 (editors' translation).

commenced an important new phase in his career
...ance of *Freud's Moses: Judaism Terminable and Interminable.*
.., Yerushalmi used a surprising text—Jakob Freud's seventeen-line He-
.·w inscription to his son Sigmund on a German-Hebrew Bible that Jakob gave
Sigmund—to reconsider the long-standing assumption that Freud was ignorant
of, indifferent to, or at odds with his Jewish identity. Yerushalmi's book entailed
a strong rereading of Freud's 1939 book, *Moses and Monotheism*, and concluded
with a daring "Monologue with Freud." Though brief (in the mode of *Zakhor*),
Freud's Moses rested on decades of engagement with psychoanalysis (as analysand and student) and years of detailed research into Freud's thought.

One of Yerushalmi's most intriguing interlocutors on the subject of *Freud's
Moses* was the French literary critic and philosopher Jacques Derrida. In 1995, Derrida published a book—*Mal d'archive: une impression freudienne*—that, while not
overtly advertised as such, was a deep and typically idiosyncratic (i.e., Derridean)
engagement with Yerushalmi's work on Freud. Derrida, like Yerushalmi, was interested in the process of the transmission of memory, as well as "the gesture of the
father" in re-inscribing Sigmund Freud into the covenant of Israel. He also focused
there on the instinct to seek out the archive, describing it as "a compulsive, repeti-
tive, and nostalgic desire for the archive, an irrepressible desire to return to the
most archaic place of absolute commencement."

Intriguingly, Derrida laid out the gist of his thinking about Yerushalmi at a conference in London in 1994 where Yerushalmi was scheduled to read the following
paper (before he fell ill and had the paper read by someone else). To be sure, Yerushalmi phrased his interest in the archive differently. And yet, he shared with Derrida a recognition of the almost fetishistic reverence for the archive by researchers.
"Series Z: An Archival Fantasy" takes as its starting point the once-sealed section
of Freud's papers (Series Z) in the Library of Congress to probe the limits of what
can be derived from archives. The paper begins with a modified version of Kafka's
great fragmentary short story "Before the Law," which, in Yerushalmi's rendering,
opens: "Before the Archives stands a doorkeeper." The doorkeepers—Freud, the
immediately succeeding custodians of his papers, Anna Freud and Kurt Eissler,
and the current guardians—seem to believe that the fate of the master's legacy,
and that of psychoanalysis at large, rests on retaining control over access to the
archive. Yerushalmi, with all his knowledge of and reverence for Freud, took issue

with this view. In contrast to those who wanted the archive to affirm the truth of Freud's teaching, Yerushalmi argued that the archive ideally "should be naive," without a desire to please this or that group of scholars. It should not be the exclusive preserve of those who participated in the events described in its documents. Nor should those who visit it assume that it contains a complete record of events. Indeed, Yerushalmi forewarned devotees of the archive against the belief that "the Past" is "something 'out there,' waiting to be recovered." In fact, he added, "[t]he archive is not a repository of the past, only of certain artifacts that have survived from the past." In offering these admonitions, Yerushalmi was challenging those who engaged in "archival fantasy"—akin to that malady that Derrida diagnosed as "archive fever."

Again, there is in this lecture something of the temperament and strain of thought of *Zakhor* from 1982. Similar to the earlier distinction he drew between history and memory, Yerushalmi drew a clear line between the archive and memory, and thereby offered an unmistakable answer to the very theme (and title) of the 1994 conference, "Memory: The Question of Archives," that brought him and Derrida to London. Just as one should not expect history to sustain and nurture memory, neither should one harbor expectations of the archive as anything more than a neutral repository. With respect to Freud's followers, he wrote, "the seduction of the archives is distracting many from the real questions" of how to understand the Master as he understood himself—and of which aspects of his legacy should be preserved. Yerushalmi's skepticism about the power of the archive to generate meaning parallels some of the skepticism (and pessimism) to which he gave voice in *Zakhor*. His essay concludes with a nod to Nietzsche and, as in *Zakhor*, Borges, when he acknowledges his anxiety that the increased amount of information available to us in our time leads neither to increased knowledge nor to wisdom.

Before the Archives stands a doorkeeper. To this doorkeeper there come men and women from many countries who beg for admittance to Series Z. But the doorkeeper says that he cannot admit them at the moment. They, on reflection, ask if they will be allowed, then, to enter later. "It is possible," answers the doorkeeper, "but not at this moment." Since the door to the Archives stands open as usual and the doorkeeper steps to one side, the people bend down to peer through the entrance. When the doorkeeper sees that he laughs and says: "If you are so strongly tempted, try to get in without my permission. But note that I am powerful and I am only the lowest doorkeeper." These are difficulties that the men and women from many countries have not expected to meet. Series Z, they think, should be accessible to everyone. But they decide that they had better wait. They sit down at the side of the door. There they sit waiting for days and years. They make many attempts to be allowed in and weary the doorkeeper with their importunity. They can perceive a radiance that streams from the door to Series Z. Finally the doorkeeper bellows in their ears: "This door was intended for all of you. I am now going to open it."

But I am already running ahead of myself with this admittedly outrageous appropriation of Kafka's parable, for which I offer him and you my profound apologies and to which, stubbornly, I shall yet return.

So far as I am aware, the only place in Freud's published works where the word "archive" appears is in the early paper (1898) on "The Psychical Mechanism of Forgetfulness" ("Zum Psychischen Mechanismus der Vergesslichkeit"). He writes: "Thus the function of memory, which we like to imagine as an archive open to any who is curious ('wie ein allen Wissbegierigen geöffnetes Archiv vorstellen'), is in this way subjected to restriction by a trend of the will. . . ." Subsequently Freud appears to have completely abandoned this particular metaphor and, I think, rightly so. Indeed, the very title of this conference—"Memory: The Question of Archives"—has made me uneasy (the original French "La Mémoire des Archives" was even more alarming), and I propose immediately to separate its two components. Archives and memory have nothing in common. Memory is not an archive, nor is an archive a memory bank. The documents in an archive are not part of memory; if they were, we should have no need to retrieve them; once retrieved, they are often at odds with memory. I shall therefore promptly banish memory from my discussion and focus on archives.

Here my malaise is of a different order. I do not want to appear before you under false pretenses. To be sure, I have spent a good deal of time in archives—in Lisbon, Madrid, Valladolid, Salamanca, Venice, Verona, Jerusalem. But though I also often move in psychoanalytic circles in New York and to a degree in Paris, my actual use of the Freud Archives has been limited. Which is to say that I come to you as something of an outsider, neither an analyst nor a historian of psychoanalysis (one book and two articles on Freud's Moses were written out of other concerns), but simply as a historian *tout court* who, as such, may know something about the nature of archives, and who also happens to have a considerable interest in both Freud and psychoanalysis.

I

"Series Z," as I need hardly tell you (the very letter sounds ominously terminal), is the section of the Sigmund Freud Collection in Washington "totally closed to researchers for varying lengths of time." Series A, E and F, have other kinds of restrictions. Series B, more happily described as "open without restriction," has the proviso that this is so "except for unpublished writings by Sigmund Freud and Anna Freud" for which permission even to photocopy, let alone publish, must first be obtained from Sigmund Freud Copyrights. What is not generally known, but which I discovered to my astonished dismay as I was forced to eliminate a short appendix when my book was already in page-proof, is that to publish even part of a Freud manuscript in German from the accessible Series B, one must also have the additional benediction of S. Fischer Verlag in Frankfurt. But I shall not weary you with my ultimately minor personal tribulations, nor shall I dwell on the fact that with regard to the Archives all scholars are equal but some are more equal than others (that is so in many other archives), nor do I intend to discuss Series A, B, E and F. The proper focus of our attention shall remain—Series Z.

Here, in all fairness, let me state immediately that the Freud Archives are hardly the only ones to impose restrictions. On the contrary, these are quite common, especially when it comes to the private papers of modern individuals deposited in public institutions. Since we are gathered in London, let me remind you that in 1909 Robert Ross, in order to prevent the manuscript of Oscar Wilde's *De Profundis* from falling into the hands of Lord Alfred Douglas, the agent of Wilde's ruin, presented it to the British Museum on condition that it be sealed for sixty years. Ross did keep a carbon copy for himself. In 1913, in a libel suit initiated by Douglas, the original manuscript was brought temporarily under subpoena from the Museum to the court, large excerpts were read aloud and its contents widely reported in the press. Douglas lost the case, but, having received a second copy for the purposes of the trial, he now announced his intention to publish it himself. To prevent that, Ross rushed his carbon to New York and had it speedily published in an edition of sixteen copies which, though full of errors and omissions, secured copyright. Ross died in 1918 and the carbon passed to Vyvyan Holland, Wilde's son. Douglas died in 1945. In 1949 Holland published the full and correct text of *De Profundis* from Gray's carbon. In his introduction he wrote: "The manuscript itself still reposes in the British Museum: the authorities there have always refused to allow anyone access to it, in spite of the fact that its contents are no longer secret, and therefore the reason for which it was sealed up no longer exists."

What is bizarre about the Freud Collection is not the fact of restriction but the manner in which the policy is implemented. Anyone, mind you, can request and receive from the Library of Congress a copy of the type-written catalogue of the collection, which laconically lists virtually every-thing in it, even in Series Z, with names of correspondents and interview-ees, but of course without revealing its actual contents. I have the 1985 version and the revised one completed in October 1993. This catalogue is itself Kafkaesque; I know of no other like it. All items in Series Z are listed under the year in which they are to be declassified, starting in 1995. Fair enough. But as one reads and re-reads these lists one begins to have the eerie feeling that not only the professed concern for living persons and patient privacy is at stake, but some insane logic all its own. Why should a photocopy of the manuscript of *Träume im Folklore*, written in 1911 in collaboration with D. E. Oppenheim and published in 1958, be in Series Z until the year 2000? Is it merely because it includes "unidentified poetry and writings by someone other than Freud"? But then what of Freud's corrected typescript and Introduction to his and W. C. Bullit's unfortu-nate book on Woodrow Wilson, published in 1967, which is placed under the same restriction? Again, why totally restrict a file on Josef Freud, Sigmund's uncle, containing "photocopies and documents regarding conviction for counterfeiting rubles, 1865–66," when Freud himself al-luded to it in *The Interpretation of Dreams*, and the documented details were published by Renée Gicklhorn in 1976 and Marianne Krüll in 1979?

But let me give some choice examples closer to my own interests. Under correspondence slated for liberation in 2008 we find "Einstein, Albert, 1931." What could he and/or Freud have been writing about? Well, who knows? But surely there could have been no scarlet passages in the item in the same 2008 column that states: "Reading Room of Jewish Stu-dents of Vienna, 1911"! In 1940 Israel Doryon published a book in Hebrew about Freud's greatly admired Josef Popper-Linkeus and prefaced it with a letter he had solicited in 1938 from Freud. Judah Magnes was the first president of the Hebrew University, of whose board Freud was a member. Why are Doryon and Magnes listed under "Year 2010"? The absurdities go on. To find under "Year 2013" a correspondence with "Maccabi World Union [Editors' note: the international Jewish sports organization], 1939," leaves one breathless, and one can hardly wait for 2013 to examine "Con-tract with Toeplitz & Deuticke [Editors' note: Freud's publishers], 1885,

1887." In the 1985 catalogue the final date for opening sealed material was 2102; in 1993 it is 2113. But enough. There are larger issues to explore.

II

What was once an intramural grumbling among scholars about the Freud Archives has by now become a loud clamor eagerly reported in the press. No doubt this agitated sensationalism is overdetermined, but two reasons immediately suggest themselves: Through her "In the Freud Archives" (1984) Janet Malcolm cleverly made the issue a cause célèbre. Meanwhile, attacks against psychoanalysis, fused with assaults against the personal integrity of Freud himself, have by now reached an unprecedented crescendo of vilification. One result is a widespread belief that the "real truth," for better or worse, is in the Archives, and that once they are fully accessible the truth will out. What both attackers and defenders of Freud have in common is a faith in the facticity of archives, in the archival document as somehow the ultimate arbiter of historical truth.

Now, this cult of the archive can be traced back to the nineteenth century when, in the 1830's and especially after 1860, governments seemed almost to compete in their eagerness to open their archives to research. Lord Acton put the reason succinctly: To keep one's archives barred against the historians was tantamount to "leaving one's history to one's enemies."

The historians came, the writing of history (at least political history) was put on a firmer basis than ever before. It was the heyday of "scientific" history, full of optimism. The "crisis of historicism" was not yet on the horizon and the archival document seemed to herald a historiographical millennium. Paleography became a science and the archivist a professional, nowhere more superbly trained than at the École des Chartes, established in Paris in 1821. By the end of the century one spoke somewhat bemusedly in France of "la fureur de l'inédit," the furor to publish the unpublished document.

Please do not misunderstand me. No contemporary historian, myself included, can be against archival research per se. It is simply that we have today a more modest and sophisticated notion of what archives and their documents really represent, their possibilities and their limitations.

So by all means let the Freud Collection be opened wide. Indeed, let me continue the parable with which I began. The doorkeeper, representing the Board of Directors of the Archives, has declassified everything. The very rubric—Series Z—has been abolished. Freud Copyrights cooperates. The men and women from many countries have packed the Reading Room of the Library of Congress to capacity; researchers on all other subjects are banished to the basement. New photocopying machines are constantly acquired to replace those so rapidly burnt out. Already after the first months conferences are being organized from New York to Tokyo, dissertations are being written, papers published, new books appear, all based on what was once Series Z. A veritable "fureur de l'inédit." The real question remains—what, fundamentally, will have changed as a result? And my provisional answer is—very little of genuine consequence. To explain why, let me first come back to the question of archives in general and then to the Freud Archives in particular.

III
I shall limit myself to four basic observations:

1. Ideally an archive should be naive, that is—it should have been created and maintained for purposes other than those which we, as historians, seek. Copies of contracts and deeds of property were preserved in archives in case any future disputes should arise, not so that we might write economic history. Tax records were kept to collect taxes, not for historical demography. The dossiers of the trials of Domenico Scandella by the Inquisition in Italy were saved in the archiepiscopal archives of Udine for the secret information of other Inquisitors on heresy and heretics, not in order to enable Carlo Ginzburg to reconstruct the mental world of a sixteenth-century Friulian miller, and the popular culture of his time, in his remarkable book *The Cheese and the Worms*.

2. Dust on the documents. Ideally the documents in the archives should have been handled by as few people as possible, and certainly not by anyone personally involved. I take this metaphor from the following incident. In 1851, the Prussian historian Heinrich Von Sybel received special permission from Napoleon III to examine the papers of the notorious Committee for Public Safety (*Comité de Salut Publique*) which functioned during the Terror following the French Revolution. They were covered with dust. The keeper said to him: "Sir, you must have some respect for this dust—it is dust from the year 1795. I can assure you . . . that since that time no hand has disturbed these papers. . . ."

3. No archive is ever complete, that is—no archive can yield

sufficient material to understand the subjects or answer the questions that its own documents present. This is so not only because so many pertinent documents never reached the archive to begin with and are forever lost to us, or because for those that have been preserved there are related documents in other archives that may be equally or more important, but because in order to be understood any archival document must be contextualized by information outside and beyond the archive, even beyond the field itself.

4. Perhaps most important—though most difficult to convey in brief compass—"the Past," by definition, no longer exists. It is not somewhere "out there" waiting to be recovered. The archive is not a repository of the past, only of certain artifacts that have survived from the past, and we encounter them in the present. The contents of archival documents are not "historical facts" except on the most primitive level—dates, names, places. The truly vital data in these documents do not become "historical" until, filtered through the mind and the imagination of the historian, they are interpreted and articulated.

IV

These remarks, incomplete as they are, should suffice to indicate some of the problematics of the Freud Archives.

The Freud Archives are, by their very nature, the very opposite of "naive." They were created by Anna Freud, Freud's devoted daughter, and Dr. Kurt Eissler, surely the most zealous guardian of his reputation, for the obviously express purpose of preserving Freud's legacy and memory for future generations. I have not a word of criticism against either of them; both acted according to the natural dictates of their feelings. But I simply cannot imagine that either of them would leave anything fundamentally compromising to Freud in the Archives. It is the difference, if you wish, between the diaries of Franz Kafka, who never dreamed that they would be published, and André Gide's journals, where one senses that as he writes one eye is gazing at posterity.

There is not enough "dust" in the Freud Archives. Freud himself radically sifted his papers several times. For years Anna had what was brought to England all to herself at Maresfield Gardens. Until his resignation from his long rule over the Archives (whose holdings, it should not be forgotten, were greatly expanded through his energetic initiatives),

Eissler had unlimited access to all its materials, and I have reason to suspect he was not the only one to handle them.

From both points of view the Archives may be regarded as tainted. To understand why they should at least initially be suspect, we have only to consider the protective mentality of those close to Freud as revealed in the way they edited some of his unpublished letters. Compare, for example, the first edition of the letters to Wilhelm Fliess, edited by Marie Bonaparte, Anna Freud and Ernst Kris, and published in 1950, with the complete edition of 1985 edited by Jeffrey Moussaieff Masson that restored the omitted passages and added over one hundred letters originally withheld. In her important book *Zurück zu Freuds Texten* Ilse Grubrich-Simitis, than whom I know of no finer textual scholar of Freud, observes correctly that other collections of Freud letters, published by people without sufficient distance from their subject, excised passages that dealt with private persons, not infrequently patients and their families.

These, however, were by no means the only criteria for omission. I should like to give you two examples from the Freud–Arnold Zweig correspondence edited by Ernst Freud and published in German in 1968. Again, I intend no criticism of Freud's son, but merely offer this as an instance of that protective mentality to which I have alluded. In each of two published letters of Freud to Zweig (December 16, 1934, and June 17, 1936), a line is missing, as revealed by the manuscripts in the Arnold Zweig archive at the Akademie der Kunste in Berlin. In the first, Freud concludes with these words: "Finden Sie nicht auch manchmal, dass dieser Jesus-Joschua ein ziemlich überflüssiger Glaubensgenosse war?" (Don't you also sometimes find that this Jesus-Joshua was a rather superfluous coreligionist?) In the second, in which Freud describes glowingly how Thomas Mann came specially to his home to read his lecture "Freud und die Zukunft" which he had already delivered in other places, he writes: "Ein edler Goi! Schön, dass es auch das gibt. Man könnte manchmal zweifeln" (A noble Goy! Nice that this also occurs. One can sometimes doubt it).

When Frau Grubrich-Simitis assures us that no previously unknown masterpiece of Freud will be found in the archive, nor evidence that any canonical work of his has been falsified (such as occurred with Nietzsche's *Will to Power*), she is undoubtedly right. "Anna Freud and Ernst Freud were cut from different cloth," as she puts it, "than Elisabeth Forster-Nietzsche and Peter Gast." Of course. But she is referring primarily to Freud's works, not to the documentary contents (or lack of them) in the

Freud Archives, while between Freud's loyal children and Nietzsche's malevolently power-hungry sister and her servile accomplice there is still a considerable spectrum of possibilities for well-intentioned intervention.

The most significant and irremediable gap in the Freud Archives is the result of Freud's own doing. "On two occasions [in 1885 and 1907]," Ernest Jones observed, "he completely destroyed all his correspondence, notes, diaries and manuscripts." The letter of April 28, 1885, to Martha, announcing his determination to thereby frustrate his future biographers, is too well-known to be quoted yet again. Other lacunae in the documentation are, as I have hinted, intrinsic to the nature of archives. We have already heard from Riccardo Steiner on how much there is in the archives of the British Psychoanalytic Society. There are other arcadias on three continents, some, like the Jung Archives, inaccessible, others not yet known or barely touched. The letters from Fliess to Freud incorporated in the 1985 edition are there only because Peter Swales, that indispensible enfant terrible of psychoanalytic historiography, tracked Fliess' daughter Pauline to an old age home in Israel and learned that she had donated all of her father's papers to the National Library in Jerusalem.

My remarks thus far are meant to point to some of the potential pitfalls of a misperception and overestimation of what Series Z may hold for us. Perhaps you find me too suspicious, overcautious. Let us, then, momentarily cast these cautions to the winds. After all, in our ongoing parable Series Z has already been thrown wide open, a stream of articles and books have been published. What now?

V

Inevitably, a huge amount of previously unknown information has thereby become available. The real question is—what is the epistemological value of this new information? The answers very much depend on what it is we want to know.

Nothing in the Freud Collection nor in any other archive can possibly decide any of the major scientific or philosophical issues that have arisen in the ongoing controversies over Freud. No document can prove or disprove the validity of Freudian psychoanalytic theory nor the efficacy of psychoanalytic therapy. Infantile sexuality, the existence of the unconscious, the mechanisms of repression, and other central tenets of Freudian theory, are not subject to archival arbitration. Thus let us imagine that our men and women from many countries have published letters from former patients of Freud, some blessing him for saving their lives and others cursing him for ruining them. Some of these letters are in themselves very interesting, even poignant, but they have changed nothing. Let us imagine that a Brazilian scholar has published an amazing letter from the Vienna Medical Society threatening Freud with ostracism for abandoning the seduction theory. Will Jeffrey Masson, in light of this, retract a word of what he has written concerning Freud's motives? I doubt it.

What do we really want to know, and how can the Archives be of help? My own order of priority would be: To understand Freud's teaching; to understand the history of the psychoanalytic movement; to understand Freud's life insofar as it relates to the first two goals.

The teaching above all, and for that we would all profit from a critical edition of the German text of Freud's writings, taking account of manuscript drafts, notes, correspondence, along the lines that Frau Grubrich-Simitis has so carefully mapped out in her aforementioned book. Note, however, that the manuscripts of Freud's works were not placed in Series Z to begin with. But what does understanding Freud's teaching mean? For me, as a historian, it entails coming as close as possible to his own intentions. This, as I have argued elsewhere must take pride of place. At least in his published works Freud was consciously trying to communicate various ideas to his readers. That these works, like all texts, also contain latent meanings of which he was unaware, that they can be approached with a variety of hermeneutic strategies, does not absolve us from rigorously seeking their conscious intentionality which, alone, can keep us from flying off the deep end. For that, not only is the value of a correct text self-evident, but any information relevant to its evolution, whether through variants or revisions, or through letters in which Freud discusses work in progress. It is in this sense that the letters in Series Z may make their most important contribution. But even then the archives are only an aid. Ultimately the student must bring to an understanding of Freud's work his or her philological, literary, and historical instincts, and an entire culture derived from other fields. Philip Rieff's *Freud: The Mind of the Moralist* (1959) remains, in my opinion, one of the most penetrating explorations of Freud's thought. And Rieff never even consulted an archive.

The history of the psychoanalytic movement (I have in mind only Freudian psychoanalysis). Here, surely, our men and women from many countries will have reaped abundant harvests. But how much wheat and how much chaff? Any history of the psychoanalytic movement cannot ignore the archives, but it must also transcend them. Once again all de-pends on how we conceptualize the problem. If we have in mind a histori-cal narrative of its leading personalities, its congresses and schisms, its dispersal after the German catastrophe of 1933 and the Austrian of 1938, then certainly these and many other aspects will have been fleshed out by Series Z. But this kind of history remains business as usual. I shall take as an instance Phyllis Grosskurth's *The Secret Ring: Freud's Inner Circle and the Politics of Psychoanalysis* published three years ago to consider-able acclaim. Assuredly the book contains new and sometimes vivid de-tails—Ms. Grosskurth had spent time in several archives, including the Rank papers at my own university, and she writes well. For me, however, the book, like so many others in the genre, represents yet another missed opportunity. That Freud's secret entourage, the "Committee" was racked by dissentions, backbiting, competition for Freud's imperious favor, was essentially known. The issue that is never addressed, is how this group of quite imperfect and in many ways incompatible men were able to sus-tain and propagate not only a therapy, but a teaching that became a vital component of Modernism around the globe. And, in a larger sense, is this not the issue for any history of the psychoanalytic movement worthy of itself—not merely to describe its inner workings or proselytizing activi-ties, but to ask what prior spiritual or cultural needs did Freud's teach-ing fulfill that enabled it to spread from a small group of Jews meeting in 1902 at Berggasse 19, to become what W. H. Auden called after Freud's death "a whole climate of opinion"?

I come finally to the vexing question of Freud's biography and here I am prepared to abandon my parable. I am only certain that the men and women from many countries will not find anything of significance about Freud's childhood and adolescence. That stumbling block to biogra-phers, especially those who are psychoanalytically oriented, will remain. Some information about Freud's parents may perhaps yet be found in Moravian and Viennese archives. As for Freud's mature life, for reasons already given I doubt that very much of a sensational nature will be found in Series Z, though of course one cannot be sure. Once again, however, I feel that the really important issues extend beyond the archives.

The first concerns the motivations of the biographers, and this can-not be divorced from the current wars over Freud nor, ultimately, from the cultural and psychological climate in which we find ourselves. That there should be widespread interest in the life of someone as famous as Freud is, of itself, natural. Many of us like to read biographies; I do so myself. But I do not know of any other personage (Sylvia Plath included), over whom biographical research is conducted in such a hothouse atmosphere and with such venom. The polarity between defenders and detractors of Freud is such as to make both sober discourse and reasonable objectivity increasingly difficult. I am fairly sure that most of the pressure to declassify Series Z has come from Freud's detractors, who are certain that dark and damaging secrets are to be found there, this being the only reason it has been kept closed. (Turned around, this has been the best argument for those partisans of Freud who would like to see it opened in order to put an end to wild speculations.)

It seems almost yesterday that Freud was, for most, a hero. By now the accusations range from malpractice to outright murder. Is it merely an inevitable reaction against a prior hagiography? Or does the age have a need to diminish its former heroes? I note that a book published in England and entitled *The Private Lives of Albert Einstein*, elicited an article in the Times of London on July 25, 1993 under the banner headline: "EINSTEIN = MC^2 (where M is for Mysogyny and C is for Cheat.)" Will the archives ever settle such trench warfare? I don't think so. What makes it worse is that where there is evidence for both virtue and vice about a historical character there is also a psychological inclination on the part of the historian (much to be guarded against) to assume that the negative is probably the more objective and truer version. The problem is at least as old as Plutarch, who wrote (in *On the Malice of Herodotus*) that "ill will in history writing is a preference for the less creditable version when two accounts of the same incident are current."

The other issue is so vital and so complex as to require a conference of its own. I have in mind the relation between biography and a person's achievement. How much of the former do we need to know in order to understand the latter? We do not even know the names of the authors of most biblical texts. Has this inhibited our understanding of Deuteronomy? So little of Shakespeare's life is known that Freud himself subscribed to the Earl of Oxford theory. Were it so, would it make a difference in our appreciation of Hamlet? How much about Freud's life must we know in order to interpret *The Interpretation of Dreams*? Or would our interpretation simply be different, with less ferreting for biographical links and more concentration on what he was trying to teach us?

Such and similar questions have often been debated in the past, but even the debate has been further complicated by the spirit of our time. It seems to me that the very questions have receded in the face of today's almost universal assumption that, especially when it comes to prominent men or women there is an inherent and boundless right to know everything about their lives, down to the most intimate details. The ethics of such probing are either taken for granted or rationalized. Thus the biographer of the American poet Ann Sexton, who committed suicide, was given access by Sexton's therapist to all the tapes he had recorded of their analytic sessions, on the grounds that she had herself been a "confessional" poet and would not have minded.

I have no ready answers to the ethical conundrum (though I hope you will not be shocked if I now belatedly reveal that at times I have a heretical empathy with the much maligned Dr. Eissler who, whatever his other follies, believed as a gentlemen of the old school that certain bounds of privacy must not be transgressed). But if not the question of ethics, then surely that of relevance must at least be faced.

To understand the time in which we live, let us observe that a well-known musicologist has taken the pains to prove, at least to his satisfaction, that Franz Schubert was not only a homosexual but a pederast. Well suppose he was. Will this information enhance my appreciation of a Schubert Lied or Quartet? (The musicologist thinks it has a bearing on the "Unfinished Symphony.") Well, that's music, you say, too abstract for direct connections. Literature, then. Some letters of James Joyce have been published which reveal that his wife Nora would on occasion oblige a sexual desire of his that can only be described as unusual even by our emancipated standards. Do these documents enable us to better understand Ulysses and Molly Bloom, or have we not more fruitfully to read Homer's Odyssey and acquire a map of Dublin? Ironically, it may have been Freud himself who first opened this Pandora's Box, but let's not hold this against him. Rather, let us ask—must we really know whether Freud slept with Minna? Those who want to discover that he really did are gripped by an unstated and faulty syllogism: a) Freud presented a public image of a devoted husband; b) Freud committed incest with his sister-in-law; ergo Freud is not to be trusted, and so neither should his work. . . .

But I have held you long enough. If I have displeased you with my skepticism about the ultimate value of Series Z, be comforted that whether or not it is declassified does not depend on me. I should like merely to summarize my stance. I believe that those on either side of the Freudian fence who think that within Series Z is to be found a decisive resolution to any of the really burning problems that face psychoanalysis and the writing of its history are deluding themselves with a credulous positivist conception of archives more appropriate to the nineteenth century than to ours. This, and not my poor parable, is the "archival fantasy" in my title. I believe equally that the seduction of the archives is distracting many from the real questions and the more important work to be done in understanding Freud and in determining what is alive and what obsolete in his legacy.

I ask your indulgence if I close on a personal, existential note. We live in a time when we are flooded with information in every field of endeavor, a deluge from which Freud scholarship is not exempt. It has become a veritable industry over which it is difficult to maintain even bibliographical control. The amount of sheer information increases incessantly. I confess that I have reached an age when I am haunted by the question of when information becomes knowledge. What I have presented here is only a special instance of that larger Angst. I am perhaps not yet old enough to seek the further line where knowledge becomes wisdom.

NOTE

This lecture was originally prepared for the conference on "Memory: The Question of Archives" under the auspices of the Freud Museum and the Société Internationale d'Histoire de la Psychanalyse, London, June 3–5, 1994. I wish to thank Elisabeth Roudinesco for having invited me, and Malcolm Pines who, when I fell ill, read my paper in my stead. I have delayed publication until now because I assumed the acts of the conference would be published as a book, but this, apparently, is not to be. As is my custom, I publish this lecture with no stylistic or other changes. The "you" in the text, originally the audience, is now the reader. [Y.H.Y.]

15 : THE PURLOINED KIDDUSH CUPS
REOPENING THE CASE ON FREUD'S
JEWISH IDENTITY

Introductory essay to the exhibition catalog *Sigmund Freud's Jewish Heritage*
(Binghamton and London: State University of New York and the Freud Museum,
1991).

This brief essay was written as part of a small catalogue published in 1991 as
an addendum to an earlier volume that had accompanied an exhibition devoted
to Sigmund Freud's private collection of antiquities.[1] This second publication dealt
with Freud's collection of Judaica objects, whose existence had been overlooked
for decades by those who knew of the careful photographic cataloguing of Freud's
home in Vienna on the eve of his departure to London. Only in 1989, after the exhibition of Freud's antiquities was already traveling, did David Becker, a graduate
student in Jewish studies at SUNY Binghamton, notice that in the front of the
photograph of a small table in Freud's study stood two kiddush cups. Closer investigation of additional photos of Freud's house yielded another discovery: a Rembrandt etching of the great Dutch rabbi Menasseh ben Israel (1604–1657).

The long-standing oversight of these and other Jewish-related objects was,
Yerushalmi announced here, "both parable and cautionary tale for what has occurred in the larger scholarly quest to understand the nature of Freud's Jewish
identity." This essay allowed him the opportunity to correct and enrich the historical record.

Yerushalmi had been reading Freud for years and had undertaken serious research in advance of delivering the Franz Rosenzweig Lectures at Yale in 1989. It
was on the basis of those lectures, and his ongoing archival explorations, that
Yerushalmi published his well-known book *Freud's Moses: Judaism Terminable
and Interminable* (1991). The new material evidence of the kiddush cups fortified
Yerushalmi's strong sense that while Freud was indeed "godless," as the Yale historian Peter Gay had asserted in his own book in 1989, he was at the same time
"very much a Jew."[2] To a great extent, Yerushalmi's perspective in this essay is

1. The exhibition was memorialized in *Sigmund Freud and Art: His Personal Collection of Antiquities* (New York: Abrams, 1989). The second volume, from which Yerushalmi's essay is taken, was *Sigmund Freud's Jewish Heritage* (Binghamton and London: State University of New York and the Freud Museum, 1991).

2. Peter Gay, *Freud: A Godless Jew: Freud, Atheism, and the Making of Psychoanalysis*
(New Haven: Yale University Press, 1989).

a direct rebuttal to Gay's conclusions about Freud and his Jewishness. Drawing on his grasp of the full sweep of Jewish history, Yerushalmi declared that "secular, godless Jews have been a ubiquitous component of Jewish modernity . . . and many have retained the most passionate Jewish loyalties, feelings, and convictions."

Freud was an excellent example of this tradition, according to Yerushalmi. In making the case, he moved beyond the well-known facts, for example, of Freud's membership in the B'nai B'rith chapter in Vienna. He argued that Freud came from a far more Jewish and religious background than had been assumed. Thus, Freud's father, Jakob, was not an antireligious "Voltairian," as Freud himself had once said, but rather a "tradition-minded Jew" who likely studied Talmud daily, kept a kosher home, and spoke Yiddish with his family (including Sigmund). It was Jakob who wrote an intricate and florid Hebrew inscription to his son when he presented him with a German-language Bible on Sigmund's thirty-fifth birthday. This provided Yerushalmi with evidence that Freud must have been concealing or even prevaricating when he said that he knew no Hebrew.

His enhanced portrait of Freud's Jewish background went hand in hand with — indeed, was the grounding for — Yerushalmi's larger claim that Freud was neither "ambivalent about his Jewish identity nor did he have any desire to discard it." The culmination of this argument would be Yerushalmi's detailed rereading of *Moses and Monotheism* (originally published in German in 1937) in *Freud's Moses*. In the following essay, he offered a brief, but significant, distillation when he declared that *Moses and Monotheism* was hardly Freud's farewell to Judaism, but rather "its triumphant vindication." Yerushalmi acknowledged that his own work of historical reclamation — both of Freud's reputation and of neglected historical material — was incomplete. New discoveries, he recognized, might unravel even more surprises and dimensions to Freud's complex personality.

In May 1938, some three months after Hitler's *Anschluss* of Austria, and only days before Freud and his family fled Nazi Vienna for London, the photographer Edmund Engelman was able to make a unique historical record of the Freud home as it appeared just prior to its abandonment. Working for three consecutive days, he photographed everything he could, including Freud's beloved collection of antiquities in their organic surroundings.

In 1976 a large selection of Engelman's superb photographs was finally published as a book titled, after the address of Freud's apartment house, *Berggasse 19*.[1] Translated into several languages, this book has had a deservedly wide circulation. Among the plates one (no. 15) is of particular interest. In a corner of Freud's study, with part of the famous couch visible on the right, we see a small table on which are arrayed a group of ancient Egyptian statuettes, photographed, in profile. Thus far, nothing unusual. But on the same table, in the very foreground facing the viewer, there also stand two goblets, one in front of the other, which are not even mentioned in the descriptive caption. Until very recently no one seemed to notice the incongruity between these goblets and the Egyptian objects. More important, apparently no one (myself included) had realized that the goblets were actually two silver Jewish kiddush cups, the one in front even emblazoned with the two Tablets of the Law.[2] In all probability, we did not *see* the kiddush cups because, aware of Freud's well-known contempt for religious ritual, we did not *expect* to see them there. And so again we experience the truism which Poe's archetypal sleuth C. Auguste Dupin knew so well, that we not only believe what we see but often see only what we believe, and that if the Prefect of the Paris police could not find the purloined letter it was because it was staring him in the face.

The same syndrome, in a sense, applies to Freud's medieval Hanukkah lamp. This lamp appeared in photographs of Freud's study taken in 1961 by the late Princeton philosopher Walter Kaufmann. Anna Freud included a "menorah" in a list of objects from her father's antiquities collection in 1974. The lamp has been on view in the room reconstructing Freud's study at the Freud Museum in London. Yet no one prior to Dr. Lynn Gamwell saw fit to draw any particular attention to it, and so there has been no reference to it in Freud scholarship, not even in the literature dealing with Freud's Jewish heritage.

The remarkable traveling exhibition of Freud's collection, assembled only some two years ago, contained not a single Jewish object. The Jewish materials now added to the exhibition were only subsequently discovered at the Freud Museum in London, and are fully described in this supplement to the original catalogue. It was only a reexamination of the Engelman photograph by a graduate student in Jewish studies at the State University of New York at Binghamton, and its enlargement to show the details of the kiddush cups, that prompted a renewed search for other Jewish materials in Freud's collection (the cups themselves have not yet been found).

But the tale does not end here. After I had finished the draft of this essay, Susan L. Braunstein returned to an even closer reexamination of the Engelman photos and, eagle-eyed, made a further discovery. In plate

23 of *Berggasse 19* (reproduced in *Freud and Art*, p. 27), she realized that on a wall near the doorway in Freud's consulting room there hung a portrait of a man that was none other than Rembrandt's etching of the famous seventeenth century Amsterdam rabbi Menasseh ben Israel! This portrait has survived in the Freud Museum in London and now joins the current exhibition (cat. no. 8).

The entire episode may well serve as both parable and cautionary tale for what has occurred in the larger scholarly quest to understand the nature of Freud's Jewish identity. That quest has often been derailed by a number of factors, notably the relative paucity of information about Freud's childhood and the parental home; the lingering inaccessibility of much archival material; the frequent lack of an extensive knowledge, not only of Freud and psychoanalysis but of Judaism and Jewish history; even the reliance on translations of Freud's texts rather than the original German. A small example of the latter will clarify what I mean. In 1883, overworked during his hospital internship, Freud wrote teasingly to his fiancée Martha Bernays: "In the future . . . I think I shall try to live more like the gentiles — modestly, learning and practicing the usual things and not striving after discoveries and delving too deep." That is, even in English, an interesting remark. But it becomes more pungent and even more revealing when we realize that, in his German letter, for "gentiles" Freud instinctively wrote "Gojim" (a transliteration in German characters of the Hebrew-Yiddish *goyim*, an often not too flattering connotation for non-Jews).[3]

One key to Freud's Jewishness may well lie in his celebrated description of himself as "a quite godless Jew" (*ein ganz gottloser Jude*), but that key, if it is to be useful, must be turned in both directions. Undoubtedly Freud was godless, and if we do not take his atheism seriously, we distort the truth. But Freud was also very much a Jew. To underestimate the depth of his Jewishness, as has happened so frequently, is no less a distortion. It falsely assumes that to be a "godless" or in the more common phrase a "secular" Jew is, if not an outright contradiction, an inevitable dilution of Jewish identity. It ignores the fact that secular, godless Jews have been a ubiquitous component of Jewish modernity, and that while they have revealed a broad spectrum of attitudes, many have retained the most passionate Jewish loyalties, feelings, and convictions.

Certainly Freud's culture, though cosmopolitan, was Germanic at its core. But culture and identity are not necessarily synonymous. Like so many other Central European Jews, what he cherished was the Germany of literature, philosophy, science. Unlike many of his Jewish contemporaries, he rarely mistook this Germany of the mind and the imagination for the real Germany or Austria, even if part of him wanted to do so. In 1886 he reports from Paris to Martha that in a political conversation on a possible Franco-German war, "I promptly explained that I am a Jew [*Ich gab mich gleich als juif*], adhering neither to Germany nor to Austria."[4] Freud's repudiation of his Germanic identity would be repeated in subsequent decades, even before the advent of Hitler. Nor was Freud, as is often assumed, spiritually and intellectually nourished merely by the traditions of the Enlightenment and of scientific positivism. In a retrospective overview of his life he states unequivocally: "My deep engrossment in the Bible story (almost as soon as I had learned the art of reading) had, as I recognized much later, an enduring effect upon the direction of my interest."[5]

To be sure, Freud himself unwittingly shares a certain responsibility for some of the subsequent controversy concerning his Jewish identity, through his frequent projection of a public persona as a universal scientist who had received the barest of Jewish upbringings, from a father whom he characterizes as an agnostic and even a "Voltairian." All too often this image has been accepted uncritically by Freud scholars, without bothering to consider how much of it may have been strategically connected to Freud's long-standing anxiety that psychoanalysis should not be perceived as "Jewish" science, and ignoring or glossing over the often dramatic gap between his public and private utterances, as well as other evidence that contradicts the prevailing stereotype.

However, a new type of Freud scholarship has recently emerged which, intent on a thorough reappraisal of Freud's Jewishness, has brought fresh tools and perspectives to bear on the subject. Often it has not even been a matter of discovering new manuscript or archival materials, but of an alert and contextual rereading of all available published texts, as a result of which we "see" for the first time what was there all along. The enterprise, of course, must still be considered as work in progress, not necessarily reaching closure on any particular point, but certainly reopening questions previously considered closed. In this limited space I obviously cannot give a fully adequate account of these new lines of investigation.[6] Let it suffice for me to indicate at least some of the contours of Freud's Jewish identity as they have begun to be clarified.

Freud's father Jacob was certainly no "Voltairian." There is now ample evidence, both oblique and direct, that even in Vienna he continued to be a tradition-minded Jew who in his leisure studied a page of Bible or Talmud daily. Even if, as some have speculated, he had become a *maskil* (an adherent of the movement for Jewish Enlightenment) in Galicia, we must remember that the Galician Haskalah was by its nature not anti-religious, but rather, only opposed to what it regarded as Hasidic fanaticism and cultural hermeticism. Jacob's marriage in Rabbi Mannheimer's Reform temple in Vienna means simply that the setting was "modern," but the wedding ceremony (like Sigmund's later circumcision) was in that period thoroughly traditional. In Jacob Freud's household most, if not all, Jewish holidays were observed, and probably the dietary laws as well. Indeed, the very violence and fury of Freud's subsequent rebellion against Jewish ritual would be almost inexplicable unless he had experienced it intimately in his childhood.

Freud's Jewish education too, it turns out, had been far from trivial. At age seven he began formal study of the Hebrew Bible with his father and, through the Gymnasium years, Hebrew, religion, and Jewish history with Samuel Hammerschlag, to whom he remained devoted. Along with German, Yiddish was almost certainly the lingua-franca in the home that Sigmund Freud left only at age twenty-six. For his thirty-fifth birthday his father presented him with the Philippson Bible from which both had once studied together, freshly rebound in leather, into which he had written an amazing and elaborate Hebrew inscription. If, as Freud later claimed, he knew no Hebrew, why did Jacob not write in German? More important is the revelatory quality of the Hebrew text itself. Long available, only now has it been properly glossed and shown to be entirely an ingenious mosaic of phrases from the Bible, the Talmud, and Jewish liturgy. Certainly it attests to Jacob's abiding command of Jewish learning. But if we trace the fragments back to their original sources, we also have a fascinating psychological subtext whose message is an appeal by the father to the son to return to the Bible, the primal wellspring of his inspiration and of their closeness together.[7]

As for Freud's own perception of his Jewish identity, we have only to review the plethora of statements scattered throughout his private correspondence and recorded conversations with his fellow Jews. His expressions of his pride in being a Jew were not merely a reflex to anti-Semitism or an attempt to transform his Jewish marginality into an asset, though there was something of that as well. Yet, faced with the same prejudice, many of his Viennese Jewish peers reacted very differently, hiding, fleeing their Jewish identities, even accepting baptism for the sake of their careers. Freud staunchly refused such evasions. Indeed, there is now ample indication that Freud genuinely believed that Jews are intellectually and morally superior to others, and that he thought these qualities to be phylogenetically inherited and transmitted. Nor did Freud's stance remain passive or abstract. He really felt comfortable only among Jews, and it is therefore no accident that the only organization which he joined at first was the B'nai Brith, that the original Wednesday evening group which became the Vienna Psychoanalytic Society was composed of Jews, and that some interesting structural parallels should emerge between the two. Though he never formally declared himself a Zionist, in 1902 he sent Theodor Herzl a copy of *The Interpretation of Dreams* with a letter hailing him as "the poet and the fighter for the human rights of our people" (see cat. No. 12).[8] Later he accepted honorary membership in Kadimah, the Zionist student organization, and became a member of the Board of Governors of the Hebrew University, and even of the honorary committee of the Yiddish Scientific Institute (YIVO) in Vilna.

In the end, of course, it is the inner Freud, his *moi profond* as the French would say, that is of paramount importance. Here certain of Freud's dreams have yielded new insight into how deeply Jewish concerns were embedded in his psyche.[9] But the depth of his Jewish passion comes through most vividly in his letters—to Arnold Zweig, for example, or Karl Abraham, or to the lately rediscovered Sabina Spielrein ("We are and remain Jews. The others will only exploit us and will never understand and appreciate us . . .").[10]

We have only to take Freud's own explicit statements with the seriousness they deserve in order to fully grasp that neither was he ambivalent about his Jewish identity nor did he have any desire to discard it. What he wanted through most of his life, and what eluded him for so long, was to understand its nature and its very intensity. The quintessential expression of this desire, echoed on other occasions, is to be found in his message to the Vienna lodge of the B'nai Brith: "What bound me to Judaism was . . . not the faith, not even the national pride. . . . But there remained enough over to make the attraction of Judaism and the Jews irresistible, *many dark emotional powers all the more powerful the less they could be expressed in words. . . .*"[11]

Only toward the very end of his life did Freud finally find the words. The result was *Moses and Monotheism*, not, as some would have it, a valediction to his Jewishness but, properly understood, its triumphant vindication.

And what of the Jewish objects now discovered and displayed? Do they change anything in our view of Freud's Jewish identity? Let us be prudent and opt for caution. The kiddush cups, I suspect, may have been an inheritance from his or his wife Martha's parents, the old Hanukkah lamp probably bought from a dealer. Godless Jew that he was, having coerced his wife even before their marriage to give up all the Jewish rituals of her natural piety and Orthodox upbringing, it would be no more plausible to assume that he used these objects for their originally intended purposes than to suppose that he actually worshiped his Egyptian deities. On the other hand, the discovery that he owned a set of the four-volume 1928 Berlin edition of the Babylonian Talmud in the original[12] (we already knew that he owned the Goldschmidt German translation) raises anew the question of his Hebraic (and Aramaic) knowledge, but this must remain, for the time being, an intriguing enigma. The portrait of Menasseh ben Israel is equally tantalizing. It hardly seems likely to me that Freud owned it merely because he was interested in Rembrandt. Freud had a long-standing interest in England, had relatives there, admired its liberties, and ended there as a refugee. Can it be mere coincidence that Menasseh ben Israel is most famous in Jewish history as having played a central role in 1654–55 in the readmission of the Jews to England, from which they had been expelled in 1290?[13] Be that as it may, the very fact that the Jewish objects, the Talmud, and the other materials now on view were kept as part of his scrupulously arranged private ambiance is sufficiently noteworthy and (such are the surprising vicissitudes in the unfolding story of Freud) may yet, with other discoveries perhaps still to come, prove significant.

NOTES

1. Edmund Engelman, *Berggasse 19: Sigmund Freud's Home and Offices, Vienna 1938*, Introduction by Peter Gay (New York: Basic Books, 1976).

2. Curiously, in other photographs of the same table taken from different angles (Engelman, *Berggasse 19*, pls. 11, 16, 19), the cups are not present. Moreover, the corresponding plate 17 in the French edition is not the same photograph as in the English. It shows the same view, but without the cups. Apparently another negative was inadvertently substituted for this printing. See *La maison de Freud: Berggasse 19, Vienne* (Paris: Editions du Seuil, 1979), p. 64, pl. 17.

I owe the following further details to Dr. Lynn Gamwell. The evidence relevant to the two Engelman photographs which do, and do not, contain the cups can be summarized as follows: Engelman took all the photographs of Freud's study on three consecutive weekdays in May 1938. Taking Engelman's recollections about the weather (which was crucial to him for the lighting of his photographs), together with newspaper reports of the weather in Vienna throughout May 1938, it is only possible to conclude that Freud's study was photographed on Monday, May 23, through Wednesday, May 25 (letter from E. Engelman to L. Gamwell, Jan. 24, 1991; *Neue Freie Presse*, Vienna, May 1938). It is impossible to determine the sequence in which these two particular photographs were made, since both were taken with a Rolleiflex camera, which has cut, unnumbered negatives (letter from E. Engelman to L. Gamwell, June 25, 1991). However, we can determine with virtual certainty that Engelman took the photographs that included the cups on Wednesday the 25th. Engelman tells us in *Berggasse 19* that after the first and second days of shooting, he went to his studio at night and made contact prints, which he put into a scrapbook for Freud (*Berggasse 19*, pp. 131, 136–40). Engelman gave Freud the scrapbook during the third day of shooting the study, when the two men met for the first time. None of the photos in this scrapbook, which includes nine photos of the table in question, contains the cups. Thus the cups must have been present on the third day only.

The opinion of the research staff of the Freud Museum is that most likely either Freud's wife Martha or daughter Anna put the cups on the table to be photographed because the two women, together with the housekeeper Paula Fichtl, supervised the picture taking (letter from E. Davies to L. Gamwell, July 1, 1991). Engelman, however, recalls that both psychoanalyst August Aichhorn and Freud himself were also present in the study during the third and final day of photographing.

In a 1974 discussion of Jewish ritual objects in Freud's study, which took place at the Freud home (now the Freud Museum) between Anna Freud, Rita Ransohoff, editor of *Berggasse 19*, and Joy Ungerleider Mayerson, then Director of the Jewish Museum in New York, Anna Freud did not comment specifically on the kiddush cups, but she did, significantly, acknowledge their presence in her father's study (letter from R. Ransohoff to L. Gamwell, July 11, 1991).

3. For the English and German texts see, respectively, *Letters of Sigmund Freud*, ed. Ernst Freud, trans. Tania Stern and James Stern (New York: Basic Books, 1960), p. 54, no. 19; *Briefe, 1873–1939*, ed. Ernst Freud and Lucie Freud (Frankfurt am Main: S. Fischer, 1980), p. 60.

4. Freud, *Letters*, p. 203, no. 94; *Briefe*, pp. 209 f.

5. Freud, *An Autobiographical Study*, in *S.E.*, 20, p. 8. The work was written in 1924. This sentence, however, was added in 1935.

6. Among the works which offer, albeit with varying emphases, a positive re-evaluation of Freud's Jewish identity through new information or perspectives,

the following may be of particular interest: Reuben B. Rainey, *Freud as a Student of Religion* (Missoula: American Academy of Religion and Scholars Press, 1975); Théo Pfrimmer, *Freud, lecteur de la Bible* (Paris: Presses Universitaires de France, 1982); Dennis B. Klein, *Jewish Origins of the Psychoanalytic Movement* (Chicago: University of Chicago Press, 1985); Emanuel Rice, *Freud and Moses: The Long Journey Home* (Albany: State University of New York Press, 1990).

Of course I do not mean to imply that there is as yet any consensus concerning Freud the Jew. Indeed, one may find a spectrum of views acknowledging but minimizing the depth or relevance of Freud's Jewishness or, in effect, denying it altogether. For a lucid review of some of the earlier literature, see Justin Miller, "Interpretations of Freud's Jewishness, 1924–1974," *Journal of the History of the Behavioral Sciences* 17 (1981), pp. 357–74.

What follows in this essay concerning Freud's Jewish identity is essentially a summary based on my *Freud's Moses: Judaism Terminable and Interminable* (New Haven and London: Yale University Press, 1991), where all the issues raised here are elaborated and documented in greater and more nuanced detail.

7. The inscription has been recently transcribed and independently interpreted by: Mortimer Ostow, "Sigmund and Jakob Freud and the Philippson Bible (with an Analysis of the Birthday Inscription)," *International Review of Psycho-Analysis* 16 (1989), pp. 483–92; Rice, *Freud and Moses*, pp. 62–84; Yerushalmi, *Freud's Moses*, pp. 70–79 and Appendix II.

8. Ernst Pawel, *The Labyrinth of Exile: A Life of Theodor Herzl* (New York: Farrar, Straus & Giroux, 1989), p. 456. I have published the original German text of the letter in *Freud's Moses*, p. 118, Appendix III, no. 1.

9. See, for example, Peter Lowenberg, "A Hidden Zionist Theme in Freud's 'My Son the Myops . . .' Dream," *Journal of the History of Ideas* 31 (1970), pp. 129–32. Cf. Yerushalmi, *Freud's Moses*, pp. 69 f.

10. Freud's letter of August 28, 1913, in Aldo Carotenuto, *A Secret Symmetry: Sabina Spielrein between Jung and Freud* (New York: Pantheon Books, 1982), pp. 120 f.; see also Yerushalmi, *Freud's Moses*, pp. 43–45.

11. Freud, *S.E.*, 20, pp. 273 f. (My italics.) Cf. his preface to the Hebrew translation of *Totem and Taboo* (*S.E.*, 13, p. xv).

12. It was first identified as such by Emanuel Rice (see *Freud and Moses*, p. 94).

13. See Cecil Roth, *A Life of Menasseh ben Israel* (Philadelphia: Jewish Publication Society, 1934); Lucien Wolf, *Menasseh ben Israel's Mission to Oliver Cromwell* (London: Jewish Historical Society of England, 1901).

16 : GILGUL

New Yorker, August 15, 2011.

Given his passion for world literature, as well as the lyrical quality of his prose and the care that he lavished on his writing, it is perhaps surprising that "Gilgul" is the first and only piece of fiction that Yerushalmi published. It appeared after his death in the August 15 & 22, 2011, edition of the *New Yorker*. The short-story form permitted him to experiment with a new mode of writing that mixed his best writerly instincts as narrator and his substantial skills as historian.

The title of the short story is a Hebrew word that connotes "reincarnation" or, more specifically in the history of Jewish mysticism, "metempsychosis"—that is, the migration of the soul from one body to another. In this sense, the story reveals Yerushalmi's great debt to and inspiration from Gershom Scholem (1897–1982), the internationally renowned master of Jewish mystical studies in the twentieth century. Yerushalmi regarded Scholem as a mentor and friend, meeting him on visits in Jerusalem and New York and corresponding with him for decades. He was also deeply familiar with Scholem's entire scholarly oeuvre and subscribed to Scholem's view that mysticism, and particularly the antinomian tendencies of the mystical tradition known as Kabbalah, were central to the history of Judaism, rather than marginal, as some nineteenth-century Jewish historians had maintained.

This story features a case of *gilgul* or transmigration of a soul as reported by Gerda, a Jewish psychic in the coastal city of Jaffa next to Tel Aviv. The psychic describes the case to a curious prospective client, a visiting New York Jewish writer and scholar named Ravitch. The narrator's report of Ravitch's unlikely encounter with Gerda includes a number of motifs familiar from Yerushalmi's own scholarly and personal life. In the first instance, a melancholic air of loss and estrangement hovers over the story and particularly over Ravitch, who was coming out of a serious depression when he left New York for a vacation in Israel. Yerushalmi engaged the theme of estrangement here through fiction, but elsewhere he probed it through the medium of scholarship, as in his sober meditations on the modern historian in *Zakhor*. For all his passion and love for his work, Yerushalmi himself had, at times, a melancholic air about him, punctuated by ever-increasing thoughts of his own mortality.

A related motif, also familiar to us, drives one of the main plotlines of the story. It concerns the original source of the soul that migrated. Gerda tells Ravitch that the soul originally belonged to one Isaac Benveniste, a Spanish Jewish physician who left the Iberian Peninsula with the Edict of Expulsion in 1492 en route to Palestine. Of course, this fictional character reminds us immediately of Isaac Cardoso, the protagonist of Yerushalmi's first historical monograph, *From Spanish Court*. Like Benveniste, Cardoso was a physician in Spain who left the Peninsula in order to connect to his Jewish roots. But whereas Cardoso made his permanent home in Italy, Benveniste never sunk roots in Palestine—or in any other locale. He could not have known in 1492, Yerushalmi wrote, that "that his wanderings in exile had only begun, that in a sense they would never end, that he would never reach his real destination." After twenty years of wandering, he finally arrived in Rhodes, where he died two years later.

At the end of her description of Benveniste's peripatetic journeys, Gerda relates to Ravitch that she had a client into whose body Benveniste's soul had migrated. She instructed this client to go to the cemetery in Rhodes where Benveniste is buried. Once there, she enjoined him to pray so that "Benveniste's soul should cease its wanderings . . . and that you, too, should at last find peace."

Later, back at his Tel Aviv hotel, Ravitch tries to make sense of his encounter with Gerda. He is overcome with a powerful sense of nostalgia for his own past, as symbolized by another storyteller, his grandmother, who transmitted to him a rich array of Jewish beliefs, customs, and superstitions. Painfully aware that he can recall but not re-create them, Ravitch returns to contemplating Gerda's intention in relating the tale of *gilgul*. He ends up in something of a Kafkaesque labyrinth, not surprising given that Yerushalmi was a great admirer of Kafka (and proudly collected first editions of his writings for his library). With a clear nod to Kafka's evocative and mystifying short story "Before the Law," Yerushalmi has his narrator provide a vexing answer to Ravitch's question as to why Gerda imparted her account to *him*: "The story was meant for you, but it is not about you." The indeterminacy, mixed signals, and failed communication represent the modern man's quest to reconstitute a living memory, a memory full of personal meaning and connection to a larger collective. It is a quest of which Yerushalmi was keenly aware and toward whose understanding he devoted a great part of his professional life, most often as an historian and here, in this one instance, as a fiction writer.

"You know," she said almost shyly, "that I have the ability, if you wish, to look into your eyes and tell you when you will die?"

"No, I didn't realize you could do that." He hesitated for a moment. "And I don't want to know."

That was how Ravitch's first encounter with Gerda had ended, four years earlier. It was Mira, his friend Yoram's wife, who had taken him to her. She'd told him that there was an amazing sorceress in Jaffa, a "good witch," with unusual psychic powers, who had been born in a D.P. camp in Germany after the war and brought to Israel as a child. "You must meet her before you return to New York," Mira had said, and since he was very fond of Mira, and because she was always capable of surprising him, Ravitch had gone along.

The apartment occupied the top floor of a decaying Arab house in Jaffa. They climbed three flights of stairs and Mira knocked four times, then simply pushed the door open. They entered the living room, where there were multicolored lights in brass lanterns, blue glass bottles from Hebron, Bedouin weavings on the walls, cushions on the floor—the kind of baroque pseudo-Orientalism that Ravitch disdained. But the location was superb. Through one of the two windows placed irregularly in the far wall, he caught sight of an exquisitely bloated red sun sinking into the darkening sea.

Gerda now entered the room and they were introduced. He guessed that she was at least in her late forties, but it was difficult to judge her exact age. Gaunt, pale, straight dull-brown hair, a cheap cotton print dress with a low neckline, her collarbones straining against freckled skin. Yet there was something girlish about her. After some initial pleasantries, she offered them sweet black coffee in Turkish cups, and when they had finished drinking she read the grounds for them. Then she laid out the Tarot. Ravitch noticed that the deck was a fine one, obviously old, beautifully illustrated, hand-colored. But all she offered in her readings was banalities. Mira would become pregnant sometime soon. Mira must avoid walking on the left side of the street. As for Ravitch, when he got home he would finish his book (Mira must have told her about the book) and it would be a success. No witch she, Ravitch mused, only a skinny Jewess playing Gypsy. He smiled to himself. Just at that moment, she said to him in a curiously insistent tone, "Please, come with me to the other room."

He followed her into a tiny bedroom. Unlike the living room, it was totally austere, its white plastered walls bare except for a small Klee lithograph. They sat down facing each other, on straight-backed chairs, near an iron cot. Well, what game will we play now? Ravitch wondered. Closer to her than before, he studied her face and realized that she might once have been beautiful. When she spoke, the timbre of her voice had changed, taking on a richer, more full-throated texture that momentarily startled him. An unfamiliar tremor flickered through his body. It was then that she made her offer and he refused.

"Well, what did you think of her?" Mira asked as they drove away.

"You certainly know some weird people," he replied with a shrug.

Four years ago, all that. He had gone back to New York and, yes, he had finished his book, though, of course, this had had nothing to do with the witch's prediction, since he'd already had a rough draft when he met her. The book, a study of the Jewish tales of Sacher-Masoch, received enough friendly reviews from the critics and deliberately misleading publicity from his publisher ("Jews . . . Masochism!") to bring him some much needed money. But Ravitch was not gratified. The moment the book was published, it was already alien to him, as though someone else had written it. He wished someone else *had* written it.

Now he was on vacation. He had gone first to Greece, but after two days in Athens, on an impulse, he flew to Israel. He was staying in Tel Aviv, a city he was not fond of. Why had he chosen Tel Aviv? Why had he even come to Israel? No answer. His habitual lucidity seemed to have deserted him. The past four years had not been good ones. His divorce. Inevitable, he thought in retrospect. And, in the course of separating, both he and Evelyn had behaved reasonably, even charitably. Yet he couldn't reconcile himself to sleeping alone, still lay awake entire nights. It wasn't that Ravitch had difficulty finding women. There had been several since the divorce, attractive, intelligent, eager to please, to console. But even now he awoke in the middle of the night, groping in confusion for the familiar, soft yet stubborn body. Then, there had been his father's death, at eighty-four, which had been surprising only in the intensity of the depression that followed. He'd felt nothing comparable when his mother had died, years before. The shock of it. He, Ravitch, who had always thought his mind inviolable, had naively conceived of depression as merely a state of being very sad. The trembling of his hands and the motor roaring loudly in the back of his skull had enlightened him. Clinical depression, a succession of doctors had explained gravely, patiently, defining his suffering. Not uncommon under the circumstances. Not severe enough for hospitalization. A cocktail of various pills, taken over three months, had rid him of the worst symptoms. Time and new habits would undoubtedly assuage his nocturnal agitation. What was left was simply the feeling of being scooped out, hollow. No other words for it. But what did it portend?

For the first few days in Tel Aviv, Ravitch contacted no one. None of his friends knew he was there. He had taken a room in one of the luxury hotels lining the beach, on a high floor with a huge picture window facing the sea. He remained in his room, took all his meals there, going down to the lobby for a drink only to enable the maids to tidy up and make his bed. Though he had brought some books, he did not read. He lay on the bed, inert, unable to focus on a thought, occasionally dozing lightly. Or else he sat for hours at the window, looking out toward the sea.

On the fourth day, in the late afternoon, he finally emerged and began to walk along the beach, the hotels to his left, the sea on his right. He walked slowly on the moist margin between sand and water, oblivious of the cries of children and gulls. Staring straight ahead, his eyes scanned the coast as it began to curve outward some two miles away. Toward the end of the rim was the other town. Even through the slight haze, you could see that it was no longer Tel Aviv. The architecture was visibly softer, older. Dun-colored houses, the silhouette of a small mosque. Dome and minaret. Jaffa.

Ravitch returned to the hotel. He called Mira, deflected her torrent of questions, apologized for not having sent a gift when the baby was born, congratulated her and Yoram. Yes, he was fine, no need to worry about him. By the way, was she still in touch with that woman—what was her name—yes, Gerda? Could he have her phone number? More questions. Even marvellous Mira could be exasperating. No, no particular reason. Just the number, please. Finally, she gave it to him.

He called immediately. "This is Ravitch. Do you remember me? We met four years ago. I was with Mira." Gerda remembered. "I want to see you again," he continued rapidly. "Actually, I must see you. This time alone."

A pause. "You can come tomorrow night at ten o'clock," she said slowly, "not before. How will you be coming?"

She gave him the address and instructions for the cabdriver. The following night, he went down to Jaffa.

Gerda opened the door and stood on the threshold without moving, scrutinizing him. She was wearing a long sleeveless black dress, simply cut, rather becoming. Her hair had been brushed back over one ear, revealing a single amber earring. "You are depleted," she said. "You need lots of sun, lots of love."

"I need more than that," he replied, wondering if it had been a mistake to come. "I need to talk to you, and not about my death. About my life."

"Of course," she murmured. "Please come in."

The living room was exactly as he remembered it. Not a single object had been shifted, nothing removed, nothing added. They sat in silence for a few minutes. Then he told her all that had happened since he last saw her and almost all that he felt now, for that was harder to articulate. Curiously, it did not take him long. While he spoke, he noticed that she was not looking at him. She had closed her eyes, as though to listen all the more intently. As soon as he finished, she looked at him again. He met her gaze without flinching. Once more, they were both silent. He felt his heart beating, but she seemed utterly tranquil, exuding a stillness that enveloped the entire room. At moments, he was aware only of the sea sounds drifting in through the windows and then fading away. When she finally spoke, it was almost in a whisper.

"What I am about to tell you," she began tentatively, "what I shall tell you, you are, of course, free to believe or disbelieve. It will make no difference to me."

"But I came deliberately to hear what you have to say," Ravitch protested. "After all, it was I who sought you out, who chose to come."

"Perhaps," she said with a passing smile.

"But that last remark of yours was unnecessary, even a bit unkind. I had hoped that your allowing me to come here meant that you might also care a bit about what is happening to me."

"I didn't say that I don't care about you. I said that whether or not you believe what I tell you will not affect me, which is something different. I said it because it is true and also because it might free you to listen properly—that is, without worrying whether by not believing me you might hurt my feelings in some way."

"I understand," Ravitch said, somewhat subdued.

"And now I ask you only to listen closely. Try not to judge until you have heard me out, although, knowing something about you, I realize that will be difficult, perhaps impossible. In any case, whatever your judgments may be, keep them to yourself. Agreed?"

"Agreed." Ravitch settled himself more comfortably on his floor pillow and leaned his back against the wall.

"I am aware," Gerda said, "that people call me a witch. It is not meant meanly and it doesn't bother me. Who knows—perhaps I am a witch. It is a venerable vocation, and its history is not without honor. Be that as it may, if I am a witch who still reads coffee grounds and the Tarot—I could feel your disapproval four years ago—I am also a very modern one. It may surprise you that I am known to a number of psychiatrists around the world, a small number, to be sure. But there have been occasions when they have tried all their own brands of sorcery on a patient, without success. Then, when they have given up, they have sent him to me."

Ravitch said nothing.

"Before I tell you my tale," she continued, "I shall ask you only one question. Do you know what *gilgul* is?"

"Given that I have been speaking fluent Hebrew to you since we first met, I find it odd that you should ask. Of course I know. *Gilgul* is the transmigration of souls. Reincarnation. Metempsychosis. Related etymologically to *galgal*—'wheel'—and *galgel*—'to roll'—neither of them inappropriate, as a matter of fact. If you mean do I know anything about it, well, yes. The soul, after death, can be reborn in the body of another human, an animal, or some other creature—once, repeatedly, or infinitely, according to the quality of the life one has lived. It's a give-me-another-chance doctrine, so to speak, ancient, ubiquitous, simultaneously comforting and frustrating. Pythagoreans, Hindus, Buddhists, and Kabbalists all believed in it and spun their own complex variations on the basic theme. I have read some of the Kabbalistic material. Do you want more details?"

For the first time, Gerda actually laughed. "Stop, Ravitch, before you overwhelm me with your legendary erudition! No more, I beg you. You have answered my question, at least on a certain level. I shall proceed to my tale and promise you no more questions."

She stretched, arching her back like a cat, folded her hands in her lap, and leaned slightly forward.

"I said that certain psychiatrists refer their failures to me. One of them is British, a psychoanalyst, actually, who practices in Manchester. It happened about eight years ago. He had a patient, a middle-aged Jew born in Bucharest, with a singularly interesting problem.

"The man was—how shall I put it—restless. Not like your restlessness, Ravitch, or that of other people. He was not an insomniac, like you, or unable to sit still in a room. He was pathologically *rest-less*, without respite. Nothing ordinary here. Let us call it an uncanny geographical restlessness."

Ravitch had not mentioned his insomnia. How does she know? he thought. Does it show? But he held his tongue.

"Yes, a geographical restlessness, rare, perhaps unique. This was a man who could not bear to live in one place for more than a short time. Sometimes after only a few months, some strange compulsion would drive him to leave for another place. You must understand that we are not speaking of wanderlust; he had no desire to travel and see the world. On the contrary, he hated this constant moving about, wanted nothing more than to fix his abode somewhere, anywhere, to have a permanent home, perhaps a family, to find repose. Instead, he had crisscrossed the whole of Europe, had been several times to America, and even once to Bolivia and Peru. He was an engineer of some sort, an eminently portable profession, but he never committed himself to large projects, knowing in advance that he would not stay long. I know he suffered! In great cities and small, he would rent a flat, begin to rearrange the furniture and to make it his own. Sometimes he even met a woman he liked sufficiently to begin an affair. But as soon as a particular job was done, sometimes even before it was completed, before he had hung a picture on a wall, before the affair had had a chance to blossom, he was off again, without knowing why, knowing only that he had to leave, that he had to uproot himself once more. Desperate, he finally sought help for his affliction. The Manchester analyst was the last of many to whom he had poured out his troubles. And then he came to me. I listened to his account, which was far more detailed than what I am telling you now, and even as he spoke I knew the real root of his troubles."

She "knew," Ravitch thought, vaguely irritated. With what assurance she said that, the arrogance of it. Yet what she had told him so far was obviously only a prelude. Despite his misgivings, he was eager to hear more.

As she resumed her tale, he noticed that Gerda's voice now swiftly modulated into that vibrant resonance which had so unnerved him at their first meeting. This time, he allowed himself merely to savor it, waiting.

"Here is what I told that driven man, almost in these words:

"'Your body,' I said, 'was born in Bucharest, but your soul was born elsewhere. You carry within you the soul of a Jew born long ago, in Spain. He was a physician. His name was Isaac Benveniste. His family had lived for centuries in Ávila. Along with the rest of Spanish Jewry, he was swept up in the great expulsion of 1492. I have reason to think that, when the edict of Ferdinand and Isabella was made public, he decided to make his way to the Holy Land. As you must realize, this was no easy task. The Jews had only three months, a period of turmoil and panic, in which to liquidate their assets and leave. There was no way for him to travel directly to the Land of Israel. Benveniste managed to get from Ávila to Valencia, where he was lucky enough to find passage on a ship sailing to Genoa.

The voyage was unusually long, the seas turbulent. When he arrived, the authorities would not allow him to remain. Since Genoa was not his goal, he accepted this rebuff with equanimity. He did not realize that his wanderings in exile had only begun, that in a sense they would never end, that he would never reach his real destination.'"

Ravitch found himself under the spell of the tale. As Gerda spoke, his breathing began to rise and fall softly to the cadence of her sentences. There was something magnificent about her now, as though she had come into her true kingdom. She had the radiance of a born storyteller, luring him, lulling him. No longer Gerda at all. Scheherazade.

"From Genoa, Isaac Benveniste made his way to Venice, and from there across the Adriatic to Ragusa. I did not give my patient all the stations along the way, only the major ones, but, Ravitch, try to trace the map in your imagination. Years of travel from one place to another, practicing medicine in small towns just to stay alive and save enough to journey farther. Wars, plagues often forced him to take circuitous routes. But always he pressed onward. Down the Dalmatian Coast, across the frontiers of the Ottoman Empire, eastward overland all the way to Adrianople, then westward again to Salonika and once more by ship through the Aegean to Smyrna. From Smyrna, he sailed finally to the island of Rhodes. Why didn't he undertake one more voyage? A few hundred miles by sea and he would have reached the Land of Israel. Who knows? He had been wandering for almost twenty years; he was old, exhausted. Whatever the reason, the will to continue had seeped out of him. He remained in Rhodes. Less than two years later, he died and was buried there."

Silence. Gerda's face now looked strained, as though she were wearied by the effort of retelling the tale.

"But that is not all you told your man from Bucharest," Ravitch said quietly. "Please, go on."

"I said to him, 'This story is, in a real sense, your own. When Dr. Benveniste died, his soul found no rest. Since that time, it has wandered, as you are wandering, born and reborn in every generation. Now it is you who carry it within you. Its restlessness is the source of your own. You will never find peace until you help it find peace.'

"'How can I do this?' the man from Bucharest demanded.

"'You should first go to the university in Jerusalem. The rational part of you must be convinced that this person at least existed. In the library, read whatever you can on the history of the Jews of Rhodes. On Jews in medicine as well—I hear they have a large and splendid collection on the subject. Since you barely read Hebrew, speak to the librarians and archivists; some may be willing to assist you. See if you can find anything about a Spanish Jewish physician named Isaac Benveniste who died in Rhodes in 1515 or thereabouts. If you succeed, and if what you find has any relation to what I have told you, then you must take the next step and follow my instructions carefully.'

"Our man was fortunate, Ravitch. He called me a few weeks later from Jerusalem and told me that, with the help of the library staff, he had followed not only some scattered information about Benveniste in various books but even a manuscript, a Spanish medical work that Benveniste had translated into Hebrew, with a colophon signed and dated in his own hand. The man from Bucharest knew that I had never looked at these materials, because the library kept a record of those who had. There was now no longer any question as to what he should do next.

"'You must,' I said, 'go to Rhodes yourself and find the old Jewish cemetery. There are only a handful of Jews left on the island since the war, but one of them will surely guide you. With him you must walk carefully among the tombstones, reading the inscriptions, until you discover Benveniste's grave. Once you find it, you will ask to be left alone. Then you must immediately recite Kaddish, as though you were a mourner. After that, you must prostrate yourself on the ground and pray. You needn't even mention God. But you must pray, in your own words, that Benveniste's soul should cease its wanderings, that this should be its final *gilgul*, and that you, too, should at last find peace.'"

"And did he go to Rhodes?" Ravitch asked.

"Yes. And he found the grave. And he did all that he had been told."

"And did he find peace?"

"He remained in Rhodes for a month. Then he came to Israel. He has been here ever since, living in the same town. He no longer travels at all."

"And where, precisely, does he live?"

"This I shall not—cannot—tell you. It would do neither of you any good to meet."

Another silence. Ravitch waited for Gerda to say something, anything, about him, but she was completely still. Suddenly, with a single abrupt motion, she rose from her pillow and stood before him. "My God!" she exclaimed. "I didn't realize the time! Already past midnight! I promised a friend that I would pick up her dog. It is ill. I must run!"

It all happened so quickly. Gerda was already gathering her shawl and a large handbag. "Wait!" Ravitch cried, leaping up. "Please wait! You can't leave yet! There is so much more I need to hear from you. This entire story you told, was it a parable for me? Do I also carry someone else's soul—is that what you mean?"

Gerda turned to him. "No," she said. "The story was meant for you, but it is not about you. And now I must really go."

"Can I call a cab and drop you off?'"

"No, the place I'm going to is right here in Jaffa. I will walk. Don't accompany me. You can remain here for a while if you like. But don't wait for me. I will not be back tonight. Leave whenever you wish. It is no problem. I never lock the door."

"Does that mean I can come again?"

"I don't think so. It will serve no purpose." And with that she walked out.

Ravitch remained standing in the middle of the room, stunned, hurt, angry. It had indeed been a mistake to come here. A sick dog! The woman was crazy—he'd already known it four years ago. In his fragile state, this was the last thing he should have done. Scheherazade, indeed. Circe! He could not forgive himself for having been such a fool, he, Ravitch. Coffee grounds, Tarot, *gilgul*—they were all of a piece, a cheap occultism, sham powers of darkness.

Dire Biblical verses welled up from the past and pounded through his head. *Turn ye not unto the ghosts, nor unto familiar spirits; seek them not out, to be defiled by them.* They knew, even then, long ago, the ancestors knew! *There shall not be found among you any one that . . . useth divination, or an observer of times, or an enchanter, or a witch . . . For all that do these things, are an abomination unto the Lord.* True, so true. For what had happened this evening, for this abomination, he was as responsible as Gerda. Guilty, the two of them, perhaps he above all. *They shall stone them with stones: their blood shall be upon them!*[1]

By the time Ravitch got back to his hotel, he was calmer. He had some vodka and hors d'oeuvres sent to his room. Hungry, he quickly devoured whatever it was they had put on the tray. Then, drink in hand, he settled into a big armchair.

He now began to review the events of the evening from beginning to end, gradually, as though projecting a reel of film in slow motion, freezing frames here and there so that he could examine them more carefully. He remembered every word of Gerda's, every gesture; nothing had escaped him. Yet he could make no sense out of what he so vividly recalled.

Who was Gerda? Different voices in Ravitch's head whispered different answers. She was a charlatan. She had read about Benveniste in some book; how else could she have known such details? Or perhaps she had invented him altogether. Perhaps the whole story of her restless client was an invention, concocted to impress him. On the other hand, there was something compellingly sincere about her. Ravitch had felt it. If a charlatan, she was certainly not a deliberate one. She obviously believed in what she did. But that did not mean that what she did or said was true. Far from it. Gerda lived in a world of fantasy. Still, her fantasies could be useful, even therapeutic, for those who accepted such things. The tale of Dr. Benveniste might have been an illusion, a hallucination, but its impact on the Jew from Bucharest was real enough. A placebo effect. Just so.

Yet even as these thoughts came to him Ravitch was not satisfied. This was just the kind of crude and sterile reduction that he detested in others, the glib psychological demolition he encountered so often at New York gatherings, everything neatly explained, nothing understood.

If this was what he thought of Gerda, why such fury when she walked out on him? Why his deep and aching sense of loss? What had he sought from her to begin with that he should feel so deprived?

The fact was, as he now allowed himself to recognize, that even at their first meeting he had sensed something remarkable about her, as though she really had access to some uncommon order of knowledge and power. Of course, he had tried his best to deny his own intuition, but it had lingered within him. When he had suddenly decided to come back to Israel, it had been because of her. That much was now clear. If he had asked to see her, it had been because he needed her help, hers alone.

So why had the evening ended in disaster? He unwound the reel again, looking, listening. The effort was strenuous and sterile.

Ravitch took a sip of his drink and felt the warmth permeate his body. His thoughts turned to his father. Vodka always reminded Ravitch—who was never a heavy drinker—of him. His father's favorite snack, fastidiously prepared by Ravitch's mother, never varied: Slices of herring and a boiled potato neatly arranged on a plate. A small decanter of vodka on the side. Afterward, some scalding hot tea, always in a glass, sucked through a lump of hard sugar. All gone now, mother, father, the samovar that his grandmother had brought from Russia to New York, long lost.

His grandmother, another storyteller. And what stories! Along with the samovar, she had brought a trunkful of superstitions, dark and marvellous, which he, as a child, had accepted without question. When once she caught his mother in the midst of altering his jacket with needle and thread while he was wearing it, she rushed to pop a piece of bread into his mouth and told him to chew vigorously in order to show the Angel of Death that he was alive, for only a shroud is sewn directly on the body. When she cut his nails, she was careful to keep the parings together and burn them. If she failed to do this, she warned, at the time of the Resurrection of the Dead his body would have to roll underground to all the places where he had scattered his parings and gather them together again. Ravitch had adored and trusted her. She'd died when he was eight. For several years after that, he had still burned his parings, but then he gave it up, and by the time he went off to university he had given up much else as well. He had left behind his childhood; his grandmother's quaint fancies; the Resurrection of the Dead, along with the parings; the Messiah, along with the Resurrection; God, along with the Messiah. For want of a nail, he now punned to himself, the kingdom was lost.

Only the classical Hebrew texts remained important in his life, his father's legacy, transmitted so lovingly that they still spoke to him. But they could no longer guide, let alone command, him. He recalled that once—how old could he have been?—his father had told him, "It is written that if all the Jews were to observe one Sabbath completely the Messiah would arrive." For weeks, this idea obsessed him. Why, he kept thinking, could all the Jews in the world not pick one Sabbath and make a pact to do just that? The nonbelievers had nothing to lose if it turned out to be false, while if it was true there was everything to be gained. A Jewish version of Pascal's wager, though he had not yet heard of Pascal.

Ravitch realized that his mind was wandering and that his eyes were moist. He was overcome with a sudden nostalgia for the child who had believed so passionately in the Redemption. But he checked himself, drained his glass, got up, and paced the room. After a while, he went back to his chair and resumed his vigil.

Why had Gerda left him stranded? Had she felt his innate skepticism rising, even though he had not expressed it? But, no, she had told her tale from beginning to end, had engulfed him in it. Why? It seemed to him now that in all she had said there was one crucial remark. *The story was meant for you, but it is not about you.* Here was the key, but it unlocked nothing. The man from Bucharest was not Ravitch. He was, if he existed at all, unique. Ravitch's problems were not his. Yet the story was meant for him. Ravitch turned and twisted the sentence in his mind, repeated it aloud, pondered and dissected it over and over until his head ached.

Finally, he gave up. No question of sleep. He merely continued to sit, immobile, glazed.

At 5 A.M., he stirred, aware, through the window, that the darkness outside was yielding to a very pale light, the first hint of dawn. He pulled on a sweater and his canvas shoes. Then he took the elevator down, passed through the back door of the hotel to the terrace, and descended the curving ramp to the empty beach. He walked a short distance and sat down facing the sea. Nearby he saw the ruins of an elaborate sandcastle that must have been built the day before. He noticed a few pieces of charred wood and a small pile of tiny scalloped shells that someone had collected and then abandoned. The light was slowly expanding over the sky. The sea was quiet, small waves breaking gently at the shore, leaving patches of white foam as they retreated. Ravitch sat very still, staring raptly at sky and water, the rush and ebb of waves pulsing softly in his ears.

He must have sat this way for some time. The sky was luminous now, the ripples in the sea glistening. Ravitch saw a young woman strolling with a little girl, the first visitors of the day. After they had passed him, they paused. The girl took a pink plastic pail she was carrying and ran to the edge of the water. She filled the pail, ran back to the woman, and poured the water on her feet. "*Yam!*" — "Sea!" she shouted triumphantly. The woman smiled. Then they went on their way.

Ravitch continued to watch them as they receded in the distance. Then he stared down at the sand. He observed a few tiny flealike insects hopping around. How do they live? he mused. What do they eat? It was warming up a little. He stood, took off his sweater and slung it over his shoulder, brushed the sand from his trousers. Then slowly, deliberately, he walked toward the water. The waves were cresting higher now, churning and crashing as they rolled in. Isaac Benveniste had never reached this, his destined shore. He, Ravitch, had arrived here. Soon he would leave. A waste.

Ravitch looked one last time to the left, around the coast, toward Jaffa. Then he turned back to the sea, scanning it to the horizon. What will become of me? he asked quietly. What must I do?

The sea heard him but did not reply. It continued to shimmer, to heave and swell, to roll its waves, ancient, majestic, inscrutable, indifferent.

EDITORS' NOTES

On the origins of this story, see the interview with Ophra Yerushalmi on August 8, 2011, www.newyorker.com/online/blogs.

1. Leviticus 19: 31; Deuteronomy 18: 10–12; Leviticus 20: 27.

INDEX

Aboab, Samuel, 162, 165, 166
Abravanel, Isaac, 5, 8, 20, 44, 133, 221–
   22, 238n16, 299, 305
Acosta (da Costa), Uriel, 134, 159,
   215–16
Ahasueros (king of Persia), 218, 256,
   260
Albigensians (Cathars), 61, 76, 108n61
Alenu, 85–86
Alexandria, Jews of ancient, 246, 248–
   49, 269n2
Alitienz, Abram, 92–93, 94
Almohades, 146–47
Alonso de Cartegena, 181, 200n24
Amitai ben Shefatiah, 308, 309
Amsterdam: De Barrios in, 128;
   Méndez in, 162; Sephardic
   community in, 129, 131, 133, 134,
   135, 152, 154, 160, 215–16, 235n6
antisemitism: assimilation and racial,
   in Iberia and Germany, 175–209;
   Christian and anti-Christian, 190,
   191; criticism of Israel equated
   with, 287; emancipation consistent
   with, 283; Jewish despair used in,
   307; Jews seen as Christ-killers,
   252; as key to Jewish survival to
   Spinoza, 214, 217–33; medieval
   versus modern, 176, 178–80,
   191–94; nineteenth-century, 263;
   political, 189–90, 194; proverbial
   Jewish traits, 182; racial, 126, 176,
   178–80, 189–94, 201n29, 203n39,
   261, 283; the state and, 264;
   varieties of, 178
apocalypticism, 53–56, 286, 291,
   293n2, 311
Arama, Isaac, 245, 256, 260
Arendt, Hannah: on Baeck, 276n55;
   Eichmann in Jerusalem, 16, 246,

266; on Jews' understanding of
   modern antisemitism, 264; *The
   Origins of Totalitarianism*, 16,
   246, 247–48, 261, 266; on political
   tradition of Jews, 16, 19, 247–48;
   Yerushalmi's criticism of, 245, 246,
   247, 266–67
assimilation: as border condition,
   176, 196; emancipation associated
   with, 232–33; in Germany, 189,
   190–91; medieval conversion seen
   as leading to, 179, 182, 189; and
   racial antisemitism in Iberia and
   Germany, 175–209; and Sephardic
   emigration, 132, 133, 152; of
   Spanish Marranos, 225; tolerance
   associated with, 214, 232, 233, 232,
   233; in transition of European
   Jewry to modernity, 261

Baeck, Leo: criticism of concentration
   camp activity of, 276n55;
   Yerushalmi's Leo Baeck Memorial
   Lecture, 3, 19, 175–209
Baer, Yitzhak Fritz: on Marranos, 158;
   on medieval Spanish Jewry, 132; on
   ritual norms shared by Jews and
   Christians, 61; on Spanish hatred
   of Marranos, 239n21; on Spinoza,
   220, 243n34; Yerushalmi's review
   of *History of the Jews in Christian
   Spain*, 18, 37–48
Baḥya ibn Pakuda, 129, 134, 137n3, 169
baptism: debaptizing, 92–93;
   emancipation through, 189;
   forced, 68, 75–76, 106n55, 143; as
   indelible, 79, 89; Inquisition and
   Jews who had accepted, 71, 74;
   Jewish physical defects eliminated
   by, 179, 192; Jewish view of, 90,

91; reception of baptized Jews in Jewish community, 78; rejudaizing bathing rite compared with, 61

Bar Kochba Revolt, 280

Baron, Salo Wittmayer: annual seminar at Columbia, 8; on comparative framework for Jewish history, 142; evaluation of Yerushalmi, 10n22; on Jewish political action, 48n10; on Jewish question at Congress of Berlin, 15; on medieval Jews as "serfs of the chamber," 16, 19, 245, 256; on racial antisemitism, 201n29; Yerushalmi as Salo W. Baron Professor of Jewish History, Culture, and Society, 11, 157; as Yerushalmi's mentor, 2, 7, 60

Barrios, Daniel Levi (Miguel) de, 128, 129–31

Baruch, Second Book of, 299, 304

Baruch of Toulouse, 67–70, 78, 91, 111n72, 120n122, 122n131

Berggasse 19 (Engelman), 334–336, 341n2

Bernard of Clairvaux, St., 179–80

Bible, Spanish translations of, 165, 166

birkat ha-minim, 85, 117n99

birkot ha-shahar, 84–85

Bloch, Marc, 29, 30, 217, 302

Bund, the, 263, 282

Burgh, Albert, 230, 231, 232

Caligula (emperor), 246, 248, 268, 269n2

Capsali, Elijah, 151, 273n39

Cardoso, Isaac, 9, 12, 20, 161–62, 223–24, 343–44

Castro, Américo, 47n4, 199n111, 200n21, 206n48, 206n49

Cervantes, Miguel de, 195, 206n49, 314

charters, 246, 252–54

circumcision: and conversion to Christianity, 93; of Freud, 338; of Juan de Ciudad, 92; of Marranos, 157, 161–63; of proselytes, 95–96; Spinoza on hatred of Jews and, 231; symbolic, 121n125

Clement IV (pope), 75, 84, 98n9, 107n54, 111n66

Clermont-Tonnerre, Stanislaus de, 261–62, 289, 295n22

"Clio and the Jews: Reflections on Jewish Historiography in the Sixteenth Century" (Yerushalmi), 11

Collingwood, R. G., 17, 49

Contra la verdad no hay fuerza (Barrios), 128, 129–31

conversion: assimilation associated with, 179, 182, 189; and dejudaization, 93; dimension of French Jewish, 71; emancipation versus, 233; Expulsion of 1492 versus, 157, 180; finality of, 90; by forced baptism, 68, 75–76; forced versus voluntary, 95; number of medieval Spanish, 181; Portuguese forced, 15, 131, 133, 151, 180, 214, 225, 306; Spanish forced, 143–44, 146, 179, 214; Spinoza leaves Judaism without, 220, 238n13; ultimate, 192, 193; by Viennese Jews, 338–39. *See also* baptism; *conversos*; relapsi

conversos: all classes as, 48n9; assimilation and racial antisemitism in Iberia and Germany, 175–209; backlash against, 182–84; coexisting with Jews, 180, 181; crypto-Jews and, 157, 158; *estatutos de limpieza de sangre* applied to, 175, 184–88; live apart in Portugal, 214; reaction to Inquisition, 196; rejudaization of,

Gamwell, Lynn, 335, 340n2

Gebhart, Carl, 213, 215–16

Germany: assimilation and racial antisemitism in Iberia and, 188–97; emancipation in, 262, 283; Freud and German culture, 336–37; Jewish charters in, 253–54; Jewish soldiers in First World War, 265; Jews and German culture, 194–95, 266; Jews support unification, 262–63

Gershon, Isaac, 167–68, 173n29

ghettos, 67, 264, 265, 267

"Gilgul" (Yerushalmi), 20, 343–56

Goldberg, Sylvie Anne, 3, 14

Golden Age, myth of, 38, 40–44

Gregory IX (pope), 81, 113n78, 255

Gui, Bernard, 62; Albigensians as concern of, 76; credibility of his data on Jewish life, 82–83, 88; and expulsion of Jews of 1322, 105n44; as Inquisitor of Toulouse, 60, 62, 65; Jewish books confiscated by, 65, 66, 73, 81; Jewish literature as interest of, 74; literary activity, 62–63; prosecutions for Judaizing, 65–66; sincerity of, 61. See also *Practica inquisitionis heretice pravitatis* (Gui)

Haggadah and History (Yerushalmi), 10

Hannukah, 281–82, 335

Hebrew language: Christian study of, 83–84; Freud's knowledge of, 334, 338; grammars in Spanish and Portuguese, 169; Marranos and, 164, 170; Maskilim abandon, 57

Hebrew University, 5, 5n11, 322, 339

Heine, Heinrich, 177–78, 196, 262

Herzl, Theodor, 283, 294n14, 339

Hess, Moses, 203n39, 283, 288

historicism, 16, 50, 323

Holocaust (Shoah): versus "Age of Aquarius," 58; could it happen again?, 268; versus earlier Jewish catastrophes, 303, 306; Expulsion of 1492 compared with, 45–46; Jewish attitudes affected by, 315; Ladino and Yiddish devastated by, 127; remembering, 50, 58–59; Zionism affected by, 282

hope, 299–317; history and, 313–14; memory and, 312–13; messianism and, 278, 299, 300, 302, 306, 310, 314; migration and, 300, 311

Ibn Adret, Solomon, 257, 311

Ibn Daud, Abraham, 147, 151, 311

Ibn Ezra, Judah, 147

Ibn Shaprut, Hasdai, 41, 146

Ibn Verga, Solomon: Baer on, 38, 46; on horrors of Spanish exiles, 299, 305; *Shevet* (*Shebet*) *Yehudah*, 17, 46, 169, 239n20, 246, 258–60; Yerushalmi's interest in, 3, 17

Inquisition: circumstances in which it played a decisive role in Jewish history, 70–71, 74, 106n50; clashes between bishops and inquisitors, 106n47; *conversos* and, 184, 196; establishment of, 44; and Jews of France in time of Bernard Gui, 60–124; Marranos flee, 160, 196; means of access to Jewish information, 83; Cristóbal Méndez trial, 162; Nazis contrasted with, 194; Papal, 62, 63, 76, 131; penalties levied by, 79–80, 112n75; sincerity of inquisitors, 61; Spanish, 62, 63, 125, 131, 226; special commissions to investigate Jewish affairs, 77; theories of origins of, 47n4; in Yerushalmi's master's thesis, 8, 18, 60. See also *Practica inquisitionis heretice pravitatis* (Gui)

143; Yerushalmi's early interest in, 5, 157, 213. *See also* New Christians

Martínez de Oviedo, Gonzalo, 258–59

Martini, Raymund, 84, 115n89

Maskilim, 50, 57–58, 338

Maury, Abbé Jean-Siffrein, 289, 295n22

Megillat Aḥimaaẓ, 309

Méndez, Cristóbal (Abraham Franco de Silveira), 162–63

messianism, 279–81; Christian, 291; and hope, 278, 299, 300, 302, 306, 310, 314; messianic syndrome, 277, 285; versus political realism, 19; in Yerushalmi's Hebrew College Address of 1970, 49, 54–57; versus Zionism, 16, 277, 278, 282–86, 314

Michel le Moine, 67, 102n33

Mishneh Torah (Maimonides), 82, 115n83, 169, 284

Moses and Monotheism (Freud), 12, 318, 334, 339

Nazis: Inquisition contrasted with, 194; *Judenräte*, 246, 266–68; seen as end of history, 55; state destruction of Jews by, 265–66; tradition of kingly benevolence comes to end with, 245; Zionism affected by, 282. *See also* Holocaust (Shoah)

Netanyahu, Benzion, 61, 158

New Christians: Abravanel on Divine Providence and, 221–22, 238n16; assimilation and racial antisemitism in Iberia and Germany, 19, 175–209; becomes official term, 227; *estatutos de limpieza de sangre* applied to, 175, 184–88; Judaizers attempt to convert, 164; Lisbon attacks of 1506 on, 15, 183; meaning of term, 137n5; research on, 216; in

Sephardic trade, 152; in Spanish civilization, 194–96; Spinoza contrasts Spanish and Portuguese attitudes toward, 225–29; Toledo attacks of 1449 on, 183, 184, 188, 226. *See also* Marranos (crypto-Jews)

Newman, Louis I., 60, 61, 76, 97n1, 98n7, 108n61

Nora, Pierre, 2, 29, 32

Oath of Abjuration, 78–79

oaths, Jewish, 78, 111n68, 111n71

Origins of Totalitarianism, The (Arendt), 16, 246, 247–48, 261, 266

Ottoman Empire: Constantinople conquered by, 150; dismantling of, 288; Golden Age of Sephardic Jewry in, 132, 151, 154; as land of hope, 311; sultans seen as protectors of the Jews, 260, 273n39

Palestinians, 290–91

"Papal Inquisition in France and the Jews, The" (Yerushalmi), 8

Paris, Disputation of, 81, 112n77

Pastoureaux (Shepherds), 67, 70, 105n44

Pérez, Yehuda Leon, 170, 171

Philo of Alexandria, 248, 269n2

Pinto Delgado, João (Moshe), 159

Pirke Abot, 165, 166

Poema de Yoçef, 130–31

pogroms: in Alexandria, 248; conversion due to fear of, 75; in Granada in 1066, 146; by the Pastoureaux, 105n44; Russian, 263, 264; of 1391, 42, 137n5, 180

Poland, 258, 262, 265, 272n32, 275n51, 311

popes: as protectors of the Jews, 255. *See also under individual names*

Portugal: expelled Spanish Jews come

154; Ladino literature, 125–37; Spinoza as, 214; under successive conquerors of Iberian Peninsula, 141–56

Sephardic Tradition, The: Ladino and Spanish-Jewish Literature (Lazar), 125–37

shamta, 86–87

shemitot, 55

Shevet (Shebet) Yehudah (Ibn Verga), 17, 46, 169, 239n20, 246, 258–60

Shmuel (Shemuel) Ha-Nagid, 41, 141, 145, 146

Shulḥan Arukh (Karo), 129, 137n3, 167, 168

Spain: assimilation and racial antisemitism in Iberia and Germany, 175–209; cathedral versus synagogue in Toledo, 309; forced conversion of Jews in, 143–44, 146, 179, 214; *Galut Yerushalayim 'asher bi-Sefarad*, 149; Golden Age of Jewish culture in, 145–46; Granada falls, 44, 142, 150; Inquisition, 62, 63, 125, 131, 226; Jews' royal alliance in, 257–58; Jews saved during World War II, 265, 274n48; Ladino and Spanish-Jewish literature, 125–37; massacres of 1391, 149–50, 157, 180; Muslim conquest, 144–47, 179; *Reconquista*, 142, 148, 149, 150; Sephardic Jews under successive conquerors of Iberian Peninsula, 141–56; Spinoza contrasts Portuguese attitudes toward New Christians with those of, 225–29; Toledo attacks of 1449, 183, 184, 188, 226; union of Aragon and Castile, 262–63; Visigothic, 143–44, 179, 258; Yerushalmi's review of Baer's *A History of the Jews in Christian Spain*, 18, 37–48. *See*

also Expulsion of 1492; Marranos (crypto-Jews)

Spinoza, Baruch (Benedictus): excommunication of, 134, 215, 223; Marrano background of, 153; myth of philosophical intelligence of, 217, 236n9; research on, 213, 214–17; on survival of the Jews, 19, 213–44; Yerushalmi's lecture on, 3, 19

Stark, Johannes, 196–97

Tacitus, 220

Talmud: on apostasy, 89–90; on astrology, 55; Babylonia as center of Talmudic authority, 144; burning of, 29, 32, 65, 66, 67, 68, 81; Clement IV calls for destruction of, 84; Freud owns Babylonian, 340; Gregory IX orders confiscation of, 255; Inquisition condemns, 81–82; investigation of 1240, 82, 83, 84, 85, 87, 111n68, 112n77, 114n81; John XXII orders confiscation of, 66–67; in Latin, 167; on ritual immersion, 93; "Talmudic mind," 207n52

Temple Mount, 286, 292

Teresa of Ávila, Santa, 195, 207n51, 207n52

Theologico-Political Treatise (Tractatus Theologico-Politicus) (Spinoza), 213, 214, 215, 219–20, 222–23, 224, 229, 231–32, 243n33

Titnem le-ḥerpah, 86–87

toleration: assimilation associated with, 214, 232, 233, 232, 233; in medieval Christianity, 252

Torrejoncillo, Francisco de, 187–88, 243n31

Tortosa, Disputation of, 42–43, 44, 180

Trunk, Isaac, 267, 275n54

Turbato corde (Clement IV), 75, 98n9, 107n54, 111n66

Unamuno, Miguel de, 216
universalism, 49, 50, 57–58
Usque, Samuel, 129, 169, 239n20, 299, 305–7

Vega, Joseph Penso de la, 153
Vera y Alarcón, Lope de (Judah the Believer), 187–88, 202n35, 230–31, 232, 243n31
Vieira, António, 228–29, 241n26
Vives, Juan Luis, 195, 207n51

Wissenschaft des Judentums, 3, 30, 141

Yehudah (Judah) Halevy, 44, 48n7, 146–47, 148, 169
Yerushalmi, Yosef Hayim, 1–21; and activism, 15; applied history of, 17; balance between existential fulfillment and quest for objectivity, 14–15; on collective memory, 29, 256, 268; at Columbia University, 10–11, 157; commitment to Israel, 5–6, 277; as congregational rabbi, 7; doctoral dissertation, 9, 37, 49; on fissures of modernity, 16; on French culture, 6, 18, 29–33; at Harvard University, 9, 10, 18, 141; higher education of, 6–9; on historian's role, 13–14; on historical objectivity, 12–13; on history and self-understanding, 44–46; on Jews and the state, 15–16; as lecturer, 2, 3; on living in midst of history, 13, 14, 50, 58; making of a Jewish historian, 3–17; master's thesis, 8, 18, 60; name change, 6;

on openness of history, 29, 32–33; original surname, 25–26; on political tradition of Jews, 16, 19; on postmodern skepticism, 12n27; on Russian literature and culture, 4, 18, 25, 27; on sacred history, 38, 45; wife of, 9, 30; Yeshiva College yearbook entry for, 6n13. *See also names of individual works*
Yiddish, 127–28, 334, 338, 339
Yom Kippur, 86–87

Zakhor: Jewish History and Jewish Memory (Yerushalmi): on deep and unrealized yearning for the past, 20; estrangement as theme of, 343; French translation of, 29, 32; Funkenstein's response to, 1; Hebrew College address of 1970 anticipates, 18, 49; on history as "faith of fallen Jews," 14, 50, 278; on hope, 300, 313; on memory and history, 14, 50, 319; organizational pattern of, 245; preface to Russian translation of, 3, 4, 25–28; reviews of, 11n; Stroum Lectures as basis for, 2, 11
Zionism, 281–83; anti-Zionist persecutions in Soviet Union, 26; colonialism equated with, 288; Freud and, 339; versus messianism, 16, 277, 278, 282–86, 314; as nationalism, 50, 288–90; religious, 293n9, 294n15; as rupture in Jewish history, 278, 282; secular, 281–82; the state and, 263; Yerushalmi's commitment to, 5

Library of Congress Cataloging-in-Publication Data
Yerushalmi, Yosef Hayim, 1932–2009, author.
[Essays. Selections.]
The faith of fallen Jews: Yosef Hayim Yerushalmi and the writing
of Jewish history / edited by David N. Myers and Alexander Kaye.
    pages cm.— (The Tauber Institute series for the study of
European Jewry)
ISBN 978-1-61168-423-0 (cloth: alk. paper)— ISBN 978-1-61168-487-2
(pbk.: alk. paper)— ISBN 978-1-61168-413-1 (ebook)
1. Jews—Historiography. 2. Judaism—Historiography.
3. Jews—Spain—History. 4. Marranos—History. I. Title.
DS115.5.Y45 2013
909′.04924—dc23
2013018730